D1345822

English Presbyterianism, 1590-1640

ENGLISH
PRESBYTERIANISM
1590–1640

Polly Ha

Stanford University Press
Stanford, California
2011

Stanford University Press
Stanford, California

© 2011 by the Board of Trustees of the Leland Stanford Junior University

Printed in the United States of America on acid-free, archival-quality paper

Library of Congress Cataloging-in-Publication Data

Ha, Polly
English Presbyterianism, 1590–1640 / Polly Ha
    p.   cm.
Includes bibliographical references and index.
ISBN 978-0-8047-5987-8 (cloth : alk. paper)
    1. Presbyterian Church—England—History—17th century.
2. Presbyterianism—History—17th century.   3. Congregationalism—History—17th century.   4. Church polity—History—17th century.
5. Reformed Church—Netherlands—History—17th century.
6. Church and state—England—History—17th century.   7. England—Church history—17th century.   I. Title.

BX9055.H3   2011
285.24209032—dc22   2010011334

Designed and typeset at Stanford University Press in 10/13 Galliard

For my parents

Contents

Tables and Figures

Acknowledgments

———◦◆◦———

The recovery of English presbyterianism is based not only on the recent iden-tification of a collection of manuscripts but firstly upon the work and gener-ous help of many others. Any attempt to account for my intellectual debts is bound to be severely inadequate. Long before I reached Cambridge, Patrick Collinson sparked my interest in the subject; it goes without saying that his research was responsible for recovering English presbyterianism in the first place. He provided invaluable references and directed me toward an impor-tant line of investigation by suggesting I interact more with congregational-ism. His kindness has been immense and his influence and support have been incalculable. He and Ann Hughes rigorously examined the dissertation upon which this book is based and helped me to strengthen the work. Ann Hughes kindly allowed me to read a version of *Gangraena* before publication. It will be obvious that this work also owes more to Peter Lake than it is possible to spell out. I am indebted to him for generously providing references, reading drafts of the first four chapters, asking precisely those questions that helped to crystallize my thought, and for discussing many aspects of the study as a whole.

John Morrill, as my doctoral supervisor, guided me from my earliest days as a postgraduate to the final stages of revising this book: he offered invalu-able guidance, challenged me to develop my work, and has continued to offer unstinted help. Keith Wrightson first introduced me to early modern British history when I was an undergraduate, and I remain ever grateful to him for encouraging me in my study. I am especially indebted to Elisabeth Leedham-Green: there are few scholars with the combined erudition, palaeographic expertise, and generosity to interpret the manuscripts that are at the core of this study. She and I spent many afternoons discussing Walter Travers and strained our eyes for countless hours to interpret his cryptic notes, which would have been a much more formidable task without her learning, insight, good humor, and encouragement.

I am further grateful to a great number of scholars who helped me with valuable references, shared their insights, and lent me resources or copies of their dissertations. Alexandra Walsham, Thomas Freeman, and especially John Craig guided me in my first faltering steps in the Cambridge University Library, discussed the earliest contents of the work, and commented upon the introduction and conclusion. Alan Ford and Jonathan Moore supported me in my initial research when I was still an undergraduate. Alice Wolfram made astute comments on almost the entire work and advised me on the final chapter. Irena Backus inspired me and offered helpful comments on Chapter 4. I hounded many other scholars in their passage through Cambridge, including Anthony Milton and David Harris Sacks. I am grateful for their conversation at Clare Hall, for their comments on drafts, and for continuing to offer guidance. John Walter very kindly read and commented on the final chapter. Christopher Brooks made helpful suggestions for Chapter 2. I am in debt to David Como and Jane Dawson for sharing their references, notes, and transcriptions for Chapter 6. Keith Sprunger very generously helped me to navigate my way through archives in the Netherlands and patiently answered many questions relating to the final chapter. Earlier drafts of Chapters 2, 3, and 6 were presented at the Religious History Seminar of the Institute of Historical Research, seminars in the University of Cambridge History and Divinity faculties, at the Reformation Studies Colloquium, and the North American Conference on British Studies. I thank the moderators and audiences for their comments, especially the convenors of the Religious History Seminar at the IHR, for sharing their extensive knowledge. My ideas took further shape by participating in the Freedom and Construction of Europe and Insular Christianity networks, and I wish to thank the convenors, Quentin Skinner and Martin van Gelderen, and Robert Armstrong and Tadhg Ó hAnnracháin, for inviting me to their conferences.

I could not have hoped for a more amiable publisher than Stanford University Press. Nor could I have asked for more helpful readers than Paul Seaver and Sears McGee, who carefully read and commented upon the entire manuscript, bringing numerous corrections to my attention. The revision of this book would have been unthinkable without the editorial help of Christine Linehan, who taught me how to write (and rewrite) entire sections. She patiently helped me to untangle my thoughts and sentences and to transform my writing into readable prose. John Feneron and Martin Hanft saw the book manuscript through to publication with alacrity.

The Governing Body of Clare Hall elected me to a Research Fellowship as I was completing the dissertation; it has been a warm intellectual home and played a formative role in the development of my work. Postdoctoral fellowships from the British Academy and the University of Southern California also provided me with invaluable opportunities to take my research in new directions. The British Academy and the USC-Huntington Early Modern Studies Institute lavishly assisted with my career development and with a subsidy for the publication of this book. Shorter-term fellowships at the Huntington Library and the American Antiquarian Society also shaped my thinking about this monograph. I am particularly grateful to Cynthia Herrup, Philip Gura, David Hall, and Frank Bremer for their support and conversation at USC and AAS. I also thank the Yale Paul Mellon Fellowship Committee for electing me to a postgraduate fellowship at Clare College, which lacked nothing, and the board of directors for the Archbishop Cranmer and Lightfoot funds, for awarding me additional grants for research in Dublin and the Netherlands.

The staff at libraries and archives offered outstanding assistance, particularly at Trinity College Dublin. Bernard Meehan and the Manuscripts Library staff of Trinity College Dublin showed more courtesy than I could have expected in numerous visits and requests over the years, and provided me with the microfilm of Travers's manuscripts from their collection. I am grateful to the board of Trinity College Dublin and to the British Library for permission to reproduce excerpts from Travers's manuscripts in this book. I am indebted to Stuart O'Seanoir and to Liz Toner-Hughes, who helped and welcomed me in research trips to Dublin. As assistant librarian, Stuart provided extensive bibliographic references on the holdings at Trinity College Dublin Library, in addition to transcribing passages from MS 292 that were illegible from microfilm. With a careful eye for detail and wide-ranging knowledge he also proofread the entire manuscript. I am also grateful to James Ha and Nawal Lutfiyya for running data for the final chapter through SPSS.

It would be impossible here to account for my largest debts, to family and friends who have supported and inspired me throughout my years in California, Connecticut, and Cambridge. I wish to offer them my deepest appreciation. I owe the most to my husband, And, for making the completion of this book and life beyond it a joy. Roth and Gabriela must be singled out for their friendship, which has personally and intellectually challenged me and remained a constant source of encouragement. Peter and Soo have been remarkable friends and examples in more ways than it is possible to spell out. My family taught me virtually everything. Peter, Jane, and James have mentored and put up with me from infancy. My in-laws, especially Chris and Margaret, showered me with encouragement. My parents have always supported me unconditionally and demonstrated throughout their lives what it means to search beneath the surface of people and events. Without their example, encouragement, and many sacrifices, I would have never attempted, nor had the ability, to write this book. This work is dedicated to them.

Preface

The genesis of this book can be traced to the summer of 2001, when I came across the biography of the Elizabethan presbyterian ideologue Walter Travers. Although still an undergraduate at the time with no intention of investigating the institutional remains of puritanism, I soon became intrigued by the later life of Travers. There seemed to be a story to tell about him and about Elizabethan presbyterianism following its official suppression in the early 1590s. English presbyterianism, which posed a threat to the hierarchy of the Church of England, was supposed to have been effectively wiped out after that time, only to reappear during the 1640s at the onset of the English Civil War. Travers remained a shadowy figure until his death in 1635, and his biographer believed that not much could be learned about his later life, since his papers seemed to be untraceable. Following leads by William O'Sullivan and Laetitia Yeandle, however, I was able to confirm attributions of Travers's papers in Trinity College Dublin and to recover additional manuscripts by him and other presbyterian spokesmen that span the half-century of apparent English presbyterian silence. These do not simply reveal the individual thoughts of Walter Travers and the continued activity of English presbyterianism, but modify traditional accounts of the religious, political, and social climate of pre–Civil War England.

A central contention of this book is that English presbyterianism, however covert, was far from being a self-contained and marginalized clerical community. Following their prosecution, and the deaths of key patrons in the 1590s, presbyterians made a concerted effort to prove the compatibility of their ecclesiology with the monarchy and to develop an alliance with lawyers against episcopal authority. They were also at the heart of some of the fiercest religious controversies of pre–Civil War England, giving rise to new puritan ideology. In addition, they placed pressure on the very nerves of society. With the help of the laity, English presbyterians established networks through centers of power and commerce in England that extended across the North Sea and the Atlantic. They also adapted to varying circumstances and incorporated diverse social groups, men as well as women.

Abbreviations

AD   H. M. Adams, *Catalogue of Books Printed on the Continent of Europe, 1501–1600 in Cambridge Libraries*. Cambridge: Cambridge University Press, 1967.
BL   British Library
DWL   Dr. Williams's Library
ERCA   English Reformed Church in Amsterdam
GAA   Gemeentearchief, Amsterdam
GAD   Gemeentearchief, Dordrecht
GAL   Gemeentearchief, Leiden
NA (Kew) National Archives, Kew
TCD   Trinity College, Dublin

AHR   *American Historical Review*
CH   *Church History*
EHR   *English Historical Review*
HJ   *Historical Journal*
JBS   *Journal of British Studies*
JEH   *Journal of Ecclesiastical History*
JMH   *Journal of Modern History*
ODNB   *Oxford Dictionary of National Biography*
P&P   *Past & Present*
SCJ   *Sixteenth Century Journal*
STC   *A Short Title Catalogue of Books Printed in England, Scotland and Ireland 1475–1640*, 2nd ed. Oxford: Oxford University Press, 1976–91.

English Presbyterianism, 1590-1640

Introduction

To suggest that English presbyterianism had a continuing history in the late sixteenth and early seventeenth centuries is to challenge the standard narrative of the period. From their first appearance in the 1570s, presbyterians emerged as leaders of a puritan movement for further reformation of the Elizabethan religious settlement. They posed a threat to its episcopally organized hierarchy by insisting on a model of government based on the equality of ministers and the inclusion of lay elders in the oversight of the Church.[1] But when the crown suppressed the movement in 1592 by arresting its leaders and depriving them of their ministry, English presbyterianism appeared to be a dead letter. Thomas Rogers, a chaplain to Archbishop Bancroft, gloated that they had "so battered the new [presbyterian] discipline as hitherto they could never, nor hereafter shall ever fortify and repair the decays thereof."[2] Modern historians concurred. According to R. G. Usher, "[A]fter the arrests of 1590 and the trials in the Star Chamber in 1592, the whole movement was tacitly abandoned by all concerned," and "there was even no continuity reaching from one to the other, from the 'Presbyterians' of Elizabeth to the 'Presbyterians' of the Civil War."[3] The sudden resurgence of English presbyterians in the frontline of the English Civil War has instead been explained by political expediency and Scottish influence.

The fate of presbyterianism makes sense in light of revisionist accounts of puritanism, which disabused readers of the view that it was a precursor to modernity.[4] As chief agitators against Charles I and William Laud, puritans were previously considered champions of liberty in explaining the rise of parliamentary sovereignty and religious toleration.[5] It has been fifty years since Patrick Collinson complicated that picture.[6] Puritanism, he argued, was indeed initially organized as a movement led by presbyterians. However, it was also compatible with episcopacy so long as bishops remained committed to upholding a reformed protestant preaching ministry.[7] Nicholas Tyacke's classic study confirmed this narrative by highlighting the relative stability of the early Stuart church and a lack of theological contention until the disruption of Calvinist orthodoxy by Laud.[8] There also appeared to be relative tranquility over the subject of church polity. Tom Webster painted a picture of Caroline puritan clergy that focused on their sociability rather than differences over ecclesiology.[9] Obviously, Webster did not approach reform from the same vantage point as continental scholars. Nonetheless, his stress on the social cohesion of reformists as opposed to their ecclesiastical divisions corresponds to wider trends in Reformation historiography. Rather than focusing on distinctions in church polity, these studies have tended to emphasize comparative development across Western Christendom, whether through a shared sociopolitical function or theological overlap between competing traditions.[10]

However, there were clear divisions between English protestants, even when it came to shared antitypes such as the Church of Rome. Anthony Milton has explored how English Calvinists posed competing arguments and arrived at different alignments of the Church of England with foreign churches.[11] Rather than identifying an organized puritan assault on the Church of England, postrevisionism has tended to stress diversity and division among the godly. Peter Lake explained the contradictory tendencies in moderate puritanism by shedding light on its contingency and strategic maneuvering.[12] The instability of puritanism appeared most vividly in David Como's recent study that unearthed a radical puritan underground prior to the proliferation of numerous dissenting sects at the outbreak of the English Civil War.[13] It is hence no surprise that Lake recently concluded that "it is becoming increasingly difficult to write a continuous history of puritanism in the early Stuart church."[14]

There is good reason for the absence of a continued English presbyterian history. The crown's prosecution of the leading presbyterian ministers appears at first sight to have silenced them permanently and driven them into obscurity. S. J. Knox observed that the suppression of the presbyterian party "for the remainder of Elizabeth's reign meant that its leaders were also silent, particularly Travers, its former outspoken exponent."[15] Walter Travers, a leading Elizabethan presbyterian ideologue, lived through the reign of James VI and I and into that of Charles I. He provides a key to understanding religious change in the early Stuart Church,[16] but until recently it has been impossible to trace his life beyond the sixteenth century because his papers seemed to have disappeared.[17] However, a cache of manuscripts recently identified as his at Trinity College Dublin, and others,[18] reveal that the "death of presbyterianism" has been greatly exaggerated. These papers provide unique insight into the continued exposition of presbyterianism by a group of clerics who led the Elizabethan movement, and who deliberately concealed themselves by carefully hiding their papers and guarding them from discovery by the authorities. Travers himself used Greek characters to encrypt several folios of English, Latin, and French in his manuscripts,[19] while presbyterian Julines Herring resorted to a more severe measure of self-censorship through his "letter martyrdome . . . wherein many of the best thoughts of his dearest Friends were committed to the flames."[20]

This is neither to suggest that presbyterianism was a majority or even a widespread position among puritans. Nor is it to imply that presbyterianism continued to be organized as a movement as it had been under Elizabeth. It is to stress that presbyterianism was nonetheless a significant position. Although seemingly a period of relative quietude, some of the fiercest debates over church government were taking place. Presbyterians remained at the heart of such controversy. Despite their cryptic nature, presbyterian manuscripts informed the printed debates over church government and provide a key to interpreting the polemical literature of the early Stuart period. Even before the reign of Charles I and the rise of Laud as Archbishop of Canterbury, they argued for the abolition of bishops and acted as a trigger in the making of revolutionary ideology. It was during these years of apparent silence that they made a concerted effort to argue that episcopacy was unbiblical, unlawful, un-English and unnatural. It was also through their underground activity that the presbyterians contributed to the birth of congregational 'independency,' which made new claims to popular sovereignty within the puritan mainstream, several decades before it was supposed to have existed.

This makes possible a multivariable analysis of ecclesiastical development as opposed to a two-dimensional model of religious fragmentation. Controversy was carried out not only between nonconformists and conformists, or separately between godly disputants, but also between diverse sets of participants. English presbyterianism developed both in response to the challenges from conformists in and after the late sixteenth century onward and from the threat of emerging congregationalists, among others, from the early seventeenth century. Not only did the number of participants and positions multiply over time, but the same debates were carried out across the North Sea and across the Atlantic. This helps to explain the development of England's religious turbulence and the chief ruptures that ultimately divided English protestants. There was of course nothing inevitable about ecclesiastical divisions. But neither were such fault-lines entirely contingent on the circumstances that have been traditionally held up to explain them. For English ecclesiology underwent continual adaptation and change well before the rise of Laudianism.

Yet presbyterianism was not simply an abstract and static concept without variation: it adapted to its circumstances and continued to inform the broader practices of nonconformists even though it existed outside a national institution in full operation. Although all lay allies were not necessarily committed to reformed government themselves, presbyterians continued to speak to a broad and socially diverse audience and to play a key role in the religious and political disputes of the period. While the definition of presbyterianism used here is a system of government adhered to and supported by a collection of individuals, it was also an alternative jurisdiction and a process used to reach a consensus, whether in theological argument, intercongregational conflict, or interpersonal disagreement. English presbyterians employed a particular pattern of ecclesiastical jurisdiction in which they weighed evidence and various testimonies to arbitrate and arrive at their conclusion.[21] This could be applied in their case against episcopacy, in their cross-examination of congregational suspects, and in their execution of discipline in their local congregations or wider communities. Because it was rooted in a shared understanding of biblical passages such as Matthew 18: 15–17, the presbyterian form of dispute resolution overlapped with others.[22] Nonetheless, it was explicitly inscribed in presbyterian government. They claimed that their government embodied the biblical prescription for reconciling parties, even if their effect could prove more disruptive than peaceful.

Presbyterian exchanges here center on points of conflict rather than agreement, because these were precisely the moments when their mechanisms became useful and therefore the points at which presbyterianism becomes distinctively visible. However, presbyterians maintained a unique position through sustaining a discourse with other puritans across the spectrum even if through polemical or politicized arguments: while they ultimately contributed to divisions among the godly, they nonetheless remained well positioned to fill the role of mediators between divergent parties. In this capacity, the presbyterians could either foster support for the English establishment or help unite activists in their shared grievances against it. At the same time as presbyterians gave further definition to distinctions between nonconformist polities, they contributed to the blurring of divisions and to the development of ecclesiological ambiguities. Their mediating role was essential to the rise of intermediary positions, such as moderate episcopacy.

Ecclesiastical ambiguity and the overlap between competing church polities have received due attention in previous studies.[23] The presbyterian perspective highlights another aspect of ecclesiastical malleability. Here a multiconfessional reading provides a fruitful approach to English history. Historians have recently explored the religious dynamics of biconfessional states and the range of confessions that an individual might encounter and convert to in the course of a lifetime.[24] The ambiguous nature of the English religious settlement also allowed room for individuals to hold competing traditions in tension and to simultaneously subscribe to multiple confessions. English presbyterians held a narrowly defined concept of the Church that was opposed to epsicopal government, while nonetheless identifying with the Church of England and a plurality of protestant traditions on the continent without considering that position to be inconsistent.[25] The existence of multilayered commitments meant that a particular ecclesiological vision could (at least in some contexts) be held in tension with alternative forms of jurisdiction.

I.

The most obvious implication of the persistence of presbyterianism is that it opens up a wider and politically charged ecclesiastical landscape out of which the abrasive Laudian measures, among other conformist policies, emerged. Just as Richard Hooker conceived of his ecclesiastical polity in direct response to English presbyterians,[26] it was in fact the specter of presbyterianism as an alternative to the Church of England that continued to fuel the ecclesiastical polity of Laudian divines such as Peter Heylyn.[27] Although frequently referring to presbyterian subversion abroad, avant-garde conformists insisted on the threat of presbyterianism at the heart of the Church of England. These writers portrayed radicalized caricatures that associated presbyterianism with even the most extreme expressions of nonconformity and separatism in order to prove that the threat of sedition still existed, which in turn served as a means of gaining promotion and furthering their own clerical careers.[28] The actual persistence of English presbyterians during this period helps to account for the radicalization of conformist policies.[29] It explains religious conflict in England through mutual antagonisms as opposed to identifying one party or another as the aggravating agent. Indeed, the peculiar developments in the early Stuart Church depended on rival ecclesiastical polities and continually underwent change in reaction to them.

What emerges from the presbyterians' clandestine activity during this period is their continued assault on the hierarchy of the Church of England. They advocated an altogether different form of jurisdiction and attacked the very nature of episcopacy, invoking the metaphor of a hermaphroditic bishop to underscore theological arguments for its abolition. But even more worrying for conformists like Heylyn were the supposed links between presbyterians and MPs. There was obviously no national conspiracy, no presbyterian plot to overthrow the state, and it goes without saying that there was no one-to-one relationship between religious and political developments in the early seventeenth century. However, it would be a mistake to overlook the continuing political aspirations and institutional ties of the presbyterians simply because their writings were circulated in manuscript among a select readership in a period when prospects for institutional reform had significantly diminished. Part One of this book argues that English presbyterians turned the accusation of political sedition and unlawful government against the bishops themselves. It was common among reformed churches under the cross in France and the Netherlands during the sixteenth century to ground their practices on constitutional principles in order to temper their illegal status.[30] English presbyterians followed suit in their own legitimacy crisis: they appealed to parliamentary statute and common law in order to bolster ecclesiastical arguments, intent on convincing lawyers of the unlawfulness of episcopal jurisdiction.[31]

However, a more complicated picture of puritanism emerges that challenges any straightforward relationship between puritanism and constitutionalism. Rather than turning to French and Dutch theories of resistance, or solely to parliament and common law, presbyterians continued to advocate a mixed polity and to appropriate the language of royal supremacy. They denied that clerical autonomy was inherent in their government, and insisted that their polity was compatible with the royal supremacy. They went further, arguing that it would prove a stronger buttress to that supremacy than episcopacy. Neither did they set parliamentary statute nor common law in opposition to the royal prerogative: they appealed to crown, parliament, and common law to attack episcopal authority and its foundations in Roman canon law.

II.

Notwithstanding the presbyterians' multilateral attack on episcopacy, the full range of puritan arguments against episcopacy can be discerned only by exploring the multidimensional nature of puritanism itself. Part Two uses presbyterianism as a point of entry into intrapuritan debates, which provide unprecedented insight into a pivotal moment: the birth of independency. This reveals that the ecclesiological taxonomy traditionally reserved for the debates of the Westminster Assembly and for the political factions of the mid-seventeenth century predated the 1640s. In fact, it appeared before the imposition of rigid conformist policies in the 1620s.

Included among Travers's newly identified manuscripts are treatises documenting the presbyterians' clandestine examination of Henry Jacob's earliest congregational experiment in Southwark in the late 1610s. They reveal that far from approving, the presbyterians directly opposed it, while carefully guarding their proceedings from being uncovered by the ecclesiastical authorities.[32] It is here that the earliest references to "independency" can be found.[33] By coining the word to describe Henry Jacob's church polity and confronting him with their objections, the presbyterians played a crucial role in the emergence of a distinct "independent" ideology that marked a turning point in history.[34] If the protracted presbyterian assault on episcopacy can be viewed as advocating a "Second Reformation," Henry Jacob can be seen to have self-consciously extended that reformation and inaugurated what might be termed a "Third Reformation."[35] While claiming to remain within the reformed Protestant tradition, rather than becoming an outright separatist, he nonetheless admitted to pushing reform further (than Calvin had) by dissolving the authority of synods. He also articulated a different understanding of the ministerial vocation, and exercise of church government at the congregational level, including the administration of the sacraments.[36]

Yet, a broader interpretation of ecclesiastical development presents another view. Historians have long attempted to trace Jacob's congregational lineage through a single church polity, whether separatism, Elizabethan puritanism, or in response to episcopal jurisdiction. A multidimensional reading of Jacob's ecclesiology reveals the revolutionary nature of his independency. In response to episcopal, presbyterian, and separatist alternatives, Jacob redefined the Church, rather than simply separating from it.[37] It is true that presbyterian reform itself may be seen to represent a much more radical reorganization of the Church akin to what one scholar has called a "disciplinary revolution."[38] Their alternative church government began from the bottom up and redefined rather than empowered royal authority in the Church by circumscribing it along consensual lines. Yet presbyterians were at pains to argue that the national church and the royal supremacy would remain more or less intact. Jacob not only dissolved the concept of a national church, replacing it with particular congregations, but he also refounded the Church of England on the principle of independence. Whereas Elizabethan separatists had chiefly appealed to a covenanted membership to underpin their polity, Jacob explicitly defined ecclesiastical liberty along neo-Roman lines, insisting that freedom in church government consisted in the absence of dependence.[39] He went further by redefining the nature of consent and arguing for the freedom of individual choice, while nonetheless claiming to remain within the bounds of England's religious establishment. This silent move to independence and peculiar ecclesiological formulation was unparalleled on the continent. In this respect, Jacob's congregationalism can not only be viewed as amounting to England's unacknowledged and silent ecclesiastical revolution but can also be seen to be as revolutionary as Luther's Reformation.

III.

Puritanism was not inherently revolutionary. The contested emergence of congregationalism reveals a crucial assumption that was shared by puritans when challenged by Jacob: the concept of a universal ecclesiastical society. As a concept that provided a theoretical basis for unitive puritanism, the idea of a single visible church needs to be stressed. The endurance of principled unity among the godly is largely missing from those accounts of puritanism and English protestantism that rely almost exclusively on sociability or a shared hostility to popery to explain solidarity. It helps to explain diverse tendencies in puritanism that agitated for decentralization on the one hand and remained committed to the Church of England on the other. Ernest Troeltsch's dichotomy between "church" and "sect" is largely responsible for the misunderstanding of English nonconformity. It has led to the assumption that presbyterianism simply mutated into either congregationalism or moderate episcopacy when suppressed. However, by revealing flexibility in puritan ecclesiology, the concept of a single visible church helps to resolve Troeltsch's puzzling dichotomy between church and sect, while also avoiding an anachronistic insertion into a separate denominational typology.[40] For the presbyterians, it meant that each and every congregation was a part of the same visible church composed of those congregations, thereby facilitating movement between the concerns of the congregation and those of the national church.

Extending beyond the writings of a small group of ideologues, this book examines the wider influences of presbyterianism in practice. Part Three explores how the presbyterians' understanding of the universal church was reflected through a basis of networks that extended throughout and beyond England and aided in the mobilization of a range of alliances. It identifies bonds among nonconformists that both reflected elements of self-government and extended beyond the congregation. Nonconformity was not by default congregational, but grounded in a broader understanding of ecclesiastical society. Presbyterian ministers exercised authority beyond the particular congregation with the support of laity, even though such lay allies might not have necessarily shared presbyterian views of church government. The emergence of a second generation of English presbyterians appears through clerical, commercial, and other lay networks that coincided with the expansion of the market in England. These were not the only channels through which presbyterianism developed, since it appears that the fear of heresy and schism also predisposed certain early Stuart puritans toward collective government beyond the particular congregation.

The concept of a universal visible church combined with confessional flex-ibility opens up the geographical scope of this study and paves the way for English presbyterian experiments overseas. The reintroduction of the concept of a universal godly society opens up new possibilities for exploring the rela-tionship between England, the continent, and the Atlantic. Part Three further explores the English Reformed Church in Amsterdam, which was established early in the seventeenth century. Alternative patterns of puritan migration can be identified that were not chiefly prompted by flight from persecution: certain puritan migrants identified with the Church of England as well as with European churches on the continent, transcending boundaries across the North Sea and the Atlantic.

The importance of history also emerges through the concept of a unified visible church. For these multidimensional and multiconfessional English controversies were located within a longer ecclesiastical tradition and broader historical genre during the early seventeenth century. The elasticity in the presbyterians' use of ancient and modern sources to establish an ecclesiastical court extended throughout history and included English protestant writers and continental contemporaries. Such proceedings transcended temporal boundaries by invoking witnesses from antiquity, thus rooting discussions in the late sixteenth and early seventeenth centuries within the context of the Church throughout history. Unresolved controversies from Tudor reform likewise resurfaced through mutual appeals to English precedent.

Another, and surprising, dimension in presbyterian elasticity concludes the story. Were the poorest artisans and laborers (both men and women) also participants in presbyterian activity in the early seventeenth century? A quantitative analysis of the social profile of the English Reformed Church in Amsterdam is made possible through the Church's detailed consistory records between 1607 and 1640. Chapter 7 uses a bivariate analysis of these records to test whether there was any relationship between the two main variables of social status and popular participation in presbyterian government. This is not to test whether presbyterianism was popular per se. Instead, it inves-tigates whether poorer men and women could be conscripted in reformed government and how they could use it to their own advantage. While the central role of city elites in supporting presbyterian ministers is confirmed, the traditional association of reformed church government and domination by members of social elites is challenged.[41] It finds the erudite discourses that took place among ecclesiastical writers to be reflected in the day-to-day opera-tion of presbyterian government on the local level. English presbyterians not only incorporated the testimony of the Fathers in their theological delibera-tions but also relied upon the testimony of poorer church members as they followed the same pattern of deliberation in their disciplinary proceedings. Poorer members, both men and women, appeared before the consistory as the chief informants, the most frequent witnesses, and as some of the most energetic participants in the debate over church government. Having experimented with the presbyterian alternative for several decades, they bear witness to the dynamic nature of English religious life before the revolutionary circumstances of the mid-seventeenth century.

PART I

English Presbyterianism and
the Church of England

CHAPTER I

Royal Supremacy

Presbyterianism, as James VI and I once put it, "agreeth with a monarchy as God and the Devil."[1] Elizabeth had been equally firm, writing to James in 1590 that "there is risen, both in your realm and in mine, a sect of perilous consequence, such as would have no kings but a presbytery, and take our place while they enjoy our privilege."[2] Charles I was emphatic that "all forms of presbyterianism were inherently subversive."[3] Central to the crown's supremacy over the Church of England was its omnicompetence in spiritual jurisdiction, replacing papal authority. Presbyterianism could hardly be taken seriously so long as monarchs believed that it infringed upon their supremacy in spirituals. For presbyterian government was based on the principle of divine right, which insisted that ecclesiastical authority came directly from God by scriptural mandate rather than by delegation through the prince. It also threatened to dissolve the crown's authority over the clergy by replacing the episcopal hierarchy with locally elected church officials.[4] That presbyterian polity aimed to topple the ecclesiastical hierarchy implied that populist forms of governance would be applied to the state and would overturn the monarchy.[5]

It was in response to the allegation that populist views of governance would be introduced in the state that presbyterians tended to stress the separation of Church and State. As Peter Lake put it, "[S]uch a distinction enabled them to argue . . . that the introduction of the discipline in the church would have no necessary effects on the structure of the authority in the state."[6] But this distinction does not provide a complete answer, since there was no positive evidence that a presbyterian system respected the royal supremacy. Furthermore, there was a danger that emphasis on the separation of Church and State resembled English recusant objections to lay authority (namely that of the prince) in the Church. For instance, Cardinal Allen argued that the Church was spiritually independent of secular authority, especially when under a heathen prince.[7]

Yet reformation of the Church had obviously relied on the intervention of the civil magistrate: Cartwright "affirm[ed] that the civil magistrate is more necessary to the Church than the sun is to life."[8] In arguing for the separation of Church and State, presbyterians were more concerned to prevent the clergy from wielding political power (as in the papal tradition) than they were to exclude lay involvement in church government. This is most obvious in their demand that lay elders be elected for oversight of the Church. Unlike separatists, presbyterians followed the magisterial reformers in affirming that the prince held legitimate authority in preserving the Church. Anticipating the potential clash between their doctrine of the two kingdoms and the Elizabethan Settlement, Cartwright employed a careful strategy whereby he "marshal[ed] the weight of his argument in favour of the view that Church and State should be two self-sufficient complete and distinct, but related, societies."[9] Peter Lake has written with clarity on this area of exasperating ambiguity:

> [In] contradistinction to the papists, Cartwright allowed the prince a right to reform the church unilaterally if and when it had fallen so deeply into corruption as to be unable to reform itself. He also retained a residual right to ignore, revoke and indeed punish the illegitimate use of excommunication by the ecclesiastical authorities. Similarly, the prince could claim a right to prior consultation before, and active participation in, church councils, but ordinarily it remained the case that the "church and commonwealth are distinguished as well under a Christian prince as under an unchristian" and the secular magistrate was, therefore, excluded from an active role in the government of the church.[10]

This is the closest definition we have of the role of the monarch in the hypothetical English presbyterian world. As it was, the allegation that presbyterianism infringed upon the royal supremacy reached deadlock in the battle between conformists and Elizabethan presbyterian ministers. On the one hand, conformists were unable to clinch the case against presbyterians at the Star Chamber trial of 1592 when "vital questions about the attitude of the puritans to the royal supremacy and to the Church of England as established by law were in general not answered or were circumvented."[11] On the other hand, this allegation, notwithstanding Cartwright's careful articulation, remained substantially unanswered; by the end of the sixteenth century it remained a primary objection to presbyterianism and silence proved to be fatal. The logical explanation for their lack of response would appear to be that there was no longer any hope of presbyterian reform—that conformists had successfully extinguished it and continued to gain preferment by imagining a presbyterian threat where there was none.

One commentator has recently observed that the absence of a presbyterian response is "quite difficult to account for" given the "large-scale treatises of

[Whitgift's] supporters" against them.[12] Indeed, the late sixteenth and early seventeenth centuries were increasingly marked by defensive assertions of the crown's supremacy, which makes sense if the persistence of presbyterianism for the duration of this period is acknowledged.[13] On one level, presbyterians in fact represented a continued challenge to supremacy by its subjection of the crown's authority to collective jurisdiction and biblical precedent.

But was presbyterianism as inherently antimonarchical and subversive as conformists had contemporaries believe? Scholars have increasingly drawn attention to the ambiguous nature of royal supremacy, which could be appropriated in diverse ways to serve both royalist and radical ends.[14] Many historians have followed Patrick Collinson's lead in viewing the government of Elizabethan England as no mere despotism, but essentially a monarchical republic,[15] and it was in this context that English presbyterianism, which itself emphasized the idea of a mixed church polity, first took root. The treatise "Reformed Church Government" sheds further light on how the presbyterians continued to exploit the concept of a mixed polity and the malleable nature of supremacy to their own advantage. It provides the most detailed presbyterian response to conformist allegations of political subversion to date and indicates that presbyterians continued to champion an alternative exposition of royal supremacy that was independent of episcopacy.

This treatise offers the same defense as Cartwright to the charge that presbyterianism conceived of the possibility of excommunicating the prince and hence could act as a stimulus for resistance: that in the Church of England as at the time constituted Christian princes were already subject to excommunication. More specifically, "[E]xcommunication hath no such force [to withdraw the obedience of subjects & depose princes]." Unlike Pope Pius V's bull excommunicating Elizabeth and absolving recusants from their allegiance to a heretical prince, presbyterians argued that spiritual censure was no basis for resistance or repudiation of the political claims of the prince, for "heathen Princes be still princes." Similarly, "[If] the husband be excommunicate he is still notwithstanding as An husband to be reverenced and obeyed of his wife. And so if a kinge be excommunicate he is still a king notwithstanding as he was before, And therefore as a kinge to be still obeyed of all his Subjects."[16]

The burden of the treatise, however, was not to refute theories of resistance, but to argue that a presbyterian polity would not detract from the queen's supremacy over the Church. It outlines a form of government that most closely represents a presbyterian polity transposed upon the existing Church of England. Thus it fused a presbyterian polity with royal supremacy, a characteristic strategy argued from the earliest Elizabethan presbyterian apologists onward.[17] In his first presbyterian treatise, Walter Travers had similarly presented an "Anglicized" model of presbyterianism, using the term "bishop" to describe the pastor of a local congregation who would exercise authority alongside lay elders.[18] Although a working relationship between the monarch and a presbyterian polity might have proved problematic, the nature of royal supremacy in the late sixteenth century did not entirely rule out a mixed polity.[19] As Paul Avis has stated, Elizabeth's supremacy "was increasingly regarded as shared with parliament: it was the supremacy of queen-in-parliament."[20] Thus Lake has warned that "before we join Whitgift and the other conformists in writing this [presbyterian] vision off as impossibly radical and un-English in its attitude to the power of the prince, it is worth pausing to consider just how closely such an interpretation fitted the situation and early history of the Elizabethan regime."[21]

The main strategy in the "Reformed Church Government" was to stress that presbyterianism could be united with royal supremacy through minimal change—namely, by the simple substitution of ministers and elders for bishops:

> Whilst some have imagined & others have not ceased to suggest, that this Cause of the Reformed Church governement doth oppugne hir Majestyes* supreme government and authority, which it doth not so much as touch much lesse violate or empayre . . . suppose that the Pastor and the other Elders in every Congregation were the Church governors (for the executinge & ministery of the Church censures) in the roome of our Bishops their underofficers & spirituall Courts, is† it not playne and manifest, √ notwithstanding √ that hir majestyes supreme governement & Authority remayneth (as is meete it should) untouched & unblemished, as is was before? For there is nothing done herein, but the substituting of the Pastor and Elders to be the Church governors . . . (in the roome of our Bishops, their underofficers and Courts as is aforesaide) and that in respect of the exercise of the church censures only.[22]

The argument for simple substitution could be made to more effect when conformist divines such as Bancroft began themselves to take on board the presbyterian principle of *jure divino* church government.[23] Divine right episcopacy could be used to affirm the royal supremacy, as in Scotland where it was endorsed by James as "Bishop of Bishops and universal Bishop within his Realm."[24] But to English presbyterians, those who supported *jure divino* episcopacy made the Church no less independent of royal control than did presbyterian ecclesiology. *Jure divino* arguments thus forfeited the conformists' strongest case against presbyterianism, that it curbed the authority of the Christian prince.[25] Thus English presbyterians could claim that their polity

*government
†no

was as fully as respectful of royal authority as that of episcopalians: "For how can hir Maiestyes Authority be any way empayred or diminished, though the exercise of the Church censures should be taken from our Bishiops, their underofficers & Courts, consideringe that although they exercise them by permission & sufferance of the Prince, yet the power & Authority thereof they clayme by Commission from god, & from his divyne institution."[26]

Despite the fact that the "Reformed Church Government" is chiefly fixed on the need to establish parity among ministers and to elect lay elders, it is clearly not describing a form of congregational government. For it affirms a single national Church and adherence to authoritative church government beyond the particular congregation. The overriding concern to demonstrate that ministerial parity was compatible with monarchy shapes the argument to such an extent that it is instead more likely to be read as advocating moderate episcopacy. Having argued extensively (in over thirty folios) against the principle of superiority among the clergy, it goes on to allow for "Bishops of the Dioceses or provinces, [or shire]* or of the whole Nation."[27] Although these were not to be altogether without function, it is clear that they were circumscribed almost entirely along presbyterian lines and served primarily as a token to close the gap between a presbyterian polity and the royal supremacy. They were to be ministers of a particular flock, exercising authority with neighboring ministers alongside lay elders. More crucially, they neither held disciplinary authority over the other ministers nor acted as moderators in synods and assemblies.

The key was that the prince had to be given some measure of authority in church government, and this was more difficult to establish in ecclesiastical appointments than in other areas of government where the queen could simply be tacked on in the final verdict.[28] For obvious reasons, if the queen were to retain her authority through appointing bishops, some form of diocesan bishop had to exist in addition to ordinary ministers. Under the hybrid "presbyterian-royal supremacy," the queen was given "nomination of thos pastors that should be Bishops of the Dioceses or provinces† or of the whole Nation."[29] But if presbyterians insisted that a superior officer such as a diocesan bishop was not prescribed in the New Testament, who could accept such office? The most appropriate solution was to apply the title of bishop to all ministers, removing any implication of superiority, while allowing some ministers to accept added responsibilities, the most substantial of which was the summoning of synods.[30]

This may appear to be a form of moderate episcopacy akin to that es-

*[crossed out]
†or shire

tablished by James in Scotland.[31] However, as this treatise argues throughout, "[T]he exercise of the church Censures which our Bishops $\lor$ & their
courts $\lor$ have got into their hands" belonged to "the Pastor & other Elders
of every Congregation who claime them of right to belonge to them."[32] For,
"[I]nequality of gifts causeth no inequality of Authority."[33] Furthermore, the
moderate episcopal model was focused on the institution of a permanent
moderator over synods. As Conrad Russell has commented in the case of Scotland, "[In] the grey area of compromises between episcopacy and presbytery,
it was arguably the difference between permanent and temporary moderators
of synods which constituted the watershed."[34] Yet the writer of the "Reformed
Church Government" explained that once the council had been summoned
authority passed to "the gathering of voices" whereby a temporary moderator
was chosen.[35] Moderate episcopacy also excluded lay officers from provincial
and national synods. The early-seventeenth-century defender of episcopacy,
George Downame, centered his attack on presbyterianism on the inclusion
of lay elders in synods even more than on the temporary moderator that they
advocated.[36] Only select clergy were to be sent to synods as representatives
of their church or diocese in Archbishop James Ussher's moderate episcopal
scheme, which, because of its very moderation, was to become a platform for
negotiation between presbyterians and episcopalians later in the seventeenth
century.[37] Yet the writer of the "Reformed Church Government" was adamant
that lay elders be included in synods. Those who chose a moderator were to
be not only pastors and doctors but also "Elders and Deacons."[38] Rather than
advocating a moderate form of episcopacy, therefore, this peculiar model
can be more sensitively described as a presbyterian government tailored to
accommodate royal supremacy.

    If there are rare glimpses into presbyterian attempts to reconcile itself with
the crown at the very end of the sixteenth century, it is also possible to discern
the role of the prince in presbyterian thought during the early Stuart period.
Travers was fascinated by Bullinger's *De Conciliis*. He thought it highly significant that Bullinger drew attention to the fact that Constantine publicly
summoned a council "not by the authority of the Empire but rather as christian emperor from the power of the church."[39] Travers's reading was not only
conditioned by his concern to counter the congregationalists but was also recorded on the eve of the Laudian campaign to roll back "protestant" advances
that had been made between the reign of Henry VIII and that of James I.[40]
Travers also noted how, with time, civil rulers eventually gained authority in
calling councils, "whence it was made by time that at length the Emperors
called and had to themselves the right of calling synods."[41] However, unable
to agree with this interpretation without qualification, Travers adds to Bull-

inger's account, "because certainly it appertains to the civil magistrate when the Church is remiss and negligent."[42] This statement indicates an important element in Travers's thought on civil authority that was left deliberately ambiguous in his printed writing—namely, in what circumstances the institution of presbyterianism would allow the monarch to exercise authority over the Church. That this would only be under exceptional conditions is made clear by the strength of Travers's language ("cessante"). Not only did Travers modify Bullinger's interpretation on this point, but he took care to emphasize what he was saying by underlining this statement. Travers's addition to Bullinger's text directly contrasts with what follows in Bullinger's historical narrative.[43]

Travers was equally concerned to observe that when princes surrendered their authority to call councils to an ecclesiastical hierarchy, the result was tyranny and civil unrest.[44] The source for this was not rebellious subjects but the tyranny of the ecclesiastical hierarchy, the exclusion of the civil magistrate, and the subjection of church councils to papal authority.[45] Travers noted the example of Alexander, who "came into the city whence also many Italian cities revolted, with him persuading subjects against their oath and loyalty to their temporal lord."[46] Bullinger had applied this argument directly to the English in 1570 when Pius V issued his bull excommunicating Elizabeth.[47] It is highly significant that Travers records passages that condemned subjects who repudiated their political loyalty on the grounds of ecclesiastical allegiance. This highlights that the presbyterians' qualified acceptance of the queen's supremacy was in fact different from the attitude of recusants toward the queen as supreme governor. The contents of *De Conciliis* that drew Travers's attention were similar to Bullinger's other writings, as he described the illegitimacy of papal supremacy, the rightful rule of the civil magistrate, and concluded with the wars resulting from papal claims to authority in the Middle Ages.[48] In Travers's seventeenth-century reading of Bullinger, we are back to Cartwright's earlier qualified acceptance of the royal supremacy that allowed for the prince's involvement in the Church on occasion and in exceptional circumstance and on the assumption that the prince was Christian and protestant.

This view is echoed in *The Letters Patents of the Presbyterie,* a treatise written in 1632 that argues against episcopal authority and in favor of presbyterian reform. Its primary concern was to demonstrate that the bishop's office was "pastoral, ouer one flocke and congregation, wherein he is an Elder, and with other Elders an ouerseer of the same."[49] Yet beyond the congregation, the treatise also affirmed the "calling of Synods to reduce doctrine, and discipline to that of the Apostles," in which lay elders were involved.[50] Written after many of the godly had become thoroughly disillusioned with the king and his ecclesiastical policy, it is no surprise to find, at the beginning of the treatise, a critical statement on the prince's judgment: "Princes are men such as trust to much to theire iudgment and protection, do oft finde themselves rewarded accordingly."[51] However, the writer nonetheless describes the responsibility of the prince in upholding the Church: the "calling of Synods . . . indeed should be furthered, cherished, and maintained by kings, and Magistrates, as by nursing fathers."[52] The writer's second reference to the role of the prince highlights the monarch's role not in the daily exercise of authority but in intervening when necessary against heresy or for reform of the Church: "That Christian Kings, as *nursing fathers* haue great authority in like cases . . . in things necessarie, as reformation of abuses supressing errours, abolishying of idolatrie, and superstitious rites and gouernments, reestablishing a preaching ministrie, and Elders, and ordaining ordinances, and ceremonies, so necessarie, as those aboue mencioned." Furthermore the writer added "that God will require it of them, if they doe not looke after these things."[53]

While a more elaborate role for the prince was offered in response to accusations against presbyterianism by the end of the sixteenth century, rare glimpses into presbyterian attitudes during the early seventeenth century reveal that presbyterians such as Travers, although unrelentingly hostile to ecclesiastical hierarchy, could still recognize that the prince might have some measure of authority in the Church.[54] As the reign of Charles progressed, it would have been increasingly difficult to sustain the hope that the prince would nurse the Church satisfactorily. In the attempt to argue that presbyterianism in no way conflicted with royal supremacy, there had been a conspicuous silence on what would happen if a prince was not Christian and protestant, or even Calvinist. If popish and "heathen Princes be still Princes," could presbyterians bring themselves to acknowledge such a prince as supreme governor of the Church of England? For although presbyterians may not have been inherently antimonarchical, their respect for royal supremacy had nonetheless always been conditional. Be that as it may, Elizabeth and James were not about to be convinced that presbyterianism was compatible with monarchy. If anything, presbyterianism had prompted them to make defensive assertions of their imperial authority, which was no insignificant consequence for political developments in the seventeenth century.[55] By the 1630s, the shrewdest polemical tactic for the presbyterians was instead to ratchet up their attack on episcopacy.

CHAPTER 2

Anti-Episcopacy

The history of the Church of England has long been driven by competing narratives of episcopacy. Previous historians focused on the puritans' implacable hostility to bishops and their criticism of the inefficiency of church courts, to explain the eventual abolition of both in the mid-seventeenth century.[1] In recent years this narrative has been considerably modified. In place of widespread anti-episcopacy, and the view that their demise was inevitable, a much more positive and nuanced picture of episcopal reputation and jurisdiction has been painted.[2] That some puritans distinguished between Calvinist and Arminian bishops suggests that they might have welcomed the idea of a moderate episcopal settlement, so long as it remained unmistakably reformed and protestant. That English presbyterians fused their polity with royal supremacy suggests that they too were prepared to accept some form of moderate episcopacy. Their persistence in the Church of England reveals that their existence was somehow compatible with the existing jurisdiction. Such a reading of presbyterianism is supported by Travers's final treatise, *Vindiciae Ecclesiae Anglicanae*, which was an extended defense of the Church of England.[3]

A closer study of English presbyterianism, however, reveals that it posed a long-standing opposition to episcopacy. While presbyterians endured prelates in practice, respected individual bishops, and defended the Church of England, they directly opposed episcopacy from their earliest days and did not cease from making broader objections to it. They challenged the very nature of episcopacy and made extensive arguments against the civil powers that the bishops claimed. Episcopacy, they argued, was not only unbiblical but unnatural. It was also unconstitutional, unlawful, and un-English.

With a view to replacing episcopacy with an alternative form of church government, presbyterians appealed both to MPs and justices of the peace, elaborating on the series of benefits (both spiritual and material) that would follow from the institution of a plurality of elders in the place of bishops.[4] In an attempt to initiate a reconfiguration of ecclesiastical and civil government along presbyterian lines, they called for a second reformation that would bring about a more godly society. Some historians have argued that the puritans' complaints and the activist drive for moral reform were in substance little different from late medieval precedents, while others have drawn attention to a willingness among establishment divines to correct abuses and reform the existing system in order to achieve a godly society.[5] Moreover, criticisms of episcopacy, even on the eve of its abolition, appeared to be suggesting no more than a return to primitive episcopacy stripped of its civil office.[6] However, presbyterian complaints were tied to an entirely different vision of government based on local jurisdiction. While at times they were content to use the term "bishop" themselves, such office was devoid of any temporal function and hierarchy and essentially defined as a local minister.[7] Contemporary critics were convinced that presbyterianism threatened radically to reorganize the entire church structure. Indeed, presbyterian discipline began from the bottom up with local and stationary courts that were embedded in the community. Although presbyterians downplayed the novelty in their ecclesiology, one scholar has argued that such a jurisdiction would have amounted to no less than a "disciplinary revolution."[8] Its fundamental reorganization of jurisdiction introduced an alternative infrastructure for religious government and instituted new mechanisms for social control.

AGAINST NATURE: THE BISHOP AS HERMAPHRODITE

When asked to describe Archbishop Whitgift in 1587, the separatist Henry Barrow pronounced: "He is a monster, a miserable Compound, I know not what to make him: he is neither Ecclesiasticall nor ciuill, even that second Beast spoken of in the Reuelation."[9] Although in public presbyterians distanced themselves from such Elizabethan radicals, they nonetheless continued to perpetuate their criticisms in the late 1590s and the first few decades of the seventeenth century. The "Reformed Church Government," for instance, compared the bishops' exercise of civil authority to "hermaphroditas that is, such as were of both sexes."[10] This caricature clearly aimed to represent prelacy as a monstrosity that collapsed civil and ecclesiastical boundaries: as in its nature corrupt and unnatural. Yet the hermaphroditic metaphor had multiple meanings in the early modern period and diverse readings of it can open up the broader social and juridical context of the presbyterians' objections alongside the theological ones.[11]

Allegations of hermaphroditism could make a theological point by means of a social statement. Transgression of gender roles, for instance, may help to explain how presbyterians maligned bishops as violators of social norms that they could use to promote an alternative view of the ministry. On one reading, the term "hermaphrodite" might characterize the bishop as a masculine female. The bishop who assumed civil office could be compared to a woman who violated order by entering into the male domain. The "Reformed Church Government" argued that clerics ought to follow Christ's model as a servant rather than ruler: for he "*came not to beare rule*, but *to serue* & therefore neither ought his ministers to beare rule in kingdoms, but to serve (as becometh them) in the Church."[12] Presbyterians further supported the view that bishops acted out of character by appealing to New Testament prohibitions against the exercise of civil authority by ecclesiastical persons. Christ's example and teaching were again a primary example for the separation of minister and magistrate.[13] Yet conformists disputed that Christ strictly prohibited the Apostles from exercising civil jurisdiction; they argued that Christ had condemned only tyrannical and unjust rule. In response, the writer of the "Reformed Church Government" defended interpretation of passages in Matthew 20 and Mark 10 as having no connotation of unjust rule but prohibiting any form of civil office whatsoever.[14]

On another reading, the term "hermaphrodite" might imply male effeminacy by association with excess, indulgence, and the lack of self-control.[15] The affluence of Jacobean churchmen was the object of envy and scorn among puritans and other critics, whose complaints of episcopal extravagance and intemperance abound.[16] Upon the abolition of episcopacy, the presbyterians planned to redistribute the wealth of the Church among clergy and the needy. Travers argued that "the neede off a great nombre may be relieued by the abundance and excess off a few," while "Cartwright admitted that there was a very close connection between the agitation against episcopacy and the desire that the property of the bishoprics should be devoted to what puritans considered the general good of the church."[17] Such criticism reached its zenith in anti-Laudian satire that played on themes such as the archbishop's insatiable appetite, habitually gorging and vomiting. It even juxtaposed physical excesses with his lack of restraint in the use of harsh secular punishments.[18] Such antiprelatical satire, which included "grotesque humour concerning body odour, festering disease, gluttony, vomiting, excretion and sexual transgression [was] firmly grounded in the cultural practices of sixteenth- and seventeenth-century Protestant polemics and their predecessors."[19]

Male effeminacy, however, corresponds more closely to the presbyterians' repeated complaint that bishops abdicated their spiritual responsibilities by enamoring themselves with worldly affairs.[20] Although puritan complaints that prelates were negligent about the care of souls in their dioceses have been challenged, the growing centrality of their secular responsibilities is clear.[21]

Presbyterians seized upon the exercise of civil office by bishops to argue that meddling in civil matters was an indulgence and led to lax oversight of spiritual matters. The writer of the "Reformed Church Government" stressed the demanding duties charged to the minister: "[If] this charge were well considered . . . ministers of the worde would have little lust & think themselves to have litle leasure to busy them selues in civill affayres."[22] For William Stoughton, civil office automatically nullified the bishop's role as cleric on account of spiritual negligence by likening it to removal for heresy and other greater offenses.[23] Indeed, the "emphasis on preaching as the chief function of a bishop encouraged men to think of him as a mere pastor," and "from the beginning it had been dangerous to episcopacy."[24]

Concern for a preaching ministry was integral to attacks against episcopacy during the early seventeenth century.[25] While rivalry for civil office may have prompted MPs to target the civil authority of bishops in the 1620s and 1630s, "such resentment, however, was reinforced by a belief that the very nature of the clerical function was so different from that of the secular magistracy as to be incompatible with it."[26] The Commons also stressed the spiritual obligations appertaining to ecclesiastical office: "Temporal office, moreover, was held to distract clergymen from their calling . . . [and] this had been one reason given for the Commons' attempts in the 1620s to remove clergymen from the commission of the peace."[27]

Beyond comparison with the transgression of gender roles, the overarching use of the term "hermaphrodite" was to argue against the blurring of ecclesiastical and civil boundaries. By extension, this presented the bishop's office as a fantastical and unnatural creation. Travers's earliest known articulation of presbyterianism recounted the bishops' gradual accumulation of civil responsibility "till they had mingled the Church and the common-wealth ciuil and Ecclesiastical matters, and confounded the Kingdom and the bishoprick together." Alluding to the state of marriage, he argued that such mingling of the civil and ecclesiastical inverted the divinely ordained state of nature: "[B]ut as that which God hath ioyned no man can separate. so we may not thinke that any man can ioynne or couple together that which he hath seuered and diuided asunder."[28] The "Reformed Church Government" likewise argued against the bishops' civil authority along natural lines: "[F]or as the state civil & ecclesiasticall be things distinct so Bishops (by the ordinanc of god) being appointed to the state Ecclesiasticall & a naturall parte thereof, can no more . . . be a naturall parte of the civil state, then the understandinge parte or power of the soule can be a true or naturall parte of the body or corporall substance of A man."[29]

Presbyterian ministers were not alone in arguing against the "mingling" of civil and ecclesiastical offices. William Stoughton has not received adequate recognition for his role as a lawyer in challenging bishops head-on with legal arguments for the lawfulness of instituting presbyterian polity. The publication of his *Abstract* in 1584 marks a turning point from mere criticism of episcopacy to arguments against its very nature. Although the bulk of the *Abstract* was devoted to arguing for the need for a learned ministry, it demanded more than improved standards in clerical training. Like other apologists,[30] he argued for presbyterian government in the place of prelates who "make a hotche potche of the Cleargie and layetie . . . a mingle mangle of Pastours, and people . . . so that by this their iumbling of offices together, there can be nothing but confusion and disorder."[31] The defense of presbyterian government in *Letters Patents* in 1632 also recounted how after Constantine with "the Empire being diuided . . . the Bishops for the most part were made councellors of the Prince, which by mixture of spirituall and temporall charges, caused their iurisdiction to increase exceedingly."[32]

That the bishops' civil office embodied, rather than simply enacted, a transgression against nature appears from further objections. According to the presbyterians, examples from the Old Testament showed "the lord leauing [Moses] onely the charge off the commonwelth [he] commited the government off the church to Aaron his brother . . . which distinction and difference was allwais diligently observed by all that cam after until king Vzziah."[33] The writer of the "Reformed Church Government" used the same argument, discounting the example of "melchisedech, both kinge and priest (gen. 14.18)" who preceded the law given at Sinai whereby the priest and judge were made distinct and were to continue as separate officers as described in Deuteronomy.[34] In explaining the distinction between the two offices, the writer made clear that the priest himself was neither to judge nor to give sentence. This was not to say that the judge did not consult the priest, but to stress that the priest and judge were two distinct persons with different responsibilities:[35]

> [T]he priests office was (in matters of controversye) to teach what was the law, and the Judges to give sentence & Judgment* according thereunto . . . for the priest and the judge be two, & expressely distinguished & severed† the one from the other . . . the priest was to direct the judge & to teach him the law: and the judge was to give sentence accordingly.[36]

Given that the offices of priest and judge were separate and could not be held by the same person, that the Court of High Commission was so offensive becomes comprehensible. As R. G. Usher showed, Bancroft was the prime

*thereupon
†from

mover in the transformation of the High Commission, which traditionally had been controlled by statesmen as a political body with power to impose secular punishments into "a permanent court of ecclesiastical law . . . supplying that coercive power which the bishops lacked."[37] In the Court of High Commission, bishops violated the separation of the two offices established at Sinai by acting as judges and further imposing secular sentences for ecclesiastical offenses.

The term "hermaphrodite" was applicable not only to the civil office of the bishop but also to jurisdictional indeterminacy. Like the physical hermaphrodite who created an early modern legal puzzle,[38] the presbyterians argued that bishops problematized juridical categories through the elision of subject matters in their courts and by their use of both spiritual and temporal punishments. They argued that all material and temporal matters were the province of the secular courts, and again presented the blurring of ecclesiastical and civil lines as contrary to nature. As the "Reformed Church Government" clearly expressed, "all Causes˙ whatsoever belong to the Commodity of this life, belong† of civil jurisdiction, & repugnant to the nature of Ecclesiastical Jurisdiction."[39]

Ecclesiastical and civil lines were further blurred by the bishops' use of the civil sword. Presbyterians argued that only spiritual censures should be administered by ecclesiastical officers.[40] Travers directly applied the separation of Church and State to church courts in his exposition of presbyterian government, the *Declaration* first published in 1574: "For as this counsell is Ecclesiasticall, and the court a spirituall court . . . distinguished by S. Paul, from the ciuill courts . . . So also the punishments is speciall and such as belongeth to the soule and Conscience, and concerneth not this life, nor those things with which the ciuill magistrate is wont to deale."[41] In this context, he argued for a distinction between ecclesiastical and secular punishment in order to counter conformists who "punish by the purse or imprisonment."[42]

This criticism of church courts was the same as that made by lawyers during the later sixteenth and early seventeenth centuries. Earlier in the sixteenth century, writers such as Christopher St. German had criticized the abuse of secular power by bishops and provided many of the same arguments that Travers would use.[43] However, Travers's explicit objection to the use of civil punishments takes on a new importance. By including these arguments in the first systematic English presbyterian treatise, Travers incorporated them into a broader argument against the nature of episcopacy, linked to his proposal for an alternative church government.

*and
†to

Complaints of episcopal negligence along with corruption of their jurisdiction were thus represented as inherent in the nature of their office, not merely a result of the personal shortcomings of Laudian bishops. In the final analysis, the "assessment of the episcopal record in its entirety enabled many members to see the Laudian bishops' secular pursuits and restriction of preaching as unprecedented only in degree, not kind."[44] This helps to explain the growing view in the Long Parliament that instead of simply aiming to remove Laudian personnel, the Elizabethan settlement should be entirely uprooted.[45] Indeed, mid-seventeenth century satirical depictions of bishops as "grotesque hybrid creatures" with "insatiable greed"[46] drew on a long tradition of Elizabethan and Jacobean criticism that represented them as unnatural beings.

THE LEGAL FOUNDATIONS OF "ROOT AND BRANCH" ABOLITION

While the presbyterians made their case for the unnaturalness of episcopacy by invoking the hermaphroditic bishop, they made the political case for uprooting episcopacy through a series of legal and constitutional arguments, which had affinities with a wider critique of the Church court.[47] As early as 1583 Stoughton insisted that bishops ought to be removed on legal and constitutional grounds. For him, the election and calling of unlearned men to multiple benefices was contrary to the Act of Submission of the Clergy (25 Henry VIII, ch. 19), a statute he later used to strike at the very roots of episcopal authority. He was convinced that prelates acted against public interest and according to private presumption.[48] Furthermore, he argued that many of the bishops' practices were uncanonical and condemned "by Prouinciall constitutions of England."[49] The writer of the "Reformed Church Government" claimed that precedent in the common law in the time of Edward III "would not allow Bishops to deale in secular causes for hindering their Ecclesisaticall function."[50] In addition to their appeal to parliamentary statute and common law, presbyterians also championed their cause under the banner of royal authority by arguing that episcopal-clericalism undermined the crown's supremacy.

Aside from the presbyterians' alleged infringement of the royal supremacy, it was their attack on bishops that was seen to be politically seditious. It threatened the removal of bishops not only from the Church but also from parliament.[51] Anti-presbyterians equated the abolition of episcopacy with revolution by arguing that removing the bishops from the House of Lords would overthrow the estates of the land in parliament and give rise to anarchy. Thus far, there has been little evidence that presbyterians involved themselves in this issue: Michael Mendle argued that they avoided the appearance of political sedition implicit in their appeals by refraining from the language of "estates."[52] However, in the "Reformed Church Government" there is not only the explicit rejection of the episcopal estate but also a series of arguments to show that the removal of bishops from the House of Lords would not alter the three estates of parliament:[53] "[H]owsoever Lords spirituall by favour of Princes have beene added & adioyned to the state . . . yet they are not to be reputed Any of the three estates."[54] Here the constitutional implications of the presbyterian ecclesiological agenda are spelled out.

> Lord Bishops be no more parte of the state now then Lord Abbots were in former tymes, whos dissolution sheweth that the dissolution also of Lord Bishops can prove no Blemish to the state for although all Lords Spirituall were extinct, yet the three Estates of the lands in parliament should remayne in their full number, & absolute perfection Iudge Dyer . . . doth reporte & record that the three Estates of the lande in parliament be thes 1. The King. or Queene the heade of the same 2. The Lords the Chiefe and principall members of this body. 3. the Comons . . . Now then suppose lord Bishops to be extinct, yet it is manifest that the three Estates of the lande Parliament do remayne still by whom lawes & statuts may be made & have the full strength, as before.[55]

In arguing that bishops be denied the title of lordship, the writer explained the distinction between the title as one signifying noble status and as one signifying civil authority: "For he is not borne A magistrate, though he be a lorde by Birth. And so he might be a lord in title & yet exercise no lordship civill magistracy or Jurisdiction in the comen weale as our Bishops doe."[56] Thus the writer complained that bishops not only seized civil authority that was not proper to the ministerial calling but also assumed a higher status by virtue of spiritual appointment. Since the presbyterians themselves had been accused of opportunism, the writer turned this accusation around by depicting the bishops as opportunists whose lordship was at odds with their true status. For even if a man of noble status were to become a bishop, "neither can he be called a Lord Bishop properly, But Lord such a one as his father was called. Let therfore all vayne cavilling goe."[57] If bishops threatened to muddle gender roles on the one hand, they blatantly subverted social order on the other.

Presbyterianism was at heart an alternative ecclesiastical jurisdiction; the "displanting" of bishops therefore also meant the "uprooting" of its "branches." Advocates claimed that it could be instituted by the simple substitution of lay elders for bishops. However, along with the removal of bishops, they intended the complete dissolution of the existing church courts and the utter repeal of the Romano-canonical tradition. The "Reformed Church Government" wished for nothing less than that "Bishops Courts . . . be dissolved, upon the placing of this reformed Church government."[58] The presbyterian assault on church courts alongside common law rivalry with the spiritual tribunals helps to explain the blossoming of civilian literature and defenses of church courts during this period. There were undoubtedly differences between ecclesiastical and legal arguments against church courts. But was there overlap between presbyterian and legal objections to episcopal proceedings? Among the lay supporters of the presbyterians were the so-called puritan lawyers who defended them before the High Commission and Court of Star Chamber during the 1590s and supplied the ministers with legal advice during their trials.[59] It appears that this was no momentary alliance. After their formal suppression in the early 1590s, presbyterians continued to direct their arguments for ecclesiastical reform to lawyers and judges. They further took it upon themselves to interpret English statute against Roman canon law and to determine appropriate forms of punishment. They even discussed the redistribution of matters tried in church and common law courts, a subject traditionally reserved for common law judges alone.

It was no coincidence that the puritans' legal opposition to the Church coincided with the height of the conflict between presbyterians and defenders of episcopacy. Travers's arguments against the use of secular punishments by the bishops and their jurisdiction over civil matters appeared on the eve of puritan legal arguments in the later sixteenth century. The fact that such criticism of church courts appeared as early as 1574 is of special significance, since Travers was renowned as a popular preacher among the lawyers in his lectureship at the Temple Church during the 1580s. Thomas Fuller recorded that "not only young students but even the gravest benchers sat at the feet of Travers, the Temple lecturer who was Hooker's great rival, eagerly making notes."[60] Indeed, the most powerful voice of opposition to the bishops' ecclesiastical jurisdiction in the early seventeenth century, Sir Edward Coke himself, "was among the Inner Temple lawyers who took notes of the sermons preached by Walter Travers."[61]

An important caveat must be stressed from the outset: rather than seeking to establish a one-to-one relationship between political patronage or argument and particular religious beliefs, the following instead attempts to ascertain the degree to which men *could* formulate alliances to establish mutually supportive programs. These alliances could exist within a diverse range of patronage links and religious beliefs,[62] contrary to contemporary suspicions that lawyers were themselves motivated by a hidden ecclesiastical agenda. Such a connection between presbyterian and legal arguments was first suggested by Bancroft, who alleged that Sir Francis Knollys "was not acting on his own account but simply as frontman for the Disciplinarian puritans who supplied him with arguments 'to manage at Court for the party.'"[63] Arguments made in parliament were obviously cast as matters of state, since the initiation of discussion on ecclesiastical matters had been strictly prohibited by Elizabeth. Lawyers carefully avoided making statements on ecclesiology in parliament. Nevertheless, they were repeatedly accused of ulterior motives after the emergence of presbyterianism in the late sixteenth century. The lawyer, clerk of the Privy Council, MP, and diplomat Robert Beale denied adherence to presbyterian polity, but the authorities were nevertheless convinced that he was a sympathizer.[64] Mark Taviner found that in practice Beale chiefly acted not as a "'man of business' in the sense of an automated instrument of the Privy Council's desires, but a man driven by his own personal political and religious ideologies and loyalties to act as he saw fit."[65] The fact that lawyers such as Beale were not always strictly bound by ties of patronage in performing their public duties demonstrates that public servants were able to favor nonconformists in practice even if they refrained from articulating the exact nature of their sympathies in parliament and even if they themselves were not presbyterian by conviction.

Scarcely any evidence has yet been presented to show that presbyterians directly supplied jurists with arguments against church courts. Even though senior lawyers, such as James Morice, who opposed the practices of bishops in church courts were well acquainted with and attended the sermons of men like Travers and John Knewstubbs, it might be argued that such ministers were not likely to have preached on this subject from the pulpit.[66] Moreover, after the 1592 trial, it appears that no presbyterian would have dared to speak against church courts or to press for presbyterian reform. According to Travers's interpretation of Thomas Cartwright's later life, "Mr Cartwright . . . never intended to incorage any man by way of schisme or any unlawfull cours to further the cause of reformation . . . confirmed . . . namly by the peaceable carige of his ministry in the midest of this church \/ [of] England at Warwicke\/."[67]

Cartwright's later career did indeed seem to demonstrate exemplary conformity. However, a manuscript copy of his letter to Sir Christopher Yelverton dating from 1603, just months before Cartwright died, is revealing. For while appearing to exercise moderation, Cartwright, who had legal experience himself, persisted in pursuing a legal course of reform. Cartwright did not need to spell out his presbyterian views in order to criticize the existing ecclesiastical jurisdiction.[68] Instead of himself launching headlong into opposition to church courts, he shared arguments against church courts with others who would take up the battle. He not only drew the connection between abuses in church courts and their contradiction of English statutes but also gave this information to Yelverton and commissioned him to further this case and to lead others on:

> I have inclosed a short survey of sundrye the abuses, of the spirituall courts, that by confrontinge them with the lawes of the lande, you might the better understande the lamentable servitude the church is in to the hande? lords and yf the lord would enlarge your Christian, heart so farre, as in subscribinge the same supplication, as the principall weather of the flocke, to goe before the rest: as I am perswaded the rest would followe with great chearefulnes.[69]

Thus, even though lawyers might not have shared all the presbyterians' religious convictions or all their political aims, presbyterians seem to have actively sought alliance and intellectual exchange. As Allen Boyer commented, Coke "remained close to the Puritans in England—whose work he aided, whose phrases he quoted, and who numbered him, with themselves, among the Lord's servants."[70] In addition to writing to Yelverton, it seems that Cartwright had given Coke a copy of his commentary on the Book of Ecclesiastes.[71] Boyer further suggests that the Elizabethan presbyterian Richard Rogers "may have known Coke as early as the 1560s," and in 1615 Rogers dedicated his commentary on the Book of Judges to Coke.[72] M. M. Knappen commented that in Richard Rogers's earlier Elizabethan career, he was "an active participant in the . . . secret presbytery movement which was at its height."[73] Although historians have tended to focus on Rogers's pastoral concerns, portraying him as a nonpoliticized puritan after the 1590s, he urged Coke to take responsibility for preserving the Church in his dedication:

> God who hath made you a principall member in this great bodie of our land, both in gifts personall and publique . . . therefore hee expects that you drop it . . . vpon his Church and Gospell . . . to the promoting and aduancing whereof, the aduantage of your Honour and authoritie (besides your other gifts) is chiefly to be employed.[74]

The "Reformed Church Government" provides evidence that presbyterians directed their arguments against church courts to lawyers and judges after their trials in the early 1590s and that their arguments were rooted in their platform for presbyterian reform. The treatise was written for an audience that included none other than the "learned and reverend Judges and other Lawyers of this Realme and all equall indifferent persons whosoever specially of thes that be in Authoritye."[75] Its main argument, that bishops could be replaced by pastors and elders with deference to "hir maiestyes supreme governement and authoritye," is immediately followed by an attack on the bishops and in particular their church courts.[76] The writer not only provided lesser magistrates with arguments against episcopal jurisdiction, he further urged them to act on behalf of the godly and to counter their adversaries:

The Judges & Magistrates of this lande must remember themselves to be Christian & protestant Judges & Magistrates and therefore sworne (in their Baptisme) to be trusty . . . unto Christ Jesus, his statues & ordinances & consequently they may do nothing against him nor any his servants that (in a godly sort) seeke the advancement of them, but contrariwise are bounde to relieve & defende them (all that they may) & to hinder & punish thos that seek to molest them.[77]

The contents of the "Reformed Church Government," which challenged the matters tried in church courts, are perhaps more surprising than the fact that it was directed to a lay audience. Much scholarly attention has centered on puritan objections to the inefficiency of church courts and the controversial procedures used by the ecclesiastical commissioners. Preoccupation with the latter is clearly reflected in the literature of the period. Richard Cosin's definitive *Apologie for sundrie proceedings by iurisdiction ecclesiastical* was devoted to defending the use of oaths, particularly the oath *ex officio mero*, in response to scribal publications made against it by James Morrice and Robert Beale.[78] By contrast with the controversy over oaths, historians have argued that the subject matter under ecclesiastical jurisdiction was relatively uncontested, except by occasional encroachments by common lawyers.[79] However, the first part of Cosin's lengthy *Apologie* was concerned with the scope of cases tried in ecclesiastical courts, which was precisely the issue to which the presbyterians turned. It is striking that even after the presbyterians were cast into prison for refusing to take the oath *ex officio* before the High Commission, they targeted the instance side of spiritual jurisdiction instead of simply objecting to procedure or to prosecution for religious dissent, moral regulation, and other criminal cases. This reveals that presbyterian criticisms were neither simply provoked by inefficiency nor by the measures used against them in the late sixteenth century. Their hostility to episcopacy was both grounded in English tradition and driven by an alternative ecclesiastical vision that extended to forms of punishment and procedure, and included the subject matter of the spiritual tribunals.

Certainly material benefits, especially for the laity, would have resulted from transferring causes from church courts to common law.[80] As tithes causes rapidly grew in the Elizabethan and early Stuart period, they began to dominate the instance business of spiritual courts and become a point of contention with competing courts.[81] It is no surprise that presbyterians argued that they be transferred to temporal courts as they were *"no more spirituall, then thefts, murders, oppressions, & other iniuryes,"* which was testified by Nowel and Foxe.[82] Whereas Cosin argued that tithes were allocated to spiritual courts by statute "in the days of K[ing] Richard II," the "Reformed Church Government" cited Judge Fitzherbert to point out that before Richard II's reign, up to the time of his predecessor Edward III, the right of tithes was determinable in temporal courts. Yet even in the present time the author pointed to diverse cases when tithes were deferred to temporal courts, and concluded that it was therefore "without inconvenience that all cases of tithes be tried in secular court."[83]

Presbyterian arguments were not simply tailored to fit those of common lawyers but in some cases extended beyond them. Next to tithes, the bulk of instance business in spiritual courts (which likewise generated sizable revenues) were testamentary causes that dealt with wills and the disposal of personal property other than land. This appeared to be relatively uncontested by common lawyers compared with tithes. Such matters, however, were disputed by presbyterians. Whereas Cosin argued that common law allowed both lay and ecclesiastical persons liberty in such matters, the "Reformed Church Government" argued that probate of wills ought to be exclusively handled by temporal courts. It supported this view by continental examples. It also argued that in England wills had only been transferred to spiritual courts "but of late time by custome." Therefore they should be "transferred from the Church to the Commen Weale . . . whereto they rightly and Antiently belonge and apertayne."[84]

Other cases presbyterians took issue with included general bastardy, dilapidations, and all actions of trespass in church yard or glebe.[85] Stoughton's *Assertion for True and Christian Church-Policie*[86] provided a similar list that should be tried in the secular courts:

> [M]atters of Wills and Testaments . . . matters of Spousals and Marriages . . . all and singular matters of defamation . . . shall bee heard, examined, and determined by the said civill and secular Officers and Iudges . . . And that all matters of Tythes, Dilapidations, repayre of Churches, and if there bee any other of like nature, with their acessories, and appendices, shall be heard, examined, and determined, by the said civill and secular Officers and Judges, in the said Civill and Secular Courts.[87]

Both writers acknowledged cases that might be punishable in either ecclesiastical or temporal courts, such as those of clergymen who had been physically beaten and sought monetary recompense, defamation cases that required punishment of sin or recovery of damages, absence from divine service, perjury, and usury.[88]

Stoughton's *Assertion* was organized around passages from the Elizabethan Admonition controversy and continued to argue for the institution of presbyterian polity.[89] Yet it appeared at the accession of James in 1604. C. W. Brooks recently pointed out that dispute over "the relationship between the temporal and spiritual jurisdictions w[as] regularly resurrected in litigation and in parliament throughout the 1590s and well into the seventeenth century."[90] The cases listed in the *Assertion* were not only raised during James's reign but also matched those drawn up in anti-Laudian tracts. Indeed, Stoughton's treatise was republished in 1642.[91] *The Letters Patents of the Presbyterie*, which was printed in the 1630s, also argued for presbyterianism by anticipating the advantage of transferring certain cases from ecclesiastical to temporal courts, "for . . . many causes are fitter for the common lawes, and those courts where the Kings Chancellour, and other Iudges sit, but only that such matters should be in the churches power, as are fit, that the church should take care of them, and iudge them."[92]

To explore the overlap between presbyterian criticisms of church courts and those of common lawyers is not to suggest that there was a direct parallel between their arguments. It would be absurd to imply that presbyterianism was the only source of inspiration for common law criticisms of episcopacy. Common lawyers could view presbyterian-clericalism as posing a greater potential threat than episcopal encroachment, which could be kept in check through writs of prohibition.[93] It would also be wrong to align presbyterianism with the common law tradition and parliament to the exclusion of the crown. Presbyterians had long appealed to the royal prerogative, claiming that the spiritual courts infringed upon it more than would presbyterian government by transferring civil matters to the ecclesiastical domain.[94] This was pressed more forcefully as bishops began to make *jure divino* arguments in the late 1580s.[95]

Presbyterian attacks upon the bishops' civil jurisdiction were of course in danger of threatening the king's prerogative courts of Star Chamber and High Commission. The "Reformed Church Government" guarded the crown's prerogative by insisting that notwithstanding the abolition of church courts, the High Commission might be preserved. The writer suggested that "instead of bishops and ministers, other divines that as yet have received no such orders nor ministerial function in the church . . . be commissioners in their rooms."[96] The bottom line was not to curb royal authority but to prohibit the appointment of bishops and other clergymen.

Rejection of the Romano-canonical tradition also served to support the case against episcopacy while preserving royal authority. Indeed, it was through such claims that the anti-episcopal and abolitionist language of "root and branch" spanned the early seventeenth century. Roman canon law had been criticized by the presbyterians as early as 1572 in the *Admonition to Parliament* as "Antichristian and diuellish, and contrarye to the Scriptures." Whitgift replied with the standard defense that canon law could be retained so long as it did not contradict Scripture or common law.[97] Turning the presbyterians' objections to canon law against them, Whitgift maintained that they threatened to alter the "whole state of the Lawes of the Realme."[98]

The "Reformed Church Government" refuted this charge by asserting that since the bishops' courts were founded "above 1000 years after Christ" at the time of William the Conqueror and "had their originall from the papacy," their dissolution would have no negative effect but instead "profit" the state by deferring "all the civil causes . . . [to] temporall courts . . . whereto they properly & rightly belonge."[99] Stoughton likewise took up the cudgels and organized his *Assertion* around Whitgift's response to the *Admonition*. He argued that the removal of bishops and their spiritual courts would not alter the "Lawes of the Realme," since episcopacy was based on Roman canon law, which had been decisively abolished: "The forraign and papall canon law, with all the accessories, dependances offices, and functions thereof, is utterly abolished out of the Realme: Therefore the same law is no part of the lawes of the Realm; and therefore also it is evident, that there will not follow any alteration of the Lawes of the Realme, by the taking of it away."[100]

Appealing to the Act of Submission of the Clergy (25 Henry VIII, chap. 19), which granted royal license over ecclesiastical legislation, Stoughton insisted that Roman canon law was permitted only by "sufferance of our Kings."[101] Richard Cosin followed Whitgift in his view that it should remain unless positively contradicted: for the statute did not apply to existing canon law, but only prohibited "new Canons, &c in their Conuocation, without the Kings royall assent and authoritie in that behalfe."[102] Yet Stoughton demanded positive proof of its legitimacy, pointing out that the Act of Submission had placed the existing Roman law under review by the crown and a committee. He argued that positive evidence had in fact been required by Cosin himself, who had dismissed Stoughton's appeal to statute in *An Abstract* on the grounds that it ought to "shew us how they have beene used and executed [in England], before the making of the [Act of Submission.]" Cosin's latter argument for positive use of law could thus be turned against his former that canon law remained unless contradicted: "[M]uch more forcibly may [Cosin's] agument be retorted . . . for sithence it hath never yet beene proved, that the forraign Canon Law, used and executed at this day, was accustomed and used 25 H 8 . . . we must still put him, and his clients to their proofe."[103]

Like the "Reformed Church Government," Stoughton's treatise reveals that presbyterian advocates and lawyers continued to exchange arguments. Presbyterian ministers had not only received legal advice from lawyers during in the early 1590s, but in turn directed their theological and legal criticisms of episcopal jurisdiction to a lay audience. On the other hand, the writer of the *Epistle Dedicatory* to Stoughton's *Assertion* claimed that some of the arguments made in this text were "discovered by the Authors means to the said learned Judge Sir *Edward Cooke*." It further asserted that the author was "esteemed learned by the best of [civilians], as also by Divines and common Lawyers, learned Sir *Edward Cook* . . . Sir *Christopher Yelverton* . . . Sir *Henry Finch* . . . and others."[104]

These disputes are as noteworthy for their duration as they are for their contents and affinities with a lay audience. Ethan Shagan recently explored how Cosin's argument with the puritans over oaths paralleled the theological points made by conformists and puritans about indifferent matters in the Elizabethan Admonition controversy.[105] It should come as no surprise that disputation over the status of Roman canon law and the matters tried in church courts were closely tied to Elizabethan religious debates. Both Cosin and Stoughton specifically wrote with reference to presbyterian government.[106] Indeed, the *Assertion*'s relation to Elizabethan ecclesiastical controversy has caused some historians to believe that the text was written earlier in Elizabeth's reign.[107] Yet Stoughton's references to "the King" and "our late Soveraigne Lady the Queene" reveal that it was at least edited in 1604, the same year as it appeared in print.[108] Moreover, it was not abandoned during James's reign but republished and directed at Long Parliament MPs in 1642. There is also evidence that it was actively read prior to republication. An annotated copy of the 1604 edition at the Huntington Library is dated "1621" and also "Juni 30 1634," indicating the reader's ongoing interest in Stoughton's text. Passages on the abolition of the canon law and against the use of temporal punishments by ecclesiastical officers are exactly those that the reader underlined in his 1604 copy.[109] The reader also took note of Stoughton's analogy to the "branches of a tree," which must "receive nourishment from . . . the root." But if a tree were rooted in the canon law, which Stoughton insisted was already abolished (even if by legal fiction), what remained but to raze the tree and its branches?

MORAL REFORMATION OR DISCIPLINARY REVOLUTION?

Anti-episcopacy was social, legal, and constitutional, yet it was also deeply moral and of course ecclesiological. The relationship between ecclesiological and moral reform was made explicit by Travers, who "extended Puritan reformation of manners to reformation of Church government."[110] This did not simply mark a difference in degree between the late medieval and later puritan reformation of manners, but a different view of how and, more important, by whom church censure ought to be administered. Indeed, the presbyterian argument for the complete abolition of episcopacy was driven by an alternative vision of church discipline. Although referred to as a "further reformation" by contemporaries, Philip Gorski has recently maintained that the implementation of presbyterian government in the early modern period would mark a "disciplinary revolution."[111] This would include the reorganization of ecclesiastical oversight through lay officers and local courts and in turn function as a mechanism for increased state control over its subjects. Even if the institution of English presbyterianism would not have necessarily amounted to a "disciplinary revolution," it would have nonetheless radically reorganized the Church of England along such lines.

A critique of popular culture, like the complaint against episcopacy, had been central to presbyterianism from its beginning. And behind the complaints of immorality lay another opportunity to castigate the inadequacies of episcopacy. The "Reformed Church Government" argued that the episcopate was failing to keep England in order and was chiefly to be blamed for England's horrendous immorality. God's anger at England's sin led to terrible judgments, such as the "late losse of so many honorable religious & prudent *priuy counsellors* taken from this Lande, and dying in so short a space one after an other" and "*the Famine of breade* and dearth of corn . . . not long since in the lande." It continued, "[B]ut then Aske the Question further and know what is the cause, the synnes of this nation be so many, so manifolde, so great, so grievous, Whereby the Wrath of god is so incensed?" The writer would have his readers recognize that the certain cause of such catastrophes was "no doubt the *Want of the Christian and primitive Church government* (which god himselfe instituted for the same purpose to keepe his Church in godlynes and holy Conversation)."[112] If the absence of a presbyterian church government was the reason for the increase of England's sins, then the writer went further, pointing his finger at bishops who hindered reformation "to the further increase of the synnes of England & bringing of them to their full ripenes)."[113] The bishops then were chiefly responsible for "all gods Wrath & vengeance against this Lande and therefore no longer to be tolerated if we love the favour of god & prosperity of Englande."[114] The London Petition of 1641 specifically linked episcopal jurisdiction and moral degradation: "The great increase and frequencie of whoredomes, and Adulteries, occasioned by the Prelates Corrupt administration of iustice, in such Cases, who taking upon them the punishment of it, doe turn all into moneyes or the filling of their purses."[115]

Preferring a plurality of church officers akin to a jury to the sole judgment of a bishop, presbyterians argued that corruption under the episcopal system was almost inevitable. The *Admonition to Parliament* (1572) was convinced that corruption resulted from the lone jurisdiction of bishops, where "favoure, affection, or money, mitigateth the rigour of [rash and cruell judgement] . . . because the regiment left of Christ to his church, is committed into one mannes hands, whom alone it shal be more easie for the wicked by bribing to pervert, than to overthrow the faith and pietie of a zealous and godlie companie."[116] The "Reformed Church Government" argued for common consent whereby "the force & sway of Many (in a Councell) must needes cary greater perswasion in the minds of all Christians then the pleasure of one preferred above the rest . . . considering then that one is more easy to fall & to be corrupted then many."[117] The office of lay elder, absent in the English episcopal order, was especially designed to keep church censure free from corruption through collective jurisdiction. Travers complained of the bishop's exclusion of elders along with other church officers: the bishop "hath destroyed the whole body, whiles he will haue it nothing but an eie; neither will suffer either the Deacons or the Elders or the Assembly to doe any thing, but onely himselfe to heare, handle, and deale with all manner of matters."[118] Thus the presbyterians again tied abuses in episcopal practice to the nature of the bishop's office while advocating a practical plan for reform through the institution of their church polity, specifically through the role of the lay elder.

The lay elder, from whom the name "presbyterian" was derived, assisted the minister in visitations and individual care for the congregation. Consistorial discipline, as initially established by the reformed churches on the continent and envisaged by presbyterians in England, was chiefly concerned with the regulation of manners and admission to the lord's supper.[119] It proposed a radical shift from itinerant governance through superintendents to regular local oversight and discipline by lay members of particular congregations. While the significance of a transition to local and stationary courts has in recent years tended to be understated by historians, its practical advantage has been well observed: "[L]ocal discipline—by justices or by presbyteries—was cheap, acquainted with local circumstances and flexible."[120] Travers explained that, through the office of elders, "euery part of the Church should haue their watchmen assigned to them, to whose office especially it should belong to marke, ouersee and obserue all mens manners."[121] The duty of such watchmen was explained in the *Admonition*: "Their office was to gouerne the church with the rest of the ministers, to consulte, to admonish, to correct, and to order all thinges apperteigning to the state of the congregation."[122] The "Reformed Church Government" similarly described the moral invigilation assigned to these "elders . . . whose office (singly by themselves considered) is to look to the manners [of] the people within their Church & congregation and to admonish the[m] whom they see offende."[123] Travers provided an even more searching description of the moral invigilation which was to be the responsibility of lay elders: "Therefore those Elders be such as . . . the Censors of Rome, who exacted and examined every Citizens life according to the lawes. So they marke and obserue euery mans manners, and they themselues doe admonish men of the lighter faults, and bring the greater to the Consistory."[124] Thus, the office of lay elder required, along with the preaching and teaching, full moral and spiritual oversight. As Travers summarized:

> [T]his oversight can haue but two parts onely, whereof the first pertaineth to doctrine and religion, the other to life and manners. Seeing then that two kindes of Elders are expresly named by Saint Paul, whereof the first sort are occupied in preaching and Doctrine, it is necessary that the other should haue charge of manners and conversation, which part onely remaineth.[125]

Whereas presbyterians found conformist religion to be vague and removed from the lives of churchgoers, their particularization of specific sins created many occasions in the reign of Elizabeth when parishioners complained that they were being attacked personally in a public sermon.[126]

English presbyterians envisaged their ecclesiastical reform as both local and national; the election of lay elders in the provinces was designed to bring about moral reform on a national scale. Peter Lake has discussed how spiritual concern and the principle of edification were projected to the entire realm through Cartwright's defense of the discipline, where "language normally applied to the internal process of individual salvation was being applied to the collective cause of national reformation."[127] By the late sixteenth century, presbyterian discipline as exercised by the collective rule of elders became further inscribed along national lines, not simply as a program proposed to parliament but as argued according to powerful precedents from the distant and recent past. According to the author of the "Reformed Church Government," "Mr Nowell . . . cleerly distinguisheth thes Elders from the Pastor of the Congregation," "Mr. Juel teacheth & acknowledgeth this to be the order of the primitive Church." Martin Bucer and Peter Martyr taught at Cambridge and Oxford "that thes Elders are gods owne expresse ordinance, & ought perpetually & unremoveably to remayne in the church" and "D. Fulk likewise hath taught the same."[128]

The authorities were well aware that the alliance between presbyterian ministers and the laity promised lay supporters not only material rewards but also the opportunity to become elected as church officers. Through the role of the lay elder, presbyterian apologists were therefore able to appeal to lay supporters, not simply by sharing a common enemy but also by sharing the goal of establishing a godly society.[129] However, it was insufficient merely to ensure the effective administration of church censure when critics claimed that the institution of their discipline would result in civil disorder. Presbyterian apologists from the earliest petitions in the reign of Elizabeth onward claimed that far from producing anarchy, the abolition of episcopacy would enhance civil authority, since ministers and magistrates would again rule within their rightful jurisdictions, which had been usurped by the episcopate. Having promised civil authorities that reformed church government was the solution to England's social and moral problems, they reasoned by extension that the establishment of a godly society would also strengthen the state. As Stoughton argued, "For the mind brought in frame by discipline, frameth the whole body to a more holy obedience, so that the magistrate therby hath lesse trouble in his office, & the common weal more florisheth in peace and prosperity."[130] Thus "Cartwright claims that crimes will be diminished if the eldership is established."[131]

The minister's public role was confined to acting as councilor to the magistrate. This corresponded to the presbyterians' interpretation of government as found in the Old Testament, where the priest interpreted the law and informed the judge accordingly. However, presbyterians went further by stressing that the two offices could bolster each other. In the presbyterians' elaboration of the relationship between church officers and the civil sphere, it appears that elected lay elders were not the only lay men promised a greater role in ecclesiastical jurisdiction. Significantly, the local magistrate was also recruited as an active partner for the minister. If, on the one hand, presbyterians vigorously argued against ecclesiastical officers discharging secular punishments for church censure by themselves, on the other they believed that civil officers were needed to deploy the secular arm to reinforce ecclesiastical sentences. Thus the presbyterians stressed the separation of Church and State by condemning the exercise of civil punishment and offices by bishops, but in speaking to magistrates they described the close cooperation of the minister and the magistrate in establishing a godly society.[132]

William Stoughton described the mutually reinforcing roles of the minister and magistrate whereby the secular arm made church censure effective:

> [N]either the magistrate without true instruction from the ministers: Nor the ministers without due authoritie from the magistrate, ought to wrest any thing into the governement of the Church, For both offices, and gouernments, Magistracie, and ministery are very holy and honourable, & beeing seuerall, tend to seuerall endes, and bring foorth seuerall euents in the administration and gouernment of the Churche: the one is the mouth: the other is the hand of God: the one by worde, the other by swoord, ought to execute the Lordes iudgementes in the Lords house.[133]

Richard Rogers's dedication to Coke included this theme: "God commandes vs, and would haue vs goe to worke otherwise, and namely, both the Magistrate and Minister to do those great works required of them."[134] Ronald Marchant has pointed out familiar passages from the *Admonition to Parlia-*

ment against church courts that are often cited but not understood within the broader call for more severe punishment of sinners by a local coalition of lay elders backed by justices: "Public penance in church was evidently not a sufficiently severe punishment in the eyes of the Puritans, and the efforts of the Lancashire justices must have come nearer to their ideal."[135] The Elizabethan Dedham Classis decided to "defer . . . obstinate sinners to the magistrate: When Chapman asked how to deal with 'some careles persons that had no regard of the word or Sacramentes,' it was noted that this problem was always coming up, and that the line now agreed upon was to complain to the magistrates."[136]

All this appears to contradict the principle of separation of Church and State. However, the difference between the argument against use of civil force in the previous context and the stress on civil reinforcements is the difference between punishments for nonconformity over religious ceremony administered by ecclesiastical officers versus punishment for moral offenses by civil magistrates as defined by the Ten Commandments. Both the severity of punishment and the justification for the secular reinforcement of sin came from the view that violation of not only the second table, but even more the first table, was a moral transgression and therefore punishable in both ecclesiastical and secular law.[137] Insofar as presbyterians believed that transgression of the first table of the Decalogue was a civil offense and caused further transgression in the second, the civil magistrate was to use force to restrain the disobedient. Cartwright is known for supporting an especially severe enforcement of law in moral matters. In accordance with his high federalism and covenantal interpretation of Scripture, unless specifically revoked elsewhere in Scripture, the judicial law granted by the authority of the Old Testament would continue to be in effect. Hence, blasphemy and even adultery were punishable by death, and civil authorities could be called upon to correct Sabbath negligence.[138] A distinguishing mark in the sabbatarian writings of both John Field and Nicholas Bound is their appeal to the justices to play their appointed part in bringing about national reform and civil order.[139]

Travers's writing in the early seventeenth century reveals his continued commitment to the respective roles of minister and magistrate. In response to congregationalists in the 1610s, Travers defended the *Declaration* from radical political implications. In so doing, he spelled out more clearly his understanding of spiritual and secular responsibilities for furthering reform, which reserved a special role for godly magistrates. While claiming due obedience to civil authorities, the rest of his statement mirrors Calvin's exalted view of ministerial leaders as advisors to civil rulers.[140] Perhaps English authorities were legitimately suspicious of presbyterian ministers who might urge others to take radical steps, even if they themselves were not the ones carrying out those actions in parliament:

> [The Declaration] never intended to exhort to any unlawfull Course, not agreeing with the peace of the church nor with obedience due to Magistrates, but that lawfully and dutifully every one would further it according to his vocation[,] private men by prayers to god ministers by preching of gods word and informing of the higher powers of the will of god herein[,] and magistrates by the Civill power and authority which they have receaved especially to the maintenance of gods trew religion worship and service.[141]

A similar division of labour can be found in Peterborough during the early seventeenth century: "Every member of the godly was expected to make a personal reaction, in his place, but the onus was on the godly minister and magistrate to take the lead both by personal example and, in the case of the minister, by stirring up the people at large to an awareness of their perilous predicament in the face of Antichrist."[142]

The call upon secular authorities for a reformation of manners is especially recognizable in the printed literature from the last decades of the sixteenth century until the mid-seventeenth century and described by Keith Wrightson as "the godly concentrated upon the exhorting of the secular authorities to instigate disciplinary action."[143] Initiatives for moral reform "swelled in the sixty years before 1640 . . . into a programme of national significance" and from 1641 was given full force.[144] Robert Brenner noted that, in the mid-seventeenth century, "the inseparability of godly magistracy and Presbyterian church polity was the basic ideologico-institutional premise from which they derived their rather variable political strategies for securing a national Civil War settlement."[145] The relationship whereby reformed discipline was bolstered by local civil officers is well documented in the literature of the period,[146] and took on a special significance among presbyterians in the 1640s. The Westminster divine and presbyterian Richard Heyrick proclaimed in 1646 that "religion shall be established . . . the peace and safety of the country shall be secured, [and] God's glory shall be exalted."[147] Heyrick happened to be kin to the Robert Heyricke of Leicestershire who in 1586, together with thirteen other men in the town of Leicester, sought to secure Travers as minister.

A critical element in this vision of a national reform by the cooperative efforts of magistrates and ministers was how it would reach into every corner of the land, and necessarily involved the whole of English society. Theoretically there was no individual from the lowest to highest who was exempt from conforming to its moral order. It is significant that the enforcement of sabbath observance can be seen even in the prohibition of commerce and other business activity by merchants and lawyers who were reprimanded along with other sabbath breakers.[148] Both presbyterian and congregationalist writers appealed to the magistracy to enforce moral order. Among congregationalists, however, church covenants ultimately placed a premium on voluntarism and sharpened the division between the godly and the unregenerate mass of English society. For example, Henry Jacob acknowledged the civil magistrate as a useful alternative to diocesan jurisdiction and saw him as a means of resolving problems instead of either episcopal or presbyterian authorities beyond the congregation.[149]

By contrast, presbyterians lacked confidence in the ability of a gathered church to maintain sufficient discipline merely by exploiting the covenantal pledge to godly conduct. Disciplining scandalous behavior, presbyterians believed, required the systematic involvement of lay authorities in a national campaign for reform. Only an alternative and comprehensive church government that promised the laity an expanded role in local jurisdiction could produce the discipline which episcopacy had failed to achieve and indeed could never have achieved given its excessively clerical structure. This alternative church government, which promised the laity a greater role in local jurisdiction, wedded criticism of episcopacy to presbyterian arguments along with practical plans for ecclesiastical reform. Thus, presbyterian ministers not only made arguments alongside jurists to assault episcopacy and ecclesiastical courts, but also sought to build an alliance with provincial magistrates that was supposed to enhance the cooperative relationship between ministers and magistrates. Presbyterian critique of episcopal jurisdiction could rouse a wider intellectual and organizational opposition to it, not simply by directing such criticism to parliament but also to counties, towns, and parishes.

PART II

The Evolution of English Ecclesiology

CHAPTER 3

The Visible Church

The conformist George Downame was putting his finger on a crucial ecclesiastical fault line when he drew a distinction between elder and newer disciplinarians in 1608: not all opponents of episcopacy used the same arguments
against it.[1] Ecclesiological debate did not take place simply between conformist and puritan polemicists, but involved a range of participants. Although
congregational government appeared to be relatively uncontested by puritans
when it emerged more visibly in the early seventeenth century, it was fiercely
disputed by the presbyterians who carried out a clandestine trial against it.
Congregationalism in part seemed to be uncontroversial, because historians
believed it was virtually indistinguishable from Elizabethan presbyterianism.[2]
They observed presbyterian agitation for ministerial parity and their relative silence on government beyond the individual congregation.[3] Travers's
magisterial presbyterian treatise of the 1570s in particular is significant for
its perfunctory treatment of synods and general assemblies, only alluding
once to synods "of more Kingdoms and countries."[4] But is the amount of
space devoted to discussing relative congregational and synodal authority on
its own an adequate means of distinguishing between these church polities?
What were the underlying assumptions of their writings? Were there differences between presbyterian and congregational views concerning the visible
church and ecclesiastical liberty?

   In 1612 Travers charted a Ramist Tree in his notebook that offers further
insight into his understanding of the relation of particular congregations to a
national Church.[5] Beginning with the Trinity, the tree descends through the
order of creation and redemption, branching into the Church, the predestined
object of redemption.[6] Next in the outline comes the form of government for
the visible Church as prescribed in the Old Testament, followed by extraordinary and ordinary church officers in the New Testament. The last branch
in Travers's tree is a presbytery divided into elders and deacons. By charting a

single unit of church officers, with no extension into a compound organization of presbyters, Travers's tree appears to locate church authority within the individual congregation.

It is striking that the visible Church appears in the singular throughout this diagram. While congregationalists did not always contest a single visible church in the Old Testament, they rejected outright the application of this model in the New Testament. Historians have argued that the early formulation of congregational thought not only provided a more systematic articulation of congregationalism but also legitimized the unique position of puritans during this period. These puritans articulated principles for their self-governed congregations and at the same time justified remaining within the Church of England; they achieved this by asserting congregational autonomy, nominalizing the authority of the bishops that they were under, and translating the established Church into plural and individual parishes with some of which they might choose to communicate.[7]

Yet the pattern for a single, visible Church appears not only in the Old Testament but also in the New, according to Travers's tree. In the left-hand corner, above the New Testament branch, there figures a crucial concept that explains how jurisdiction through presbyters at the congregational level did not necessarily conflict with the concept of a visible Church through the combination of particular congregations. Travers states that "congregations are called the Church through synecdoche."[8] He is introducing the term "synecdoche" (a part representing the whole) to indicate that particular congregations represented the visible Church as a whole. By contrast, the leading exponent of congregational polity, Henry Jacob, applied "synecdoche" to the visible Church with respect to "people of a particular Congregation (having Ministers, yet without and beside their Ministers) are called the Church."[9] This key to interpreting Travers's understanding of the Church in the New Testament provides the conceptual framework for the tactical flexibility in presbyterian thought; it explains the relative ease with which they moved from the particular to the national Church.

There is therefore no reason to assume that because Elizabethan presbyterians were preoccupied with church government on the congregational level they did not hold a strong commitment to a national Church complete with authoritative classes and synods. Elizabethan presbyterianism initially emerged as a proposed solution to the national Church where "the whole question of what a protestant national church should look like was thrown open in the debate about presbyterianism."[10] One tactic used by presbyterians to argue that their polity would require minimal change to the existing national church was to propose a simple substitution of pastors, teachers, elders,

and deacons for bishops. The "Reformed Church Government" was preoccupied with parity of ministers at the congregational level while interpreting
provincial and national ecclesiastical authority as if to follow automatically by
implementing presbyterianism only at a local level.

When the legitimacy of ecclesiastical authority beyond the individual congregation came into question in the early seventeenth century, presbyterians
offered an extensive defense of the authority of synods. Their exchange with
congregational defendants demonstrates that they viewed the universal nature of the visible Church to be crucial. Yet in the course of debating the
authority of synods and definition of the visible church, the congregationalist Jacob came to his fullest articulation of ecclesiastical liberty, which reveals
yet another split between presbyterian and congregational thinking. Whereas
the presbyterians used parliamentary example to argue that the authority of
synods did not undermine the liberty of individual congregations, Jacob argued for freedom along neo-Roman lines as the absence of any dependence
that might conflict with self-government. The presbyterians appealed to the
testimony of antiquity themselves,[11] but they were nonetheless skeptical of the
use of classical authors and ideas in the dispute over ecclesiology. Not only
did they deny that ancient Greek authors could be used to support the congregational exegesis of "ecclesia" in the New Testament, they also refuted the
neo-Roman concept of freedom that underpinned congregational polity.

This is not to suggest that there were only two ecclesiological categories
among the godly that remained static in the early seventeenth century. Rather, the presbyterians' theological exchange with emergent congregationalists during this period had several effects. On the one hand, it intensified
congregational and presbyterian proclivities and sharpened divisions among
the godly that predated and defined later divisions among the divines of the
Westminster Assembly. That congregationalism did not develop simply in
response to episcopacy but also in reaction to presbyterianism in England,
the Netherlands, and even in New England changes our understanding of
the development of ecclesiology during the first half of the seventeenth century. While the presbyterians defended the role of synods and the universal
nature of the visible church, they also defensively argued that their polity
guarded individual and congregational liberty. Despite the dominant narrative of an almost exclusive tendency toward congregational autonomy, there
was flexibility within nonconformist ecclesiology that allowed for ecclesiastical liberty and authority beyond the particular congregation. Yet presbyterian exchanges with congregationalists during this period also contributed to
the development of further ecclesiological ambiguities. This cautions against
forcing the godly into distinct denominational categories at the same time as

it explains how church government became a central contention that chiefly defined divisions between the godly.

"INDEPENDENCY" EXAMINED

Henry Jacob's congregation in Southwark remains one of the most significant sources for early English congregationalism. "[In] 1616 Jacob founded the church in Southwark which claims to be the first continuing Congregational Church on English soil—and thus earned from his son the title, whether proper or not, of England's 'first Independent.'"[12] Jacob's son was apparently not the only contemporary to believe that Jacob was the "first Independent." That Jacob conferred with Travers and other ministers in 1616 before establishing his congregational experiment has long been known to congregational historians, who have assumed that this exchange represented the "apparent approval of these London puritan leaders."[13] This is disproved by Travers's manuscripts held at Trinity College Dublin Library. Travers and a panel of presbyterian writers (collectively referred to as "the examiners") penned a rigorous argument for presbyterian church government directed against Henry Jacob (the so-called "defendant"). The manuscript treatise, partially in Travers's hand, was part of a prolonged exchange in which presbyterians were committed to legitimizing the authority of synods, national assemblies, and ecumenical councils more extensively than in any treatment of this subject known during the height of Elizabethan presbyterianism. The position taken by the "defendant" directly corresponds to Jacob's arguments in many of his writings, particularly in his *An Attestation of many Learned, Godly and famous Divines.* According to the examiners, "[T]his defendant and his followers" had violated the "golden rule" never to "be author of any new opinion in the church" which "new opinion and before unheard of paradox" rejected the Church of England's authority over congregations, while regarding some assemblies in England to be true churches.[14] Judging from the title to which the presbyterian manuscript refers, the debate began with objections from presbyterian examiners that provoked an "answer & reply" from the "defendant." The presbyterians responded with an "examination of the answere & reply" that in turn prompted the congregationalist to pen his "defence of certaine Christians who by some are unworthily and unjustly traduced by the name of a new separation." It is to this "defense" that the presbyterians' second examination responded.

The authority of church councils became a particular bone of contention between Henry Jacob and his presbyterian opponents, but this was not the only concern that his examiners raised in objecting to his government, at least according to their account of the controversy:

[Y]ou say, that for shortnesse and sparing of labor, you will leaue all the rest of the examination, and handle onely one poynte. . . . This poynte is in effect that euery perticular congregation and parish church should bee so absolute for the spirituall government of it sel[f] as it should not bee subordinate, nor subiect to any ecclesiasticall assemb[ly] to giue an account to them for any thing they doe, or receive any ordinances from them, as hauing authoritie ouer them.[15]

The presbyterians objected to the reduction of the debate to this question alone, arguing that "such proceeding can not bee any iust and sufficient answer to our examination of many divers matters."[16] Jacob's response and the presbyterians' rebuttal indeed proved that the divisions between them were related to a whole set of other concerns, not least the definition of the visible Church and its implications for the relationship between particular congregations.

In his printed treatises Jacob argued that "under the Gospell Christ never instituted, nor had any one Universall visible church (that is Politicall) either proper, or representative; which ordinarily was to exercise spirituall outward government, over all persons through the world professing Christianity."[17] He argued in *Reasons Taken Ovt of Gods Word* that "only a *Particular ordinary constant Congregation* of Christians in Christes Testament is appointed and reckoned to be a visible Church."[18] For "the Church of Corinth, and of Antioch, and of Thessalonica . . . and of other Churches . . . were so many proper, and distinct Churches in those times, and independent one of another; & so were contrary to the forme of the Iewish Leviticall Church before notified."[19] In his *Confession and Protestation* Jacob similarly stressed that the visible church was "a free congregation independent."[20] Here, in the language that Jacob used to describe the visible church, are the origins of "independency."

The presbyterian "examiners" alleged that the "defendant" "affirm[s] a church to bee an ordinary congregation and that independent."[21] They proceeded by refuting Jacob's definition of the Church and essentially accusing him of interpreting the New Testament through a prior commitment to an altogether different church polity:

This independency hath so deceived you even as it is with them that have such a desease in their eyes as they can see nothing but it semeth unto them to bee of a red colour so you can never see the word church in the new testament but it seemeth to you to signify a church independent.[22]

Margaret Sommerville observed that in the mid-seventeenth century, congregationalists such as John Goodwin and William Bartlet rejected the term "Independency," regarding it "as a nickname fastened on them by the Presbyterians."[23] In these manuscript debates it appears that presbyterians not only used the term "independency" to refute their adversaries during this period but had coined it to single out the importance of the concept to Jacob's ecclesiology by the late 1610s.

Jacob directed his interpretation of the visible church in response to episcopal authority as well as to his presbyterian adversaries. He replied to the presbyterians by arguing that New Testament references to "ecclesia" in the singular indicated "an ordinarie Congregacon; & not any provinciall nor universall Church nor ruling sinod."[24] That the "sense of the word ἐκκλησία Mat. 18.17" was "of a parish and not of any sinode, senate, or consistory" could be demonstrated "by all Greek authors" as well as by the New Testament and by Christ.[25] Jacob further supported this interpretation by appealing to the Zurich reformer Heinrich Zwingli[26] and a host of other ecclesiastical writers: "But all authors of credit doe give to the word Ecclesia . . . the sence only of one ordinarie Congregacon, they never giue it the sence of all, the destinct Congregacon through a nation or province, much les through thee world nor yet doe they ever take it for a sinod; not for a sinnat or consistory nor for any supreame person."[27] By arguing that the visible church was a particular congregation, Jacob was doing more than simply redefining the relationship between the individual and national church: he was introducing the idea of independence to government within the congregation by shifting authority away from the clergy in a council or synod and instead locating it in the collective membership of a congregation.

In response to Jacob's interpretation of the Church of England as plural and individual parishes, presbyterians insisted that the visible church was denoted in the singular by "several places in the new Testament, where in the holy ghost doth call the professors of a nation by the name of a church in the singular number & not churches only in the plurall."[28] They pointed to Acts 7: 38 and 2 Corinthians 10: 32.[29] Countering Jacob's reading of Matthew 18: 17, they claimed that "Mr Beza directly declareth that the word church ἐκκλησία is sometimes taken for an assembly of professed christians," and added that "this Beza that speaketh thus against you was publike reader and professor of the greek toung at Lausanna." The presbyterians also cited Chrysostom's exposition of the word "ecclesia" in this passage "for the company of the governors & overseers of the church whereby it is evident that this sense agreeth well enough with the greeke tounge."[30] Church Fathers and reformers also played an important role in ecclesiological debates beyond the specific exegesis of "ἐκκλησία" in Matthew 18.

The presbyterians' exegesis of these particular texts again reflected flexibility between the particular and general visible church. "We find the use of this word so generall and so large as it noteth any meeting or comming together of the people not only ecclesiasticall but civill, and those not ordinary & lawfull as where the courts of iustice sit, but even also extraordinary & the concourse of the people in an uprore or tumult."[31] They argued that Christ's own understanding of the Church in Matthew 18: 17 referred to an ecclesiastical court and not to the entire membership.[32] After making this point, they argued that "the speach of our Saviour Christ as it is reported by the Apostle Matthew Tell the church. wherby church hee understandeth any* assembly administring discipline† as of the perticuler church called the presbytery by the apostle Paule so also of other Synod, lesse or greater."[33] They tied their interpretation of these specific biblical passages directly to their view of the particular and general visible church:

> [W]ee say that the words tell the Church are no more spoken of consistories of particuler congregations then they are of Synods. For by the church there wee understand every assembly or ecclesiasticall \/ meeting \/ of the church that hath power to administer discipline. So tell the church (that is to say) tell the ecclesiasticall assembly which it concerneth either the consistory of a particuler congregation or a Synode lesse or greater to which it may belong.[34]

In objecting to Jacob's interpretation of Scripture, they claimed that the Church "significations being so many and so divers it is a wonder that you can find it no where sygnifiing any other thinge in the new testament then‡ a parish independent."[35]

The presbyterians also took issue with Jacob's argument that "all Greek writers" could be conscripted in favor of congregational interpretation. Here the hermeneutical and exegetical distinctions between presbyterian and congregational defendants came more to the fore. According to the presbyterians, the New Testament Greek used by the Apostles and Evangelists in many instances held a different meaning from the Greek of classical antiquity.[36] They preferred to draw from the language of the Old Testament to support their interpretation of the New Testament Scriptures, stressing the continuity between the Old and New Testament models of the visible church. They thereby denied that "the speach of the New Testament must be allwaise taken as it was used by the ancient Grecians," and argued that "besides the greek in the New Testament doth hold much of the Hebrew toung so as the phrases and speeches are oftentimes Hebrew. which are called Hebrainses."[37]

These arguments, however, did not convince Jacob. Instead, the presbyterians' examination of the defendant deepened Jacob's convictions that the particular congregation was the only form prescribed in the New Testament

*assemb
†as~~of~~
‡such~~as~~

for the visible church. The debate over the nature of the visible church was directly related to the authority of synods. It was especially the relationship of the individual congregation to other congregations in Jacob's interpretation of the New Testament that the presbyterians refuted. They denied that the existence of parochial assemblies implied that they exclusively exercised independent authority.[38] Although there were "indede parochiall assemblyes in the new testament as where mention is made of the churches of galatia, Asia, Macedonea & such like," they reasoned that "in other places it signifyeth men chosen by the congregation for the administration of discipline as Mat 18 ver 17 Act: 15.4 or for other purposes as Acts 15.4."[39]

Jacob rejected the validity of a diocesan and national church, yet he did not deny that synods could make doctrinal judgments and decrees.[40] For Jacob, the shift from ecclesiastical jurisdiction at the congregational level to provincial or national levels threatened the freedom of the individual congregation and subjected its members to diocesan episcopal authority. By rejecting the concept of a visible church beyond the congregation, congregationalists were able to undermine the basis of episcopal authority and free the individual congregation from the jurisdiction of prelates. Downame specifically argued that the primitive churches were diocesan. In countering this, Jacob argued:

> For where each ordinarie Congregation hath their free consent in their ordinarie governement, there certainly each Congregation is an intire and independent Body politike Spirituall. . . . So that these Congregations admit not (where they are) any proper Diocesan Church, or larger: neither doth the proper Diocesan Church (or larger) admit intire and independent ordinary Congregations. . . . They are indeed . . . such as cannot stand together possibly.[41]

According to Jacob, Downame's insistence on a diocesan church amounted to creating "two wayes to heaven, two wayes and formes of administring Christes Visible Church, of Calling the Ministerie, of exercising holy Censures."[42] It is again significant that he used the same argument of mutual exclusivity to defend himself from the presbyterians who, he claimed, sought to "prove a universall or a provinciall Church using government to be Christs ordinance in the Gospell."[43]

Denying that congregational and provincial governments were mutually exclusive, the presbyterians argued that "you say . . . both cannot bee, that is an universall church and a parish church independent. But take away your independency which word you have no where in the new testament but have devised it of your own brayne and these two formes may well stand* together."[44] It was crucial for them to affirm the liberty of particular congregations "to order their own ordinary afayers by their owne consent" without the over-

*stand

sight of other ecclesiastical authority.[45] However, they argued that it did not follow that congregational consent conflicted with other levels of ecclesiastical jurisdiction.[46] They used a political analogy to illustrate the compatibility of congregational and synodal jurisdiction: "[By] a like symilitute of cytyes that rule themselves by their charter yet, so as they are subiect to ordinary courts of iustice and to the extraordinary court of parlament."[47] Using this example they also affirmed that synodal authority was congruent with congregational liberty:

> So are parishes free to order thier soscietie by their owne consent according to gods word, yet if theire bee cause they are to give account of what they doe and to receive and keepe such godly cannons and rules as any higher ecclesiasticall authoryty over them shall iudge to bee necessary for them. Herby it appeareth that the liberty of parishes agreeth well with the authoryty of synods.[48]

Here, in response to the presbyterians' appeal to parliament, Jacob came to his fullest discussion of freedom. Moving outside English example, he outlined a definition of freedom along neo-Roman lines. He argued that higher authority was incompatible with local jurisdiction (as presbyterians had argued in the example of parliament) because freedom excluded the possibility of any dependence on a higher authority: "[An] ordinarie congregacon is never absolutely depending on any other in any matter ecclesiasticall, whatsoever; but (in case others leave them & stand against them) they are sufficient of themselves by Christs ordinance."[49] Although there is no indication in these debates that Jacob drew this concept directly from classical texts, he would not have needed to look far given the continued currency of neo-Roman views of liberty in the early seventeenth century.[50] Regardless of how Jacob arrived at his position, his opponents claimed that he had departed from the received view of freedom. They objected that "it is no bondage to the churches to bee ioyned together in an union and leauge to help and assist one another with all the good meanes that god hath giuen them." Directly challenging Jacob's view of ecclesiastical liberty, they asserted "neither is it to bee esteemed to bee a freedome to be subject to none."[51]

These debates exhibit that by the second decade of the seventeenth century a clear division between English presbyterian and congregational thought already existed. This division did not exclusively revolve around the authority of synods, but was also tied to competing conceptions of the nature of the visible church and the definition of ecclesiastical liberty. Whereas Jacob's rejection of a general visible church had initially been in response to episcopacy, it was also used against presbyterian polity. Among Jacob's list of "oposites & adversaryes" he not only named "D. Downame" and "D. Sutcliffe" but also "Mr Travers."[52]

CONGREGATIONAL CROSS-EXAMINATIONS
IN THE NETHERLANDS

Subsequent to Jacob's "independent" experiment in Southwark, the Netherlands proved to be a crucial locus for the development of congregationalism. Not long after the presbyterians interrogated Jacob in the late 1610s the English presbyterian John Paget, who was based in Amsterdam, subjected candidates for the position of copastor to a similar experience through his rigorous screening on questions of church government.[53] Paget suspected the candidates of tending toward congregational views and tested their ecclesiological convictions by asking a set of questions specifically designed to expose their position on the authority of synods and administration of the sacraments. It seemed obvious to many of the members of Paget's congregation that the primary aim here was to exclude these specific candidates, despite his claim that he sought agreement.[54]

Responses to Paget's objections to congregationalism began in the 1620s and lasted until the end of the seventeenth century, which attests to his success in provoking the radical tendencies that he perceived in those who eventually left for New England.[55] The effect that Paget had on neighboring English ministers in the Netherlands cannot be overlooked in explaining the development of congregationalism among the leaders of the New England Way. It might even be compared to the effect that Bancroft's scrupulous investigation had on the presbyterians. However, it is equally important to note that these exchanges also brought the disputants closer to each other at the same time as they deepened mutual hostility and division. In response to congregationalists, presbyterians such as Paget stressed the congruence of congregational liberty and synodal authority. It is noteworthy that in certain polemical contexts presbyterians focused on the liberty of the congregation within presbyterian government. This shaped the semantic development of presbyterian defenses against congregationalism, even as it has often blurred the divisions between presbyterian and congregational thought.

Just as Jacob's examiners used political analogy to describe the compatibility of congregational and synodal authority, so Paget explained that "though particular cities in and for themselves have power to execute judgement, and to punish offences committed among them; yet this hinders not but that if they judge unjustly or abuse their authority, that they themselves may then be judged of others."[56] Paget used positive language to discuss ecclesiastical liberty by reversing congregational arguments for autonomy and by drawing on examples from the Old Testament. He described synods in terms of "the liberty of Appeales, from one Ecclesiasticall judicatory to another, from the judgement of a particular Church unto a Synod Classicall, Provinciall, or Nationall."[57] He cited Exodus 18: 22–26 and Deuteronomy 17 to illustrate that "there was a law appointed touching Appeales from subalterne or subordinate Judges."[58] Not just church officers, but all members of the Church were entitled to this liberty. For "what reason had [Davenport] in describing the use of Classes to mention this onely, that they were for the help of Pastours, seing both they & those judicatories, Deut 17. 2 Chron 19 were for the help & benefit of every member of the Synagogues then and the Churches now, as well as for the help of Pastours?"[59] In fact, Paget argued, this liberty specifically supported the relief of the poor "for under the Law the poore being oppressed in judgement by unrighteous Iudges in one place, they cryed for help by appealing unto a superiour Syndedrion, and there found releafe, and so were redeemed from deceit & violence."[60]

Paget not only followed earlier presbyterians in arguing for the liberty of particular congregations within presbyterian government but also placed the same emphasis on continuity between Old and New Testament models of church government. In responding to Jacob, the presbyterians expounded New Testament Greek with reference to Old Testament Hebrew;[61] the continuity between the two models is also mapped out in Travers's Ramist tree of 1610. English presbyterians similarly emphasize the continuity between the two testaments in the late sixteenth century. As Rembert Carter has pointed out: "Thomas Cartwright had accused Whitgift of making the Jews different from Christians: 'your words seem to give suspition of a difference between the Jewes and us, what is that?'"[62] Paget similarly interpreted church government under the new covenant through the prophecy of the Old Testament. He argued that the liberty of appeals applied equally to Christ's kingdom according to the prophecy of Psalm 72.12,14: "What an unworthy counceit is this, thus to dishonour the New Testament, as if God had shewed more grace and provided more help for afflicted soules under the Law, then under the Gospell?"[63]

Paget's other arguments matched those of his presbyterian predecessors. Just as presbyterians had argued that government by particular congregations and provincial synods were not mutually exclusive in earlier debate, so Paget argued that "it followes not because severall Congregations have their due power, that therefore the power of Classes is an undue power."[64] Presbyterians understood "ecclesia" by synecdoche to shift from the single congregation to a universal Church. During his Elizabethan career, Travers had originally made this transition from the "simple" unit of elders in a particular congregation to the "compound" of elders in synods in his *Declaration*.[65] Paget described Dudley Fenner's discussion of elders in Matthew 18: 17 in like terms: the verse applied to elders in an individual congregation as well as to those combined in a synod through "a double Synecdoche, when the assembly of some Officers in a particular Church is called with the proper name of the Eldership . . . and whereas the assembly of such men in a Synod is an Eldership as well as the other."[66] Paget made the same argument himself in response to the congregationalists' application of Matthew 18: 17 to the individual congregation, also referring to Deuteronomy in discussing this passage:

> [T]here ariseth hence no prejudice to the authority of Classes or Synods. The authority of particular Churches and the authority of Synods may well subsist together . . . if a particular Church hath intire power, in and of itself to perform all Gods ordinances; then hath it power to unite itself with other Churches combined in Synods, and to submit unto the judgement thereof, according to the divine warrant & ordinance. Act 15.2. &c. Deut 17.8."[67]

What emerges from presbyterian responses to the congregational challenges is crucial: there was a distinctive order of church government expounded in this flexible reading of Scripture that was useful in responding to both conformist and congregational adversaries. By placing ecclesiastical authority in each congregation before the synod or assembly, presbyterians called for a "bottom up" style of church government which countered conformist ecclesiological formulations that began with the bishop and descended to local jurisdiction. Yet presbyterians also used this order of church government to claim that the liberty of the congregation was compatible with other levels of ecclesiastical jurisdiction, since it was only when government on the local level failed to provide a satisfactory solution that other ecclesiastical bodies were needed. This order of authority implied that even if synods ultimately exercised greater ecclesiastical authority than the individual congregation, church government within a congregation was neither derived from nor necessarily dependent on a higher ecclesiastical body. The presbyterians' description of an aggregate power of congregations combined in a synod in effect reinforced that of the particular congregation. As they stated in their examination of Henry Jacob, "[If] particuler churches haue authority to heare and order complaynts then much more assemblyes gathered by order and authoritie of more churches then one have this authoritie and power."[68]

However, while presbyterians recognized power to have originated in the congregation, they believed that it was invested in appointed officers and did not share the congregational principle that it was derived from the collective membership of the congregation.[69] What this crucial aspect of presbyterian thought does reveal is that presbyterians were not only concerned to defend the authority of synods but also to preserve the proper role of congregational government in response to congregational writers. In various contexts it could be strategically useful for presbyterians to focus debate on the ordinary exercise of ecclesiastical authority within the congregation. As the debate with Jacob shifted to the role of synods, his examiners explained that they were not insisting on a universal visible church proper: "Ffor we doe not say, that ther ought to be one generall Councell residing in one place, & continuwally imployed in governing all the Churches of Christ."[70] Acknowledging the ordinary government of churches on a congregational level, they were concerned to defend the concept of a universal Church as represented through authoritative church councils "when ther is necessary cawse."[71] As the examiners explained,

> [W]hen inferior meanes are not sufficient for any necessary buisnesse of the church: and namly for manteyance of our holy fayth & both for convincing and also condemning of contrary erors herisies and heritickes, that it is christes ordinance that then and in such causes by extraordinarily by the common care of all Christian churches and specially of their faithfull pastors and teachers . . . chosen men should bee called and assembled to gether from all parts to consider of such important and necessary affares of the church and according to gods word.[72]

It has usually been emphasized that Paget, through his strenuous efforts to drive a wedge between presbyterian and congregational polities, managed to alienate certain English clerics before they had embraced congregational ecclesiology. As Alice Carter wrote, Paget has been "variously dubbed 'a busy body,' 'unscrupulous' and 'biassed' and 'the Presbyterian watchdog of the English Church at Amsterdam . . . by Congregational historians."[73] Yet it is noteworthy that in the process he himself adopted congregational rhetoric to defend presbyterian government against congregational charges of clerical tyranny. The tactical flexibility of presbyterian discourse was useful for answering both conformist and congregational opponents. It also left room for ambiguity in the exact relationship between the visible church as a particular and general body. Such ambiguities were not necessarily disposed to congregational polity; key aspects of presbyterian thought can only be fully understood with reference to discussion of the visible church as a whole.

NEW ENGLAND ON TRIAL

If English presbyterians questioned Jacob's congregational experiment in Southwark in the 1610s and those with congregational inclinations in the Netherlands during the 1620s and 1630s, it has seemed that there was no presbyterian inquisition of congregationalism in New England during the 1630s. By the late 1630s rumors of radical New England practices had reached English nonconformists and prompted eleven ministers to inquire, in a letter signed by a group of nonconformist ministers, about the government of the

New England churches. That one of the signatories later migrated to New England has suggested to historians that there were no presbyterian overtones to this exchange.

In light of the flexibility of presbyterian thought it is worth reconsidering the English critique of New England church polity. The chief respondent to the New Englanders' defense of their government was John Ball. Although heralded by English presbyterians of the mid-seventeenth century, Carol Schneider said of Ball's writings that "the first and most striking aspect of all three tracts by 'the Presbyterians' Champion' is that they share much common ground with what are usually taken to be congregational views on church order and governance."[74] Again, there is no basis for assuming that congregational views lurked within the "ambiguities of the Cartwrightian tradition." However, Tom Webster draws the conclusion that during this period "this tradition seems to have been almost the exclusive property of the Amesians."[75] Citing Ball's silence about synods, Webster concludes that "plainly, this was not a Presbyterian accusing a 'non-separating Congregationalist' of Separatism, but one non-separating Congregationalist (or, as I would prefer, one Amesian) accusing another of going beyond the standard set by Parker, Baynes and Ames."[76]

However, presbyterian debate with congregationalists was not limited to the role of synods alone. Relative silence on this topic, and the proportion of writing devoted to it, are not always on their own an adequate measure of ecclesiological commitments. John Paget's brother Thomas and his copastor Julines Herring were committed to presbyterianism before departing for the Netherlands, and others who signed this letter also became outspoken advocates of presbyterianism in the mid-seventeenth century.[77] Their involvement in questioning the New Englanders indicates that even if not all the signatories shared the same ecclesiological convictions, certain presbyterians were involved in questioning New England radicalism and were concerned to challenge their church practice without directly raising the role of synods. Although synods were not included in the questions sent over to New England, the English were in fact deeply concerned with the relationship between congregations in addition to how particular congregations were governed individually.

Indeed the theological discourse of New England congregationalism was shaped by the discussions on the visible church of the 1610s and 1620s. Schneider's view, which has largely gone unchallenged, is that for over thirty years before the civil wars, "nonconformists had generally argued that the first churches were parochial, and therefore not diocesan."[78] However, there was extended debate over this question among nonconformists during the 1610s and 1620s. In writing against the New England congregationalists during the 1630s, Ball argued, against Henry Jacob, that in the New Testament the visible church was composed of multiple congregations: "[W]hen a church did comprehend a citie with its suburbs and the contrey circumjacent . . . it might well be that the number did so increase through the extraordinary blessing of god . . . that they could not well meet ordinarily in one place, and yet might and did continue one society."[79] Ball also employed the synecdoche used by presbyterians to translate the individual congregation into a single visible church composed of many congregations: "The increase of churches doth require an increase of ministers, and if they grow to bignesse more then ordinary, an increase of places for their assembling, when the essence of the visible church is not changed, nor one multiplyed or divided into many."[80] On the key question of a single visible church in the New Testament, Ball wrote: "May we not well think that the Church at Jerusalem . . . that this church did quickly rise to such bignesse that they could not well assemble in one congregation, as we call them? And the same may be said of other churches before mentioned."[81] For Schneider, this seems an "unexpected argument" in Ball's treatise, given his previous discussion of church government in the context of individual congregations. Instead of exploring how a given congregation might have related to other congregations, Schneider dismissed this crucial concept as "a minor rather than a major point in Ball's argument. It was used not to counter congregational ecclesiology, but to check its potential excesses."[82]

But Ball further applied the implications of a single visible church in the New Testament to church government: "What then remaineth, but that they might assemble in divers places, and yet hold communion in laws, ordinances, government and officers?"[83] These comments, which were a response to Henry Jacob's defense of congregational autonomy, directly challenged Jacob's understanding of the physical gathering of saints in a single congregation as the visible church. As Ball argued, "To meet together therefore in one place is not so essentiall to the church, but it may continue one in laws, ordinances, government and communion, though in respect of multitude, distance of places, and many other occurences they be constrained to assemble and hold their meeting severally."[84] He also objected to the congregationalist's rejection of authoritative synods and their consequent inability to suppress heresy: "If subtile Heretikes arise, and seduce, and draw away many from the faith and the body of the society be not able to convince them, either they must be let alone or cast out without conviction, for neighbouring Ministers stand in peculiar relation to their flocks onely, and must not meddle beyond their calling according to your tenet."[85] He further argued that neighboring ministers ought to be involved in the placement of ministers, contrary to congregational practice. Yet instead of allowing for the possibility that Ball's concept of the particular congregation agreed with synodal jurisdiction, Schneider concluded that he subscribed to the notion "that Scripture provides more than one model for church organization."[86]

English clergymen were not alone in challenging New England congregationalists' understanding of the visible church. Certain preachers in New England began to make this argument after Ball's exchanges. John Paget claimed to have convinced the leading nonconformist ecclesiological thinker, Robert Parker, to accept the lawful authority of synods. Congregationalists also claimed Parker as a supporter of their government. There is an irony in Parker's role in inspiring New England congregationalism in that his son Thomas and his nephew James Noyes who settled in Newbury, Massachusetts, were among the most vocal protesters against it there.[87]

Echoing earlier presbyterian arguments on the compatibility of congregational and synodal authority, Noyes stated: "Let this be the conclusion: All congregations have a divided power, but not an Independent power."[88] Just as earlier presbyterians had been concerned to affirm congregational liberty within presbyterian oversight, Noyes argued that "a particular congregation needs the protection of other congregations."[89] He used the synagogue as an example to demonstrate this point: "The Synagogues in *Israel* had a divided power, yet dependent upon the Temple: they could excommunicate, *Joh.* 9 and in all probability, the Priests and Levites in the Temple did not admit such as stood excomunicate in the Synagogues until the case were decided."[90] According to Noyes, this pattern also applied to the Christian Church, where "the Apostles, &c. were members of no visible Church, if they were not members of a visible Church Universal."[91] Citing Calvin's *Institutes*, he gave further arguments for the universal visible church in the New Testament:

> It is correspondent to Scripture-phrase; the visible Church is termed in Scripture one Universal Church, *Matth.* 16.18. the Universal Church is one visible Church, because it is described as acting visibly in the administrations of the Keys: This may be more fully proved in another place. In *Eph* 4. the Universal Church is one visible Church, because it is described by its visible Officers, Apostles, Prophets, Evangelists, Pastors and Teachers. *1 Cor. 12*, the Universal Church is one visible Church, because it is described by its visible Officers in like manner. *Rev* 11.1,2,3, the Universal Church is described as visible, by one city, by one court; and is called the outward court, and so distinguished, as it is visible, from the mystical Church, which is resembled by the Temple.[92]

Matthew 18: 17 was central to presbyterian arguments against congregationalism. Noyes asserted that this passage referred to church officers and not to all the members of the congregation: "ἐκκλησία is used for any assembly in the new Testament." Noyes cited earlier Elizabethan presbyterian commentators among other exponents of presbyterian government: he noted that "Mr *Cartwright* alledgeth many places of Scripture to shew that church in this place, signifieth the Presbyterie."[93] He made the same use of the Old Testament model of church government as had his predecessors to establish this interpretation of the word "ecclesia" in the New Testament:

> Our Saviour may well be supposed to conform his speech to the old Testament, rather then to the new Testament, to the use of the phrase, at that time when he spake, not so much to the future use of it, in the new Testament. . . . Our Saviour doth manifestly allude to the Presbyteries of the Jewes, and gives the Christian church a pattern from the practise of the Jewish church. One would not think that our Saviour should speak of an unknown church, and not describe it, because he directs the disciples to repair to it: to direct one to a place unknown and unknowable, is but labour in vain. Besides, those phrases heathen and publican, and two or three witnesses, do argue that our Saviour referred his speech to the Jewish church.[94]

Thus, Noyes not only drew upon Elizabethan sources to defend the authority of synod, but he presented the same exegesis of key biblical passages to make the same arguments as were produced in earlier presbyterian debates with congregationalists. He also relied upon his uncle, Robert Parker, to reinforce his argument for the unity of the visible church: "What is done by one gate in *Jerusalem*, is done by the whole city (*intuitu,* though not *interventu totius Ecclesiae*) as Master *Parker* distinguisheth to another purpose."[95] Citing his use of the existing scholarship, he commented that "I might now charge the multitude of Interpreters both ancient and modern, but it is done already by others."[96]

It appears that there was a relatively short interval between Ball's debates with the New England clergy at the very end of the 1630s and the Newbury ministers' expression of presbyterian sympathies. There is reference to presbyterian sentiments in New England as early as August 1641, when somebody noted that "of late divers of the ministerie have had set meetings to order church matters, whereby it is conceived they bend towards Presbyterian rule."[97] On December 17, 1643, Thomas Parker wrote to a member of the Westminster Assembly describing their presbyterian meditations over the course of several years: "My cousin Noyse and myself, have seen such confusion of necessity depending on the government which hath been practised by us here, that wee have been forced much to search into it within these two or three yeeres."[98] According to Parker, Noyes had waited a long time before acting on his presbyterian convictions and raising his objections to congregational practices in 1643:

This Reverend Author, who (amongst others) is not satisfied touching the Charter of the Churches where he lives, and cannot yet finde in Scripture that the Lord Jesus did ever give them Commission to the *full* exercise of that Government which is there Established; he did after long silence, at length acquaint his People, and the Reverend Presbyters of that countrey with his doubtings concerning the way they went in.[99]

On September 4, 1643, "Winthrop states that an assembly or synod of all the New England elders, being about fifty, and such ruling elders as desired to sit with them, convene at the college in Cambridge."[100] As Felt recorded, "The principal occasion of such a meeting was, that several ministers endeavored to promote Presbyterianism, especially those of Newbury." At the meeting the Newbury ministers offered an extended defense of presbyterian government.[101] It is significant that by the time of this meeting the New Englanders had already come to identify presbyterian government with the Westminster Assembly, even though scholars have argued that it was far from clear by this date where the assembly would stand on the question of church government. Robert Paul has argued against any substantial English presbyterian presence in the assembly until after late December 1643, attributing the main presbyterian strength to involvement of Scottish commissioners.[102] However, Felt quoted a primary source which stated that at the New England meeting, "Hutchinson says that the movement was made 'to set up Presbyterian government under the authority of the Assembly at Westminster.'"[103] This meeting not only preceded the assembly's debates over church government which began in October 1643 but was also prior to the reception of the Scottish Commissioners on September 15, 1643.

Given that the deliberations of the assembly were private, it was presumably through private correspondence that the New Englanders gathered their impressions of a presbyterian temperament among assembly divines. The Newbury ministers had worked closely with William Twisse, the prolocutor of the assembly, before their departure for New England. Furthermore they had corresponded with at least one of the members of the Westminster Assembly by December 1643. Other New England clergy also corresponded with those in England. "About the same date," according to Felt, "a different writer, in this country, sends a communication to another clergyman in England, concerning the same matter." In this letter the author complained that just as prelates had persecuted the godly in England, so did the presbyterians keep a close watch on their activity, extending this persecution to those in New England: "England was never quiet, but worse and worse since it hunted almost a little nation of saints to New England; though W. Rathband, joining issue with A.S., will follow them with a blotting pen in print, even to that kingdom too."[104]

It is possible that the Newbury ministers supplied the presbyterian William Rathband with the supplementary information he used to write his *Narration* of the New England way, against congregational government. As Rathband mentioned in his preface, "That my selfe by divine providence had sundry intelligences lay by me, which ioyned to what was already printed might either make the storie compleat, or else might occasion and spurre on some other (perhaps of themselves) to publish a better."[105] Regardless of Rathband's unnamed sources, his agreement with the Newbury presbyterian ministers on the nature of the visible church and on presbyterian government is evident, and his efforts to refute New England congregationalism were clearly resented. It is no surprise to find that Rathband described the universal visible church with reference to both the Jewish and Christian community of saints:

> As all the scattered Jewish Churches are called one flock, 1 Pet. 5.2. and all the Gentilish Christian Churches present were called one little Sister, Cant. 8.8. And the Jewish Christian Churches yet to come are called one Bride, Revel. 19.7. And the Scriptures oft speake of many Churches, or al, as one in the singular number, 1 Cor. 19.32 Ephes. 3.10. Gal. 1.13. by reason of some bonds by which they are united together: And our brethren themselves do sometimes acknowledge an universall visible Church (though usually they deny it) as Apol. p 16.21.37.40. yea, and officers too of that Catholique Church, *viz.* Apostles and Evangelists, which therefore (whiles they remained) baptized persons into that Church, wheresoever they met with them without any respect to a congregationall Church, as themselves acknowledge.[106]

Rathband was also the prime mover in the publication of John Ball's treatises, including his extended refutation of New England congregational practices. On the general visible church, Rathband even cited Ball: "The Apostles Churches (most at least if not all) consisted of so many thousands as possibly could not meet all conveniently together in the same place, and at the same times for all Gods publike Worship to Edification. For which see more in Master Rutherfords and Master Bals late Treatises."[107]

Sargent Bush has highlighted the significance of "the year 1643, when the synod at Cambridge fulfilled Hooker's dream in establishing a formal confederation of the several New England colonies."[108] It was at this point that the New Englanders addressed criticism of their church polity from abroad, when "the first concerted efforts by New England ministers to answer questions and criticisms from abroad, some of which had begun before the Westminster Assembly was convened, but all of which after July 1, 1643, became relevant to that body's deliberations."[109] Yet it is important that, during this period, the New England congregationalists responded to presbyterian criticism at home and abroad. Already by September 1643 New England presbyterians had developed their arguments against congregationalism and attempted to act on their convictions; this local pressure on local congregationalists during a critical period in their development reveals that just as Henry Jacob defended his actions against presbyterian criticism in England, so did the New England congregationalists face opposition on the question of the nature of the visible church from presbyterian critics at home and abroad. New Englanders had not simply developed their ecclesiological views in response to presbyterians once they had crossed the Atlantic: both Hooker and Davenport had been interrogated by John Paget. Their views of church government were also apparently informed by earlier congregational exponents. Thomas Hooker took particular note of Henry Jacob's definition of the visible church. In his undated manuscript notes, Hooker cited Jacob and wrote, under the heading "What the church is visible," that "a visible church is a number of faythfull people ioyned together by ther willing consent in a spirituall outward society or body having power to exercise government & all gods spirituall ordinances, in & for it self immediately from Christ: Jacob."[110]

Contrary to the assumption that the dominant understanding of the visible church among early seventeenth-century nonconformists applied exclusively to a particular congregation, it is clear, rather, that it was a point of serious contention among those inclined to presbyterianism and congregationalism. That John Ball's works were written after nearly two decades of debate over the nature of the visible church warns us against dismissing the significance of the concept. That his works were posthumously published (and even quoted on this subject) by advocates of presbyterian government in the Westminster Assembly, including Simeon Ashe, William Rathband, Daniel Cawdrey, and Edward Calamy, further challenges the view that congregational definitions of the visible church dominated nonconformist ecclesiological thought.[111] Richard Heyricke, a supporter of presbyterianism in the mid-seventeenth century, interpreted the visible church in the New Testament to be composed of multiple congregations in his sermon at the Collegiate Church in Manchester in 1640.[112]

Given that arguments between presbyterians and congregationalists in the first several decades of the seventeenth century involved competing definitions of the visible church as well as the authority of synods, it is no surprise that this was also the case in the grand ecclesiological debates of the 1640s. As Elliot Vernon has shown, "[T]hroughout the Assembly debates, this argument for unity and catholicity was linked by the Presbyterians to the view that the New Testament polity was an association of congregations under the authority of presbyteries and synods,"[113] that "underlying the debate between the Independent Burroughes and the Presbyterian Calamy were conflicting understandings of the nature of the scripturally instituted church" and that "Calamy's scriptural exegesis pointed to the idea that the New Testament described the church militant as one, catholic body."[114] In the several decades prior to the Westminster Assembly, presbyterians affirmed their understanding of a single visible church in the New Testament by Old Testament church polity. Rembert Carter argued that presbyterians in the mid-seventeenth century similarly "had a keen sense of the unity of Scripture" and "in general favored an appeal to the Old Testament for much of their polity," pointing out that the presbyterian "Thomas Edwards calls attention to one error of the time: a denial of the Old Testament affecting Christians under grace. Some, he complained, do not read the Old Testament nor bind it in the same volume with the New."[115] Many congregationalists, such as Thomas Goodwin, objected to this reading of the New Testament and argued "though Christ might speak in the Language of the Old Testament, it is not necessary that his meaning should be, that the Churches in the New Testament, should be formed according as the Old were; but the contrary."[116] However, there had been a relatively small number of outspoken advocates for congregationalism early in the Westminster Assembly; this minority was ultimately unable to outmaneuver their opponents who disagreed with their definition of the visible church. As Vernon stated, by "March [1644] the majority in the Assembly concluded that the scriptural church of Jerusalem consisted of many congregations under one presbytery."[117]

ECCLESIOLOGICAL AMBIGUITIES

Competing interpretations of the visible church, however, did not directly translate into presbyterian and congregational divisions. Nor did all presbyterians agree on their interpretation of certain passages in Scripture, nor did they simply defend the authority of synods strictly through an Old Testament grid. According to Carter, "Isolated individuals from the Presbyterian ranks insisted on an exclusively New Testament polity," and "within Presbyterian ranks there sometimes appeared a note of dubiety concerning Old Testament proofs."[118] If English presbyterian polemicists contributed to the deepening of divisions among the godly, it is also worth considering their contribution to the development of ecclesiological ambiguities and the blurring of presbyterian and congregational governments.

If there was ambiguity and flexibility within presbyterian rhetoric, there was also room for interpretation within congregational government.[119] The New England divine Giles Firmin is an example of those inclined to congregational polity in the early seventeenth century. For Firmin, "New England showed traces of belief in a universal 'Catholick-visible-Church.'" He was committed to unity within the Church of England and interpreted conservatively New England practice whereby "many settlers acted as if being a member of a particular church meant membership of a wider Church. When they moved to a new town, they took letters of recommendation to the minister there, rather than transfer to a new church."[120] Before returning to England, Firmin may have been in contact with others who would have held a similar interpretation of the visible church as a universal body. Nathaniel Ward of Ipswich, Massachusetts, was one of the New England presbyterian sympathizers; he was a colleague and the father-in-law of Giles Firmin. It is possible that the Newbury ministers were in contact with the clergy of Ipswich and may have shared their views on the universal nature of the visible church. A collection of sermon notes held at the Massachusetts Historical Society, dating from the 1640s, reveals that a "Mr Noise" preached to the Ipswich congregation in 1646.[121] Yet, more important than the various factors that may have ultimately shaped Firmin's understanding of a universal visible church is the fact that this did not necessarily lead him to a full acceptance of presbyterian government and the authority of synods. Rather, it appears that he "devised arguments that crossed party lines, to unite against sectarianism."[122] His position confirms the complexity in the development of ecclesiology during the early seventeenth century and the ambiguity in various ecclesiological formulations.

The example of Giles Firmin is not the only one to show how presbyterians contributed to the richly complicated proliferation of ecclesiological ideas. A prominent nonconformist text in the realm of ecclesiological debate in the early seventeenth century was *The Reply* to George Downame's defense of his sermon. Contemporaries identified Richard Sheerwood as its most the likely author; little is known of him apart from his participation in the petition at the accession of James VI and I to the English throne.[123] Although Downame does not name Sheerwood as his refuter, he does charge his opponent with espousing "the newfound parish discipline" in contrast to the elder disciplinarians who accepted the authority of spiritual assemblies beyond the individual congregation. The author himself defended the "new-found parish discipline," including himself among those targeted by Downame. Again, even though congregational views were developing and denominational categories may not have been rigidly defined during this period, Downame had already set up a division by identifying a distinction between the elder and new-found disciplinarian puritans. There appear to be distinctly congregational elements in the *Reply*'s argument against diocesan episcopacy. The definition of the Church (*ecclesia* in the New Testament) was as a local congregation according to the classic congregational argument. The text also identified church authority as deriving from individual members of each congregation instead of assigning it directly to church officers.[124]

Thomas Paget offered a different reading of the text and account of the controversy. According to him, the refuter denied congregational sympathies, claiming to have written against Henry Jacob in support of authoritative church assemblies.[125] Furthermore, the *Reply* was ultimately endorsed by the staunch presbyterian John Paget, who was not only involved in editing the second part of the *Reply* but also made modifications to those parts of the text that he found to clash with the authority of spiritual assemblies.[126] Although Thomas mentioned John Paget's involvement in editing the *Replye* in order to demonstrate the breadth of his influence among nonconformists, it is not unlikely that Paget contributed to the arguments made in the *Replye*, which would explain the defense of the authority of spiritual assemblies in the text.[127]

A more explicit endorsement of spiritual assemblies appears in a third part of the *Reply*, which defended the role of the elder. This section is not included in extant copies of the first two parts of the *Reply* and until now has not been known to historians. However, in the library of Trinity College, Dublin, there is manuscript copy of the last seven chapters of the third part of the *Reply*, which reinforce Thomas Paget's arguments. In the eleventh chapter of this section, the subject of spiritual assemblies naturally follows on from a discussion of the plurality of elders who governed by common consent. To argue that presbyters ruled by common consent before the rise of schism was to concede that "among the ordinary Church-officers the Presbiters were at first under the Apostles trusted with the government of the Churches by their common counsell[,] their counsell ergo ought not to be excluded but rather still to be used in matters of Ecclesiastical government." Furthermore, the *Reply* argued that "according to Jerome, Moses did not rule alone, but that bishops ought to govern in common with the presbiters," for the singular rule of bishops was "by custom and not by Lord's ordinance."[128] Yet the writer insisted that "it were madnesse to imagine that all superiority should therefore be condemned . . . who doth not know . . . governing Elders and Deacons are esteemed inferior in degree unto the Pastors or ministers of the word, and that among the Pastors in their Presbiteriall or Synodicall meetings a preeminence of order is given to the one who moderateth the Assembly for the time."[129] It can thus be concluded from the third part of the *Reply* that whereas Downame sought to drive a wedge between the elder disciplinarians and emerging congregational puritans in his writings, the *Reply* countered such categorizations, including elements that can be identified with both congregational and presbyterian exponents. It strategically aligned itself with the widest possible witness by drawing on the testimony of church Fathers, early English protestant writers and the reformers.

Thus, if it was possible for some such as Firmin to espouse the concept of a universal visible church without necessarily accepting a full presbyterian government by synods and assemblies, for others it was important to define the Church as a particular congregation while nevertheless embracing the authority of synods. Presbyterians contributed to yet further complexities in ecclesiological formulations. John Paget's influence on Robert Parker's ecclesiological thought and treatise *De Politeia Ecclesiastica* was perhaps more substantial than his editorial involvement in the *Replye* to Downame. He claimed that "after much conference with [Parker]" on the subject of church councils, "[Parker] plainly changed his opinion" and "so becoming a member of our Classicall combination, yet did he never testify against the undue power of the Classis."[130] An attempt to categorize Parker's position, especially if based on John Paget's account, is likely to be misguided. Yet defining his ecclesiology is essential given the profound influence of *De Politeia Ecclesiastica* on the development of congregationalism in New England: "Both Presbyterians and Congregationalists claimed the book as supporting their side," although "the book has served the Congregationalists much better than the Presbyterians, and it is more accurate to treat Parker with the discussion of the early Congregationalists."[131]

As scholars have suggested in their analysis of Parker, it may not be accurate to define congregationalism in the early seventeenth century simply in terms of the rejection of authoritative synods. Equally Parker's definition of the visible church and the relative authority he allocated to particular congregations and synods do not establish a straightforward congregational tendency. The ambiguity in his text reveals that presbyterian-congregational debates produced polarization as well as modification of church polities.

In his *De Politeia Ecclesiastica*, Parker, like Henry Jacob, identified the visible church as a single congregation: "[T]he name Church, which in Scripture is ever used in the singuler but for one congregation; as it is used in the plurall when scripture speake of the saints of a province or nation, as of many Churches, & never in the singuler 1 Cor 16.19, 2 Cor 8.1 Gal 1.2.21. Act 9.31 & 15.41." He used this definition to counter conformist arguments directly, for "in all Downams Table he can find only Act 7.38 in which the whole Nation is called a church which was for that as thet it was but one congregation."[132] A primary concern for Parker in refuting Downame's definition of the Church, however, was not the extent of ecclesiastical jurisdiction but the political prescription: "Downams instance of the Jewes Church which was but one because it was one common wealth, & subject to one high Priest is light. 1. though the Jewes were subject to the Romane Emperour, yet that made them not one Church as we see Act 9.31. Gal 1.21."[133] If the visible church was not to be defined along political lines, nor should it necessarily be limited by the number of those who gathered in one place for worship as Henry Jacob had argued. Parker considered the Jerusalem church to be "many thousand beleving Jewes in Jerusalem, yet that hinders not their being one congregation, as was the whole Nation of the Jewes in the Wildernes, being one congregation, which Luke calls the Church, as Moses called it the Congregation: . . . And to what church did Paul & Barnabas give account at Anteoch, but to that Church which had sent them forth? Act 13.1.2."[134] However, while Parker defined the visible church as a single congregation, he nevertheless used the same pattern and language as Travers to explain the nature of the visible church. For Travers the particular congregation as well as the combination of congregations was the visible church, beginning with "the first and more simple" college of elders in a particular congregation "whence also the latter doth wholy spring."[135] Parker similarly identified the two forms as the visible church, using the same language as Travers:

> From the Church in generall as the subject of Ecclesiasticall Policie we come to the kindes of Churches visible *which* are two. . . . [T]he first is a collection of faithfull men into one congregation which is called by the generall name A Church. The Church which springeth of the first is a combination of many first Churches gathered into one companie, called a Synod.[136]

Further ambiguities in Parker's treatise can also be explored in light of his concern to refute conformist arguments for diocesan authority. The order of ecclesiastical authority was foundational for his argument against episcopacy. From Matthew 18: 17 he concluded "that the words tell the church belongs to perticuler church meetings first, properly, imediately & essentially & to synods only by consequence is cleare."[137] In response to Downame's discussion of diocesan authority, Parker argued that "the keyes were not given first to synods; or if so, yet not only to Provinciall & Diocesan but also Parish Churches."[138] He emphasized that not only did congregations hold power and exercise authority initially, but also with greater frequency: "[It] is inconvenient to take authoretie from perticuler Churches & to rule by Synods wc are rare . . . Field hath no thing to answer but Synods of ould were frequent & though he sheweth reason Synods may now be frequent yet can they not be so frequent as the Churches causes require."[139]

However, while locating power and authority in each congregation "first, properly, imediately & essentially," he also cited Whitaker's understanding of Matthew 18: 17, which attributed greater authority to synods than to congregations: "[F]or if every perticuler church have more autoretie then Peter then much more the universall church represented in generall councells."[140] Synods also had authority over a congregation "when her misgovernment is in question." For just "as a Pastors fault is not subject to censure of any one of his Church, but to many, so if a Church erre she is to be corrected by no one Church, but in a Synod of many." Parker explained that by "right of ap-peale" synods checked the standing of individual congregations, "yea though she erre not, yet if any suppose she erreth the synod may heare the appeale & that Church is bound to answer."[141] He also acknowledged the fallibility of synods. Congregations themselves retained the right to appeal, and there-fore the superiority of synods over congregations did not necessarily deprive congregations of their original power and authority: "[T]hough a perticuler Church be inferiour to the Synod yet the power of all Parish Churches is grater then the synod for they may by a new Synod repeale the former."[142]

Parker's congregational sympathies might have been expected to have emerged more clearly in his discussion of the Church's power over ecclesias-tical officers, which was a case congregationalists often made. As Parker put it, "[E]cclesiasticall power commeth from the church to her rectors, not from Bishop to her."[143] He also denied that rectors received power and authority from ordination by bishops, rather that "the Pastors as other officers have authoretie immediately from Christ, & in that respect is superiour to men & Angells Gal 1.8. as being in Christs steed." However, direct reception of authority did not exempt pastors from church censure "because the holyest men may erre to the Churches hurt; therefore though his authoretie be not subject to the Church yet the person to whome the Church comitted the administration of that authoretie, is subject to her." As indicated by the state-ment "[E]cclesisaticall power commeth from the church," Parker appears to have ascribed even more to the Church. Yet the three respects in which "the Churcyh ha[s] fullnes of power" over her officers that Parker described did not necessarily diverge from the views of Paget and other presbyterians: "first in the end," by which Parker meant that ministers were appointed for the edifica-tion of the Church not the Church of her ministers: "[T]he Ministers are only the churches the churches are not the ministers."[144] "Secondly in applying it to the person," whereby the Church held the authority to call ministers to a particular congregation. "Thirdly in ruling the use of it if it be abused."[145] For the right to censure the pastor was a "necessarie defence of the church, which can not be safe without power over her rectors."[146] This was not to say that church officers derived their power or jurisdiction from the Church. In coun-tering Downame and the conformist writer Thomas Bilson, Parker stressed that "Presbyters are dispensers or stewards from God, & therefore receive from him their Jurisdiction & power of exercise as well . . . though they be ordained of Bishops or whomsoever yet receive they no authoritie, jurisdiction, or power from them to exercise."[147] Thus, even here in the discussion of the Church's power relative to her officers, there is no straightforward departure from presbyterian government, so that it is still possible to argue that Parker's *De Politeia* was not simply akin to congregational polity but was also congruous with presbyterianism not only with respect to church assemblies but also on the crucial subject of the extent of congregational authority.

What appears to reveal Parker's proclivity to congregationalism most starkly is his argument that the authority of the synod was conditional upon the consent of the congregations. Parker alluded to this while explaining that the authority of combined congregations gave synods greater force: "And that synods have their power from perticuler Churches appears by their binding such Churches as by their Deligates gave consent without which consent synods could not bind them."[148] Since "they are confessed but to represent the Church," Parker argued that synods "neither bind any which send not to them as Bilson." Parker cited the moderate puritan William Whitaker to argue that the condition of congregational consent did not apply in the example of Acts 15, since "the Synod at Jerusalem, whose decrees bound other Churches, not as by ordinarie right of a Synod but by the authoretie of the Colledge of Apostles."[149]

Ecclesiological thought among nonconformists did not simply develop as varying responses to episcopacy but was also shaped by the debates between presbyterians and congregationalists, persisting throughout the first several decades of the seventeenth century. Presbyterians reacted to congregational developments, and at the same time the pressure they exerted on those inclined toward congregational government had a range of effects. English presbyterianism alters understanding of the emergence of congregationalism no less than it alters understanding of the evolution of conformist thought in the late sixteenth and early seventeenth centuries. Contrary to the traditional paradigm, the distinguishing marks between presbyterianism and congregationalism cannot fully be ascertained simply by an affirmation of authoritative synods or a lack thereof. It was not the authority of synods alone but also the nature of the visible church that divided presbyterian and congregational thinkers. As they came to espouse different definitions of liberty, the extent of common consent and the exact nature of ecclesiastical judgments also became crucial factors.

CHAPTER 4

Common Consent

From the tyme of the Apostles of this sayde age which was a
1500 yeere and some what more hath not one not so much as
one witnesse truly vouched to testyfye either for the absolute
independency of parishes or agaynst the lawfull authorytie of
Synods.[1]

"Examiners" against Henry Jacob the "Defendant"

On one level, it can be argued that episcopal, presbyterian, and congregational advocates all shared the view that government had a consensual basis.
The principle of consent, however, was deeply divisive in both theory and
practice. The Elizabethan apologist for episcopacy, Richard Hooker, argued
for an initial consent of the governed that subsequently delegated authority
to the prince and the episcopal bench. Presbyterian and congregational writers, on the other hand, argued for the perpetual gathering of a plurality of
voices. They used this principle to challenge the superiority of bishops over
pastors and to argue for the inclusion of the laity in the government of the
Church. Nonetheless they disagreed on its nature and extent. Did consent
chiefly derive from the congregation as a whole or from the collective decision of church officers in a consistory or synod? What was the role of consent
throughout history, especially in biblical, patristic, and modern times? How
did judgments of ancient and modern councils and ecclesiastical writers relate
to unresolved debates on English ecclesiology? Were ecclesiastical determinations in themselves authoritative acts or statements?

What remained unquestioned was the importance of interpreting the
meaning of consent through historic precedent. While on one level history
served a polemical purpose in these debates, it was also part of a longer ecclesiastical tradition that turned to history to define and express confessional
identity. For presbyterians history was not simply a storehouse of examples
that they appealed to in order to refute the arguments of their adversaries. It

played an essential role in their deliberative processes and bore witness to the necessity of collective judgment and jurisdiction through councils and synods. Indeed, as the presbyterians conscripted ancient and modern witnesses and the decrees of church councils into their deliberations, they regarded this as an extension of the principle of consent for the resolution of their theological conflict. The practice of weighing various testimonies to arrive at a decision did not apply only to theological argument but was also used to determine disciplinary cases. In this respect presbyterians' understanding of ecclesiastical history put them at odds with their congregational adversaries over what authority the sources and debates carried, even if they shared the mode of argument. Notwithstanding disagreement among the godly over the nature and extent of common consent, history and contemporary examples clearly played a central role in their deliberations. Their mutual commitment to historical sources and examples may even have brought them closer to each other than either side was likely to have admitted. Ecclesiological development was not only the product of a multidimensional debate among English ecclesiologists, but was inextricably linked to history and other contemporary controversies.

THE FREEDOM OF CONSENT

Even if the basis of government were consensual, conformists argued that on account of the bishops' superior status, they were not bound by the consent of ruling elders in the ordinary exercise of their jurisdiction. As early as Whitgift, certain conformists traced the apostolic origin of episcopacy, chiefly through the examples of Timothy at Ephesus and Titus at Crete (who were referred to as "episcopoi" in the Greek New Testament). Its apostolic origin did not necessarily mean that the office was perpetually binding. But late Elizabethan and Jacobean divines who held a more exalted view of episcopacy asserted that these bishops were to be recognized as such by their title in the New Testament as well as by their exclusive function of jurisdiction and ordination as prescribed by the Apostle Paul in his epistles.[2] Such arguments tended to take the superior status of bishops itself as evidence against rule by common consent. A sermon of George Downame's in 1608 is one such example. Particularly concerned to defend the episcopal office, using the status of Timothy and Titus,[3] Downame argued that neither a continuous nor a perpetual residence was required: an "ordinary abode" in Ephesus and Crete was sufficient for Timothy and Titus to have acted as bishops.[4] In response to early examples of government by consent, Downame pointed to Jerome's understanding that presbyters ruled by consent until the rise of schism led to the necessary introduction of episcopal superintendents. Common consent for conformists could thus be acknowledged as the basis of government, but nevertheless be superseded by the authority of bishops and thereby omitted from the daily exercise of church government.

The presbyterians in turn asserted that the jurisdiction and ordination of Timothy and Titus were not reserved for any such superior office. On the grounds that Timothy and Titus exercised an itinerant ministry fulfilling similar duties outside Ephesus and Crete, Cartwright and Travers argued that these men belonged to an altogether different category of "Evangelist," which office was extraordinary and came to an end along with that of the Apostles.[5] The writer of the "Reformed Church Government" similarly argued that because Timothy

> served as an attendant upon the Apostles . . . was called by title and did the work of an Evangelist . . . he was such as one as was evermore at the appointment of the apostle, either to goe with him or stay so where ells, or to send to Churches & to doe always, as he should direct him. . . . Paul appointed him sometyme to Macedonia sometyme to Corin . . . to Thessalonica sometyme to this Church & sometyme to that . . . .[6]

Nonconformists especially targeted Downame's reliance on Jerome. In the *Replye* to Downame, the writer objected that in the latter example Jerome included elders of Ephesus, and that this undermined his previous arguments from Ephesus.[7] He further asserted that Jerome acknowledged no such distinction between bishop and presbyter in 1 Corinthians 1:12 following the rise of schisms, and therefore could not have claimed that the rise of schism during the Apostles' time led to the introduction of superior ecclesiastical officers.[8] Although it is not clear when the author believed that the introduction of bishops took place, it is clear that he thought that there was no room for ecclesiastical superiority among ministers in this interpretation.[9]

For presbyterians, the superior status of bishops was especially offensive, because it undermined the principle of common consent in synods. According to Travers's reading of history, after introducing a slight degree of superiority among ministers, the bishops' tyranny came to extend over spiritual assemblies.[10] Once episcopal authority replaced the authority of synods, the *Letters Patents* described how the personal ambition of prelates continued to undermine the role of synods, whereby "synodall iudicatures was reiectd almost by all, because it did diminish the Episcopall . . . for proceeding against the persons of the Bishops, no man desiring to facilitate the iudicature against himselfe, the restoring of it to parochiall Synods, vnto which it did formerly belong."[11] The writer of the "Reformed Church Government" argued "that god himselfe hath instituted Synods otherwise called Councells for determining of all errors & heresyes which might arise & for preserving the Church in unitye."[12] He insisted on strength in numbers, "for the fource & sway of Many (in a Councell) must needes cary greater perswasion in the minds of all Christians then the pleasure of one preferred above the rest."[13] The author further claimed that doctrinal error naturally followed from episcopal government which neglected the principle of common consent: "[T]he humane devise of erecting a Bishop or primate in Nation to rule the rest (whereby all the rest were made subiect to one mans pleasure) was a very vayne devise & to intollerable in the Church which ought to be governed . . . by the Pastors together in common."[14] The writer of the *Letters Patents* drew an explicit link between episcopacy and Arminianism, claiming that "even as at this day in England, the Supporters of the Hierarchie, and Arminianisme prevaile by the same reasons."[15]

Although the fault-line between the godly on the principle of common consent may not be immediately apparent, presbyterians and congregationalists were deeply divided as the issue related to the nature of ecclesiastical judgments and to their broader understanding of church government. The link between the authority of synods and the suppression of heretics had been the presbyterians' strongest card, and they likewise used it to oppose congregational autonomy. The synod at Jerusalem in Acts 15 was central to the presbyterian argument that synods were the divinely appointed means for preserving doctrine:

> For by this it is manifest, that when the churches are troubled with false doctrine and teachers and specially when such are spread farre & neare, this is the principall, if not the only remedy that the church hath to supresse such errours and heresies and to restore the doctrine of the gospel to her soundnesse and place agayne.[16]

Against Jacob's rejection of this example, the presbyterians defended the synod as a perpetual authority that continued after the apostolic age.[17] They supported this view on account of the participation of other church officers in post-apostolic church practice: "Besides these it was ordinary that the churches seend not only to the Apostles but also to the elders of that church of Jerusalem. And this also, that the messengers are received, as of the Apostles so also of the church and of the elders."[18]

Jacob objected that this was no example of spiritual censure, but merely instruction, to which the presbyterians responded: "[D]oth not the delivering & declaring of the doctrine of the gospel imply all ways (though much bee not sayde at every tyme) the iust wrath of god upon the disobedient."[19] Presbyterians understood Acts 15 not only in the name of the "Apostles, but also in the name of the Elders and the brethren, that the offenders are sensured ver 14[,] that they were commended which opposed to them ver 26."[20]

Against Jacob's argument that the synod was an extraordinary meeting that no longer held any currency, the presbyterians insisted that there was "the farest presedent that might bee, both of the extraordinary and ordinary synods of the church."[21] They claimed that all churches were to submit to such councils not only on the authority of Acts 15 but also that of the Pauline epistles. In writing to the Church of Corinth, the presbyterians argued that

> the Apostle heere intended not to perswade a voluntary humilitie but a necessary subiection ffor to what end els shuld hee make mention of the word of god that came from other to them, & also to other churches. Besides this may bee proved by the disorders reproved thus out this epistle such as were schismaticall factions, the ambitious vanyty of some preachers . . . ffor remedy whereof and perticulerly of the disorders mentioned in the church the Apostle draweth them to the consideration of the word of god in all churches.[22]

Jacob never questioned the necessity of suppressing heresy. Rather, the debate between him and his presbyterian opponents was essentially over the nature of common consent, ecclesiastical judgments in synods and whether such judgment implied authority over individual congregations. While presbyterians argued that bishops undermined the common consent of synods, Jacob argued that synods were in conflict with the common consent of congregational membership. For him, "Church-government ought to be exercised alwayes with the peoples free consent," which was impossible under a coercive ecclesiastical body beyond the individual congregation.[23] This view of consent was deemed a "weightier issue" even than the definition of the visible church, which "followeth by a necessarie consequence from it."[24] He reasoned: "For where the peoples free consent is orderly and conveniently practised alwayes in the Church governement, there the Body of the Church can not be so large as a Diocese, much lesse a Province or Nation, and least of all so large as a Vniversall Church."[25] Jacob thus defined the visible church according to the principle of free consent and ecclesiastical independence.

Since freedom was already implicit in the concept of consent, Jacob's use of "free" with "consent" would suggest that he began to distinguish his consensual views from an unfree or less free form of consent. On one level, Jacob stressed that consent ought to be carried out with the "cognition" and understanding of the congregation.[26] Yet implicit in Jacob's discussion of consent was his understanding of independence. Although he allowed for pastors to hold the ordinary sway in congregational government, he nonetheless placed the weight of ecclesiastical power and authority with the people, removing its dependence on a representative council. He argued that electoral power and authority rested directly in their consent and active "willing" of a candidate to office by the people.[27] "The essence of Ministers calling under the Gospell, is the Congregations consent."[28] Thus, the calling of the minister was created by the consent of the people, the elders simply serving as moderators of the action. Jacob had argued that power was held by the people while authority was ordinarily exercised by the clergy. But the distinction became blurred in Jacob's discussion of consent. Jacob not only placed the weight of elections in congregational consent, but also argued that the execution of ecclesiastical censures was located in the entire congregation directly as opposed to being seated in an ecclesiastical council. He argued that excommunication rested in the consent of the people because it was ultimately enforced by the people. They were instructed in 1 Corinthians 5:13 to "Put out from you this wicked man."[29] It was necessary to argue that both power and authority stood in the act of consenting by the entire congregation in order to argue for ecclesiastical independence and to counter any form of government beyond the particular congregation. He thus made the argument for congregational power and authority explicit, reasoning that because "Christ simply commanded Church government by the Churches free consent. Therefore [both] the authoritie and power of Church government doth stand in the Churches free consent by the absolute and immutable commandement of Christ." Congregational consent was thereby translated into a direct source of power and active exercise of authority rather than rendered the passive or negative role that had been taken for granted in traditional ascriptions of consent.[30]

In addition to arguing that consent be "free," Jacob required that it be "always" and "in all things" by the people. The potential burden of the entire congregation to consent in diverse matters was called into question by Jacob's examiners, who argued that it was unbiblical, unreasonable, and uncharitable "that all the people of a whole Congregation should leave their businesse & the duties of their calling which they are to follow for the necessary maintenance of their families to hear & determine the causes that dayly might fall out amongst them."[31] The necessity of establishing ecclesiastical independence makes sense of Jacob's concern for the direct consent of the people, because it guarded against any power or authority outside of the particular congregation. Although ministers administered the ordinary affairs of the church, it was necessary that "in maters of waight the whole Congregation doe first understand thereof before any thing be finished, and the finall act be done in the presence of the whole Congregation, and also that they (the sayd Congregation) doe not manifestly dissent there from."[32]

Presbyterians did not discount congregational consent in their government. They affirmed "that perticuler churches are free and have power to order their own ordinary afayers by their owne consent without leave and order from any other ecclesiastical authority."[33] However, they denied that power or authority rested in congregational consent. Jacob's presbyterian examiners objected that he redefined the nature of consent by imputing the power to punish in it: "[H]is owne words 'power to consent' . . . hath no sense for to consent is no matter of power."[34] For example, they stressed the decision and declaration by the elders in excommunication, rather than the enforcement of it. Furthermore, consent did not necessarily include the direct participation of congregational membership in every decision, such as determinations made by a synod. That both power and authority rested in the ecclesiastical council, rather than in the people, makes sense of the passive nature of consent in both election and church discipline. Travers argued that the people "allowed" the judgment of the elders. The form in which consent was made could likewise be passive. "The Elders going before, the people also follow, and having heard and understood their sentence and decree, may either by some outward token or else by their silence allow it if it be to be liked of, or gainsay, if it be not iust and vpright."[35]

Given that they agreed on the principle of common consent, but disagreed on its nature and extent, it is predictable that such judgments themselves became central to presbyterian and congregational debate. According to the presbyterians, testimony throughout church history and among contemporaries countered congregationalism: "[F]rom the tyme of the Apostles of this sayde age which was a 1500 yeere and some what more hath not one not so much as one witnesse truly vouched to testyfye either for the absolute independency of parishes or agaynst the lawfull authorytie of Synods."[36]

APPROPRIATING ANTIQUITY

If it was within the context of refuting episcopacy that divisions among the godly appeared more visibly, it was also within this context that they made further use of ancient and modern sources. While such sources were applied to other theological considerations, it was in the debate over common consent that they were most significant. It is also important to recognize from the outset the interest of presbyterians in patristics, which may not be reflected in their writing on church government. Travers's independent reading and translation of the Fathers, for example, reveals a familiarity with patristic sources that is not apparent from his printed treatises.[37] There were clearly other than immediate polemical purposes for appropriating antiquity. Irena Backus recently examined Calvin's reliance upon post-apostolic practice and especially the writings of Jerome and Gregory I to frame an ecclesiological code upon the scriptural principles outlined in the New Testament.[38] Protestants loved Jerome for arguing that the hierarchy of the Church of Rome was of human origin. Given the influence of Calvin and other Protestant writers on English presbyterians, it will come as no surprise that Jerome became a crucial source for refuting episcopal authority. Earlier Elizabethan presbyterian exponents, however, tended to withdraw from extended debate with conformists using patristic sources. Their primary concern all along had been to convince conformists to use Scripture rather than tradition in determining church government.[39] Why, therefore, did they increasingly use nonbiblical sources in their arguments in the later sixteenth and early seventeenth centuries? [40]

It seems that English presbyterians began to use their knowledge of the church Fathers more boldly in ecclesiological debates in response to conformist challenges and in their debate with emerging congregationalists.[41] As the writer of the "Reformed Church Government" explained, since "the adversaryes make their appeal from the late writers to the ancient fathers . . . I have endeavored to shew the truth of this cause both by scriptures & ancient fathers."[42] The charge against them hitherto had not been their complete neglect of patristic sources but their selective use.[43] The writer of the "Reformed Church Government" explained his practice, which of course was to privilege the testimony of the Fathers insofar as it agreed with Scripture. He supported this principle by citing the Fathers themselves: "St. Jerome saith All that ever we speake we ought to proue by the Scriptures," and Augustine likewise argued that "by the authority of the Scriptures let us weigh matter with matter, cause with cause, reason with reason," and that "we do no injury to Cyprian whilst we distinguish any of his writings whatsoever from the canonicall authority of the divine scriptures."[44] In short, the writer believed that the Fathers themselves sanctioned the selective use of their writings, where Augustine gave the direction that "this kind of writing is to be reade not with a necessity to beeleve them, but with a liberty to judge of them." Similarly, "this Rule and direction likewise giveth St. Jerome in the reading of the Antient fathers . . . to be read for his learning . . . but yet so that we choose the good in them and refuse the contrary."[45] The writer thus both justified a selective use of patristic sources and explained how this did not conflict with his commitment to *sola scriptura*:

> [As] all triall of truth is to be reduced to the divine scriptures, so whensoever any of the antient fathers them selves be produced, either in point of the doctrine or disciplyne, for proofe of any thinge which they helde or practised without warrant of the Scriptures, or contrary thereunto, they should cary no credit or estimation*as themselues haue giuen warninge, taught yea & practised toward other antient fathers before them) . . . for even them selves have taught, how farre We ought to credit & reverence them . . . to be reade, non cum credendi necessitate sed cum iudicandi libertate, not with a necessity to believe them but with free liberty to judge of them & to take good & refuse the bad in them, as in the likewise to be done in the Writings of all other Men.[46]

He also drew from both Jerome and Augustine to defend this position, avoiding the tendency among some protestants to prefer Augustine to Jerome, especially in support of *sola scriptura* and *sola fide*.[47] In addition to citing Jerome in support of ministerial parity, the "Reformed Church Government" attempted to list further patristic sources to argue against the superiority of bishops: "Ignatius . . . *that to every church there was one Bishop Elders Deacons, and a communion table*";[48] Augustine "saith that Episcopus the bishop was nothing ells but primus presbyter the chief pastor"; and "Ambrose likewise saith the same that he & a pastore had both one ordination & moreover that both were pastors."[49]

The author of "Reformed Church Government" also cited historical sources in order to establish the status of bishops among the church Fathers: "Bishops likewise in Cyprians tyme were correspondent that is pastors of several flocks & particular congregations," which could be seen "by the councell of Carthage in Cyprians tyme, wherein were . . . bishops of villages & small townes."[50] Eusebius was unsurprisingly a frequent source: "[We] shall fynde it a common thinge with him to note the Bishops he speaketh of to be parish bishops: for example he affirmeth Abilius the third Bishop of Alexandria to be a Parish Bishops there . . . even to the tymes of Hirome."[51] In such examples, presbyterians were not only engaging in an exchange of patristic citations with their conformist opponents, but justifying presbyterian government by historical precedent.

Such precedent was especially effective for refuting congregational autonomy. Presbyterians argued that following the synod of Jerusalem and into the post-apostolic age, synods continued to play a vital role in suppressing heresy: "[T]he 4 chiefe and most famous generall Councills, which by playne evidence of the holy scripture convinced and condemned those heresies and heritikes and manteyned the holy apostolike and orthodox faith and doctrine in the church."[52] Travers found examples in Bullinger's history of provincial synods before Constantine, recording, "[T]hus in the first church the neighboring bishops, having been warned, and the ministers convened a [regional] synod spontaneously by necessary demand. And they held synods few and particular. Ecumenical and universal."[53] From Bullinger's history Travers recorded the controversy "whether Christ was the son of god before he became incarnate," noting that when "Berillus the bishop of the Arabs of Bostrensium" denied the deity of Christ, "he was convicted and converted toward the right faith by Origen."[54] Further examples of Origen's success were commemorated: "Origen indeed convicted others, who said that souls decay with bodies until the resurrection."[55] In such Travers is alluding to crucial doctrines that were placed in the hands of the council. The cumulative implication was that the Gospel became vulnerable without the authoritative decrees of church councils.

In addition to stressing the use of early synods for the suppression of heresy, presbyterians drew from the testimony of ancient worthies, noting both their quantity and quality: "[So] these 4 first generall counsills above yeld us of the fathers themselves above a thousand witnesse beside an infinite multitude of other that were present at them."[56] Both "the number and qualitie of the persons in such counsills" reinforced the legitimacy of the first four councils.[57] They further argued that the first four councils were not simply concerned to provide counsel but also to exercise authority over particular congregations: "[A]nd not only these but also all other Counsills which did likewise make cannons and governed the churches subiect unto them." It appeared to these writers that censure followed judgment since "some recon to the second counsil at Nyce, about 70 Counsills and Synods wherof some had in them a 100 some 200 other 300 and some above 600 Bishops. All which if they were reckoned what a number of witnesses would all these come unto which all manteeyne the authorytee of Synods and argue the subjection of perticuler churches unto them."[58] Thus, just as the presbyterians had argued from the historical practice of the Church when countering the superiority of bishops over other ministers, so they used historic example, ancient witnesses, provincial synods, and the first four councils to maintain the post-apostolic use of authoritative spiritual assemblies.

THE TESTIMONY OF THE REFORMERS

The wider witness of the continental reformers was also useful. In response to conformist challenges there was a double polemical advantage in appealing to a broader range of continental divines: not only to demonstrate that presbyterianism was practiced outside of Geneva and Scotland but also to place the testimony of bishops in direct opposition to that of the reformers. The central influence of the Genevan divines on English presbyterians is undoubted, as both Cartwright's and Travers's citations of Calvin and personal associations with Beza make clear.[59] But the extent to which English presbyterians were familiar with and inspired by other reformed churches on the continent tends to be obscured by the conformists' polemical writings and representation of presbyterianism as directly descended from Geneva and Scotland. Travers's personal reading reveals that in fact he was familiar with a broader range of writers than anti-presbyterians would suggest. It is clear from titles in the catalogue of his bequest to Sion College Library and his personal reading lists and notes, that his ecclesiological interests continued into the early seventeenth century and that he was familiar with the writings on church government of authors such as Johann Althusius and Heinrich Bullinger.[60] Travers's notes on the *De Conciliis* and *De Origine Erroris* further reveal his close reading of Bullinger on church councils and his active use of these texts in his argument against congregationalists in the early seventeenth century.[61]

One immediate polemical reason for citing modern sources was to discredit the judgment of conformists. As the writer of the "Reformed Church Government" spelled out:

> Who are most likely to hold the truth? Whether Mr. Sutcliffe Mr. Saravia, Bridge Mr. Whitgift, Mr. Hooker or Mr. Calvin Mr. Beza, Mr. Martyr Mr. Bucer Mr. Tremelius & the rest between whom there is no comparison either for skill in Tounges, great Readinge, sounde Judgements, paynefullness in labour shewede for the good of the church or approved sincerity.[62]

The third part of the *Reply* cited the reformers in order to offer an alternative interpretation of the Fathers as well as to note the judgment of the reformers. The reformers' interpretation of Jerome, for instance, demonstrated their opposition to episcopacy and at the same time set Downame's use of Jerome against that of the reformers. According to the *Replye,* the magisterial reformers understood "Hierome in plaine words sayth that betwixt Bps and Presbiters there is noe difference . . . that when one was chosen to be sett ouer the rest, it was done for remedy of schisme &c. and hence they thus inferre: Hierome here teacheth that the distinct degrees of Bps and Presbiters or Pastors were ordeyned by mans authoritie only."[63] The *Reply* also drew attention to Bucer's citation of Ambrose in support of the lay elder: Bucer disliked "the Bishops and teaching Presbiters thrusting out of office the ruleing elders . . . he sayth. Ambrose complayned even in his times, that the church began to be governed by the learned only, and not as before (ex omnis generis piis hominibus) by godly men of all sorts."[64] Such patristic citations supported the argument that the reformers disapproved of *jure divino* episcopacy. However, the examples from Jerome also conflicted with the *Reply's* earlier argument that Jerome did not acknowledge the introduction of such superiority immediately after the rise of schisms during the time of the Apostles. In this context, it appears that patristic citations were secondary to ascertaining the judgment of the reformers. While the reformers' use of the Fathers may have inspired later English interest, English ecclesiastical debate could nevertheless depart from the reformers' interpretation of them.

Anthony Milton has drawn attention to the pressure that continental reformed Churches placed upon English conformists as the practices of the

Church of England diverged from those on the continent in the early seventeenth century.[65] Given presbyterian pressure on episcopal government at that time, it is interesting to observe Travers's early use of neighboring reformed churches against Richard Hooker's teaching on predestination in the 1580s. According to Travers, he challenged the Master of the Temple Church, "whereas [Hooker] had taught certain things concerning predestination otherwise than the Word of God doth, as it is understood by all churches professing the gospel, and not unlike that wherewith Coranus sometime troubled this Church."[66] Travers further explained his use of the reformed Churches as a test for orthodoxy, "in which conference, I remember, when I urged the consent of all churches and good writers against him that I knew; and desired, if it were otherwise, to understand what authors he had seen of such doctrine: he answered me, that his best author was his own reason."[67]

Conformists themselves relied on continental reformers: "Whitgift showed a deep familiarity with and respect for the writings of numerous Continental reformed divines."[68] However, if opponents of episcopal government used the reformers to attack conformists, so conformists could also respond by showing that modern writers were at odds with the Fathers. Robert Parker complained of the conformists' overriding dependence on the Fathers: "But with [Downame] in matter of fact our Fathers testimonie is of more weight then all Disciplinarians in the world. Thus the fathers are exalted the modernes depressed, the Hierarchie is established upon the foundation of the Fathers which can not faile, the Presbyterie on Modernes can not stand."[69] Whereas "Downam perversely . . . charging the moderne with partialetie from which the Fathers are free," Parker objected "Downam concludes a partie is partiall. But I say to the contrarie, he which upon diligent triall joyneth to the truth though he becometh a partie, thet is not partiall as he is which upon respect of some person or other respect taketh part in a cause not well understood."[70] Parker instead pointed out the deficiencies of the Fathers when compared with modern writers:

> The Fathers had not our meanes of knowledge: the skill of tongues, the polishing of arts, building & indowing Colleges, the art of Printing as a gift from heaven, like that of tongues, as Fox after a sort compareth it, all wc worthy meanes our age hath injoyed aboue the ages of the Fathers. . . . But saith bancroft could the Fathers defend the truth against the greater heresies, & could they not know the true Discipline?[71]

Opponents of episcopacy defended the use of modern writers in their arguments. But even if these witnesses could be cleared of partiality, they nevertheless became divided between nonconformist parties.

In deliberations over church government Parker pointed out the use of modern writers as a witness both for determining doctrinal controversy and for settling discipline and church order. The presbyterians likewise drew upon them in their examination of Jacob's congregationalism and in disputes over church councils: "[T]hese men in their tyme enlightened and adorned the chiefe places, and doctrines of Christian religion and are able to shew us the truth of that \/ before these witnesses \/ where of they agree to testifye."[72] Just as presbyterians had used modern ecclesiastical writers to challenge episcopacy, so they argued that they gave no support to Jacob's congregational enterprise.[73] The reformers, Jacob's examiners argued, "with great iudgment and wisdom they have taught the contrary."[74] John Paget likewise commented that "against this authority of Classes and Synods divers opposites have risen up and have pleaded for a new kinde of Discipline, contrary to the order of all Reformed Churches, and contrary to that Reformation which the ancient Non-conformists in England have so much desired & laboured for."[75] In his *Narration* against New England congregationalism, William Rathband was concerned to refute "such things onely or for the most part, wherein there lies some difference betweene them and us, or other the best Reformed Churches."[76] The reformed Churches were likewise on the minds of the Westminster divines: Samuel Rutherford warned against making the "Reformed Churches a rule, yet it will be thought gracious to all reformed churches that this assembly should take a course in which we should simbolize [our agreement]."[77]

While the debate with conformists could involve setting ancient writers against modern, so debate among the godly became a matter of pitting modern writers against each other. Presbyterians wrote: "If wee should passe by Zwinglius the defendant would complayne seing as it semeth by his often producing of him and that with more grace then hee doth any other (yet is hee very worthy all the honor that is done to him and more) that hee resteth specially upon his testimony." They dismissed Zwingli's anticonciliar statements, as cited by Jacob: "[A]ll the testymonyes here alledged out of him are only against popish council and not simply against all councils and synods.[78] . . . [It] is in no sort credible that Zwuinleus intended to condemne all Counsill."[79] Here they cited Bullinger, arguing that "the next sucessor of Zwinlius in the charge of the church of Zurich expressly sayth these 4 general Councills. I desire utterly no thing to bee derogated from the determinations of fayth propounded unto us by those 4 generall and aecumenicall Councills but receaue them without all contradiction and reverence them most religiously yet I attribute greater authoryty to the holy Scriptures then to any Councills."[80]

The testimony of the Zurich divines was crucial in the contest between Jacob and his presbyterian examiners, and especially useful for supporting reformed church government since Bullinger had been a favorite writer among conformists. However, it was ultimately the collective judgment of the reformers that the presbyterians used to argue for the authority of councils: "[We] have the testimonies of the principall Doctors and teachers of the church, the chief lights of the earth and the flower of Christendome."[81] As the presbyterians incorporated Zwingli and Bullinger into the canon of reformers, a crucial aspect of their reading and use of them appears. They interpreted the judgment of one writer through other contemporary writers and ultimately placed the highest value on their collective, rather than individual, view. They were thus able to discount variance in opinion among them. For example, they applied the principle of consent to Zwingli's conflicting interpretation of "ecclesia" among the reformers, weighing the judgment of one against the others: "[As] for Zuinglius though he were a very worthy man yet the other three may easily overway him."[82]

Variance in the judgment of an individual reformer, such as Martin Bucer, was resolved by interpreting the reformer against himself. Assigning relative weight to Bucer's views, Thomas Cartwright established a hierarchy in his writing, which descended from published work to informal correspondence.[83] Public judgments also took precedence over private writings among Protestants on the continent, who placed the greatest weight on the decrees of early church councils.[84] Cartwright described this principle for councils in general when writing to Arthur Hildersham: "I thinke the Councells and Canons have the first place as those which being made with greater assistance carrie the most credit."[85] Confessions were clearly a useful source for arguing for the legitimacy of church councils and for countering claims to episcopal hierarchy. "Concerning the Helvetian confessions," Jacob's opponents argued, "the ellection of ministers is not of necessytie to bee allwayes of the voyces of the people but they may bee also by other to whome the church hath committed the charge in trust."[86] Arguing that the reformers were not in favor of superiority among ministers, the *Replye* drew from "Articles agreed on by Melanchthon, Bucer, Calvine and other learned men [which] doe plainely plead for a parity of ministers as well in the exercise of Discipline . . . as in the administration of the word and Sacraments."[87]

English presbyterians did not neglect contemporary synods:

> [T]he number of Synods nationall and provinciall of this last age of the reformation of the church and this age wherein wee now are with the cannons of the old synods and of the men and should note the persons that excelled in them and were replenished with manifold spirituall grases for such service wee might say that our witnesses are like the stars of the firmament of heaven for their great multitude and excellent glory/ notwithstanding an infinit number you may consider of some few perticulers which wee haue heere downe before you.[88]

Jacob's examiners further explained that "for where synods are established there is no independancie but synods are in use and the churches of a Belgike Ffrench Germane Bohemian [ ] and all other churches in Europe and as in them so in the whole land so as not so much as . . . their owne is independent although they boast it so to be ffor."[89] Naturally they also claimed the Synod of Dort as a prime example of authoritative government beyond the congregation. Just as synods had played a role in preserving orthodoxy in the Acts of the Apostles and in early church councils, so the Synod of Dort fulfilled the same need.[90]

Jacob had stated all along that "I grant Synods may discusse and determine of errors and may pronounce them wicked and accursed errors."[91] In responding to presbyterians, the congregationalists conceded that synods "did not only meet togeather & consult, but also they did define, determine, and decree certain pointes." Jacob further allowed that "yea they delivered the same to divers Churches to be kept, who had no deputies for them present in that Apsotolike assembly." However, all this, Jacob argued, did not constitute an authoritative ecclesiastical act; "Howbeit these Apostles delivered abroad these their Decrees only so, and in such wise, as informing and teaching all men thereby what they ought to do: that is, in maner of doctrine."[92]

Presbyterians did more than point to the synod of Dort to exemplify the role of spiritual assemblies in making ecclesiastical judgments and in preserving true doctrine. It might be foreign testimony in support of their argument, but it also involved the English. Not only were there English delegates, but nonconformists such as William Ames had contributed to the synod's deliberations.[93] If the presbyterians cited the reformers' interpretation of the Fathers, examined references to the Fathers to elucidate the judgment of the reformers, and used the reformers to interpret each other, they further turned to English sources and the nonconformist tradition as arbiters in their dispute with congregational writers. English history, in addition to early church history and decrees from contemporary synods, took on a particular significance.

THE ENGLISH PROTESTANT TRADITION

Presbyterians urgently needed to respond to conformist assertions that presbyterianism was simply a foreign (Genevan and Scottish) discipline. This meant that the testimony of the English protestant tradition carried especial weight in both defending presbyterianism and countering episcopacy. The importance of English tradition in opposing ecclesiastical courts and episcopal jurisdiction more generally was also significant.[94] Since English presbyterians argued that episcopacy had Roman roots, rival claims to the English protestant tradition were at stake for both parties. This occurred as early as the Elizabethan controversy between Cartwright and Whitgift:

> The debate had become a struggle for the English protestant tradition, in the course of which both men claimed the support of a whole series of continental and English divines. . . . Within the English tradition both Cartwright and Whitgift regularly cited such luminaries as Nowell, Foxe and Jewel. At one point they indulged in a bizarre contest to see who could say the nicest things about John Foxe and followed this with a rather unseemly struggle for the posthumous good opinion of Jewel.[95]

The tactic of the "Reformed Church Government" was precisely to claim presbyterianism as English and prove it to be most genuinely Protestant. It argued that at the time of Edward VI further ecclesiastical reform had been anticipated with "plaine Direction thereunto, saying in the Booke of Common prayer . . . Brethren in the primitive church there was a godely discipline etc. which is much to be wished until it may be restored againe."[96] It followed that "The Booke of Comon prayer (which is authorized by Act of Parliament) doth give leave and incite men to seeke after the Discipline in the primitive church, until it be restored."[97] More specifically against the superiority of bishops over other ministers, the writer claimed that John Foxe "disalloweth all lordly Bishops, condemning all civil magistracy in them, and likewise all Authority & power coactive in them over pastors."[98] The writer also cited William Fulke's antipapal arguments against Gregory Martin, whereby he "defended that by divine institution Episcopus & presbyter be both one, and so sheweth that by the word of god & his apoyntments A bishop is not superior to a pastor," and that "the elders with the pastor were the governors and exercises of the discipline otherwise called the church censures."[99] Jewel's testimony against Harding similarly affirmed "that a Bishop by divine ordinance is not above a pastor."[100] The "Reformed Church Government" and the *Replye* to Downame's Defense quoted the same passage from Robert Barnes's sixth article to argue that bishops were only pastors of particular congregations.[101] The *Reply* further used William Tyndale as an example who "acknowledgeth no[e] other Bp by the word of a God then an Ouerseer of a Congregation or parish."[102]

More was involved in this exercise than simply stringing together antiepiscopal phrases by English writers. The aim was to answer conformist allegations that presbyterianism was a foreign import by proving that it was implicit in early English historical practice and that the superior authority of bishops was a papist invention. According to this narrative, ministerial parity existed in England until the introduction of superior ecclesiastical officers through human tradition during the Middle Ages:

[In] the . . . Nation of England in no longer tyme then the dayes of William the Conqueror were there Bishops of Townes & Villages (As there was then the Bishops of Thetford, the Bishop of Dorchester &ct.) . . . this kinge William made the Councell holden at London Wherein was decreed for the furter honore of Bishops in this [En]gland.[103]

It was significant that most such English Protestant citations were from debates with Roman Catholic apologists. By arguing that the superiority of bishops was a medieval papal invention based on canon law, the presbyterians could argue that not only did it run counter to early English practice and the judgment of early Protestant writers but that following the English Reformation, it was abolished along with Roman canon law and thereby became contrary to English statute. The polemical value of this argument was one of the reasons for Stoughton's writing being reprinted in the mid-1640s, as the epistle dedicatory explained: "[He] discovers the foundation of the Hierarchie to be totally illegall, and to bee abolished by the abolition of the Papall Canon Law, which appears to be abolished by the statute of 23 of Henry 8 cap 9."[104]

Presbyterians also turned to early English precedent for evidence against congregationalists and in support of authoritative synods: "[L]et it be remembred how of old in our owne countrie, the like testimony hath bene given to shew the authority of Synods. We read of a provinciall Synod at Thetford in the time of Theodore, Archbishop of Canterbury, *Anno D. 680* where it was ordained that Provinciall Synods should be kept within the Realme at least once a yeare." They also cited that "another Synod was held at Winchester, *Anno D.* 1070. where *Stigandus* Archbishop of Canterbury was deposed for receyving his pall from *Benedict* the fift: and another was after held at *London,* where many decrees were made in the time of *Lanfranck,* the Arhcibshop, &c."[105]

English examples included the use of leading nonconformists such as Cartwright. According to John Davenport, "[In] [Cartwright's] judgement, other Churches have no power of hindring a faulty election, but by admonition, which power every Christian hath in another, for his good,"[106] while Jacob maintained that "Mr Cartright is to be remembred . . . before teaching that the Assembly acts 15 at jerusalem was of no higher authoritie then the Church of Antioch," concluding that "this is quite contrarie to the examiners."[107] Jacob's opponents rejected his citation of Cartwright on Matthew 18 as "a most grosse abusing of that worthie servant of Christ."[108] Jacob also argued that according to "[t]he declearacon of discipline commonly said to be Mr Traverses . . . nothing bee donn: not only against the good will thereof or unknowne to the same, but also not with out the consent & approbation of it."[109] He concluded that "it seemeth that the church is rather governed by all, then by a few."[110]

This brings us to a critical historical dimension in English presbyterianism. Just as Jacob and his examiners had argued over Cartwright's views after his death, so they offered different interpretations of each other's own views. The examiners defended their own earlier writing against Jacob's interpretation. Travers, in particular, protested that "as for the wordes of the declaration exhorting to proceed to such a further degree of reformation . . . they doe not exhort to further it by any unlawfull meanes such as are schisme."[111] Travers's interpretation of his own writing in the early seventeenth century reveals that treatises published in the late sixteenth century could be reinterpreted despite an author's defense of his own work. It is significant that in these disputes, historical events and ideas were neither detached from contemporary events nor simply introduced as examples; they mattered in themselves and took on a separate status, even from the voice of the author. Since Travers's writing in the late sixteenth century had become canonized in English history, it could potentially be used to trump his judgment in the early seventeenth century.

In this respect, history had a distinct role to play in these debates and was neither introduced solely to make political applications nor simply cited to win theological arguments. As Irena Backus has demonstrated, it is misleading to refer exclusively to the polemical uses of texts and to overlook the significance of historical understanding and the character of the sources used in theological debates.[112] Arnaldo Momigliano likewise argued that historical evidence was essential not only for writing ecclesiastical history but also for defending theological arguments.[113] He explained that this had always been the case, because by its very nature the Church was grounded in historical precedent.[114] This historical dimension to presbyterianism, which appears as part of the ecclesiastical discourse of the late sixteenth and early seventeenth centuries, was therefore part of a much longer tradition in ecclesiastical writing.

COMMON CONSENT ACROSS THE CHANNEL AND ATLANTIC

Debate over common consent continued, since the rival interpretations of Elizabethan presbyterian thinkers had again thrown the exact nature of synods into relief. Did classical activity essentially consist of admonition and counsel? Or did the classis and synod by nature exercise authority over particular congregations? John Paget found Robert Parker particularly useful for arguing that synods were authorized not simply to give counsel but also to exercise authoritative jurisdiction: for Parker "speakes of such subjection as is distinguished from receyving of counsell and admonition . . . the Church erring & offending is bound to receyve counsell or admonition from any one particular Church, though it be not subject to the jurisdiction of any one in speciall, but onely to many in a lawfull Synod."[115] According to Paget, Parker believed "that Synods have power of jurisdiction which is more then counsel." This could be demonstrated by Parker's use of John Reynolds's distinction whereby "*Questions* of the Church were sent unto them that had no jurisdiction over those that propounded them: but the *causes* of the Church, not so: They in Africa were forbidden to appeale unto them beyond sea; viz. for the decision of their *personall causes*, which yet were to be judged by the synods in Africa."[116]

Paget especially stressed that according to Parker the judgment of synods in itself constituted an authoritative act that was categorically different from mere consultation and recommendation to neighboring ministers. Jacob and other congregationalists had stressed the physical gathering of a congregation in the exercise of church government.[117] By contrast, Paget cited Parker to argue that a physical meeting was not essential for arriving at collective judgment:

> If all Congregations be equall, what shall be done in case of Schisme and Heresy, when there is no Synod nor Christian magistrate? He answers, *The time scarsely falles out, when no Synods can be had: or if Synods be wanting, yet Churches may communicate together by letters: and although there be no authority in one Church above another; yet many Churches joyned together, either in a Synod, or by letters, have authority over one Church offending.*[118]

Paget's citation of Parker to argue that "deposition of Hereticks was an act of jurisdiction in Synods" is a remarkable example of how English nonconformists did not simply rely on a collection of modern writers in support of their discipline. Here a collective judgment is documented by the use of sources throughout history extending from Jacobean to Elizabethan testimony to the Reformation interpretation of early church practice. As Paget noted, Parker "confirmeth it by the testimony of D. Whitaker, alledging that Calvine sayd well, that by brotherly charity, not by naked authority, but by letters and admonitions and other such meanes Hereticks were deposed in the time of Cyprian."[119]

Paget also attempted to extract an acceptance of authoritative synods from Ames's later writings: "[T]hough he did never plainely retract that which he published yet he shewed himselfe divers times enclining to a change of his judgement, yea & sometimes acknowledged that Synods had power to judge of causes, and by their sentence to decree the excommunication of such as had deserved the same."[120] He drew attention to an ambiguity in Ames's judgment on heretical churches, yet only managed to conclude that Ames had at least acknowledged that in actual practice ecclesiastical sentences followed synodal judgments.[121] But for Paget only one logical conclusion could be drawn from the right of synods to condemn heretics: "[It] is manifest and undenyable that in the censuring of Hereticks that erre in matters of faith, there is an Ecclesiasticall judgement belonging unto men, and a definitive sentence to be pronounced against such."[122] Though Ames did not reach the same conclusion, for Paget it was enough that he admitted little difference in practice: Ames "addes in his answer to the same question, touching whole Churches & members of another Church, that though they may not properly be excommunicated, *yet for manifest heresies or great faults, they may be condemned, forsaken, rejected, which is proportionable to excommunication.*"[123]

Had heresy not arisen in the New England colonies, perhaps apologists for the New England Way would have felt less need to respond to Paget's argument against this particular aspect of congregational polity. The synod of Dort had long since established the heterodoxy of Arminianism, and the New Englanders could expect no such heretics among their ranks, at least not among the first generation who had set out to establish the model godly city. It was not the rise of Arminianism that troubled the New England colonists, but Antinomianism, the view of works that freed the saints from the demands of moral law. David Hall has observed "the shift in the ministers' thinking about the nature of their authority" following the Antinomian controversy of the late 1630s.[124]

> The Congregationalism of the thirties was radically experimental in the way it allowed the minister and church members to share authority. But the shock of the Controversy recalled the ministers to a more traditional assertion of their prerogatives. Thus the Congregationalism of the Cambridge Platform (1648) reflected the temper of the forties, just as the Antinomian Controversy had reflected the temper of the thirties.[125]

While it is not of immediate concern to examine the relative authority of church members and officers in this context, it is worth noting that an increased conservatism among certain New England clergy who inclined to presbyterianism in the early 1640s followed closely upon the Antinomian controversy of the late 1630s.

Congregationalists indeed developed their description of the role of synods during the 1640s. There is a fuller statement in Cotton's *Keyes to the Kingdom*, which has "been generally accepted as the most complete and influential statement of . . . early New England Congregationalism."[126] Cotton explained that while the synod's judgment against obstinate congregations did not amount to the power of excommunication, it did provide the means of restraining heretical congregations and preventing their doctrines from spreading: "And if the Church offending shall not yet hearken to their Brethren, though the rest of the Churches have not power to deliver them to Satan, yet they have power to withdraw from them the right hand of fellowship, and no longer to hold them in communion of Saints, till they approve their repentance 6 Isa."[127]

James Noyes believed that "if there be granted a consultative or Doctrinal power, *vi officii*, to Synods and Councels, it must be also granted (for the same reason) that there is a corrective power in Synods and Councels. Authority destitute of a corective power in particular Presbyteries, is not adequate to its end."[128] Like Paget, he understood the right of suffrage as an authoritative act in itself where "to direct with judicial authority, is to command with coactive power." Furthermore he argued that this authority extended beyond the suffrage:

> What spirit should be present at the instant of excommunication, but his spirit of Apostolical inspection or authority? Spirit here is to be interpreted, *quoad materiam subjectam* a truth is, the Church of Corinth (according to the original) is not made the nominative case to the act of delivering up to Sathan, only it is required that it be done when the church is gathered together. The Apostle then did excommunicate virtually and *preceptive*, the church of Corinth *obedientialiter*. Mr *Cartwright* and others do consent to this assertion.[129]

Citing Cartwright to support his interpretation of the synod's power of excommunication, Noyes specifically directed this argument against his New England congregational brethren. He further argued that their willingness to withdraw from heretical congregations in effect amounted to excommunication: that "in this case non-communication is at least a defensive Excommunication and an excessive infliction of evil."[130]

John Davenport denied that withdrawal from a corrupt congregation constituted a form of excommunication and protested that the presbyterians misrepresented the nature of this penalty.[131] The crucial difference in judgment pronounced in this instance was that it did not extend to the final step of excommunication in Matthew 18 as demonstrated "by proportion, according to Math. 18. For, there Christ doth not allow them, who have proceeded in Admonishing, but to the second step, to forbear communion with the delinquent: whereas these Neighbour-Churches are but in the second step. *Yet*, they say, *they may forbear communion with them*."[132] Congregationalists' withdrawal from obstinate congregations was doctrine-specific, and not applicable to other cases of discipline: "[T]hough Churches may withdraw from a Church, that is obstinate and impertinent in some cases, (without any such solemn sentence of Non-communion declared by a Synod) yet, not for such causes as a delinquent Brother may be Excommunicated by a Church, according to Mat. 18."[133] As Davenport explained, "[T]hese cases, wherein communion may be regularly *Withdrawn* from a Church or Person, are onely such as Subvert the Fundamentals of Religion."[134]

However, Davenport also added a comment which revealed that there was in fact some flexibility and that there were exceptional cases for determining matters beyond fundamental doctrines of religion: "Yet this they may not regularly do meerly for their Dissenting from the Determinations of the Synod upon conscientious grounds, and in lesser matters."[135] Since congregationalists argued that the nature of synodal judgment was merely consultative, synodal activity and ecclesiastical determinations could extend beyond decisions on doctrine. This is attested to by their willingness to engage in extensive debate over the subject of church government which involved a wide range of ancient and modern witnesses and even contemporary judgments. For presbyterians these sources were more than mere references for winning theological arguments; they were participants in ecclesiological debates which were themselves an expression of reformed church government. By contrast, even if congregationalists were to have ultimately conceded that synods could play a role beyond essential doctrines, they rejected the presbyterians' view on the authority and nature of those judgments.

Debate over common consent was if anything dynamic. It not only took place as a multidimensional conversation among a range of ecclesiologists across the channel and Atlantic but also conscripted a wide range of ancient and contemporary sources to its aid. The printed literature of the period is better understood when interpreted alongside the manuscript debates that took place, for they provide unique insight into the role of history in ecclesiological writing by explaining their use of sources. The examiners, for example, supported their citation of patristic sources by noting that it was the quality and the quantity of the evidence from the Fathers that made them reliable witnesses against Jacob. By the end of the sixteenth century, the writer of "Reformed Church Government" not only cited a diverse selection of Fathers, but also justified his use of this material according to their own criteria. This again demonstrates that English presbyterians placed themselves in a long ecclesiastical tradition that weighed various evidences to arrive at a conclusion. In practice presbyterians also established a hierarchy among sources that assigned relative values to individual judgments. They weighed modern writers against other modern writers, and the judgment of one particular reformer could be overruled by the views of others. Modern writers were also interpreted with reference to ancient writers. English history had a distinct role in legitimizing church polity, while the reformers could enter directly into contemporary English disputes to discredit Church of England apologists and congregational advocates.[136] Practices in early church history and ecclesiastical acts passed through ancient councils and contemporary synods carried particular force.[137]

While presbyterians employed this hierarchy of testimony in their erudite theological discourses, they also applied it in the consistory in the day-to-day operation of church government. They prioritized formal statements from ecclesiastical authorities, demanded authentic documentation from public institutions as evidence, and took note of the quality and quantity of witnesses in weighing personal testimonies.[138] This practice did not only apply to the routine operation of government and locate presbyterianism within a longer ecclesiastical tradition but also situated it within a wider genre of historical method among contemporaries. Scholars have examined the central role and the development of historical thought among English humanists in the early seventeenth century.[139] J. G. A. Pocock and Glenn Burgess have also noted an ecclesiastical drive behind antiquarianism in late-sixteenth-century England that contributed to it.[140] It is significant that this did not come solely from Church of England apologists but also from its critics. In their critique of episcopacy, in arguing against church courts, presbyterian clerics and secular writers drew upon the same historical examples.[141] While the historical dimension to English presbyterianism can and ought to be distinguished from that of conformists and humanists, it coincided with these developments and therefore should be considered alongside them. It appears that there was an intellectual overlap between ecclesiastical and secular writers that did not only intersect in their common opposition to episcopacy but also through their shared use of history.[142] If the principle of common consent provided an ideological foundation for lay involvement in the Church, it also provided other crucial points of contact between clerical and lay developments.

A closer analysis of the use of historical sources also counters an interpretation of ecclesiastical polemic as static. Rather than producing arguments according to fixed ecclesiastical categories, disputants modified their positions as they responded to each other's arguments, and did not invariably become further polarized in their understanding of the issues under question. Despite the obvious cleavage between presbyterian and congregational thought on the nature of common consent, their differences on this subject became less marked than in other matters which had an immediate bearing on the practice of congregational government and on their status in relation to the Church of England.

CHAPTER 5

Presbyterian "Promiscuity"

Differences between presbyterian and congregational ideas of church government became increasingly apparent in the course of the early seventeenth century, even if further nuanced. Presbyterians pressed congregationalists on the radical implications of their polity, including their understanding of individual liberty. Congregationalists in turn argued that presbyterians unlawfully granted clerics the authority to minister "promiscuously" outside their situation in a particular congregation. Their disagreement extended to government within the congregation; for congregationalists further accused presbyterians of promiscuity in their practice of infant baptism and admission to church membership. While the nature of the visible church and common consent directly fed into these controversies, it was ultimately membership in the Church of England that became the crucial issue in their deliberations.

THE FREEDOM OF CHOICE

That Jacob no longer adhered to the traditional form of consent, but understood it to be the source of power and authority in government, suggests the beginning of a critical process: the transition from the individual will holding a negative role to resist authority to "the more novel attribution of a positive role . . . in the constitution and legitimation of that authority."[1] Implicit in his argument for independence and the freedom of consent was the freedom of choice. Congregational consent in elections, for instance, involved the exercise of free choice. Jacob suggested in his *Christian and Modest Offer* that such choice was freely made by the absence of interference with its decision. Here he contrasted free consent with a situation in which a congregation was "urged to conclude" or decide on a matter.[2]

Exactly how Jacob defended his Southwark congregation is not known, for his last printed treatise appeared in 1616. However, in his manuscript response to presbyterian allegations, Jacob departed radically from contemporary assumptions by arguing for the freedom of choice more explicitly. Defending himself and his followers against the charge of schism, he claimed that "it is noe sinn . . . to leave a true Church: & to goe to another, viz. to leave the Corrupter & goe to a better."[3] Jacob had argued earlier that such freedom of choice applied to every individual believer: "Seing under the Gospell there are more free societies of Christians, mo[re] visible Churches politike, then one in a Country, and some more sincere then some. And all true Christians are commanded of God to keepe their owne soules sound and cleare from contagion."[4] Yet he further explained to the presbyterians that freedom of choice was not simply made possible as a consequence when the option to choose became available. It existed as a right of the individual believer: "[N]ow under the gospel there is choyse, which under the law was not and to say the contrarie namely that now we have not choice (so we doe is in & with the best order we can) is a groce error in them or in any other devines."[5] Thus, to remove the freedom of choice was "to hould mens soules in spirituall snares & boundage."[6]

Not only did believers have the right to choose the society with which to commune, but they also had the right to establish a spiritual body politic. Jacob argued that "to gather & begin churches under the gospel is no extrordinari worke: nor peculer to the Apostles, seeing now still it may bee donn somewhere."[7] Since power and authority in election stood in the consent of the congregation, it was conceivable for people to create a church. Even without a minister, a body of believers could gather together and elect a pastor and become a church proper. This argument comes full circle in Jacob's initial definition of the church: "For where each ordinarie Congregation hath their free consent in their ordinarie government, there certainly each Congregation is an intire and independent Body politike Spirituall, and is indued with power in it selfe immediately vnder Christ."[8] Ecclesiastical independence not only contributed to Jacob's redefinition of congregational consent but ultimately made room for the freedom of individual choice. The development of individual liberty was undoubtedly part of a much longer and more complex process.[9] What is striking about Jacob's example is how quickly the freedom of individual choice emerged out of his early exposition of ecclesiastical independence.

PRESBYTERIANISM AND PUBLIC INSTITUTION

The radical implications of congregational polity prompted the presbyterians increasingly to stress the formal authorization of clerical vocation through the Church as a public institution. In his earlier writing, Travers had found biblical warnings against the presumption of entering the ministry without a lawful calling.[10] He argued that a lawful calling "hath all times been holden so necessary, that no man hath beene thought to exercise any lawfull authority therein, who had not first of all in his owne conscience witnesse of the calling of God thereunto, and after also of the Church appointing him according to Gods decree and ordinance."[11] His conclusions from these examples are particularly revealing in a treatise written in the late sixteenth century as a critique of episcopacy. Defining vocation and the visible Church itself as public by nature, he condemned the presumption of those who entered into the ministry without such authorization:

> So that if he hath forbidden any man to enter into the Church, to take upon him any publike person therein, or execute any office, but unto which he is chosen and called by him, if he hath grievously punished the transgressors of this law, who despising his commandement, and going without the bands that they were compassed with, breake into other mens ground, and haue been so bold to prophane the holy charges with their defiled hands, let us see and be carefull that there be no such thing amongst us.[12]

Presbyterians likewise stressed the legitimacy of vocation through its public authorization by the Church as a formal institution when complaining against congregationalists who in their view privileged private opinion over public institution. According to Henry Jacob's presbyterian examiners, "[T]he substance of a lawfull calling to the ministery" did not solely consist of a learned godly minister commissioned to preach the gospel. Ordination was necessarily a public and not private action. The minister must "be ordained thereunto by such order as is established by publike authority for that purpose, as ours is by the authority both of parliament and convocation."[13]

The public nature of clerical calling dovetailed with the general applicability of ministry within the universal visible church. However, here the presbyterians emphasized the public nature of ordination in the Church of England to distinguish it from all private acts that they believed could not validate the clerical vocation. In the ordination controversy of the mid-seventeenth century, presbyterians were among those for whom the Church as an institution had the utmost priority: "The presbyterian Lazarus Seaman . . . insisted that the power to grant the right to preach did not belong to the people alone, but to the Church as an institution."[14] Richard Greaves explained how presbyterians like Seaman insisted on the necessity of ordination, since "requiring ordination to preach obviously placed primary authority in the hands of the Church. Advocating lay preaching, on the other hand, immediately raised the possibility that the seat of authority might be shifted from the institution to the individual."[15]

There had of course been a long tradition of private godly gatherings in

the form of prophesyings, religious exercises, and fasts in the English nonconformist tradition. Presbyterians argued that there was a difference between
this and the Church as an institution and debated upon this subject with
Jacob. The presbyterians accepted that "they may and ought privately by communication and conference make knowne one to an other in private manner
the truth of the gospell." Yet such private gatherings could be distinguished
from seditious assemblies by the institution of ecclesiastical officers: "But to
plant a church and call ministers and elders they can not lawfully doe ffor*
heere wee have neither precept nor promise, nor example in the Scripture."[16]
Paget believed that Davenport's private gatherings came dangerously close to
becoming a separate church by the regularity of his preaching on the Lord's
Day.

> Mr Davenport . . . did he not cease to preach in a private house . . . Under the name
> of catechising he tooke a text of Scripture, and expounded the same unto them, and
> so in a private house kept a publick and solemne exercise in a large roome, furnished
> with benches and seates for commodity of hearers . . . more than an 100 persons
> have bene there sometimes gathered together: and ordinary time being kept upon
> the Lords-day in the evening, when the sermon in our Church was ended.[17]

Arguing that the nativity of the Christian church was established by Apostolic authority and by extraordinary means, the presbyterians insisted that
after the establishment of the early church no private persons could presume
to enter the ministry. If no private person could presume to enter the ministry, neither could he plant a church. For if "it were a presumption for a
private person to arrogate to him selfe the execution of an ordinary ministery
it must neds bee a greater presumption for such to attempt the planting of
churches."[18]

VOCATION

The presbyterians' understanding of lawful ecclesiastical calling as a public
act was tied to their view of common consent and the general nature of the
visible church. It was also rooted in their broader understanding of clerical
calling—that is, the outer calling by the visible church, not with the inward
calling of individual ministers. In the *Declaration*, Travers stressed the necessity of vocation for all ecclesiastical officers, including lay elders and deacons.
It was the appointment of God to any ecclesiastical office "in such sort and
manner as hee hath ordained for euery officer to bee appointed by."[19] This
involved a twofold process: election and ordination. As Travers maintained,
"[E]lection is the appointing by the Elders, the rest of the Church allowing

*their of

it, of a fit man to the bearing of some office in the Church,"[20] and "ordination is a setting a part of the party chosen unto his Office, and as it were, a kinde of investing him into it," in which "a certaine order and ceremony is wont to be used, whereby the parties chosen enter, as it were, into the possession of their office . . . consisteth especially in two ceremonies: Namely, in prayer . . . and laying on of hands."[21] According to Travers, a plurality of elders held "the right and authority of ordaining," and there was historical evidence "that in all ordinations there were more that laid on their hands, or if one did it, yet all this matter was ruled by the authority of the Councell of the Church."[22]

The plurality of elders to officiate in election and ordination was again a crucial element in presbyterian arguments with both conformists and congregationalists. In responding to conformists, presbyterians used the principle of common consent to oppose the individual role of a bishop in the ordination and election of ministers. According to Travers, it was necessary that in election and ordination: "[T]here must be more to deale therein, and that so great and so waighty a charge, and belonging to the especiall and singular commodity or discommodity of the whole Church ought not to be committed to the authority of any one, but be ordered and ruled by the iudgement and consent of many."[23] Although the use of the word "consent" is often associated with respect for the liberty of the congregation, it could also refer to the collective act of church officers outside that particular congregation.[24] Instead of identifying the necessity of consent as located in the congregation, here Travers referred to the collective act of church officers: "That the twelve called the Disciples together, and the words of the plurall number which he useth in every place of this history doe manifestly proue that nothing was done here by the private commandement or counsell of any: but that contrariwise all things passed by the common consent and authority of all the Apostles."[25] The "Reformed Church Government" urged participation beyond both the individual judgment of the bishop and the particular congregation: "*[If] the ordination be rightly observed* it is to be done not by one alone but by more, namely by the pastors otherwise called Bishops next adioyning to that Churches & people which is destitute."[26] Presbyterians used the same argument for election. The *Admonition to Parliament* had called for a plurality of voices in the election of ministers, which Cartwright defended by arguing that "it is very dangerous to commit that to the view and search of one man, which may with less danger and more safety be referred unto divers."[27] John Ball had also argued that "it is a dutie of Neighbour-Churches to lend their helpe to their brethren in the choice and election of their Minister. When the Scripture willeth that one should admonish another, it is not onely a command to every singular man towards his fellow, but also to any whole company too."[28]

Likewise, the presbyterians' understanding of a universal visible church directly fed into their argument for the general nature of clerical vocation, particularly of ordination. The example of neighboring church practices was useful when challenging the Church of England's episcopal orders, especially when conformist writers espoused *jure divino* episcopacy, which implied that non-episcopal forms of ordination were illegitimate. As Anthony Milton has noted "[O]ne of the main objections expressed against the doctrine of iure divino epsicopacy was that it arguably served to unchurch the foreign Reformed Churches."[29] This objection had been made by Travers in the late sixteenth century, prior to arguments for *jure divino* episcopacy. When Travers's foreign presbyterian ordination in Antwerp came into question during his ministry in the Temple Church in the mid-1580s, he defended his ministry in *A Supplication Made to the Council* by arguing that "when I was at Antwerp . . . I see no cause why I should have returned again over the seas for orders here; nor how I could have done it, without disallowing the orders of the churches provided in the country where I was to live."[30] Explicit in this defense is the concept of a universal church and the consent among reformed churches in the act and recognition of ministerial calling. "My calling to the ministry" he proclaimed, "was such as in the calling of any thereunto is appointed to be used by the orders agreed upon in the national synods of the Low Countries, for the direction and guidance of their churches; which orders are the same with those whereby the French and Scottish churches are governed."[31] He continued that "if any man be lawfully called to the ministry in those churches, then is my calling, being the same with theirs, also lawful."[32] Travers further claimed that a genuine clerical calling gave license to exercise ministerial acts within the universal visible church, and that all jurisdiction exercised by public ecclesiastical authority was therefore universally valid:

> The communion of saints (which every Christian man professeth to believe) is such as, that the acts which are done in any true church of Christ's according to his word, are held as lawful being done in one church, as in another. Which, as it holdeth in other acts of ministry, as baptism, marriage, and such like, so doth it in the calling to the ministry; by reason whereof, all churches do acknowledge and receive him for a minister of the word, who hath been lawfully called thereunto in any church of the same profession.[33]

Common consent and the general nature of the visible church were also central to the congregational-presbyterian debate over clerical calling. Both presbyterians and congregationalists rejected the need for episcopal ordination. But whereas presbyterians such as Travers appealed to foreign reformed churches to criticize the argument for episcopal ordination, congregationalists tended to place greater weight on the role of congregational consent in ministerial appointments.[34] Within congregationalism the consent of the congregation ultimately became the legitimizing factor in the calling of a minister; less emphasis was placed on the ordination of the minister than among the presbyterians.[35] According to Jacob, "[T]he essence of Ministers calling under the Gospell, is the Congregations consent,"[36] and since ministers were called through the consent of a particular congregation, they were not authorized to exercise ecclesiastical jurisdiction beyond that congregation.[37] This was argued not only among emerging congregationalists in the early seventeenth century but also among congregationalists in the debates of the Westminster Assembly during the mid-seventeenth. Speaking for the congregationalists Phillip Nye argued that "we suppose a minister may be a minister that is not ordained."[38] He also said that "I put a difference betwixt calling & ordination. Ther may be an effectuall calling & a minister to all purposes wher that solemnity of ordination is not used."[39]

It is striking to find that Jacob argued similarly against the separatist Francis Johnson in his *Defence of the Churches and Ministery of England* at the end of the sixteenth century.[40] In this treatise Jacob claimed that clerical calling in the churches in England was valid so long as the congregation consented to the ministers' election, regardless of corruption in episcopal ordination: "[N]otwithstanding, he being made a Pastor, (though 'unlawfully') by the Prelate; yet, by their mutuall accepting and ioyning together, hee is now verily a Pastor, yea their Pastor, true and lawfull."[41] As Slayden Yarbrough pointed out, this "emphasis on the free consent of congregations in choosing a pastor, a key element in Jacob's later thought," is a striking emphasis to find at this date.[42] It is in Jacob's concern here to reject separatism and defend the Church of England that is seen an early commitment to a central tenet in his later congregational polity prior to his disappointment following the Hampton Court Conference in 1604.

Jacob's presbyterian opponents firstly argued that congregational participation was not absolutely essential to clerical vocation, where "sometime the word essentiall may be used to note that which is either absolutely necessary to the making of any thinge so as without the same it could be noe such thing or that helpeth to the better making of it."[43] Moreover, they

den[ied] that the consent of the people was in any place or time absolutely necessary so as that a minister every other way sufficiently ordained should for \/ want \/ of the consent of the people be esteemed to be noe minister. But for the better being, & for divers conveniences & commodities it helpeth . . . that the consent of the people be had to the choise of a minister that is to serve them for this will be a good meanes of their better affection & love to him which will much further the blessing of his labor, amongst them.[44]

They further insisted, as they had with respect to the authority of the synods, that the involvement of neighboring clergy did not necessarily infringe upon congregational liberty. Here is evidence of the presbyterians' tactical flexibility between congregational and classical or synodal participation in the election of ministers. According to Jacob's presbyterian adversaries, "the defendant proveth heere by many witnesses that perticuler congregations have a right and graunt from god to chuse their owne ministers." They argued that "this needeth no witnesses nor prooffe," since congregations held a role in the election of ministers in presbyterian government.[45] Furthermore, they claimed that "the liberty of parishes agreeth well with the authoryty of synods. So that to say the churches are by their consent to chuse their owne ministers therfore they are not subiect to any synods is a ridiculous speach and setteth downe for disjunctives & oposytes those that are not such."[46]

John Paget had likewise affirmed the congregational role in ministerial election:[47] "I acknowledge (as I have also divers times publikely taught in the exposition of these 2 places) that the free consent of the people is required unto the lawfull calling of a Minister: neither is the same denyed or excluded in our practise."[48] He detailed the process of ecclesiastical appointment, which included congregational consent as a final validating act:

> The Synods of these reformed Churches describing the order to be observed in the calling of Ministers, doe require a choyse to be made by the Elders and Deacons, approbation of the Magistrates, allowance of the Classis, & in the last place consent of the Congregation, before whom the names of the persons called are publikely propounded from the Pulpit divers Lords dayes, that they may take knowledge of the matter & witnes their consent or dissent as they shall finde occasion.[49]

The particular order prescribed was, of course, crucial. According to Travers, church officers directed the whole process: "[T]hey goe before the people in the election, that they trie and examine those that are to be chosen, that they iudge of their worthinesse, and publish unto the Church, whom they haue thought meete and worthy, that being allowed by the consent of all, they may be received."[50]

Yet for all the importance that Paget ascribed to congregational consent, he qualified it by arguing that "if any particular Churches doe offend in choosing unlawfull and unfit persons, then are Classes and Synods to judge thereof, and to hinder such elections."[51] John Davenport objected to this: "To keepe out Ministers, whom the Church desireth, being free from haeresy or schysme, is not in the power of the Classis, by any warrant from the word, or by any order established in the Synods of these countryes."[52] In response Paget defended the involvement of the classis by stressing that it only became necessary when election could not be settled within the particular congregation.[53] Here again

presbyterians stress circumstantial necessity and not the perpetual involvement of the classis, which Paget explained by reason of the fallible nature of
ecclesiastical determinations.[54]

In addition to stressing common consent, presbyterians marshaled their
argument for the universal nature of clerical vocation to counter congregational and separatist arguments.[55] Jacob's presbyterian examiners stressed the
universal nature of vocation, the public nature of episcopal ordination and
the validity of ordinations performed in other churches: "[We] speak of our
Church in England and the order established here in it[56] \/ for \/ the making
of ministers by the publike authority of the Civill and ecclesiasticall estate,
and consequently of other Churches established in the like manner."[57] Whereas
Jacob had stressed congregational consent to refute Francis Johnson, Paget
appealed to the involvement of neighboring ministers in ordination to argue
against separatists in Amsterdam. In his *Arrow against the Separation of the
Brownists*, Paget stressed the value of "the help of neighbour ministers for
performing the work of ordination in other Churches . . . from the necessity of many churches that often want fit persons among themselves for the
performance thereof."[58] John Ball likewise defended the universal nature of
clerical calling in his refutation of the separatist John Cann.[59] The presbyterian
Lazarus Seaman made a similar argument in the debate over ordination in
the Westminster Assembly: " < I grant > the ordinary power of ordaining to a
church belongs to the presbitery of that church, but then consider this: when
a perticular church hath noe presbitery, ther must be a power of ordaining
somewhere."[60] The presbyterian Richard Vines argued that cures could either
be fixed or unfixed to a particular congregation: "[In] case [the power of
ordination] be over many severall congregations, whether fixed or unfixed"
was "indifferent as to the poynt of ordination."[61] Stephen Marshall, also a
favorer of presbyterian government, supported Vines's argument by referring
to "the church of Jerusalem, & the scripture hath noe wayes declared whether
those congregations are fixed or not. The scripture hath left it indifferent &
therefore it is indifferent."[62]

The congregationalists were not convinced. Goodwin complained that the
flexibility allowed by these categories was simply another way of underpin-
ning presbyterian authority: "That which makes the distinction is the suppo-
sition of a presbyteriall government over many congregations."[63] Phillip Nye
also rejected the presbyterians' concept of the transferal of authority between
a general and particular body. More specifically, he questioned the use of
analogy to legal transaction as with feoffees: "I stumble at that expression
given to them as feofees in trust; when we must find out some that must be
trusted with it."[64] It was partly the support of civic institutions and in par-

ticular the feoffees for impropriations that sustained presbyterian ministers during a period when they were under threat from the authorities. If the presbyterians insisted on ordination through the Church as a formal institution, they nonetheless relied on lay patronage, which operated with relative autonomy from the Church of England to secure a preaching ministry. Here the distinction between ordination and election was vital in their justification of the legitimacy of their nonconformity.

The general nature of clerical vocation had immediate ecclesiological resonances, since it was a principle that licensed clergy to exercise their ministry beyond their ordinary sphere of jurisdiction. Countering congregational government in New England, James Noyes maintained that ministers held a license beyond their particular congregation whereby "the Churches do mutually allow and ratifie one anothers acts: One Church admitteth Members for all Churches, and one Church electeth Officers for all Churches; one gate of *Jerusalem* admitteth into the whole City, *Rev.* 21. One Elder hath a general relation to the universal Church, as well as a special relation to his particular Church."[65] John Ball's exchange with the New England clergy on behalf of the other English divines "revealed great commonality with the fundamental assumptions that guided the organization of New England's churches."[66] On the question of whether the minister could perform ministerial acts outside his particular charge, however, Ball differed: "In Ordination, Presbyters are not restrained to one or other certaine place, as if they were to be deemed Ministers there onely, though they be set over a certain people. . . . [So] the Ministers in respect of their communion, must and ought upon occasion to performe ministeriall Offices towards the faithfull of distinct societies."[67] He was particularly concerned to refute the exclusivity he saw in congregational arguments and the implications this had for other churches. He challenged those who "say, it is a false Church constitution, if the Minister bee not chosen and ordained by the congregation alone, where he is to administer."[68] But by insisting on congregational consent along with other criteria as absolutely essential, the New Englanders were in danger of condemning the Church through all the ages, for "if so then there was never any one age, wherein the Church-constitution was not an Idoll, and the worship of God performed in that Societie, leprous, uncleane, poysoned with Idolatry."[69]

It is also noteworthy that Ball used the lawfulness of ecclesiastical acts performed in synods as an argument for the general nature of clerical vocation: "[If] a Synod consisting of sundry members of particular Churches . . . shall joyn together in prayer and communion of the Supper, wee can see no ground to question it as unlawfull. . . . The Minister therefore may do an act of office to them that be not set members of his flock as he may stand in

Relation to them for the time."[70] The weight of Ball's argument came from his understanding of the unified nature of the visible church: "A Minister chosen and set over one society, is to looke unto his people committed to his charge ... but he is a Minister in the Church Universall, for as the Church is one, so is the Ministery one, of which every Minister (sound or Orthodox) doth hold his part."[71] Thus his commitment to a single visible church was clearly significant: "[F]or if he be not a Minister in other Churches, then are not the Churches of God one, nor the Ministers one, nor the flocke which they feed one, nor the Communion one which they have each with other."[72]

Ball's works were posthumously published by advocates of presbyterian government in the Westminster Assembly, including Simeon Ashe, William Rathband, Daniel Cawdrey, and Edward Calamy, and during the debates over ordination Calamy made the same argument for the universal nature of vocation: election to a particular congregation did not undermine the general nature of clerical vocation. For Calamy, to require election before ordination was to "imply that a minister is only a minister of that perticular congregation to which he is designed."[73] But, according to the presbyterians, ordination was of a general nature, "the setting of a man apart to the office of a minister." Whereas "election is to this or that place, ordination is to the office."[74] That ordination was performed through particular congregations did not conflict with the authority to ordain vested in the universal visible church, since "a thing may be given to the church generall and yet the exercise of it must be in perticulars."[75] Calamy also referred to Ephesians 4 to show the broader nature of the ministerial charge, supporting this reference by commenting that "Mr Travers interprets that teachers, ministers of the gospell not designed to perticular chardges. Pastor is one ordained & elected."[76] While not all those with presbyterian sympathies agreed on whether election necessarily preceded ordination, the ordination controversy revealed that many shared a concern for the universal nature of vocation. William Gouge commented: "What is given to any integrall number is given to the whole; the visive faculty is given to the < ey; > it is given to the whole."[77] Stephen Marshall argued that "the body of Christ is but one. . . . The conection of all those he calls his visible church on earth & to this visible church, the number of them that professe him, to all those hath he given his holy ordinances. Distributive perticulars, 'receive them,' but not given to them only, but because they are a part of that body of Christ."[78]

PRESBYTERIAN "PROMISCUITY"

Along with the general nature of clerical vocation, presbyterians argued that the preaching of the word and administration of the sacraments were ministerial acts and therefore also necessarily public and general by nature. As Cartwright put it in the Admonition controversy, "[No], not then is the word of God, nor the sacraments, privately preached or ministered, nor ought to be."[79] He consistently argued for the public administration of baptism by attaching it to arguments for the public nature of preaching: "For, as of our Saviour Christ's preaching in public places, and refusing private places, we do gather that the preaching of the word ought to be public; even so of St. John's preaching and baptizing in open meetings we conclude that both preaching and baptizing ought to be in public assemblies,"[80] and "For, if it be in the power of the church to order that baptism may be ministered at the house of every private person, it is also in her power to ordain that the word be preached also privately."[81]

This not only challenged the Church of England's permission to midwives and laymen to baptize in private places in necessary circumstances, but also in respect to their person: "[F]orasmuch as St Paul saith that a man cannot preach which is not sent, no, not although he speak the words of the scripture and interpret them; so I cannot see how a man can baptize unless that he be sent to that end, although he pour water and rehearse the words which are to be rehearsed in the ministry of baptism."[82] Whereas Whitgift responded by arguing that "the force and strength of the sacrament is not in the man, be he minister or not minister, be he good or evil, but in God himself, in his Spirit, in his free and effectual operation,"[83] Cartwright argued that "whether he be good or an evil minister, [the sacrament] dependeth not; but on this point, whether he be a minister or no, dependeth not only the dignity, but also the being of the sacrament; so that I take the baptism of women to be no more the holy sacrament of baptism, than I take any other daily or ordinary washing of the child."[84] In the process of their polemical exchanges, Whitgift and Cartwright came to use the arguments of their opponents to defend their respective positions. Throughout the Admonition controversy, Cartwright had stressed a level of independence from the Church of England through spiritual sanctions found in Scripture and directed by the Holy Spirit, while Whitgift had stressed the discretion of public authority to underpin the case for conformity.[85] Yet on this issue Whitgift defended the Church of England's practices by arguing that "the life of baptism" was found in its "essential form": "[To] baptize in the name of the Father, of the Son, and of the Holy Ghost; which form being observed, the sacrament remaineth in full force and strength, of whomsoever it be ministered, or howsoever by ceremonies or other additions it is corrupted."[86] Cartwright, on the other hand, insisted on the public institution, preaching of the word and calling of the minister to argue for stricter requirements in the administration of infant baptism.

He had similarly stressed the validity of sacraments administered by ignorant preachers if performed according to these essentials in arguing against the separatist Robert Browne, who compared Cartwright's reasons to "wynde blowen out of a bladder."[87]

In the debate between Henry Jacob and his presbyterian examiners in the early seventeenth century, the presbyterians came to stress even more fervently the legitimacy of baptism according to the essentials noted by Cartwright in the Admonition controversy. Jacob prioritized congregational consent as an essential component of the administration of baptism just as he had argued it to be a legitimizing factor in clerical vocation. He pointed to corruption in the Church of Rome to reject the presbyterians' emphasis on the public authorization of ministerial acts, saying "that theire baptisme is not trew but all falce as it commeth frome the Pope and his clergy but trew Baptisme as the preists' $\lor$ administer it $\lor$ with the peoples $\lor$ consent and as the peoples ministers $\lor$ and not otherwise."[88] Travers had argued against reordination by stressing the general nature of his ecclesiastical calling; he also supported his position by pointing out the implications of reordination that would involve "the making void of al former acts of ministry" and "the renting of the Churches one from another; and rebaptization of those who had been by such baptized before, and the anulling of marriages solemnized before by others."[89]

In response to Jacob, presbyterians similarly pointed to the general nature of ecclesiastical calling to argue that baptisms administered by the Church of Rome were valid, for "in respect of their publike calling we doe not utterly $\lor$ dis $\lor$ annull their ministery nor their baptisme but rest in the baptisme ministred by them without baptizing againe." They reasoned that "the mercy of god in the midst of the infinite corruptions of popery graciously preserved the words of our Savior in the institution of baptisme free from corruption and alteration and partly because it was ministred by[†] those which hold their calling by publike authority that directed them to such a vocation as was allowed[‡] amongst them."[90] To accept the legitimacy of Roman baptism and the calling of such priests, they argued, was not to hold "popish priests to be justified for sufficient ministers of the gospel because they are made by publike order. . . . For in that Antichristian Church they are not ordeined to preach the gospel as ours are but to $\lor$ sacryfyse $\lor$ for the quick and the dead."[91] They argued that Jacob himself accepted certain aspects of the Roman Catholic ministry by recognizing that Roman priests could hold a legitimate calling so long as the congregation had conceded.[92]

*and ministry
†those
‡amo

Yet subsequent controversy over the administration of the sacraments was less to do with who administered the sacraments as with who ought to receive them. Presbyterians had complained of the indiscriminate administration of the sacraments in the Church of England. Cartwright argued that "papists, being such as which are notoriously known to hold heretical opinions, ought not to be admitted, much less compelled to the supper."[93] He also objected that Whitgift "doth make the holy sacrament of baptism . . . a common passage whereby he will have clean and unclean, holy and profane, as well those that are without the covenant, as those that be within it, to pass by; and so make the church no household, but an inn to receive whosoever cometh."[94] However, presbyterians were neither challenging the sufficiency of a public confession by individuals or by at least one parent for the baptism of infants, nor suggesting that communion and baptism only be administered to the true elect. Rather, they were insisting that the heretical, excommunicated, and obstinate and openly scandalous persons be denied these covenantal signs.[95] From this perspective, there was room for erroneous views by members that "be not in those points which raze the foundations of faith, because they still, notwithstanding their error, are to be counted amongst the faithful, their children pertain unto the promise, and therefore to the sacrament of the promise."[96] In addition, there was room for unregenerate participants who outwardly conformed as well as those who sinned and might still be among the elect (even if they were not yet aware of their condition).[97]

Not all the godly agreed with opening so wide the gate to the administration of the sacraments. In practice, presbyterians and congregationalists held similar policies about the lord's supper. Although they did not always agree on the qualifications required for communicants, both stressed the need for close examination of candidates while also admitting nonmembers to partake in communion upon the production of testimony to their confession and good "conversation" (or life and manners.) Yet, as the question of infant baptism would reveal, this did not necessarily indicate that they shared similar views on the dispensation of sacraments. Congregationally inclined clergy followed Jacob in mandating congregational consent, whereas presbyterians stressed the general nature of ecclesiastical calling to legitimize the sacraments. By insisting on the necessity of congregational consent, congregationalists refused baptism to the openly scandalous in addition to those who were not members of the particular congregation in which the sacrament was being administered. When Paget posed twenty questions to test the orthodoxy of Thomas Hooker, it was not only the authority of the classis that Hooker refused to accept, but also the baptism of children presented by a parent who professed faith but was not a member of the Church.[98] Paget similarly orchestrated John

Davenport's exclusion from the office of copastor by using the same inter-rogatories, whereby "regarding 'promiscuous' or 'unlimited Baptisinge of all infants, which were presented in the Church,' [Davenport] could not satisfy his conscience."[99] As Paget argued, whereas Davenport "judge[s] it a sin to baptise the infants of such parents; we judge it a sin to deny baptisme unto them."[100]

That the presbyterians and congregationalists came to disagree on the subject of infant baptism was not simply an extension of their theological polemic. Under Paget's ministry the English Reformed Church in Amster-dam practiced a wider administration of infant baptism than the Lord's Sup-per by baptizing the children of members who were under suspension from communion.[101] Since suspended status did not necessarily remove individuals from membership, it followed that their children were also received into the Church. Congregationalists objected to the presbyterians' wider acceptance into membership. Hence it is not surprising that they also protested against the presbyterians' baptism of infants whose parents were not members of their congregation. Presbyterian and congregational disagreement over member-ship is best demonstrated by controversy over the Church covenant, which was a set of statements used in the admission of new members that bound them to the authority of the particular congregation. In the late sixteenth century presbyterians claimed that the introduction of the covenant was the result of separatist influences.[102] In the early seventeenth century, the English Reformed Church in Amsterdam similarly resisted the introduction of a cov-enant, receiving new members into the Church upon their confession with no explicit contract and "without public examination of them before the whole congregation." By contrast, Thomas Hooker and other proto-congregational ministers insisted on a covenant and examination.[103] In this controversy con-gregationalists did not simply disagree with presbyterians on how particular congregations related to another; they objected to the presbyterians' promis-cuous ministry and administration of sacraments among neighboring church-es as well as to their "promiscuous" admission of members to the congrega-tion. The Newbury ministers in New England scandalized congregational ministers by their broader membership policy. Thomas Lechford recorded in 1642 that "some churches are of opinion, that any may be admitted to church fellowship that are not extremely ignorant or scandalous" and that "the Newbury church was 'very forward to practice' this rule."[104] Woodman, the chief critic of Thomas Parker's ministry in Newbury, objected that "Parker had imposed his 'change of opinion and practice' regarding admission and discipline upon the congregation" and that in this practice Parker was "seeking to 'set up a prelacy [of one], and have more power than the Pope.'"[105]

Although some scholars such as Tom Webster and Carol Schneider have argued that disputes over infant baptism and membership were unrelated to other ecclesiastical controversies concerning the relationship between congregations, they were in fact directly linked to the presbyterians' and congregationalists' disagreement over the scope of ministerial duties and the nature of the visible church.[106] It was specifically in the context of defending the presbyterians' practice of infant baptism that Paget argued for the general nature of ministerial duties: "[If] either the faithfull Pastours were taken away by death; or if through weaknes of gifts they were not able to stop the mouthes of adversaries, what remained then to be done, but to seek the help of neighbour Ministers for their assistance."[107] More explicitly, he argued that

> for the Administration of the Sacraments, it is also a duety of the ministry, to be performed by a Pastour to more then the members of his particular congregation: and this not onely by admission of the particular members of an other Church to receave the Lords Supper with them in their Church upon occasion, which the Brownists themselves doe allow; but also when need requires to administer the Sacraments, both of Baptisme and the Lords Supper in neighbour Churches that are destitute, being required thereunto.[108]

New England congregationalists responded to interrogatories on church membership and infant baptism with "one and the same defence," explaining that for "Church communion we hold onely with Church members admitting to fellowship of the seals the known and approved, & orderly recommended members of any true Church."[109] According to Ball's summary of this defense, the New Englanders' arguments for the administration of the sacraments stemmed from their definition of the Church as a particular congregation: "Seeing the churches in the Gospell are congregationall, and that Baptisme and the Lords Supper (being Church priviledges) belong onely to the Churches, it will follow . . . baptisme and the Lords Supper being Church priviledges, belong onely to the members of particular Churches, and their seed."[110] However, Ball responded by challenging the New Englanders' definition of the visible church: "If by the Church be understood the Society of men, professing the entire faith of Christ, the seales are given unto it as a peculiar priviledge; but if by the Church you understand onely a congregationall assembly in Church order, the seales were never appropriated to it."[111] It is apparent that these debates were related to a host of ecclesiological concerns that had already surfaced before Thomas Hooker and John Davenport left for New England. Although Tom Webster and others have warned against interpreting the theological exchange between English ministers and New Englanders in 1637 through the subsequent party support and publication of these debates in the 1640s, there is the opposite danger of misinterpreting them by removing them from their prior context. Early seventeenth-century nonconformist ecclesiology was far from a homogenous tradition dominated by agreement on an essentially congregational polity; rather, it was one in which the godly fiercely debated the nature of the visible church and the extent of common consent, ministerial duties, administration of the sacraments, and admission into membership. It was important for presbyterians to inscribe their action and government within a public institution and to affirm their commitment to the Church of England, which proved to be one of their most powerful tactics in arguing against congregationalism.

REACHING A VERDICT

Such ecclesiological trials did not culminate with membership in a particular congregation, but membership in the Church of England. Membership of the Church of England was ultimately the line between nonconformity and schism, a line which Professor Collinson has called "a tiny ditch, but a Rubicon nevertheless."[112] Since separatism hinged on the lawfulness of association with the Church of England, the central question was whether that Church was indeed a true one. For those who believed that it was based on an unbiblical model of government, its status depended on whether church government was an essential mark of a true visible church along with sound proclamation of the gospel and due administration of the sacraments. The notion that English presbyterians followed Beza who had departed from Calvin by demanding a more exalted view of ecclesiastical discipline was first proposed by anti-puritan writers. According to Richard Bancroft, "*Calvin* did carrie himselfe in this cause" of ecclesiastical government with moderation, "modestie" and "humilitie," "yet *Beza* is of an other opinion. . . . It is chiefly he, that hath set the pretended reformers, in this whole land, so much a gogge against Bishops."[113] In recent years, scholars such as R. T. Kendall and Stephen Brachlow have defended variations of the thesis through their examination of subsequent doctrinal and radical ecclesiological developments. Brachlow argued for "the coupling of ecclesiology with soteriological assurance . . . in the writings of Elizabethan precisionists" and cites "the views of Cartwright and Travers (against Whitgift) that church polity was a matter of faith."[114] That English presbyterians subscribed to three essential marks in the visible church has continued to inform modern studies, including Tom Webster's analysis, which questions Humfrey Fen's presbyterianism on the basis that he "held on to a two-mark doctrine of ecclesiology."[115]

However, contemporaries did not always claim that presbyterians regarded discipline as an essential mark of the visible church. Robert Browne complained that Cartwright held that "though they haue not the discipline commanded by Christ, yet they are the Church."[116] He further cited that "Master Cartwright . . . sayeth that faith in Christ is the essence, being, or life of the church: as for discipline it is but accidental, and therefore the Church of God may haue her being and life, and be named the church of God, without discipline."[117] This understanding was not simply affixed to Cartwright's writing in his later career. In his treatise against the separatist Francis Johnson at the end of the sixteenth century, Henry Jacob offered a similar interpretation of earlier Elizabethan presbyterian treatises: "The Admonition. T.C. his Replies, Demonstration, declaration, and the Defence of Discipline. . . . None of all these doe graunt any thing to be wanting with vs that is necessary to the being of a Church simply, nor to the *being* of a true Ministery or Sacraments: But onely to their well and *convenient* being."[118] It is worth pointing out that when Travers compared discipline and doctrine to "two sisters who are twins" in his *Declaration*, it was to stress that discipline was necessary for the preservation of essential doctrines, not to impute it with soteriological significance. As Travers explained with reference to the Roman Church, "The stories do testifie, how that by little and little with the corruption of discipline, doctrine also began to bee corrupted."[119] The parallel Travers drew between discipline and doctrine in the *Declaration* was therefore a description of an interdependent relationship.[120] As Lake has noted, Travers affirmed that discipline was necessary, "but not 'so simply absolutely and immediately,' 'but yet necessary as means ordained of God for the better furtherance of our salvation.'"[121]

However, if Jacob maintained that Elizabethan presbyterians did not hold discipline as essential to the visible church by the end of the sixteenth century, it was not long before he began to expound a moral imperative for disciplinary and ceremonial practice in his writings in which he argued that discipline could not be compromised, since it was commanded in the Decalogue as a part of worship. Brachlow has identified (even if misapplied to Cartwright and Travers) that "the conviction of the radicals about the soteriological significance of ecclesiology found its biblical source in their perception of the import of the second commandment in the Decalogue and its value for maintaining the covenant bond with God."[122] The imperative for disciplinary and ceremonial matters to which Brachlow refers appears in Jacob's *Plaine and Cleere Exposition of the second Commandement* (1610): "[A]ll places touching sacrifices and offerings, and ceremonies, formes of churches, and priests of mans ordinance . . . all these are forbidden in the second commandement."[123] Jacob further argued that "it remaineth certain & sure; that the forenamed matters with us in controversie (viz. Diocesan and Provinciall Churches, Bishops, & Government; the Surplice, Cope, Crosse in Baptisme, & Kneeling &c.) are substantiall points of Religion, and of Gods worship, & are contained properly in the 2d Commandement, & namely in the Negative part thereof." He concluded that "all religious Signes & Ceremonies in Scripture . . . are parts of this 2d Commandement, & are very parts of Gods speciall worship instituted, true, or false: they are all matters of doctrine, matters of Faith, matters of substance in religion, yea matters of salvation, & necessary more or lesse either to be used or refused."[124]

By the 1610s, Jacob not only stressed the moral imperative of disciplinary and ceremonial matters through his interpretation of the second commandment, but also offered an alternative reading of earlier presbyterian treatises. His examiners who took issue with his Southwark congregation objected to his view that Cartwright had imputed a soteriological significance to ecclesiastical discipline in the Admonition controversy:

> [Out] of Mr Cartwrights reply you site no words but only quote two places whereof the one is his first reply. . . . [T]he words are not here set downe but they are these discipline and government are of the substance of the gospel. . . . [H]eere you may see that hee sayth not of the substance of the church but of the substance of the gospel. And the reason is manifest because . . . discipline and government are taught in the gospel and so are parts of it, but they are no parts of the church. The other place is Reply the 2 part 1 pag 247; Heere indeed at the last wee are directed to a place . . . but the words are necessary to salvation are not there and for the other it is to bee noted that hee sayth not, discipline is of the substance of the church, but that it is required to the substance of the church that is that it is requisite, meaning to the better being and to the longer preservation of the church.[125]

Through the examiners' response to Jacob it is evident that Cartwright wrote an antiseparatist treatise which has hitherto remained unknown: "Mr Cartwright . . . never intended to incorage any man by way of schisme. . . . [He] left evident testimony in perticuler in his booke against Harison upon the 122 psalme."[126] They further argued that "in generall this hee confirmed by all his exemplary lyfe and virtuous conversation and namly by the peaceable carige of his ministery in the midest of this church [of En]gland at [War]wicke,"[127] and explicitly defended "our English churches . . . to bee trew churches of Christ (notwithstanding any thing that yet nedeth further reformation) by the doctrine of Salvation which is trewly taught in it according to gods word and by the due use and administration of the sacraments." They further added "therefore it is a most unworthy act to strike our Church with these side blows as if it were of the darkenesse and not of the light."[128]

According to the examiners, Jacob had recently changed his views: "[It] is not many yeares since you thought you" could remain in the Church of England without spiritual peril, yet "how you come to see this now, which you had not seeme so many yeares, it appeareth not. . . . [It] seemeth that you are merly deluded."[129] They claimed that the defendant was responsible for "setting up a new church of your owne when and where you will."[130] And they specifically objected that Jacob led others astray by teaching that "everyone ought to make himselfe a member of such a perticuler congregation as you fancye to be free and independent and not subject to yeld account to any higher ecclesiastical authority."[131] According to the examiners, Jacob had implied that he "who joyneth not with this new church hath not god for his father."[132] It was precisely this withdrawal from parishes in the Church of England in the late 1630s that prompted the ministers in England to ask the opinion of the New England clergy on the Church of England, and which led to the inquiry headed by John Ball. As the writers explained, diverse men and women in England "have left our Assemblies because of a stinted Litergie and excommunicated themselves from the Lords Supper."[133] The question at issue was not the New England congregations' own neglect of prescribed forms of prayer and worship (such as the Book of Common Prayer), but whether their arguments against it served to justify (and implicitly require) others to withdraw from communion. As Ball stressed, "The thing we craved resolution in was, whether in your judgements all stinted and set formes of prayer and Liturgies be unlawfull."[134] Thus while presbyterians and congregationalists developed varying responses to episcopacy, and arguments against each other, their debate over ecclesiology was also shaped by the concern over separation and their relationship with and to the Church of England.

New England congregationalists refused directly to say whether those in England should withdraw from worship in their local parishes: "As for our Judgement concerning the practice of others, who use this Liturgie in our native Countrie . . . we have always been unwilling to expresse our mindes there against unlesse we have been necessarily called thereunto, and at this time we thinke it not expedient to expresse our selves any further concerning this matter."[135] John Ball pressed the matter further by probing the New Englanders' objections to set liturgies, finding "that your reasons why you accept not of a stinted Lyturgie be ambiguously propounded, for sometimes you plead onely for your libertie herein . . . and sometime you speake so, as they that looke at Stinted Lyturgies, as Images forbidden in the second Commandement will easily draw your words to their meaning."[136] In his *Friendly Triall*, which directly followed on the initial inquiry, Ball proceeded to argue against the moral imperative that underpinned their objections to stinted liturgy and ecclesiological purity more generally: "False worship forbidden in the second commandment is opposite to the true worship which must in speciall be instituted by God: But a stinted form of prayer is not opposite to that worship which must in speciall be instituted by God."[137] It is significant that Ball concluded his trial of the New England congregational clergy by refuting Henry Jacob's exposition of the second commandment. He defended the general nature of the visible church in response to Jacob; here he also stressed that only two marks were essential to it: "Wheresoever we see the word of God truly taught and professed in points fundamentall, and the sacraments for substance rightly administered, there is the true church of Christ, though the health and soundnesse of it may be crazed by many errours in doctrine."[138]

Jacob's response to the presbyterians again provides further insight into how he justifies his actions. He bases the establishment of his congregation not on the principle of free and voluntary consent on the part of his adherents, nor on the rejection of the authority of synods. Jacob was not simply arguing that individuals had a freedom of choice and liberty to establish a new ecclesiastical society; he was arguing that they had a moral obligation to the second commandment to do so. The imperative to observe unadulterated worship did not conflict with Jacob's view on whether congregations in England could be considered as true churches, but it left little room to justify active participation in such worship, even in particular parishes within the Church of England. Jacob explained that he and his followers believed that they must "refuse to be constant members of a universal church using government or of a provinciall likewise or of a parrish being a professed & proper parte of ether of them, other wise we transgress the 2d commandement in ye decalog: as in a plane & cleere exposition, thereof published Anno 1610 is made manifest."[139]

This statement was the incriminating evidence that the presbyterians used to clinch the debate and reach their verdict: "[T]hat you depart from us of necessity and such like seeing then your selves professe and that thing it still is evident that you make a schisme and rend both your[self and] others from our church how can you bee free from schism."[140] They determined that "neither is any thing that yet you have sayde whereunto you reserve your selfe sufficient to free you from this crime," and continued, "[As] for your distinctions of being trew churches in one respect and not trew in another they are deceitfull illusions. . . . [As] a man cannot bee a man living in one respect and dead in another so neither can a church that is a trew and living church in any respect bee a false and dead church." Thus they reached their verdict through the very imperative that Jacob had used to justify his actions in addition to his selective rejection of particular aspects of the Church of England. However, instead of simply disagreeing with Jacob's distinction between the particular and general church, they argued that it collapsed in practice and in Jacob's defense of congregational procedure. In other words, Jacob had separated from the Church of England in its particular parts and as a whole:

[Y]ou answere that you leave not our churches as they are trew churches but as they are churches provinciall . . . in which respect you say they are not trew churches and therefore you are bound to depart from them in whole & from all parts of it that thus obvertly and openly professe your departure from us both from our whole church and from all the parts therof how doe you think that you should escape both the crime and punishment of schisme.[141]

They thus concluded that "amongst many notable sentences . . . we advise you to marke well these two: the first that to make a schisme in the church is no lesse evill then to fall into herycye. The other that the very bloud of Martyrdome is not able to blot out the offence of schism."[142]

While the examiners had not proceeded against Jacob for his emphasis on congregational consent, denial of synodal authority or definition of the Church of England as plural congregations in the first instance, they found a basis for building a case against him when he began to expound the moral imperative for withdrawing from worship that had justified the setting up of his congregation in Southwark.[143] Having failed to convince the defendant that his actions amounted to schism, the examiners were left simply to pronounce sentence against him. Their exasperation could almost pass for that expressed in response to modern political events: "[It] is a wonder that one man alone can bee so peremptory, in such a cause and so imboulden him selfe as to stand in the face of so great & noble an army of the lord of hosts."[144] Jacob may have anticipated the troubles that were to come for nonconformists in England, but his examiners were no less aware that the establishment of his Southwark congregation marked a significant turn in the history of the church that was to have repercussions well beyond the seventeenth century.

PART III

From Theory to Practice

CHAPTER 6

Presbyterianism in Practice?

However vehemently presbyterians opposed congregational ecclesiology, in practice there might seem to be an undeniable gravitation toward congregational autonomy. This is most notably illustrated by the proceedings of the Dedham conferences recorded in the 1580s that reveal divisions of opinion on matters ranging from doctrines on the Sabbath to points made in the Book of Discipline. The authority of the conference was undermined by Bartimaeus Andrewes's removal to Yarmouth, despite the conference's ruling against it, and then by William Negus's eventual decision to quit his congregation for another, when, again, the conference had clearly pronounced against it. The Dedham conference is an apparent hiatus in the history of English presbyterianism. Although it attempted to assert authority over individual ministers, it had no means of coercion without the formal establishment of a presbyterian system and its wholesale national adoption in the Church of England.[1] Congregational autonomy, on the other hand, was feasible within a halfly reformed national church.

Even in such uncertain times, however, there were instances when censure from the classis could prove effective. In 1583 it was exercised by John Field and the other brethren of the London classis against none other than the Admonitioner Thomas Wilcox for committing a disgraceful act. Wilcox, like Andrewes, resisted, and suspension from his ministry and excommunication initially proved ineffective. However, when the classis eventually withheld his maintenance he submitted.[2] Financial support was of course significant: the support of the Dutch classis was one reason why English congregations in the Netherlands, which had wavered between presbyterianism and congregationalism throughout the seventeenth century, gravitated toward a presbyterian church structure. Lay economic and institutional support through lectureships proved essential in placing nonconformist ministers in England, while further serving to secure them in their posts. Lay patronage was of course no mere economic investment in preaching; it was also an assertion of authority in local and national conflicts as well as a civic contribution to the cultivation of a godly society. What emerges from these examples is a picture of puritanism in practice that could, and did, find it necessary to exercise authority beyond the particular congregation contrary to the traditional paradigm that has tended almost automatically to collapse English nonconformist activity into congregational autonomy. Presbyterians did not only define the Church as a community beyond a particular locality; in practice they depended upon wider institutional support that reinforced their authority in the face of controversy and in their defense of orthodoxy. Conflicts within, without, and between congregations can reveal presbyterian inflections in English nonconformity, as a number of instances can exemplify.

THE ENGLISH MERCHANT ADVENTURER CHURCH

The English Merchant Adventurer church in Antwerp, of which Travers became the first minister in May 1578, was one such. Just as Travers received presbyterian ordination in Antwerp, which came under question in England and became a matter of public contention,[3] so there was more room to practice presbyterian government there. In 1579 Archduke Matthias helped to secure the religious liberty of the Merchant Adventurer church, which found further warrant for its reformed practices through the support of Ambassador William Davison and Robert Dudley, Earl of Leicester. This allowed the Church room to depart from the practices of the Church of England insofar as it "conformed . . . to the Government established in the Churches of the United Provinces."[4] Indeed it conformed to the reformed polity of the Netherlands rather than to the episcopal order of England: "The polity of the church was entirely presbyterian, the officebearers being minister, elders and deacons, and the characteristic discipline being duly administered."[5]

Travers's assiduous records of the operation of the Merchant Church are included in one of his theological notebooks at Trinity College and fill a substantial gap in the sources for this congregation. They confirm that the Merchant Adventurer church was indeed actively presbyterian. Agendas for consistory meetings outline the order of activity, stressing prayer before and after the meeting, as one would expect in a puritan assembly.[6] Moreover the agenda is marked by its specific concern for the duties of the officers of the Church. Beginning with the election of elders and deacons, the duties of the seniors (or elders) including announcements to be made to the congregation are outlined.[7] Elsewhere there are several accounts referring to the activity of the diaconate, including visitations to church members and the expenditures that were made by the deacons.[8]

Travers noted details of church discipline, including those admitted to the sacrament of the lord's supper, and he accompanied these lists with instructions on examination and even strict censure. Cases of members who were not admitted to the sacrament are recorded, as well as the actions taken by officers to encourage the disobedient to repent.[9] It is noteworthy that the execution of this rigorous discipline did not provoke any apparent objections from English merchants. When the governor of the company, Nicholas Loddington, interrupted Travers during service in 1579, it was not because of any particular reformed practices but because of Travers's failure to use the Book of Common Prayer.[10] Further controversy arose when "Travers desired a certain person to be appointed as deacon, and the congregation refused to accept his nomination."[11] Yet even here, the controversy was not over the order of discipline itself but in deciding who was a suitable candidate. Two other events in 1579 have indicated that the Church was unsettled, and although their nature is unknown, they have suggested that "this Antwerp ministry, [Travers's] first experiment in the actual application of the discipline, must have been very disappointing."[12] Explaining Travers's departure for England, Knox stated that the "succession of adversities must have led Travers to realize that his ministry was not having the success that was desired, and that, even though the prospects in the homeland were not rosy, a longer stay in Antwerp was inadvisable."[13]

However, there is no indication that it was the institution of presbyterian discipline that was causing problems. In fact, Travers's personal papers directly counter any impression of this. In 1580 he drew up a list of the pros and cons of returning to England, carefully concealing his process of decision-making by encrypting his writing in French in Greek characters. While he was concerned about the "the possibility of . . . [the discipline] not being well used in < my > absence," this appears seventh in his list of thirteen reasons for remaining at Antwerp and is the only mention of a practical difficulty which threatened the continuance of presbyterian discipline. Travers's other reasons included "the troubles in England" as well as "the Bishops." He also feared offending those in Antwerp by leaving. This included his prospect of marriage to a certain "TK" and "the offence of a very audacious hardness in leaving TK here." If the prospect of marriage weighed against Travers's return to England, the chief reason in favor was not the practical difficulty of the ministry but "the death of my mother." Second was his opportunity to "stay with my friend[s]", and third "certain large expenses." His fourth reason involved the "troubles on the part of the governour (which offence ought to be avoided)." Travers's decision to leave cannot therefore be characterized as simply a flight from opposition. There were other practical concerns: "the smallness of profit on account of the frequent journeys of the merchants," "the removal of the merchants house, the constant to-ing and fro-ing of the merchant households," "the air of this place, the diet," and "there being concern for health, that if you live here for long, you will for ever be ill & little able to serve the ministry, falling into sicknesses which I fear for their causes my natural indisposition."[14] Travers was also concerned to return to England because of "the lack of fit people to serve the church" and his dislike for "voluntary exile."

Travers's complaint of "the constant to-ing and fro-ing" of English Merchant households points to the routine traffic between England and Antwerp and the direct link between the English Merchant Adventurer in Antwerp and the company's base in London. There were also close links with nonconformist groups in East Anglia: the "men of Antwerp," including merchants and clothiers, who were "to be found among the more substantial members of the Dedham ministers' congregations."[15] Not only did the English merchant community constantly travel between Antwerp and England, they also stayed in close communication with one another. If Travers did not share his list of pros and cons in the Antwerp church with Cartwright, whom he secured as his replacement in 1580, he did write to him about the activity of the Antwerp church in the course of his ministry. In the midst of his controversy with the governor of the company in 1579, Travers secured the support of Davison and Walsingham.[16] It is also clear from his private papers that he sought the advice of other godly clergy, writing "to Mr Fountain, Cartwright, Grindall (et) cetere to talk of the order of our English Kirk."[17] It is especially interesting to find Grindal being consulted by the Antwerp Merchant Adventurer congregation during his later career when he seemed to have become more moderate.[18]

It appears from Travers's notes that he too was in the habit of "to-ing and fro-ing" between England and the Netherlands, for he returned to the Merchant Adventurers in July 1592. While most of the main presbyterian organizers were still recovering from their imprisonment in the Fleet, he left London on an eastbound excursion, and before the close of the day he noted that he was approaching the coast of Kent.[19] He and his companions stayed overnight "fines terrae," spending the next day at "Margorita,"[20] before crossing to the Low Countries. It was a short journey, for on July 24 their destination was in sight, as Travers wrote "appulimus Midd[leburg]."[21] The Merchant Adventurers congregation, which had moved from Antwerp to Middleburg, was in a fragile state, torn by the controversy that had arisen under their previous minister. After Cartwright had come Dudley Fenner (d. 1587), and then Francis Johnson (1590–92), who was writing against separatism as late as 1591. However, by 1592, Johnson had turned an ecclesiastical somersault, expressing separatist sympathies, falling out with his own congregation and with the Dutch Reformed ministers and resigning the pulpit by April of that year.[22] Just as Travers found support from clergy in England amid his difficulties with the governor, so the Dutch consistory in Middleburg turned to the London-based Dutch reformed church to fill the empty pulpit with a minister agreeable in church government.[23] Although it does not appear that Travers himself filled the empty pulpit, he was apparently sent over.

On July 29, 1592, as part of their reordering of this church, the merchants went on to address the administration of the sacraments. Just as Travers had listed the names of communicating members in his earlier ministry, so on his return to the Merchant Adventurer Church, he again kept track of those admitted to the lord's supper. The names that appear in his records largely correspond to the list of Merchant Adventurers compiled by Theodore Rabb.[24] Additional names, given by Travers in a separate list, may be identified as members who were "of the churche & not of the company," including "servants strangers" and a Thomas Brown of Flushing.[25] On the same day Travers noted an essential piece of information that indicates the ecclesiastical complexion of the merchant church. Included in their activity is the decision to elect new elders.[26] Travers kept an account of this process: by August 17 nominations were finalized, and by August 20 elders and deacons had been ordained.[27]

PRESBYTERIAN AND CONGREGATIONAL "TO-ING AND FRO-ING"

Travers was followed at the Merchant Adventurer Church by other English presbyterian preachers. Matthew Holmes, an early Elizabethan presbyterian from Warwick, was a minister there from around 1596 until 1597. Holmes was also one of the first fellows of Trinity College, Dublin, where he risked his career to help secure Travers the post of provost. A manuscript copy of Holmes's treatise against the Jesuits in 1598 is still preserved at Trinity and includes statements clearly in favor of presbyterian church polity. Other evidence of the same theological persuasion can be found in his sermons at Middleburg, which are also now at Trinity. While attacking both Brownists and Roman Catholics, he also anticipated in his sermons that reform of the Church would come through the civil magistrate. In one sermon he preached against "Brownistes & Donatistes, who reason thus, yf a poll[uted] person tasted of the supper th[en] it is uncleane."[28] That these sermons were delivered in the Low Countries explains his sensitivity toward separatist tendencies and his concern to refute them in his preaching. In another instance he raised objections to their illegitimate calling and lack of clerical qualification: "The

Brownists who teach in the church, never elected or ordeayned to the teachers office in the same, neyther fit to dooe such dutyes." He asked, "[S]hall all the bodye bee eyes, all pastors & Doctors? Therfor they shall make a confused bodye & thus buildinge the tower of Babell, noe marvell yf God confound their language."[29]

Holmes was succeeded by another minister with direct Elizabethan presbyterian links. Although omitted from the roster of those who served the Merchant Adventurer church, the will of Edward Gellibrand indicates that he was minister there until his death in 1601.[30] Despite variation in subsequent years, there are indications that the English Merchant Adventurers church persisted in its presbyterian practices until as late as the 1630s. According to Ambassador William Boswell's account of the life of the Church in 1632/3,

> [ffor] theyr Church, although your Lordship seme to require my Certificat of theyr constitucons onely in case of other obstinacy, yet I take leave to signify that I fynde the Disciplyne therof Presbyterian and that the Company fell into this Fashion at the first Graunt of Free Exercise of Religion unto them, and hath soe continued from tyme to tyme, and from place to place of theyr Residence.[31]

John Forbes, of Aberdeenshire, was the resident minister of the Church at that time. Following Holmes and Gellibrand, he came to the merchants in 1610 with not only his own Scottish experience but also having visited many reformed churches on the continent, particularly in France.[32] If it comes as a surprise to find Boswell classifying the English merchant congregation as presbyterian as late as 1632, it is not surprising to find that there was lively disagreement and unresolved tensions within it. As Boswell reported, "[T]he distance between the Deputy (Mr Misselden) and Mr Forbes the present minister with the company is soe great and irreconcilable as I have not been able to bring the Minister and Company to meet in a communion."[33] Deputy Edward Misselden was apparently a "known agent of Laud," who was concerned to include the Church of England's liturgy and forms of prayer, which were omitted by Forbes, in services.[34] But the more weighty issues in the Church during the early 1630s seem to have arisen from a shift in the minister's own sympathies. Like Francis Johnson, "Forbes and his elders . . . governed the church according to Presbyterian standards, at least until the 1630s, when Forbes began to innovate and move the church into freer, more Congregational directions . . . assisted in his church innovations by Thomas Hooker, his assistant 1631–33 and by Hugh Peter and Samuel Bachelor."[35]

The examples of Johnson and Forbes emphasize the fluidity of early modern religious history. Many puritans would never fit the agenda of any one party; their theology evolved throughout their careers, and cannot be placed consistently in any one ecclesiological camp.[36] Such men cultivated general puritan sympathies but engaged with a diverse range of puritan ideas; they should not be forced into artificial subdivisions. This is particularly true when investigating ecclesiology, but is a challenge in any attempt to identify the specific character of individual puritans. Nonetheless, the issues at stake in ecclesiastical debate, which intrinsically affected the life of the Church, were evident, even if certain individuals did not come to clear conclusions about where they stood as the battle lines were being drawn. There were men like Forbes and Goodyear who wavered, and there were others who were firmly fixed on one side or the other. That said, a definite presbyterianism persisted among the English congregation in the Netherlands not only in the late sixteenth but also through the first forty years of the seventeenth century:

> The most long-standing theological position of the Netherlands Puritans was Reformed or Presbyterian. Beginning with the Merchant Adventurers church of Cartwright, Travers, and Fenner, the church practiced Reformed worship and church government. During the seventeenth century, the chief Dutch Presbyterian defenders were the Pagets (John, Thomas, and Robert) and some of the Scottish preachers. In fact, Michael Watts credits the Dutch Presbyterians with the most consistent Presbyterian stand of their day.[37]

It is worth re-examining the factors that may have contributed to the gravitation toward presbyterian government of English congregations in the Netherlands during this period. In some cases the process of ordination, along with the personal persuasion of individual ministers, would suggest presbyterian inclinations. At Dort "the English ministers, especially [Robert] Paget, accepted the Presbyterian system enthusiastically and administered the church with discipline and order. . . . In 1633 the English applied to the Classis of Dort for membership, so that 'in all incidents and difficulties they might address the classis.'"[38] Recorded on March 7, 1638, in the classis minute book is the presbyterian order of "Mr Robert Paget [who] succeeded Mr Dibetius. . . . His Ordination was solemnised by Mr Rulits, Minister of the English Church at Amsterdam (he being requested thereunto by letters sent both from the Magistrates of this City, and from the Eldership of this Church)."[39]

On the other hand English churches initially established along reformed presbyterian lines could also move in a congregational direction:

> The Rotterdam English Church was an ordinary English Reformed Church during the Barkely years, 'sub ordine presbyteriali, cum nostra Belgica. . . . After the first decade however, Hugh Peter, who came in 1629 . . . led it into a period of exceptional activity, transforming the presbyterial church of the 1620s into a model Congregational church of the 1630s.[40]

In the first phase of the English church in Flushing, "the longest-established minister was Thomas Potts (chaplain 1605–16), entertained with a stipend of

£120 a year," who in 1617 became copastor with John Paget in Amsterdam. When the Church was re-established "on June 19, 1620, John Wing was ordained as minister of 'this renewed English Church' with assistance from John Paget of Amsterdam, Willem Teellinck of Middelburg, who preached the ordination sermon, and other Dutch ministers and magistrates."[41] However, despite Wing's reformed ordination, the Church at Flushing became largely congregational. When it approached Thomas Potts, Jr., to supply the vacancy at Flushing in 1645, he complained of "the churches lack of meanes and not combining with other churches," following which, in September 1645, it joined the Walcheren classis.[42]

Oscillation between reformed and congregational practices was not simply a function of the profile and preferences of individual ministers. The English churches' relationship with and financial dependence upon the Dutch reformed classis also played a part. The English congregation in Utrecht depended on the city and province for half of their financial support and the congregation for the other half: "[T]he church prided itself on being an officially sponsored English Reformed Church with close and genial connections to the magistracy." Although the personal sympathies of the English ministers at Utrecht varied, after "1629, the English church was put under much tighter supervision, and their ministers were compelled to conform by taking classis membership."[43] When the English church in Zeeland received financial support from the city during the 1630s and 1640s, the Church conducted its election of ministers according to Dutch practice. It appears that the Dutch classis offered both financial and ecclesiastical reinforcement to the English churches: "Classis membership brought the English churches of Zeeland greater ecclesiastical respectability and gave them access to financial support."[44]

MORE PRESBYTERIAN PREACHERS

Not all the English churches in the Netherlands depended upon the Dutch for financial support. If the Golden Age of Antwerp had come to an end by the last years of the sixteenth century, the Golden Age of Amsterdam was just beginning. There was no coincidence in the establishment of an English Reformed Church in Amsterdam during this period; the Church was specifically chartered in 1607 to provide wealthy Englishmen with a respectable alternative to the English separatist community.[45] If the various examples of English presbyterianism have been overlooked by historians convinced of ineluctable trends toward congregational autonomy within English nonconformity, they have been able to discount English presbyterianism in Amsterdam only by dismissing it as an anomaly. Thus Tom Webster has described "the lonely struggle of John Paget, minister of the English reformed church at Amsterdam, to keep the Presbyterian flame alive," concluding that "Paget is best understood as a member of the Dutch Reformed classis, of Scottish extraction, and should be seen as a dissenter from the mainstream of alternative English ecclesiologies."[46]

Paget of course played a vital role in the development of English ecclesiological debate, not only through his controversy with proto-congregationalists but also through his involvement with Robert Parker, and in Richard Sheerwood's *Reply* to Downame. Paget's legacy and influence on Parker extended to his son Thomas and nephew James Noyes in New England. Ann Hughes has noted that the chief presbyterian popularizer of the mid-seventeenth century, Thomas Edwards, "kept in close touch with developments in the Netherlands, as all his books reveal, and was to seek refuge with Paget's old congregation in the summer of 1647. Here there may well be an important source for his zealous Presbyterianism—or more properly for his enduring opposition to 'toleration.'"[47] Thus, even if Paget were to be described as a presbyterian of "Scottish extraction," he cannot conveniently be omitted from a consideration of English ecclesiology by simply assuming that he was an exception. As a thriving and thoroughgoing English presbyterian church with rich documentation, the Amsterdam English Reformed Church deserves further scrutiny, in particular for the nature of popular participation in it.

But was John Paget an anomaly?[48] According to his own testimony, he had been a zealous protestant from his youth.[49] He matriculated sizar at Trinity College, Cambridge, in about 1592, which puts him "slap bang in the middle of the Cambridge of William Perkins and Laurence Chaderton."[50] He subsequently ministered in Nantwich, Cheshire, from 1598 until his ejection for nonconformity in 1604. By January 1605 he had departed for the Netherlands, where he was to serve as chaplain to English troops there, and subscribed to the Dutch confession of faith. Upon his arrival, he claimed that he "reioyced to find those things that I had desired before and this without variablenes,"[51] demonstrating a pre-existing commitment to reformed church government. This draws attention to his career in Cheshire, a noted center of English nonconformity where he was certainly no anomaly.

The radical nonconformity of Cheshire market towns has been characterized as "overwhelmingly inclined to Puritanism":[52] it has been argued that the county's social and administrative self-sufficiency contributed to the rise of puritanism there.[53] Another factor was the surprisingly cooperative relationship between puritans and the authorities in north-west England. "While Whitgift was demanding conformity in his own province, Puritanism in the diocese of Chester was being actively encouraged from above."[54] As John Morrill explained, "[T]he Bishops of Chester were not particularly concerned to extirpate Puritanism, rather they saw it as an ally against Catholicism. It thus grew throughout the county, particularly in the central and eastern hundreds. . . . The result was that by the 1610s there was a distinctive lay Puritan movement in the diocese as well as strong clerical roots."[55] The bishops' laxity meant that there was a significant delay in cracking down on puritan practices in the early seventeenth century, which Laurence Chaderton sought to defend.

There is also evidence of the direct influence of Elizabethan presbyterianism in the north-west in the person of Christopher Goodman, who played an active role in promoting preaching exercises in Chester during the 1580s "which provided for thrice-yearly synods to be attended by the Lancashire clergy."[56] During the early 1590s Goodman continued to defend the role of lay elders, citing Titus 1: 5. He also continued to challenge "the Lordly title of Bishops, as also their dignity and dominion which they usurp over their brethren, fellow ministers, and over the church of England."[57] That he remained in Chester until his death in 1603 suggests that his influence continued until the beginning of the seventeenth century. Edward Fleetwood, of Wigan, was another Elizabethan puritan who was active in promoting the exercises and in mobilizing puritan forces in Lancashire. Like Goodman, Fleetwood lived until 1600; and his correspondence with the presbyterian Humphrey Fen is extant.[58]

Paget's vigorous opposition to Henry Jacob and congregationalism, partly because it made its way into print, made it impossible for historians to miss his devotion to presbyterian church order. Yet there were others, although less in evidence, who proceeded along parallel lines. Consider the case of Julines Herring, one of several ministers silenced during the 1630s by the anti-Calvinist Richard Neile, archbishop of York from 1632 to 1640. Herring preached at Calke in Derbyshire from 1610 until 1618, where "amongst many others, Master Simeon Ashe received some of his first impressions, and bent towards Religion whom Master Herring loved from his child-hood, and who lived in his heart and Prayers unto his Death."[59] Herring was forced from his position on account of his nonconformity and moved to Shrewsbury where William Rowley procured a ministry for him at St. Alkmond's. His reputation as a popular preacher and nonconformist while in Shrewsbury is memorable for Laud's determination to "pickle up that Herring of Shrewsbury."[60] Although Herring "was suspended from the use of his Ministry, through the mediation of Friends, the suspension was divers times taken off, and then brought on again by Persons of contrary minds. . . . Thus he continued in Salop for the space of seventeen years."[61] Herring next moved to Wrenbury in Cheshire before he was summoned to Amsterdam in 1637. The burgomasters and classis at Amsterdam at once approved of Herring as a convinced presbyterian preacher, and since "there was now no longer any shadow of doubts as to where the Begynhof Church stood in matters of ecclesiastical government . . . Paget was able to retire with a tranquil mind."[62] Herring soon followed him in guarding the consistory's prerogative in the election of church officers.[63]

Herring was connected to earlier Elizabethan presbyterians. He received his BA from Sidney Sussex, Cambridge, in 1603 and before he began preaching at Calke is known to have preached in Coventry, where "he had special encouragements in the study of Divinity, from Master Humphrey Fen,"[64] whose firm presbyterianism is well documented in the preamble of his will. Herring's wife was Christian,[65] "the [third] daughter of the one-time minister to the English Church at Flushing,"[66] Edward Gellibrand, a presbyterian organizer of the Oxford classis, who ended his career in the Netherlands, as minister to the English Church in Middleburg. In his will he mentioned this daughter.[67] Although Herring would never return to England, he remained committed to the further reform of the Church of England, "begging fervently [in his prayers] that the Lordes and Commons in Parliament might be preserved from the two destructive Rocks of pride and self-interests . . . for the Nonconformists cause in England, and set up the Presbyterial Government according to the Scripture Rules." Furthermore, "[It] was no small offence unto him, to hear of the Letters which came from some Independents at London into Holland, wherein falsehoods were reported, to the reproach of some Presbyterians, his known godly Friends in England." When one of Herring's sons prepared to return to England, "he warned him to take heed of joining with any party, against the Presbyterial Government of the Reformed Churches: For I am sure (said he) it is the Government of Jesus Christ."[68]

If Herring's wife was of impeccable presbyterian lineage, he also found a suitable copastor with whom he labored for most of his ministry. Thomas Paget, brother to John, had been silenced along with Herring in the diocese of Chester before leaving to take part in the work at Amsterdam.[69] Paget was succeeded at Blackley Chapel in Lancashire by the later Westminster divine William Rathband, who inspired the Beswickes, whose descendants "were among the first to raise and support a presbyterian meeting-house in their native village."[70] The record of the consistory's search for an assistant pastor shows that there were other suitable candidates for the position. On October 7, 1639, it held "an extraordinarye meetinge to consult about choyce of a minister, upon the deputyes relation from the Lords of Libertye to inquyre for a fit pastor." The minutes continue, "[At] which metinge sundrye having bene named, the number was reduced to these 4: Doctor Jenison, of Newcastle upon Tyne, Mr Thomas Paget, of Blakely nere Manchester, Mr [Brinsley] nere

Yarmouth, & Mr Simeon Ash livinge with the Lo: Brooke in England."[71] Ashe participated in the "examination" of the New England way, along with Herring, Paget, and Ball. Elliot Vernon notes Ashe's connection to other ministers who were involved in writing that letter during his ministry in Staffordshire, including Arthur Hildersham, John Dod, John Ball, and Thomas Langley.[72] John Ball too came to his religious convictions at Cheshire, and it is possible that he first developed his concern for matters concerning church government there. Ball, together with Julines Herring, had avoided subscription by receiving ordination from an Irish bishop. Upon Herring's call to Amsterdam, it was Ball he especially missed, "adding withal, Master Ball hath conquered my passions." Then "upon the final salutation they comforted each other with this consideration, that though they should never see one another again on earth, yet they should meet in Heaven."[73]

Other ministers in the Cheshire area appear to have shared their ecclesiological concerns. An unidentified preacher in neighbouring Manchester by the name of Oliver Thomas was brought before the ecclesiastical commissioners for his direct assault on the Church of England's polity in the 1630s. He was found to be preaching that "all subordinate magistrates had their authority only from the Devil. And that he and you with others of that congregation had endured the yoke of them a good while but now you were in a fair way to be freed, or words to the same and life effect."[74] John Ley, born in Warwick, was a puritan from Cheshire who eventually developed anti-episcopal sentiments. Although initially open to a moderate from of episcopacy he nonetheless emerged as a leading presbyterian, president of Sion College, and member of the Westminster Assembly.[75] If puritanism in the north-west produced men like Ley who at least leaned toward presbyterianism, it also became the home of the presbyterian Richard Heyrick (1600–1667) of Merchant Taylor's school, St. John's College, Oxford, and later warden of Manchester collegiate church. Heyrick became a member of the Westminster Assembly and a leader of presbyterianism in Lancashire.[76] He was from a long line of Leicestershire Herricks, son of the goldsmith and Leicester MP Sir William Hericke. It is likely that he was kin to Robert Heyricke, who in 1586, with thirteen other Leicester men, sought to secure Travers as minister.[77] Thomas Case has a similar profile—also a pupil at Merchant Taylor's school, a student at St. John's, and later a presbyterian member of the Westminster Assembly.[78] Although Case was from Norfolk, and may, like John Ley, have been inclined to a moderate form of episcopacy, his early connection with presbyterian-minded men in the north-west is clear from his preaching itinerary. He was invited by Heyrick to preach in Manchester during the 1630s, where he was brought before the 1638–39 consistory court for having "delivered many dangerous and unsound doctrines and uttered many passages both privately in conscience and publicly in your sermons . . . manifesting your great dislike of the government and discipline established in this our Church of England."[79] Such a network of puritan ministers in the north west reveals the collaboration and collective development of men who may not have been convinced presbyterians in the 1630s but nonetheless operated in a way that could easily translate into a classis.

That it is possible to identify certain puritan clergy in Warwickshire as inclined toward presbyterianism in the early seventeenth century comes as no surprise given the influence there of Cartwright and Fen. A key source is the diary of Thomas Dugard, incumbent of Hartlebury, Worcester, who was linked to a cluster of puritans who later emerged as presbyterian divines in the Westminster Assembly: "[T]he diary reveals a quasi-Presbyterian clerical community and indeed, makes it not surprising that in the 1640s and 1650s, the clergy in Warwickshire, as elsewhere, accommodated themselves very easily and even welcomed a moderate Presbyterian established church."[80] The papers of Robert Smart, vicar of Preston Capes, Northamptonshire, who was deprived in 1605, reveal evidence of continued nonconformity.[81] There were others too who persisted such as Robert Cawdry, rector of South Luffenham, Rutland (1576) and vicar of Melton Mowbray. That Robert Cawdry's son, Daniel, also vicar of Melton Mowbray, was a presbyterian divine of the Westminster Assembly who later combated congregationalists further indicates the probability of presbyterian undercurrents in the puritanism of the midlands in the early seventeenth century, if not through a coherently organized force, at least through kinship and personal influence. These networks extended beyond Northamptonshire and even England. From the correspondence of Robert Paget it appears that he was in touch with Cawdry in 1661.[82] Herring had already established contact with ministers in Northampton and with Jeremiah Whitaker in particular before his departure for the Netherlands.[83]

The godly clergy in London of course constituted a central organizing force in mid-seventeenth-century English presbyterianism. William Gouge's godly lineage is well established. Theodore Herring acted as his assistant and was possibly a relative of Julines Herring.[84] It is also significant that Gouge was apprentice to Stephen Egerton, whose Elizabethan career included participation in presbyterian activity.[85] It is probable that Egerton, who was based in London and lived until 1622, exercised considerable influence on the London godly circle that later formed the presbyterian party in the assembly. This circle identified with earlier Elizabethan attempts for further reform: "[F]or the London ministers and the more zealous members of the laity a chance was seen to carry on the work of reform that had halted in Elizabeth's reign."[86]

There was undoubtedly ambiguity in the Smectymnuus tracts, traditionally regarded as the first presbyterian manifestos of the Westminster Assembly. Nonetheless, the Smectymnuus "approvingly quotes the confessions of the French and Dutch Presbyterian churches." Moreover the Smectymnuans, "Marshall, Calamy, Newcomen and Spurstow would, by 1644, become firm advocates of the divine warrant of Presbyterianism."[87]

In London there was another factor that contributed to the emergence of a second generation of English presbyterian ministers that was no less significant than its predecessor. Presbyterians argued strongly for collective judgment and jurisdiction through councils and synods as a means of suppressing heresy. The strategic significance of this argument for the mobilization of presbyterianism in the mid-seventeenth century (particularly in London) appears in the writings of the arch-presbyterian heresiographer, Thomas Edwards. In Edwards's *Antapologia*, "the crucial advantage of Presbyterian government was in countering 'those many errours, divisions, evils which fall out in your way . . . all men know 'tis better to prevent the plague and taking in poyson then to expell it; government is for prevention as well as recovering.'"[88] "In *Gangraena* also he claimed a consistent opposition to separatism and error: 'I preached against, and upon all occasions declared my self against the Brownists, Separatists, Antinomians and all Errors in that way, as well as against Popish Innovations and Arminian Tenets.'"[89] Regardless of the exaggerations apparent in Edwards's writings, the threat to orthodoxy perceived by the author and his audience had some basis in the reality of doctrinal developments that had already appeared prior to the public proliferation of radical sects in the mid-seventeenth century. The orthodoxy of puritan divinity had been put under threat not only by the rise of Arminianism among Caroline conformists but also by the existence of a radical puritan underground that contributed to doctrinal convulsions within it.[90]

There are a number of possible interpretations for the godly yen for sociability; it would be wrong to impose a single explanation. In addition to its attractions in response to official persecution, there was a need to resolve internal conflicts and disputes among the godly and respond to what they deemed heterodoxy. Peter Lake and David Como described the means by which the godly resolved theological disputes as the "self-righting, indeed, on some readings the pseudo-presbyterian, mechanisms of the godly community whereby the doctrinal probity and spiritual charisma of ordinary ministers of the word were invoked to end the dispute."[91] Divines such as Thomas Gataker and Samuel Ward clearly preferred to resolve contentions privately through informal arbitration that would ideally keep disagreements from erupting embarrassingly into public affairs.[92] Yet "the nature of the consensus appears to have been a good deal more unstable than previous accounts have led us to believe."[93] This was particularly acute in lay challenges to orthodoxy, as in Arthur Hildersham's response to the heretic Edward Wightman. After attempting to convince Wightman of his error "in private conference, in the presence of Master Aberly, the Minister of Burton," Hildersham then "took occasion in the next Exercise held at Burton . . . publiquely and at large to confute his error."[94] Conferences provided a crucial mechanism for dealing with heretical opinions when they had advanced beyond the level of personal admonition without having to resort to the formal jurisdiction of the Church of England.

Preoccupation with maintaining orthodoxy and active theological consultation with other clergy were obviously not signs of presbyterian activity in themselves. But in some instances they appear to have coincided with the development of presbyterianism before the summoning of the Long Parliament. Thomas Parker's hostility to heresy in the New England antinomian controversy in 1637 is one example: "Parker was militant enough that Wilson invited him twice to preach against antinomianism in Boston (and thus brave Vane's grilling after his sermons)."[95] Robert Jenison maintained close correspondence with Samuel Ward and through Ward with Thomas Gataker on the subject of predestination prior to his public confutation of Yeldard Alvey's Arminian teachings in 1631. Jenison's preoccupation with doctrinal threats from Catholicism to Arminianism in Newcastle during the 1620s and 1630s is apparent in his writings.[96] That the consistory of the English Reformed Church in Amsterdam had short-listed Jenison as a candidate for copastor by 1639 reveals that he was already approved and known for his reformed qualifications prior to his deprivation and departure from Newcastle.

Some presbyterians were concerned to stress church unity alongside their defense against heterodoxy. They spoke against heresy and schism, closely associating the one with the other, sometimes joining them together. John Paget believed that there was a link between separatism and heresy, claiming that "it is apparent that three or four hundred of the Brownists have brought forth more Apostate Anabaptists and Arians sometimes in one yeare then ten thousand members of the Reformed Dutch Church in this citie, have done in ten yeares or more."[97] Concern for maintaining orthodoxy and the unity of the Church appeared in Robert Jenison's sermons published in the 1620s and 1630s. He listed heresy and schism along with hypocrisy as the chief threats to religion: "Religion hath three enemies: Heretickes, Schismatickes, Hypocrites."[98] The threat of Roman Catholicism and Arminianism at the local level preoccupied him; these concerns may have contributed to the development of his presbyterian view and career as a presbyterian minister in Newcastle during the mid-seventeenth century.[99] While Jenison's name appears among nominees for the position of copastor in the Amsterdam English Reformed Church, the name of the fourth short-listed candidate is omitted. The most likely suspect "nere Yarmouth" is John Brinsley, who began his preaching career there in 1625 and continued to preach in the area throughout the 1630s despite royal displeasure at his nonconformity. It would not be surprising to find this famous lecturer mentioned in the Amsterdam English Reformed Church's minutes in 1639, given his staunch presbyterianism in the 1640s. Brinsley's writings were also swiftly put into print in the 1640s, commissioned by parliament. Both heresy and schism are common themes in his writing.[100] If diverse networks and persecution by authorities were important factors in uniting the godly, certain ministers also argued for ecclesiastical unity and stressed the need for maintaining orthodoxy in the face of heresy in the early seventeenth century.

LAY PATRONAGE AND INSTITUTION

Clerical collegiality helps to identify the strength of ministerial connections that reinforce the continuity between the Tudor and the early Stuart godly communities. It reveals varying networks of likeminded ministers and the links that played a crucial role in their spiritual experiences and in the development of their theological views. But an examination of godly bonds would be incomplete without taking into account wider networks that included patronage and lay participation in nonconformist activity. If presbyterians stressed public institution in defending clerical vocation, they also turned to institutional support for reinforcement in the face of persecution from the authorities. This involved support beyond the particular congregation that did not necessarily involve presbyterian government, but could easily translate into a compatible means of coercion against the wishes of the membership of a particular congregation in the face of local conflict.

Just as the English churches in the Netherlands had turned to the Dutch for economic help, so those in England depended on financial support from godly laity outside their own particular parish. Patrick Collinson has described how "puritans had mechanisms, in their lectures, fasts and communions for reaching into their pockets on behalf of total strangers. This was a kind of informal Presbyterianism in voluntary action . . . to relieve not only the poor of the parish but 'other churches in their afflictions and wants.'"[101]

Another form of informal presbyterianism can be observed in the placing of presbyterian preachers through town and borough lectureships. The role of the laity in this extended beyond the initial appointment. Corporation lectureships were well suited not only to protecting preachers from ecclesiastical authorities but also to supporting them in the face of local controversy. That such lectureships were perceived as part of a national presbyterian plot to subvert the English establishment is a tribute to the machinations of anti-puritan propagandists who made the relationship between the two explicit. But could organized lay puritan cells potentially be used to convert the existing government to a presbyterian church? According to Peter Heylyn, lectureships were

> borrowed by Travers and the rest, towards the latter end of Queen Elizabeth's reign, from the new fashions of Geneva; the lecturer being super-added to the parson, or vicar, as the doctor was unto the pastor in some foreign churches . . . to advance a faction, and to alienate the people's minds from the government and forms of worship here by law established.[102]

Lectureships were in fact a long established means of meeting lay demands for supplementary preaching. When Samuel Clarke advised the Northampton corporation in 1638 that "the Thursday lecture and sermons on Sunday in the afternoon should be forborne in these infectious times," he commented that "they then raised a report of me that I was about to starve their souls."[103] Just as Richard Fletcher in 1575 had identified "Cranbrooke clothiers" as "some of [the puritans'] artificers and pragmaticall prentices,"[104] so John Shaw as late as 1633 described how it [had been] a custom for the merchants and other tradesmen that lived in London, so many of them as were all born in the same county, to meet at a solemn feast . . . together in London, and there to consult what good they might do to their native county by settling some ministers (or some other good work) in that county."[105] The religious motivation for lay patronage through lectureships cannot be overlooked; for example that of the puritan gentry, "whose support for the cause needs no other explanation than their godliness.[106]

That apart, kinship and other relationships were important in building solidarity and trust within godly communities. The presbyterian Robert Jenison, who had lectured at All Saints in Newcastle for twenty years, "had strong local connections with some of the powerful families of the area, being the younger son of a prominent townsman."[107] Both his father and uncle had served as mayor and sheriff in the late sixteenth century, and Jenison's uncle, who was elected mayor in the early seventeenth century, ultimately became a strong patron of nonconformist activity as Sir John Marley reported to the dean of Durham:

> [It] is reported Dr. Jenison is coming home, but that is not great matter, he may be looked to; but what is worse, there is an intention to make Robert [Beckwith] mayor at Michaelmas next, who is the doctor's half brother and strong for that faction, and I am sure most who know him think him good for little else.[108]

Jenison's uncle, Robert Beckwith, was indeed a strong supporter of puritanism in Newcastle. The wealthy merchant John Fenwick was apprenticed to him in 1612 and publicly expressed sympathies for presbyterianism, even more so than Jenison himself, by the late 1630s.[109]

The Haberdashers' Company was notable for its success in securing puritan preachers in the first four decades of the seventeenth century; its activities were influenced by such Elizabethan luminaries as the Culverwells and Charkes who had been involved in presbyterian activities. The advowson to St. Alkmond's Shrewsbury, where Herring lectured before leaving for the Netherlands, was conveyed to the Feoffees for Impropriations. Closely involved in St. Alkmond's was the "powerful Drapers' Company of Shrewsbury, who leased their splendid Hall . . . at 4 pounds a year" to Herring.[110] Herring's uncle was a member of the company and a bailiff in 1580.[111] The activity of the feoffees in Charles's reign highlights the strategic alliance between the ministers, merchants, and lawyers who composed that body. Wilfred Prest mentions the intersection between the Inns of Court and London merchants during this period where "many lawyers . . . intermarried with London mercantile families,"[112] as did presbyterian-inclined ministers: John Brinsley married the daughter of Edward Owner, "MP for Yarmouth and a leading member of its oligarchy of puritan merchants";[113] Thomas Case's second marriage to Ann, "daughter of Oswald Mosley of Manchester, and widow of Robert Booth of Salford brought him into the heart of the lay puritan elite in the north-west";[114] George Hughes, who became the chief presbyterian minister in Exeter during the mid-seventeenth century, married the daughter of "a former sheriff of Coventry, whose family name was Packstone."[115]

The authorities were less concerned with relationships that bound lay and clerical nonconformists together than with those between puritan ringleaders in London and local officials in towns and boroughs.[116] The trial of the feoffees had allegedly uncovered a calculated plot to secure subversive ministers all over the country, in which, according to the authorities, market towns had been specifically targeted. William "Gouge's son and biographer admitted that the Feoffees concentrated on cities and market towns."[117] The geographic pattern was certainly significant. "The accusation that the Puritans concentrated their propaganda efforts on populous towns goes back at least to 1584," or in Patrick Collinson's example to 1575, and as Christopher Hill commented, "[T]he possible effect on the return of M.P.s was certainly a curious coincidence."[118] Nonconformists mobilized networks that had long been established between commercial centers in England and radical reform movements in the late sixteenth and early seventeenth centuries. In addition to self-sufficiency, the religious influence of London, strengthened by a strong economic relationship through trade, contributed to the growth of puritanism in north-west and East Anglian market towns.[119] In describing the development of puritanism in Newcastle, Roger Howell similarly observed that it "had, by its extensive trade, particularly in coal, more contact with London and the South of England and with the Continent than any other town in the North."[120]

The close communication between Antwerp and England, exemplified by the Merchant Adventurer church in the late sixteenth century, and that between ministers in Amsterdam and in England during the early seventeenth century, was echoed by links among the laity. Thus "trade to Amsterdam and the Baltic areas brought Newcastle merchants into contact with the Reformed churches there."[121] One of the reasons for the authorities' protests against Brinsley's appointment in Yarmouth was that "diverse of that town have continual intercourse with those of Amsterdam, and sundry schismatical books have thither been imported."[122] Wealthy merchants were not the only laymen with contacts in Amsterdam. In 1626 the widow Anne Bramsonne transferred her membership from the parish of Saint Giles without Cripplegate in London to the Amsterdam English Reformed Church where "somme her especiall good ffrends nowe resident and dwelling there."[123] One pauper heard of the deacons' distributions in the Amsterdam English Reformed Church and traveled to Amsterdam, only to be rejected and sent back to England.[124]

The informal association of the godly worried anti-puritan activists less than organization through institutions that could do more to undermine the authority of the Church of England. This is seen in the central charge against the feoffees: they acted as a corporation without being legally incorporated.[125] Indeed, the feoffees' endowment was not used simply to position puritanism strategically; they further used their shares to displace ministers of whom they disapproved, and even "occasionally went farther and paid a stubborn incumbent to surrender his place."[126] The Haberdashers were prepared to use coercion to place their appointed ministers and support them in the face of hostility from ecclesiastical authorities, and thus incurred the wrath of the king, who, referring to their appointment of puritan ministers to Bunbury, said he would not "endure that anie lay persons, much lesse a corporation, have power to place and displace curates or beneficed priests at their pleasur."[127] Despite displeasure of bishops and king, Haberdasher's was able to protect its preachers according to the statutes of Thomas Aldersey, who had purchased the advowson of Bunbury from Elizabeth:[128] "[It] was precisely this entire dependence on the laity that made the lectureships so thoroughly objectionable."[129]

But the authority of the Haberdasher's is highlighted to a greater extent in other instances, where conflict arose over the nomination of a minister. Such was the case when the company appointed the presbyterian Laurence Potts of the Merchant Adventurer Church in Middelburg to the lectureship at Newland in 1615. Laurence Potts was the brother of Thomas, who had been John Paget's first copastor at the English Reformed Church in Amsterdam, and was also a native of Cheshire. What is the more surprising than the appointment of this English presbyterian minister to Newland, where there was a strong anti-puritan faction, is the Haberdashers' success in keeping him there for the rest of his life (he died in 1627).[130] This was achieved despite opposition from certain members who believed that they were entitled to choose the lecturer, and proceeded to make several unsuccessful attempts to eject Potts. The conflict between nomination by the Haberdashers and approval by church members raises the question of the delicate balance between the judgment of ruling elders and the consent of the Church's membership according to the presbyterian model. Support from the classis when members of his congregation expressed their opposition to him proved to be vital to John Paget's lengthy ministry in Amsterdam: "At every step during the Paget years, the English church relied on the Dutch Reformed Church and the magistrates for guidance; Paget depended on this broader institutional support."[131] The clash between Thomas Potts and the Newland membership quite strikingly demonstrates that, in the face of conflict, the godly laity was prepared to override the wishes of a particular congregation.

The godly laity of Newcastle (which included Jenison's half-brother) reacted similarly when Jenison was deprived. Although he eventually left Newcastle, "the Puritans succeeded in forcing out the other loyal lecturer, Thomas Stephenson, and installing a Puritan temporarily in his place."[132] Yarmouth townsmen were not successful in asserting their legal right over the appointment of their lecturer when the king "barred Brinsley from preaching in Yarmouth . . . and imprisoned four of the puritan aldermen." Nonetheless, "despite these restrictions Brinsley continued to minister to the townsmen, with large numbers travelling to Lound to hear him preach."[133]

The corporation in Exeter interceded on behalf of their lecturer in the early seventeenth century. In the controversy between the local incumbent and the corporation's lecturer, "the magistrates damped the fires of internal faction while Lord Zouch blocked a suit in the Star Chamber brought by the disappointed Whitaker against Warren and his supporters in the town."[134] The corporation in Plymouth was less successful in securing their lecturer, when the king and Laud "not only blocked the election of the corporation's nominee but decreed that the corporation's next choice would be Thomas Bedford." Nonetheless, "the corporation had its revenge in 1642 and 1643, when Wilson and Bedford were removed and George Hughes, one of the leading Presbyterians in the West, was elected both vicar and lecturer."[135] Example of lay intervention can also be found in the late sixteenth century when a dispute between two lecturers erupted in Ipswich. This involved the senior lecturer Dr. Norton and none other than the presbyterian William Negus, who would subsequently defy the Dedham classis in his decision to leave his position for a better living. In this instance, Negus had the support of the council, which intervened and "ordered Norton to leave in April."[136] Negus's successor was the presbyterian Robert Wright, who like Travers had been ordained at the Merchant Adventurer Church in Antwerp. The council controlled this lectureship through the stipulation that Wright arrange for a substitute in his absences and that he not "take any other pastoral or ecclesiastical promotion without the consents of the Bailiffs for the time being."[137]

Town councils and livery companies were obviously not committed to any overt presbyterian agenda. The Haberdashers appointed a range of puritan ministers and some who wore more conformist colors. Even during the Middle Ages the company had similarly "acted as a trustee to fulfill the pious wishes of its former members, in managing the resources they left to provide intercessory masses for the benefit of their souls."[138] But such examples are nevertheless illustrative of how presbyterian-minded ministers could be employed through such bodies and continue to exercise an influence in the early seventeenth century. They also clearly reveal the central role that the laity played in securing reformed preachers, and how lay involvement did not inevitably lead to independency. Lay patronage of nonconformist ministers was capable of presbyterian inflections in the face of conflict, not only by asserting autonomy from the hierarchy of the Church of England but also by overriding the wishes of a local membership. The economic grip that the laity enjoyed in the early seventeenth century meant that in certain instances they were even more successful in asserting their authority than the Dedham ministers had been in the 1580s.

If the relationship between presbyterian ministers, merchants, and magistrates was not simply an incestuous one, their alliance might also be understood through their complicity in the formal mechanisms for establishing order in a local and national context, whether through charitable acts to relieve the deserving poor or through the prosecution of misbehavior and criminal acts. The exercise of authority beyond a particular locality was not a foreign concept in the late sixteenth and early seventeenth centuries. The expansion of the market in the late sixteenth century extended transactions and networks "in increasingly lengthy chains of obligation" that pushed economic activity beyond the local and face-to-face context and contributed to increased levels of litigation. Both the ubiquity of the law throughout the country and the role of city officials were essential in the process of regulating trade and resolving disputes.[139] A closely regulated system of trade could help to prevent disputes, as demonstrated by the role of the marketplace as "open and expressly public places where buying and selling could be regulated within set hours, where public weights could be used, and where attempts could be made to deal with market offences."[140]

It is possible to identify overlaps between lay and clerical commitment to such regulation in the language that they used to describe officers appointed for moral and commercial oversight.[141] A manuscript treatise in the Huntington Library, written by the Merchant Adventurers around 1588 (just after the presbyterian ministry of Dudley Fenner, who had succeeded Cartwright and Travers), demonstrates the same preoccupation with orderliness as manifested by the presbyterians. The presbyterians' appellation of lay elders as overseers is echoed in the merchants' discussion of the regulation of customs at "the porte of London . . . appointed shipps have their *overseers*, whome they call Appointers, and other officers to take view of their packs . . . and other parcels."[142] Like the lay elder whose role concerned the regulation of life and manners, these officers were also responsible for keeping moral discipline and order, whereby "the maister as his factor and other servants and dependants within dew order by their good government, Religious exercise and strict discipline, to which end they have their governor, Assistents, preachers, and other officers beyhond the seas, whereby disorder and licentiousness . . . is restreyned and mett withal."[143] The language used to describe civil magistrates could likewise echo that of presbyterians when referring to their church officers. For Robert Jenison, civil magistrates were "Ministers of God." If JPs were described as "the eyes" of justice, so too were lay elders "the eyes" of the congregation according to presbyterian writers such as Matthew Holmes and Walter Travers.[144]

This language reflected more than an overlap in terminology, since commercial, ecclesiastical, and judicial responsibility could be closely intertwined. The Merchant Adventurers described overseers who were not simply commercial invigilators, but were also responsible for the regulation of life and manners. Lectureships were neither simply pious acts of charity nor were they simply mechanisms for asserting authority through a series of power struggles between members of a local parish and against the king's deprivation of presbyterian preachers. Insofar as the lectureships secured preaching that in turn was supposed to induce piety, they were a moral investment. And if civic and religious interests were brought together through such investment, so were ministers and magistrates who each played key roles in establishing a godly society. So what of the alliance between ministers and magistrates that was evident, for example, in the presbyterians' criticism of episcopal shortcomings? When Jenison referred to civil magistrates as "Ministers of God" in 1620, he was envisioning that they would work alongside ministers of the Word.[145] It was up to civil magistrates to "draw out the sword of iustice against Seducers," while "Gods Ministers [contributed] . . . by teaching, and as the Lords dogs and housekeepers by barking tell you of the approach of enemies."[146] This was in the hope of protecting both local and national interest from God's judgment "not onely in whole Kingdomes and States, but also in particular Cities, Townes and Corporations."[147]

An extensive survey of the relationship between ministers, magistrates, and merchants has not been required to demonstrate that lay alliances with godly clergy were not necessarily predisposed to independency. Far from being individual clerics detached from each other and from the laity during this period, presbyterians operated within wider networks of association that were not always propinquitous. They extended beyond local communities for economic, administrative, and theological support, not only through Cambridge and Oxford colleges and because of the need for sociability. Such networks were facilitated by the activity of English presbyterians at the very heart of commercial centers during their Golden Ages: Antwerp in the late sixteenth century, Amsterdam in the early seventeenth century, and by the mid-seventeenth century the presbyterians had established a headquarters in London. In the early seventeenth century networks that extended throughout England were particularly dense in Cheshire, and many of those who were to emerge as presbyterian advocates preached in Manchester, "the very London of those parts."[148] This reveals an opposing strain within high Calvinism that coincided with the rise of commercial leaders in England. It did not revolve around individualistic interest and fixation upon proving elect status, but rather a corporate spirit united in public institution and committed to a highly regulated system of invigilation.

CHAPTER 7

Popular Presbyterianism

PRESBYTERIANISM AND THE POOR?

Predicated on the active participation of the laity, presbyterianism relied on the cooperation of church members no less than on the voluntary initiative of elders for moral surveillance and disciplinary control.[1] However, the precise role of the membership in reformed discipline has attracted less attention than that of lay leaders. Indeed, church members often appear as passive recipients of a moral reform imposed by an elite group of church officers.[2] What can be said of the poorest members in the exercise of reformed discipline? Did they simply appear as objects of discipline? Or did they themselves engage as agents and initiators in moral reform?

There was of course a polemical purpose for presbyterians in specifically identifying with respectable citizens. On the one hand it countered accusations of popular anarchy. On the other it targeted popular culture and plebian immorality as a critique of episcopacy.[3] However, polemical contexts in which presbyterians were particularly concerned to retain respectability cannot be taken as a straightforward indication of the nature of popular participation in presbyterianism. Root and Branch petitioners in London deliberately used higher ranking members dressed in their most impressive apparel to discount conformist allegations that their main support came from men and women of lower social status.[4] In printed polemic, "Presbyterian authors such as Hall and Edwards constructed their relationship to the 'popular' in contradictory ways, depending on the rhetorical context of particular passages."[5]

While it was in their interest to present themselves to parliament as composed of the better sort, in other contexts English presbyterians addressed themselves to a wider popular audience. The presbyterian propagandist Thomas Edwards's "lecturing and publishing in the 1640s is only explicable as part of a dynamic campaign for broad public support, a campaign he felt he had some chance of winning,"[6] while the presbyterian Thomas Hall "claimed that he was writing for a broad, even poor readership."[7] At times John Paget also used radical social rhetoric. He claimed that presbyterian government was specifically designed to function on behalf of the poor "for under the Law the poore being oppressed in judgement by unrighteous Iudges in one place, they cryed for help by appealing unto a superiour Synhedrion, and there found releafe, and so were redeemed from deceit & violence."[8] He also denied partiality in the administration of discipline in his own personal ministry, claiming that "according to my power, I have laboured that the censures might be executed in due maner, for discouragement, not of the godly, but of the ungodly and offendours; and as well against the richer as the poorer sort, without acception of persons."[9] It is interesting that Paget claimed to have laboured not only among the poor within the English Reformed Church but also those outside it:

> For the visitation of the sick . . . according to my power and above my power, both to rich & poore, to English and Dutch, to the members of the Church, and to them that are no members of the Church, to such as were diseased in body, and to such as have bene afflicted in minde . . . I have not refused to visit many visited with the Pest, to comfort them in the time of their anguish: Yea in the most infectious places, as where in one poore family, the floore hath bene covered with death, some persons being already dead of the plague, and some ready to give up the ghost, lying so thicke on the ground, that I could scarsely set my foote beside them, being six of them in one small roome, 3 dead, and 3 dying upon their pallets; yet have I with cheerefulnes and comfort gone among them, to exhort them, to pray with them, and to minister the consolations of Christ unto them as need required.[10]

Travers's undated translation of Chrysostom's sermons on the parable of the rich man and Lazarus warned of prejudice against the poor, teaching that "neither is he a rich man, who is furnished with many things, but he which hath no need of so many things: neither is he a poore man, which possesseth nothing. . . . For we ought to iudge of poverty & wealth by the purpose & resolution of the mind, & not by the measure of a mans substance."[11] So far this would accord with traditional accounts of protestant relief of the poor, which involved the distribution of alms to the respectable and deserving poor after close scrutiny of their moral character.[12] However, there were varying levels of emphasis on discrimination and even arguments for indiscriminate charity: "Well into the 1630s, furthermore, we find even the 'hotter sort of Protestants' arguing that charity should be given indiscriminately."[13] Travers's translation can be counted among the works that advocated indiscriminate relief of the poor through private charity.[14] For "it is a robbery of the poore, not to relieve their necessity" and those with substance were therfore obli-

gated to provide "hospitality & relieving of all such as are in necessity." This
point in the introduction was rephrased by Travers, who edited his sentence
to make the indiscriminate relief of the poor even clearer. He crossed out the
word "necessity" and inserted a statement that described obligation to even
the ungodly, completing the sentence with: "all such as are in need euen
though they be wicked because of their necessitee."[15] The sermon went on
further to instruct people to give "not inquiring diligently into him that hath
neede. For the necessity onely of the poore man, is worthy of releefe. And if
any man at any time come to us with this necessity, let us not be curious to
know any more. For we doe not give to the manners, but to the man, neither
doe we shew mercy to him for his vertue, but for his calamity."[16]

Presbyterian attitudes toward the poor can hardly be measured simply
through Paget's defensive self-appraisal of his personal charity or Travers's
translation of Chrysostom's sermons, which held a devotional value no less
significant than a message which for a puritan might strike us as socially radical. As Andy Wood has put it, "Beyond the populist discourse of the Level-
ler movement lay the grim reality of parish politics in the mid-seventeenth
century," which the "rhetoric of urban radicals, however impassioned, was insufficient to bridge."[17] Patrick Collinson has similarly cautioned against overlooking the distinction between principles expounded in "religious courtesy
books" and actual practice.[18]

How might the actual role of the poor be discerned? The best work on
the social profile of puritan communities has appeared in detailed microhis-
tories,[19] and for presbyterianism and the poor, the English Reformed Church
in Amsterdam can provide a useful case study. The church's detailed records,
which cover the years 1607 to 1640, provide a point of entry into the nature
of popular participation among a diverse membership composed of both men
and women, rich and poor. While confirming the central role of the elite in
the leadership of the Church, it challenges the view that there was little room
for voluntary participation in presbyterian government by the laboring and
poorer members. Like the various institutions that offered support for the
London poor, the English Reformed Church in Amsterdam functioned as a
public institution that distributed alms and redressed the grievances of the
poor.[20] As a diverse range of humble men and women were incorporated into
membership, they made a considerable contribution to the discipline of the
Church through their active participation as witnesses and as initiators of
disciplinary cases. In examining practices within English presbyterianism in
the Netherlands there is no suggestion of direct translation into presbyterian
experiences in England. Rather, the flexibility within the English presbyterian
community is being tested and the extent to which such a community could

(and in this case did) incorporate a broad social range. What is revealed is that English presbyterianism could encompass a wider social range than hitherto realized. This was not simply a rhetoric that promised social benefits, but active participation by the poor, by members of lowest social rank.

PRESBYTERIAN "PROMISCUITY"

That congregationalists objected to the presbyterians' broad or "promiscuous" practices with regard to infant baptism and admission to membership raises the question of whether English presbyterians actually did admit a wide range of members. Did membership extend so far as to include radical separatists? Paget's moderation in accepting former separatists into membership and the Reformed Church's less stringent requirements may have encouraged the transfer of membership from the separatist to the reformed church.[21] If the presbyterians stressed the need for a general allegiance to the Church of England, they neither insisted on an explicit acceptance of its set liturgy nor did they require a separate covenant for admission to membership. Although a trajectory of increasing radicalism is often charted in nonconformist studies through separatist conversion stories, John Paget's antiseparatist propaganda was actually successful in converting some English separatists in Amsterdam to his presbyterian congregation.[22] When the English Reformed Church in Amsterdam was established it was with the clear intention of converting English separatists at the Ancient church to the reformed church. There had indeed already been some movement from the separatist to the Dutch reformed church before the English Church was set up.[23] In the course of his long ministry, Paget attacked the separatist church when it was in a particularly vulnerable state as a result of internal tensions and other conditions.[24] Under such circumstances "waverers and compromisers" at the Ancient church could be persuaded to the English Reformed Church;[25] during this period "Paget's anti-Separatist work was remarkably successful, so much so that few Englishmen were dropping away to Separatism and some of those already in Separatism were won back."[26]

It has been argued that the "English Reformed Church's broader practice of infant baptism attracted members of the Ancient Church."[27] This is supported by examples of members of the Ancient church who became members shortly after having their children baptized in the English Reformed Church.[28] Thus the baptism of infants whose parents were not already members of the English Church appears to have contributed to its growth. Between 1607 and 1640 more than two hundred baptisms of the children of nonmembers took place. More than thirty of the heads of households involved became members in the year of the first recorded baptism of one of their children, and between

1617 and 1638 twenty-six heads of households became members at least a year after a first recorded baptism. In some of these cases the mother had been a member prior to the first baptism. Whether or not the practice of a more open baptism expanded the membership of the English Reformed Church, there is a clear indication in the first several decades of the seventeenth century of a commitment to infant baptism by those families who felt it necessary to have their children baptized before becoming members themselves.

According to Carter, separatists who began to join the English Reformed Church because of its lower threshold included "such pillars of the Ancient Church as Samuel Whittaker and his wife Deliverance, daughter of Robert Penry."[29] In 1621 the acceptance of former separatists into the English Reformed Church was made solely based on their admission that the Church of England was a true church:

> We whose names are underwritten do acknolwedg that we hav here to fore gone astray in that separation which we have made from the church of england, and are sorry for the offence that we have given thereby; we do now hould the same to be a true church of christ, purposing also, as occasion shalbe given, to communicate therwith in the publick worship of god: and for the present our desir is to be admitted for members of this reformed english church, whereto we do now offer in respect of any differences formerly professed by us, purposing to rest in peace, and by all good means to seeke the edification thereof.[30]

Overall, at least forty separatists joined the English Reformed Church between the years 1607 and 1640, of which fifteen joined in August 1521.[31] However, while former separatists constituted an important and active group, less than 5 percent of the total membership of the English Church could be identified as having come from the Ancient church. This highlights the significance of their involvement while also focusing attention on those in the community who had not migrated from separatism.

MEMBERSHIP IN THE AMSTERDAM ENGLISH REFORMED CHURCH

If one intention in the foundation of the Amsterdam English Reformed Church was "to undercut the Separatists," another was "to provide spiritual benefit for a friendly and economically important immigrant people."[32] "[B]esides the civic and ecclesiastical authorities in Amsterdam, the leading English merchants, few of whom were to be found among the separatists, were also in favor of a Church of their own nationality, even, or perhaps especially, though it was to be Calvinist and not Episcopal in organisation."[33] At least three of the merchants who participated in the search for the first minister were among the first officers of the Church.[34] Merchants and others of high status continued to play an active role in the leadership of the Church as elders and deacons,[35] as is to be expected in light of known lay alliances between presbyterian ministers and city elites. However, it would be rash to conclude that the English presbyterian community consisted of an alliance between wealthy citizens and presbyterian clerics to the exclusion of men and women of lower social status, without a close examination of the profile of the Amsterdam English Reformed Church.

Between 1607 and 1640 more than 900 members appear in the consistory records of the English Reformed Church, though there were undoubtedly some who did not appear.[36] It is possible to divide almost 700 of these into a hierarchy of high-, intermediate-, and low-status occupations (more than eighty were identified) or wealth categories by using information from the records.[37] The occupational groupings used do not provide a precise guide to the status of Englishmen in Amsterdam during the early seventeenth century. Since criteria other than occupational information have also been used to categorize individuals, not all those following the same occupation will be placed in the same category. However, in almost all cases where additional information could be found, social status confirmed the hierarchy of occupations.[38]

Members of higher status consisted primarily of merchant families—a total of fifty-eight members inclusive of dependants. Clergy and their dependants followed, twenty-eight altogether. Goldsmiths also fell into this category, along with professionals such as surgeons, the public notary, and the scholar, since such persons were grouped with other wealthy citizens by Amsterdam officials during this period.[39] The consistory records also revealed the wealth of several members through their substantial charitable donations and their home addresses on Warmoesstraat.[40] A further few individuals were placed in this category because they paid the 200 penning tax collected from those members whose immovable property amounted to more than 1,000 guilders in 1632.[41]

Low-status members were usually weavers, seventy-five of whom, with their dependants, were members, as were twenty-three laborers and a smaller number of glovers and sawyers. These four occupations correspond to the low-status clusters identified in the occupational hierarchies of London during the early seventeenth century.[42] A number of button-makers, dyers, and card-makers also came into this category (almost all of whom worked as servants, received alms, or identified themselves as poor), together with uppermen whose work as assistants to bricklayers placed them below the intermediate status. At least some members of each of these groups can be shown to have either received alms or also worked as servants, a further confirmation of their low status. Masons and millers (nine in all) may also be placed in this group, as they consistently appear in the lower occupational ranks in Brodsky Elliott's study.[43] Eight more servants, not already accounted for, complete the total of 316 members of low status.

Evidence of receipt of alms prior to and in the years 1640 and 1641 confirms "poor" status. Fourteen members can be identified as in receipt of alms prior to 1640 through references in the consistory minutes. The only surviving alms lists (for 1640 and 1641) reveal that an additional sixty-seven members including dependants, not already categorized as lower-status group by occupation, received provision from the Church. The use of alms lists for 1640–41 to identify the poor can be legitimately challenged, since poverty was not a permanent state: "[P]eople moved into and out of poverty in the course of a life-time."[44] Yet the list appears to be an accurate indication of status for most of the people on it, since within a decade of receipt of alms at least forty-two individuals found it in their interest to come fully under the care of the Church by becoming members. The alms list is particularly helpful in identifying status, since occupational detail is frequently omitted from the consistory records from the late 1630s, and consequently during those years more members fall into the unknown status category than in previous years.[45]

Most members of the Church (sixty-four of the eighty occupations) fall into the intermediate-status category. Although, inevitably, analysis tends to highlight comparison between high- and low-status occupational groups, this is not to suggest the insignificance of those who fell in between: the work of Paul Seaver and Peter Lake has shown that turners and boxmakers of London such as Nehemiah Wallington and John Etherington played an active role in the world of puritan politics and theological development.[46] That Wallington himself eventually became an elder of the London presbyterian classis in the mid-seventeenth century reinforces the significance of middling artisans in the early-modern English presbyterian community. However, because vivid examples of middling artisans involved in the London puritan scene are already known, the participation of poorer men and women is of particular interest if the social range of the godly community is to be fully tested. Members of intermediate-status occupations do not feature in this analysis because they are less precisely defined and necessarily over-represented. All occupations that may have ranged between status groups were placed into intermediate status unless clear indication of high or low status could be found. Although some members who belong to higher- and lower-status groups are therefore absorbed into the intermediate-status group and under-represented in the figures that follow, this method was used in order to ensure that those who were placed into higher- and lower-status groups could be identified with some certainty. Given the conservative figures used for high- and low-status members, the findings are particularly illuminating.

TABLE 1
Membership Profile (ERCA, 1607–40)

	High status	Intermediary status	Low status	Unknown status	Total
Men	83 (15%)	146 (27%)	198 (37%)	112 (20%)	539 (59%)
Women	43 (12%)	66 (18%)	118 (32%)	143 (39%)	370 (41%)
TOTAL	126 (14%)	212 (23%)	316 (35%)	255 (28%)	909
Officers and family members	33 (43%)	8 (11%)	20 (26%)	15 (20%)	76
Former separatists	11 (28%)	3 (8%)	15 (38%)	11 (28%)	40

Of the membership of the English Reformed Church, the status of approximately 28 percent could not be determined, a high proportion of them women. Given the nature of the records, which included occupational detail but rarely included information on other sources of maintenance, this was predictable. Overall, women constituted 41 percent [370] of the membership. Members of high status were the smallest percentage, at 14 percent [126], a conservative figure; 23 percent [212] were of in intermediate status, almost 10 percent more men than women. Figures for intermediate status are perhaps smaller than might have been expected, given that some members of higher and lower status are likely to have been included in it. A striking result emerges. Contrary to expectation that the demands of presbyterian discipline were too rigorous for laborers and others with less leisure to devote to religious observance, there was in fact room for the less learned and poor within the English Reformed Church in Amsterdam: at least 35 percent (316) of the membership, more than three hundred men and women, were of the lowest social ranks. It might be the case that the high proportion of poorer and low status members is due to the survival of the 1640 alms list, which facilitates the identification of more of the poorer members than those in other status categories. Yet lower-status men and women would still constitute the bulk of the membership even if those who received alms were discounted from the analysis. Furthermore, even if the status of those in the unknown group were to be disclosed, members of the lowest-status group would nonetheless constitute a considerable proportion of the membership.

A large number of lower-status and poorer members joined the Church following the first baptism of a child. However, since there was considerable range in status among members who joined at this point, there was not necessarily any material motivation. Nonetheless, it is possible to entertain this as one explanation for some of the poor, since the Church distributed alms

TABLE 2

Number of Baptisms (ERCA)

High status	Intermediary status	Low status	Unknown status	Total
100 (16%)	190 (31%)	196 (32%)	135 (22%)	621

that could certainly act as an incentive for a pauper who faced the demands of providing for a growing family. At least 44 percent of those who either became members in the same year or following the first baptism of a child in the English Reformed Church were in the lowest social category. Six of the twenty-four fathers who became members in the same year of their first child's baptism were weavers. Distribution of alms thus probably contributed to the growth of the Church among poorer members. In April 1633 "Cuthbert Rocksbey and his wiffe haueing desyred to be members of this church, being demanded the cause why he came out of England acknowledged that the paresh where he liued allowed him but 6 pence a weeke which he saith could not helpe but littell for the defraying of his charge."[47] In the years 1640 and 1641 a total of seventy-three members, nearly 20 percent of the entire membership, received alms.

Of course, not all members of low status received provision from the Church. Assessment of poorer members is complicated by the fact that lists of the deacons' distribution exist only for the years 1640 and 1641. The omission of occupational detail in the consistory records beginning in the late 1630s has resulted in a larger number of members whose status is unknown by 1640; however, at least forty-two members who can be identified as within the lower-status group in 1640 do not appear on the alms list for that year. Unfortunately for Cuthbert Rocksbey, the English Reformed Church was not inclined to accept poor members simply on account of their need for charity. When Rocksbey unashamedly explained his reason for seeking membership, he was turned away by the consistory and "admonished to macke his returne againe into his owne contrii."[48]

How did such a large population of poor members gain admission into the English Reformed Church, and what exactly was their role in the growth in membership of the Church? Instead of instituting church covenants that bound new members to the Church through a set of agreements, the English Reformed Church relied on testimonials to vouch for the "good conversation" of individuals seeking membership. Consistory records indicate that nearly 100 members entered into membership upon a testimonial letter from another church. Of these it is possible to identify the occupation or status of approximately sixty-seven. At least fifteen testimonial letters were presented by merchants and other wealthy members, which came mostly from within the Netherlands, including Delft, Utrecht, Middelburg, and Harlem.[49] Twenty-four testimonials were in behalf of members with apparent intermediate status,[50] but the largest number was in behalf of those of lower identifiable status. At least twenty-seven of the sixty-seven testimonials of known status were presented by poorer members, which is almost twice the number of testimonials presented by those of identifiable high status. Poorer members migrated from within the Netherlands, from Utrecht, Brill, Leiden, Delft, Dort, and Flushing. Some also brought testimonials from a wide range of parishes within England, including a weaver from Colchester, a mason from Sussex, an upperman from Southwark, and a chain-maker who received alms from the Church and came from Warwick. Two servants also came from London, which was undoubtedly the origin of most members who migrated directly from England.[51] All but one of the London testimonials dated from 1624 onward reveal that some of these members would have experienced the religious turbulence in London resulting from Laudian policies prior to their departure. While the motivations for English migration to Amsterdam are not entirely clear, what is evident from the membership testimonials is that the poor did not automatically gain admittance and access to the benefits of the Church when they found that they had an extra mouth to feed or when they faced financial insecurity.[52] If Paget's and Travers's translation of Chrysostom's sermons spoke of indiscriminate charity toward the poor, acceptance into membership was another matter; the requirement of valid testimony to an upright life and good conversation strictly limited membership in the English Reformed Church to the respectable poor. Given that evidence of some religious devotion through regular attendance of church services and good behavior among neighbors was a prior condition for membership, distribution of alms cannot be taken to have been the only incentive drawing poor members into the Church.

Most commonly, membership was not through letters of transfer from another church but through testimony from at least two members of good standing in the Church. Witness on behalf of new members did not only constitute the basis for most admissions, but is also one of the most complete records of membership participation. Between 1607 and 1640 a total of 700 testimonials were given by witnesses who can be identified as members of the Church. Testimonials from each status group roughly correspond to the proportion of their membership, with members of high and low status contributing at a slightly higher rate than their membership. Overall, high-status members contributed 20 percent [136], intermediate 24 percent [168], and low-status 40 percent [275]. It is not surprising to find that testimonials

TABLE 3
Status of Witnesses for New Members (ERCA)

Status of witness	Status of new member				
	High	Intermediate	Low	Unknown	Total
High	43 (32%)	18 (13%)	34 (25%)	41 (30%)	136 (20%)
Intermediate	17 (10%)	64 (38%)	50 (30%)	37 (22%)	168 (24%)
Low	27 (10%)	51 (19%)	119 (43%)	78 (28%)	275 (40%)
Unknown	16 (14%)	28 (24%)	36 (31%)	37 (32%)	117 (17%)
TOTAL	103 (15%)	161 (23%)	239 (34%)	193 (28%)	696

made by each status group were highest in behalf of new members of the same group. Likewise, it is not surprising to find that a number of high-status members acted as witnesses for lower-status applicants. Forty-three testimonials by members of high status were offered on behalf of members of lower status. What is more surprising is to find the high number of testimonials from members of the lowest-status category. The role of these humble men and women in testifying for those within their own status category, a total of 119 testimonials altogether, is the highest level of testimony offered by any one category. Even more striking is that at least twenty-seven men and women of low status testified in behalf of men and women of high status. Contributing, as a whole, 275 testimonials (roughly 40 percent of the total recorded testimonials), members of the lowest status played the most active role in the admission of new members into the Church.

Not all humble applicants felt it necessary to be supported by witnesses in the Church; nor did all the poorer members enthusiastically endorse potential members of their own social status. In February 1623 the wife of a miller, Jane Claprise, "desiring to be a member of the church, but neither bringing any witnesses of her conversation, & withall having bene complayned of by divers & being admonished to agree with those that were offended by her," was not admitted into the Church. The most likely objector to Claprise was Susanna Clerk, the wife of a laborer, who on December 21, 1622, appeared before the consistory in her dispute with Claprise.[53] Dismissing those who opposed her membership, Claprise "answered that she would submit herself to none but to God & her husband & giving other stoute wordes, it was therefore signifyed unto her that she must cary herself more peaceably & give satisfaction to those she had offended before we could admit her."[54]

Others were also refused membership upon report of previous sins. In February 1623 the pointmaker "Thomas Ewer was not admitted to our communion for as much as he was complayned of to have slaine a man at Steenberghen wch he also confessed." The consistory chastised members who had acted as witnesses for such candidates. Michael Steed, also a pointmaker, was called before the consistory on March 15, 1623, "having given testimony for Thomas Ewer . . . it being shewed that the person commended by him had run into a great scandall & that he ought not so rashly to have given his testimony, wherein he acknowledged his fault & professed that he was sory for it & would be more carefull hereafter in giving his testimony."[55] There were clearly consequences for testifying for members with known sins. The credibility of individual testimony was vital for members of every wealth category and served as a more valuable commodity than material assets in the presbyterians' disciplinary economy.

DISCIPLINARY DISCONTENTS

Consistorial discipline, as initially established by the reformed churches on the continent and envisaged by presbyterians in England, was concerned with enforcing religious observance and moral behavior chiefly through regulation of admission to the Lord's Supper.[56] The consistory of the English Reformed Church in Amsterdam visited all members of the Church before communion, strategically dividing the congregation between the elders. In 1607 they resolved that "for the better preparation of those which shall be partakers of the Lords table it is thought good that the communicants shall be visited att their houses & confermd withall there." They decided "that the number of the communicants shallbe divided into two porcions, that they may be there conveniently visited & confermed with all."[57] This practice continued throughout the seventeenth century and appears in the standing orders of the consistory dated in 1657.[58]

As the designated "eyes of the church," lay elders were particularly open to being criticized for intrusive investigations and partial judgments. Poorer members did not simply complain against these proceedings, but drew religious analogies to criticize the consistory. William Edmunds, a weaver, was admonished by the consistory "of some offence comitted in his house" following which the consistory also "reproved [Edmunds] for reproching the visitation of members before the communion, & for comparing it with the auricular confession of the papists, & for his wilfull persisting in the maintenance of his opinion."[59] In 1613 another weaver, Edward Hawkins, "acknolwedged his falt in comparing the eldership to deall as hardly with hyme as the comessary court in england."[60] Such criticism of the consistory's discipline reveals that anti-episcopal sentiments did not only resonate in England under immediate persecution by bishops; anti-episcopacy was also felt and expressed among poorer Englishmen in the Netherlands during the 1610s, before the damage done to episcopal reputation by Laudian policies in the 1620s and 1630s. This language still held currency in 1639 when Thomas Wortley complained "both against our Deacons, for beinge proude & against us, as though it were with us as ye prelates in Q. Marys tymes."[61]

Visitation before communion was one among many means by which the elders identified sin and misbehavior. From the very beginning, they also summoned absentees from communion before the consistory.[62] Indeed, absence from service or communion was the most frequent cause for which members found themselves before the elders and was one of the first checks on the standing of members. Between the years 1607 and 1640, the consistory recorded more than eighty summonses for absence from service or communion.[63] In England, absence from communion was common among recusants and radical protestants with troubled consciences, and could therefore be taken as an indication of deep-seated religious discontent and as a form of resistance to authority.[64] The weaver William Edmunds not only criticized visitation by elders but also withdrew from communion, even though he was not under suspension.[65]

However, from the surviving communion lists from the 1630s and 1640s, it appears that this form of resistance was not widespread. On average there were approximately twenty absentees, less than 5 percent of the total membership, including those barred from the table because of suspension and others whose absence the elders excused on account of sickness or travel. Exceptions, however, occurred in the mid-1630s. The communion lists dated to 1635 reveal that nearly sixty members absented themselves from two consecutive celebrations of the Lord's Supper. In what amounted to a form of public demonstration against Paget, at least nine members stayed away from communion in 1634 following their support of the unsuccessful candidacy of John Davenport for the position of copastor. Though not all of Davenport's supporters appear on the absentee lists, many of those who do appear were directly opposed to Paget's proceedings against him. Chief among those who protested was William Best, a hatmaker and deacon who had already crossed Paget over the Sabbath and was to seek his revenge in what could be seen as a sequel to the duel between Stephen Denison and the boxmaker John Etherington.[66] "[It] is clear that the hostile attitude Best was later to adopt towards Paget about Independency, was due partly to Paget's earlier objections to Best and his wife keeping the shop open on the Sabbath."[67] It is significant that the leading anti-Paget demonstrators were not a rag, tag, and bobtail of discontents: several were merchants and at least seven of the nine can be identified as higher-status members of the Church.

Nine men, along with twelve additional signatories, described as the "burthened and oppressed members of the English Church in Amsterdam," pub-

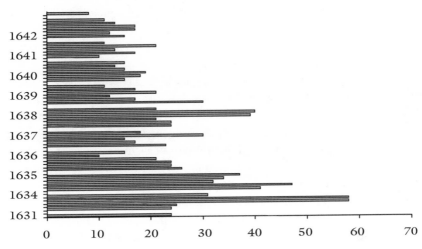

FIG. I. Absence from Communion, 1631–43 (ERCA).

lished their grievances against Paget in 1634 and defended their withdrawal from the sacrament: "Whereas offence hath bene taken that some of us whose names are underwritten, did absent ourselves from the Lords Supper the last communion day; we thought it good to give the reasons of our absences in writing."[68] They argued, "[H]owsoever we doe not thinke that the personall sinne of any man can defile the ordinances of God to us, if we be meet and fit to partake thereof; yet we know that a man may make himselfe partaker of other mans sins by neglecting his duety in seeking reformation, and so communicate unworthily."[69] Paget argued against them that "where Christ commanded to observe the Sacrament of his Supper, in remembrance of him; where the H. Ghost requires that we should not forsake the assembling of our selves together. These expresse commandements haue bene transgressed by these that withdrew themselves."[70] He further argued that "the preposterous order of these men is inexcusable, that first separated from a solemne act of religion with the Church of God, and afterwards came to tell the cause thereof; doing that in the last place which should have bene done in the first."[71]

While the publication of these exchanges was occasioned by a public withdrawal from communion, the debate had in fact developed directly out of the congregational-presbyterian contention between Paget and the pastoral candidates. These lay members objected that by disqualifying Davenport, Paget had deprived "the Church of that liberty and power which Christ hath given it in the free choyce of their Pastour, contrary to Act. 6. v. 3 & 15. v. 23."[72] "Secondly, by his pressing others upon the Congregation, abusing his interest in the Magistrates & Classis to that purpose."[73] Thus while some merchants may have supported presbyterian preachers against local hostility, others intervened in behalf of congregational-minded preachers, protested against Paget's appeal to the classis, and found themselves at the center of the ecclesiological debates that were to shape the New England Way.

Among Best's twelve supporters were some of the poorer former separatists such as Thomas Adams, who was receiving alms from the Church at the time of his protest, having come into membership in 1621. Through Adams's involvement it is clear that poorer men could do more than mimic anti-episcopal and anti-Roman language as a form of religious insult against the consistory. They too were caught up in the ecclesiological controversies of the early seventeenth century. Adams complained that the Church "had the name of a reformed church and he wished it might so be but he did not see how our practise agreed with reformation and thought he had the word of God for it."[74] Not all the poor in the Church can be regarded as passive recipients of relief who outwardly if ignorantly conformed (or did not conform). These were poor members who were theologically informed, actively engaged in the ecclesiological debate, and prepared to challenge the proceedings of the consistory according to their understanding of reformed ecclesiastical polity.

"TELL THE CHURCH"

If the consistory routinely summoned absentees from service and communion, for other offenses they crucially relied on the membership for the identification of scandal, discovery of information and administration of discipline. Just as they were frequent witnesses for new members and constituted a large proportion of the Church's membership, lower-status men and women were active accusers. At least forty reports against members came from men or women of low social standing, the largest number from any status category. By bringing matters to the attention of the consistory, poorer members played a key role in targeting certain members and shaping disciplinary priorities. Two of the lengthiest disciplinary cases, which occupied the bulk of the consistory's business during the 1620s, involved allegations of adultery. The first was made by Adam Dixon, a self-identified pauper, against Priscilla Hallowell, who does not appear to be of low status. The other case was against one of the congregation's wealthiest members, John Webster, by his servant Clara Jones.

In addition to sexual misdemeanors, members also reported general misbehavior that usually involved excessive drinking. When the tailor Thomas Bagnalt approached the consistory in 1621 to ask "counsail how to proceed with one whom he found drunken publiquely upon the street, & had now admonished him . . . the counsail of the consistory was, that thomas bagnall

TABLE 4

Status of Complainants and Defendants in Disciplinary Cases (ERCA)

Status of complainant	Status of defendant				
	High	Inter-mediary	Low	Unknown	Total
High	1	1	7	3	12 (13%)
Intermediary	3	6	10	3	22 (23%)
Low	3	12	20	5	40 (42%)
Unknown	2	2	12	5	21 (22%)
TOTAL	9 (10%)	21 (22%)	49 (52%)	16 (17%)	95

should a now for the present take an other with him & admonish him both of his fault in drunkenness."[75] From one perspective it would appear that the consistory's reliance on such accusations helped to breed disharmony by encouraging mutual suspicion and a culture of complaint. Richard Flower, a servant who had been accused by Isabell Barrell and Elizabeth Jordan of drunkenness, "was reproved for quarellinge with those who testifyed of his fault to ye Consistory . . . & his aptnes to blame ye witnesse against him."[76] Mutual accusation and further contention can also be seen between Henry Poulter and Margret Allen, wife of the goldsmith Thomas Allen. The poor also complained against the poor. When the mason Roger Jones testified against Anne Sims's husband for abusing alms, she retaliated by complaining against participants in Jones's late-night drinking parties, which consisted of other poorer members in the congregation. In the year of 1609 alone she reported against the laborer Ralph Young for his involvement, against Ambrose Kettering, another laborer, against Elizabeth Blowfield, the wife of a servant, for slander, and against Richard Plowes, a sawyer, for "keeping a suspicious woman."[77]

Yet sexual scandal and misbehavior were not the chief causes for complaint to the consistory. More recorded appearances before the consistory were related to interpersonal dispute than any other single category including absence from service or communion.[78] Appearances before the consistory for absence from service or communion may have gone unrecorded, and many disciplinary cases related to a range of offenses and cannot be precisely numbered, but nonetheless a high proportion of appearances did involve interpersonal disputes.[79] At least twenty-five members who appeared before the consistory were involved in a dispute with another member of the congregation. Disputes were neither necessarily nor chiefly between unrelated members of the Church. At least twenty-four members were involved in disputes with kin, some of whom were not church members. Spouses of members in particular approached the consistory even though they were not members themselves.[80]

TABLE 5

Relationships in Disputes (ERCA)

Status	Member	Kin	Nonmember
High	2	1	1
Intermediary	8	8	1
Low	10	11	0
Unknown	6	4	1
TOTAL	25	24	3

Florence Stevens complained to the consistory against her husband, John Stevens, in January 1617 before she appears on the consistory's register as a member herself in 1619. Some complainants, neither members themselves nor related to any member, resorted to the consistory after the magistrates had failed to redress their grievances. The servant Clara Jones who had accused John Webster was not a member of the Church. Anne Sims, who almost single-handedly disclosed all Roger Jones's drinking partners to the consistory, was apparently also in the habit of accusing others who were not members of the Church. The consistory recorded "a greevous complaynt made against Anne Sims, by a woman called Henne Woodard who said the Anne Sims had accused her about stollen cloth."[81]

Given the number of disputes brought before the elders, it is no surprise that they endeavored to avoid causing further provocation through their disciplinary procedure. In cases that involved general suspicion and complaint made by neighbors, the consistory could conceal the identity of individual accusers. In many of these cases the consistory did not bother to list particular names in their records. One upperman, John Greene, complained against the surgeon John Nicholas for "want of Christianity in not dealing privately with him" before reporting him to the consistory. Yet the consistory "admonished [Greene] of his fault, & required [him] to confesse his errour, seing the matter was deemed publique & did not neede a private dealing of necessity."[82] In 1639 Anna How, the daughter of an upperman who received alms from the Church in 1640, was reported to the consistory for her drunkenness, and she "confessed yt shee hath bene druncke sometymes & yt shee goes in bad houses, as wel as good, but it is to get worke, & to bringe it backe & fetch monye for her worke." The consistory suspended Anna on account of "the general report of her drunkennes & frequentinge houses of ill report." Anna "being in a great passion desired to knowe her accuser," but the elders were unwilling to disclose this information. "To prevent wranglinge," they "iudged it not fit to name ye persons who testifyed against her wher upon shee sayd, wee dealt not uprightly."[83] Two of her accusers, Thomas Adams and Miriam

Skates, had made a series of allegations against Anna's mother in 1627. Had Anna discovered the identity of all her accusers this might have been another case of dispute between kin. The consistory noted in September 1635 that upon the general rumor of Anna's misbehavior, the accusation was not only advanced to the consistory by complainants against Anna's mother but also "confirmed by Elizabeth Ratliff, & by her owne father Marten Hanewell."[84] Martin had experienced other difficulties in disciplining his children. He not only confirmed the general suspicion of his daughter's misbehavior, but in October 1629 had reported his son's breach of the Sabbath and drunkenness to the consistory.[85]

It would be hasty to conclude that the consistory was eager to accept all complaints for the sake of disciplining its members. Just as in theological debates involving the testimony of the Fathers and reformers, the consistory took into account the quality and quantity of the witnesses produced to support accusations as well as the way in which complaints were made.[86] The particular order that they followed was that set out by Christ in Matthew 18.17, which instructed personal admonition before involving others and finally bringing the matter to the attention of the Church. If on the one hand the consistory readily accepted complaints against sins that had become publicly scandalous, on the other they chastised complainants who approached the consistory before personal consultation and an attempt at reconciliation in private matters. Thus, members who complained to the Church ran the risk of coming under censure if they failed to follow this order. It was, for example, enforced in the case of Goodwife Coldgate, who "was reprooved because she dealt not with Anna Miller privately before she brought this matter to the consistory."[87] The consistory was equally prepared to rebuke members for dealing harshly with individuals by personal admonition. The weaver Edward Hawkins, who compared the consistory to the bishop's commissary court in 1613 in its routine visitation of members, was himself found guilty by the consistory of dealing harshly with other members: in April 1613 he was "complayned of for his forward dealing with Robert Bulward admonishing him of his syne & for his slandering the eldershippe of partialitye acknowledged his fault."[88]

Adam Dixon had been under suspension for various offenses prior to and at the time of reporting against the Hallowells. In 1616 "adam dixson acknowledged he hade sclandred the deacons in saying they were the cause of his childs death.[89] Still under suspension in June 1621, he lost all patience and "charged the consistory to keepe him from the Lord's table only because he was a poore man."[90] Nonetheless in the following November he approached the consistory bringing the Hallowell affair to their attention. This only worked to Dixon's disadvantage, since the defendants charged Dixon with perjury for breaking his oath in disclosing the Hallowell affair. Dixon may have presumed that by supplying this information to the consistory, the elders might have been more inclined to release him from suspension. The consistory, on the other hand, must have suspected that Dixon acted out of malice against Bartholomew Barrell, who, along with Thomas Hallowell, had accepted a bribe to conceal Priscilla's affair. For in September 1621, the tailor Bartholomew Barrell and stone-carver Robert Bulward explained that they had intervened in Dixon's dispute with his wife, reporting to the consistory that "they had heard the controversie betwixt Adam dickson and his wife . . . and that they had now reconciled them."[91]

When Dixon approached the consistory again and "demanded how long we would keepe him from the communion, the answer was till he cleared himself from periurie." Here Dixon's response to suspension is quite reveal-ing. He threatened "that except he wer admitted quickly he would appeale to the Dutch Classis. We answered he might if he would."[92] Dixon was not the only poor member to threaten appeal to the classis. In 1632 the glover George Hewett "was admonished of his drunkenness . . . hee in coller sayd yt wee weare partiall & yt hee would accuse us unto the classes & appeale thether & refused our admonition remayning obstinate."[93] Thus, while some of the lowest-standing members complained of the consistory's partiality, they nonetheless saw fit to work within the reformed ecclesiastical polity to redress their grievances. If congregationalists had interpreted Christ's injunction to "tell the church" in Matthew 18.17 as referring to the entire membership of a particular congregation, there were plenty of poorer members, such as Martin Hanwell and Anna Sims, who found it useful to direct their complaints to the local consistory, which could protect their identity. When complaint to the consistory developed into complaint against the consistory itself, such members were also well aware of a hierarchy to which they could appeal. Thus, while certain poorer members such as Thomas Adams may have objected to the intervention of the Dutch classis in their criticism of Paget, others were prepared to "tell the church" by appealing to the classis against the consistory's judgment.

PUBLIC OR PRIVATE OFFENSES?

When Bartholomew Barrell approached the Amsterdam English Re-formed Church consistory in 1621 "desiring that one of the members of the church might [be] excluded from the Lords Supper for speaking against him & his children," the consistory asked him "whether he had dealt according to order." For Barrell, the order set out in Matthew 18.17 to which the consistory referred did not apply in this instance, since "the matter was publique & neded no private dealing." Yet the consistory "demanded farther for witnesses to shew the matter to be publique" and explained that "the consistory could not so hastily suspend any member of the churche without witnesses." Barrell insisted "that he neded to bring no witnesses in this case" and "thereupon charged the consistory with unrighteous dealing."[94]

The disagreement between Barrell and the consistory over what constituted public versus private offenses and over the requirement of witnesses points to a recurring area of ambiguity. Key issues in earlier ecclesiological debates involved flexibility in defining the boundaries of the visible church, the establishment of authenticity through public authority, the weighing of various evidences, and the taking into account of the quality and quantity of witnesses. These issues reappeared in the execution of ecclesiastical discipline. In particular, the flexible definition of community contributed to the already existing ambiguity in determining public and private boundaries. This was crucial for the consistory, since its ability to mediate between private and public knowledge by sentencing private and public confessions reinforced its disciplinary authority. However, at the same time that such flexibility provided the consistory with additional leverage, it also left room for objections by poorer members, some of whom found that flexibility worked in their own interest, while others used it against the consistory.

The consistory demonstrated a consistent concern for the public nature of sins. As Alice Carter had remarked in the case of drinking, the consistory appears to have been "less concerned with intoxication in private than with its public manifestation, especially when the Church as a whole was brought into disrepute."[95] Godderd Brooke was brought before the consistory in September 1610 for "his scandalous dronckeness," whereupon "both brethren of the congregation & also Brownists have takn offence there at & speak evill of the congregation thereupon."[96] Public profanation of the Sabbath was similarly noted in distinction from nonattendance of divine service. As recorded on August 28, 1631, "Susanna Bullerd beeing admonished to desist from the publiqe breaking of the Saboeth persisted obstenaetly accusing sondry members of the lyke & would acknolidg no falt, so was suspended from the tabell."[97] When Nicholas Joyner charged Humphrey Bromly for "breach of the Saboth daye as wytnest in publyck shewes" in 1619, "the sayd homfrey Bromly did confesse his falt & promysed to leave it also did acknowedg that nichlas Joyner myght lawfullye bring his complaynt to the church without prayvate admonytyon seyng the falt was publycke."[98]

The fluidity between public versus private sins appears in a number of disciplinary cases, particularly (as one might expect) in domestic conflicts. In some instances the consistory received complaint from a spouse.[99] In February 1619 the consistory recorded that

> whereas james Rassell & Barbara his wife being in strife one with a other, she complayning of the strokes he gave her, & he of her evill & provoking speeches, & both of them being ready to leave & forsake one another, by much perswasion they were at length reconciled, both of them confessing their faults & promised to live peaceably & christianly together, giving their hands one to another, for confirmation of their promiss.[100]

But where domestic disputes or abuse became public knowledge, it was considered an offense to neighbors and to the Church as a community. In February 1619 "edward ppotter beinge complained uppon by thoms banc for beating his wyfe aknowldged his falt & promesed amendment."[101] Francis James's neighbor Heiniick Jansen reported that he had "pushed his wife with his foote & gave her a bope on the eare with the back of his hand." Another neighbor, "Ffoppe Luitkins saith that a week afore May Francis James took the panne from the table with baken in it, & cast it on the floure & then troade the panne in peces." These two neighbors along with Nummelie Pieters further "witnes[sed] that he sayd he would not worke so long as there is a stone upon the house."[102] On August 5, 1637, "Richard Flower being complayned of for drunkenes & beating of his wife, & this to the scandall and offence of his neighbors who dwell in the streete nere unto him, was therfore sent for unto the eldership & seriously & sharply rebuked for his sinne." Upon his acknowledgment of fault and promise of amendment, "it was also signifyed unto him that if the lyke complaynt should agayn come unto us, hee must then acknowledge his fault before the whole congregation to give satisfaction unto them."[103]

Through their efforts to bring reconciliation between husbands and wives, the consistory was therefore at the same time attempting to reconcile such members with the Church as well as with the local community. For offense against his wife on April 22, 1626, "Thomas Bibroth coming of himself to the consistory shewed his desire to be reconciled with the church acknowledging his fault in going from his wife, & desired to know what he should further do that he might come to the Lords table, as he had done in former time."[104] Likewise, on February 1, 1623, Ambrose Kettring "coming to the consistory & desiring to be reconciled to the church confessed his fault in drunkennes, striking his wife, & neglect of gods worship in publique & being demanded further whether he would be content to acknowledge his fault at the Lords table the next communion; he promised that he would be ready so to do; which by the eldership was also thought meete."[105]

Florence Stevens's disciplinary history reveals how unresolved domestic dispute could develop into dispute with the consistory itself. She had first complained to the consistory about her husband in 1617. She then appeared in the consistory records on September 13, 1620. She was "suspended or ferbyden the tabell of th Lorde, for obstynatly refusyng to come to the congregacyon except monye were lent her to redeme her clothes out the lombard."[106] The following year the consistory noted that she came and "acknowledgeth with many teares that she is heartily sorrowfull for giving us such iust occasion to suspend her and promiseth to be diligent in hearing the word preached and to avoyde giving offence as formerly she hath done."[107] Florence Stevens's contention with her husband, however, brought her before the consistory again in October 1625.[108] In this instance Florence "being admonished of her evill language to her husband & of her provocation of him would not acknowledge her fault, avouching she had done nothing that she had cause to be sory for.[109]

Florence now found herself involved in a dispute with both her husband and with the consistory, and when she appeared before the consistory again in November 1625, she was prepared to be reconciled neither with her husband nor with the Church. On the one hand she "complayned of his drunkennes, that he did not provide for her & that she would not give him a bit of bread though she should see him dy in the streetes." She apparently held the Church responsible, and "threatned also that she would go away & leave her children to the church, to be maynteyned by it."[110] Five months later she followed through with this threat, "being sent for to the Eldership & admonished of her rude & unchristian behaviour with the deacons in bringing her bed into the church & violently casting it among the deacons in their meeting; bringing her children also & left them with the deacons, saying they should keep them." By thrusting her children into the care of the Church, Florence further blurred private and public boundaries, even subverting the boundary between public and private responsibility.

Florence wanted to end her relationship with the Church, which would have made her eligible for charity elsewhere: "[S]he desired that we would excommunicate her & prayed unto God we might never rest untill we had excommunicated her & sayd that we must & should keep her children, that she could live well enough herself & had in trust in her house a thousand guilders from others." Instead the consistory refused to excommunicate Florence, and "it was signifyed unto her that she was suspended from the Lords Supper & advised to bethinke her selfe better."[111] Several years later, in October 1629, Florence still "desiring of the Eldership a certificate that she was none of the church,"[112] "it was answered that she was not yet excommunicate & therfore we could not give her such a certificate; but in stead thereof she was admonished of her former obstinacy & contempt of the church."[113] By December 1629, having been denied relief from the Church for nearly half a decade, Florence "complayned that we made no ende" whereby "the consistory layd her sins before her & shewed her owne obstinancie to be the cause of the delay at length she confessed that she was sory that she had offended both God & the consistory." Thus, nine years after her first suspension, Florence was restored in December 1629, and "the consistory signifyed to the Deacons that upon her confession of her fault, we thought they should do well to contribut to her . . . [at] their discretion considering her charge and also the consistorie released her of her suspension."[114] But on May 17, 1634, Florence Stevens was once more brought before the consistory being "reproved for whoredome and Adultry." Now widowed, Florence appeared before the consistory again on June 25, 1636:

> havinge comitted adultery & having bene suspended from the Lords supper, was admonished to make publicke confession of her fault which though shee had longe refused to doe, yet now at last she came & signifyed she was willinge to submit her selfe according to the order of this church, to giue publicke satisfaction for her offence & so it was agreed & appoynted by the consistory, that at the next communion which was to bee on the 29 of the month shee was to present her selfe in the church & at the table to make public confession of her fault."[115]

Even as Florence made a public confession before the church community, she had already granted herself absolution through private conscience, again subverting the consistory's public and private distinctions.

EVIDENCE AND REPENTANCE

After fifteen years of ecclesiastical discipline, Stevens realized that it was in fact easier to repent than to obtain a demission from the Church. If the consistory was reluctant to accept the scandalous into membership and to suspend members for private sins without sufficient evidence, once members found themselves under the discipline of the Church, it appears that the consistory was equally unwilling to release them from suspension without sufficient evidence of repentance, even if such discipline extended over the course of many years. The suspension of Francis and Elizabeth Blowfield from the Lord's Supper for their absence from church spanned Paget's entire ministry at Amsterdam.[116] Whereas Francis Blowfield was called before the consistory for his absence as early as 1607 and was suspended until at least 1629, his wife, Elizabeth, remained under suspension from the Lord's Supper from 1622 until the late 1630s. During Francis Blowfield's suspension, his master had also made a complaint against him, and his contention with a neighbour was also brought before the consistory in 1608. The presbyterians held a tight grip on

TABLE 6
Disciplinary Sentences and Status (ERCA)

Status	Summon	Admonition	Suspension	Excommunication
High	28	6	9	0
Intermediary	102	19	28	2
Low	153	21	40	3
Unknown	74	13	31	1
TOTAL	356	59	108	6
Men	246	39	72	3
Women	102	19	34	2

its poorer backsliding membership and were reluctant to remove them from oversight: in the same year that the consistory disciplined Blowfield for his absence and received complaint from his master, they nonetheless baptized his daughter, recording on August 17, 1608, that "this day was baptised the daughter Francis blowfield named Rebecca."[117] This was precisely the sort of practice that would have confirmed congregational views of presbyterian promiscuity in administering the sacraments.

However, discipline in the English Reformed Church in Amsterdam was, if anything, rigorous. The consistory's decision to restore recalcitrant members strictly demanded the presentment of authentic evidence from public institutions, a credible confession, and evidence of genuine repentance. In cases such as debt, which were also a civil offense, the consistory was particularly circumspect when presented with evidence to prove satisfaction of creditors. Richard Haynes was summoned to the consistory in January 1637 on account of his debt after three years of suspension, and "exhorted to haeste his agrement with all his creditors & to bringe a testimony of the same under his creditors hands.[118] By 1639 Haynes had finally convinced the consistory "upon certificate of his satisfying some Creditors & having Attestation from ye rest yt they were content to wayt til god should inable him." Yet the consistory also expected that "accordinge to the rule of the synod & custome of the consistory one Elder viz Mr Beuchamp & one Deacon viz Mr Denman to receiue every 6 monthes the account of his gaynes & expences & the overplus to bee reported to the consistorie for the use of his creditors."[119]

The consistory was similarly conscientious in cases involving violence. In February 1623 John Hebson finally satisfied the consistory, "having long desired to be receved againe to the communion of the church, & bringing a certificate vnder a Notaries hand of some that witnessed the man formerly wounded by him did not dy of the wound."[120] The consistory required the same level of evidential authenticity for establishing marital status. In March 1623 "Andrew Ruymien having had two proclamations of his mariage & it being signifyed unto us that he had no sufficient testimony out of England of the death of his former wife, was advised by us to go unto the Commissaries & to stay the proceeding in his mariage untill he had more perfect testimony about this matter."[121] The consistory also rejected Humfrey Bromly's evidence of his wife's death, which consisted of "a letter [dated at Norwich, June 20, 1622] . . . by one francis de Keyser wherein it was sayd that having made enquirie touching Mary Austen at Windam and Norwich he heard that she had bene whipped in the Bridewell at Norwich & lead out of the city but he had no further certainty where she was some saying that she was at London, & some that she was dead." They explained "that they held not this testimony sufficient, because it was but from one person & uncertaine also: It was required of him to bring testimony that was authentique as from magistrates, ministers, churchwardens or the like to shew that he is lawfully discharged from her by the law; & that her parents have no further action against him."[122]

There is obvious concern to establish authentic evidence in the readmission of members to communion through signs of genuine repentance. Early in the records the consistory took special note of manner and posture in confession of sins. In February 1608 "David henrickes being convicted of much lewd behaviour acknolwedged his fault with teares & promised amendement,"[123] and approaching the consistory again the same month "on his knees confessed his fault & besought forgevnes of god & our prayers to god for him."[124] However, several months later, in April 1608, the consistory again suspended him, and on account of "his droucekeness it is apoynted ther he shalbe excluded from the lords table without publishing his name & his debarring to be signified by 2 elders."[125] It was insufficient simply to show conviction upon confession; the consistory expected further fruits of repentance through the turning away from previous sins. In July 1622 "thomas greenhill was sharply admonished and reproached by the consistory, because he shewed not such signes & fruits of repentanc for former adultery and drunkenesse as was meete but still frequented tap houses and was unquiet in his house, sometimes lying out of his house two nights together: ffor which causes he is now suspended from the Lords table, till we may see some the reformation of his conversation."[126] When Florence Stevens "acknowledged fault and was willing to undergoe the censures of the church by publycke acknowledgment," the consistory required further evidence that "her repentance must be made to appeare by her lyfe and conversation."[127] However, unlike the consistory's expectation that members present evidence authorized by public authority, requirements for signs of genuine repentance were open to interpretation, negotiation, and objection.

DISCIPLINARY RESPONSES AND PUNISHMENTS

At every step of the disciplinary procedure, poorer men and women were far from passive subjects. They complained against the consistory, actively testified in behalf of and accused other members, and reinterpreted public and private boundaries. When the consistory demanded additional evidence of genuine repentance from Florence Stevens, she responded by challenging the consistory's theology, which she regarded as "a popish proof." Stevens appears to have been exempting herself from the consistory's requirement for outward signs of moral reform, appealing to the doctrine of justification by faith alone: "[S]hee was confident of pardon soe regarded not much what men sayd or did."[128] This was dismissed by the consistory as simply reflecting "ignorance."

Yet Florence Stevens's objection is a vivid example of how even a poor widow and delinquent member could challenge the consistory's procedure with a confidence in her own theological understanding and in the puritans' standard appeal to conscience.[129] While many studies of puritanism and women have tended to anticipate their role in the leadership of the Church as preachers or prophetesses, recent work has explored the ways in which puritanism empowered women through the traditional conventions of godly community.[130] The example of Stevens reveals that women not only appropriated puritanism through their nonconformity and exemplary piety in the domestic sphere but could also appropriate their arguments and work within reformed religion to make theological statements in the consistory as members of the Church through the ordinary disciplinary procedure. Her example not only demonstrates how women engaged with church officers as members, but also broadens the scope of theological interaction among the godly to include women of low status; this complements known challenges to (and almost all other interactions with) puritan clerics by well-educated women such as Ann Hutchinson.[131] The implication of Stevens's contacts with the consistory is therefore at least twofold: it challenges assumptions about the level of theology and ecclesiological controversy with which poorer women were capable of engaging, and it reveals that there was room within the disciplinary procedure for women as members to engage theologically with clerics and other church officers.

While Stevens provides a powerful example of a poor woman holding her own against the consistory, it would be misleading to suggest that cases such as hers were common. Samuel Merideth, of unknown status, would have preferred any form of Christian discipline to presbyterian government. On July 24, 1630, being sent for & required to give a reason of his absence from the communion & from the church refused to give a reason thereof, saying that he was free to go whether he would he was not bound prentise to the church that very man was to answer for himself onely in contemptuous & reprochfull maner he spoke evill of the reformed church & praised the papists Anabaptists Lutherans for the kinde done to him with some reproches of particular persons & being desired to stay & heare what we would say unto him he refused to heare or tary & went abruptly from us.[132]

There were at least nine different instances in which poor or low-status members denied charges or remained obstinate after witnesses had testified against them and after admonition from the consistory.

However, defiance of presbyterian government was not representative of all responses to the consistory's discipline, not even among the poorer members. Dependence upon relief from the Church may have been the reason why large numbers of low-status and poorer members submitted to the discipline of the Church. In at least twenty-five instances, members of this social group responded by promising amendment. At least thirty-six members of this category were suspended, out of which as many as twenty-five approached the consistory for readmission to communion. Two of the six excommunicates also gained readmission. In July 1610 the barber Gilbert Much, "being reproved for his heresee did with great obstinacy reject & dispise all that was sayd unto him for his conviction out of the worde of god & at his departing did protest that he will never come before us more, although we should send for him a thowsand tymes.[133] However, in December 1620, after being excommunicated by the consistory with the consent of the Dutch classis, Much "revoked his errours of denying the godhead of christ & acknolwedged his fault desiring to be received promising at the next communion to confesse his sin openly before the congregation at the table of the lord."[134] What is noteworthy is that, again, the church member is taking the initiative.

When members sought readmission to communion it was usually granted upon confession before the consistory or publicly before the church community. In 1618 John Jordan (the younger), a well-off member of the Church, appeared before the consistory to confess his sin "in that he hade contended so much with the consistorye about sett formes of prayer," promising to "walke peaceablye among us." He did this "in the presence of this consistorye, & of three brethren that he brought with hymme viz john Somers thomas Bagnall, and Nichles joyner & her upon he was freed from suspentyon."[135] Richard Troutbeck, of unknown status, had wounded another man in combat and been required by the consistory and Dutch classis to make a public confession. He would have preferred a private confession before the consistory with several additional witnesses to public confession. In October 1629 he "came to the

TABLE 7

Responses to Discipline and Status (ERCA)

Status	Denial or obstinacy	Promised amend- ment	Consist- orial confession	Public confession	Readmis- sion request	Readmission from suspension	Readmission from excommuni- cation
,h er-							
,h er-	3	5	1	1	7	3	0
nediary	4	24	7	1	14	11	1
w	9	28	14	8	28	19	0
known	8	9	7	3	9	6	0
TAL	24	66	29	13	58	39	1
n	14	45	23	9	41	27	1
men	9	19	6	4	17	11	0

consistorie to desire that he might not confesse his fault at the table, but here in the consistorie. The consistorie answered as afore, that he was to confesse his fault at the table, as the classis had signifyed to him he was exhorted to humble himselfe and to conform himself to the discipline of the church."[136] In April 1610, David Henrick (also of unknown status), "desiring humbly to be agayne receaved & admitted to the Lords table," was asked by the consistory "wether he would at the communion table acknolwedg his fault publicquely in regard of his great offence & his often falling into the sam agyn after he had at other tymes bene readmitted." Unlike Troutbeck, Henrick "answered, that he was not only willing & content to doe it or what so ever should require, but hee rather should be so then otherwise, that all the church might take knowledge of his amendment."[137] These members were apparently disinclined simply to accept the consistory's sentences: they voiced their opinions on the consistory's decisions, attempting to negotiate or expressing their approval in order to provide further evidence of the genuineness of their repentance.

There was ambiguity in the determination of what constituted private ver- sus public offenses, and members of the Church challenged the consistory's definitions. It is perhaps unsurprising to find that there was both ambiguity and flexibility in the consistory's requirement of private and public confes- sions. The issue of whether the consistory or the entire membership of a congregation heard confessions related to the definition of the visible church. Congregationalists stressed the consent of the entire membership, while pres- byterians placed prerogative first in the consistory. Some members of the English Reformed Church in Amsterdam believed that officers of the Church were obliged to acknowledge all faults related to their ministry before the en- tire congregation, since their errors were by nature public. The embroiderer

Thomas Farret, who received alms from the Church in 1640 and would later sign William Best's petition against Paget, made such an argument against Thomas Potts in 1622: "[H]aving formerly delivered a writing to the consistory wherein [Farret] set downe his reasons why he would have Mr Pot to repent publiquly the omission of a psalme after the communion, it was signifyed vnto him that the Eldership . . . did iudge his request to be unreasonable."[138] While Potts had argued that "sins were not to be publiquely repented of, unless they were heynous & notorious, not lesser matters as sleeping in the church & the like," Farret "replyed that if a minister should sleep in the pulpit in the sermon time, he ought to repent publiquely, though a private person ought not."[139] Here a poorer member of the Church is objecting to something other than a sentence on his own affairs. He was also concerned with the disciplining of others and demanded public confession from church officers.

Public offense did not always involve public confession in the English Reformed Church. In April 1608 the tobacco-pipe maker Thomas Lawrence, who appears to be of middling status, "was warned [ ] & did this day appeare unto whom was objected his Keping company with a suspitious woman; his having her to kepe hi house &c." At first Lawrence "denyed any falth matter: yet att last being pressed to tell the trueth, confessed that he had comitted uncleanes with her & thereupon the grevousnes of his sin being layd before him, he was warned to refrayne from the communion." Despite his initial prevarication the consistory appears to have been convinced of his sorrowful response, and decided "that the fact should be signified at the communion table, but his name not named, because he seemed penitent."[140] In a period when reputation was vital to men and women whatever their status, the consistory's power to publish or withhold information from the Church undoubtedly added to the impact of their disciplinary sentences. If a member such as David Henrick had no reservations about confessing his sins publicly, there were others who pleaded with the consistory out of fear of the damage that would be done to their reputation by a public confession.

But the consistory's discretion between public and private confessions did not go unchallenged. It was precisely the flexibility within the presbyterian discipline that provoked Thomas Adams to confront the consistory in 1627, objecting that though the Church "had the name of a reformed church & he wished it might so be but he did not see how our practise agreed with reformation."[141] Adams's complaint was made in the context of the private confession of Elizabeth Hanwell, whose offense Adams believed to require a public confession before the entire congregation. Just as Farret had argued that Thomas Potts ought to repent before the entire congregation for his omission of the psalm in service, Adams complained that Hanwell "having called the whole church a generation of vipers was not brought to publique repentance."[142] Other members added their complaints to Adams's, even if without full knowledge of the particulars of the Hanwell case.[143]

The consistory denied that "she should confesse her fault more publiquely before the whole congregation," which they argued was "contrary to our practise." According to the elders, "[E]ven of late since this controversy began, greater sin complayned of to the consistory, hath bene reconciled passed over without confession thereof at the L. Table." They particularly noted Hanwell's submission to the consistory:

> that we do not iustify E.H. in any of her evilles. . . . But for as much as she hath alwayes submitted her self unto the iudgement the consistory receyved their rebukes & confessed her fault in every thing so far as the consistory would require of her, professing her repentance & that with many teares from time to time, have therfore thought it meet . . . she should be againe admitted vnto the same.

They also took into account her circumstance, that "much hard dealing hath bene used towards her & that by sundry provocation she hath bene drawne to the more evill, being in a great measure deprived both of her good name & consequently of her meanes to live which in speciall maner depended vpon her credit." They further argued that "we have also considered her great infirmitie both of body & minde, sometimes falling downe . . . & for this cause also we have had the more regard of her estate that no extreme or dealing should be used to her."[144]

The defendant in question, Elizabeth Hanwell, was the wife of Martin Hanwell, an upperman who received alms from the Church in 1640 and reported his own children to the consistory. The consistory's judgment in favor of Elizabeth does not appear to have been simply due to her husband's cooperation with the consistory in reporting his children's sins. In denying accusations of stealing a blanket and a pair of knives, Elizabeth could not have come up with a better line to vouch for her piety: "[As] she should be saved, she had no other blanket."[145] While the initial complainants, Thomas Allen and Miriam Scates, accused Elizabeth Hanwell of stealing and then lying about a pair of knives, these allegations appear to have arisen from her contention with Rebecca Barlow, who had appeared before the consistory on account of her dispute with Hanwell in December 1626.[146] In 1627 Barlow produced a line of witnesses to testify against Hanwell, including the separatist Richard Matley, who "testifyed that Eliz. Hanwell had often rayled on Mrs Barlow & called her hypocrite: That once she called Her fletchers whore." Matley's wife and Margret Allen "did also testify that Eliz. Hanwell had called Mrs Barlow & Thomas fletcher the divell & the pope."[147] Even here in Hanwell's insulting her superiors, there were signs of her zealous protestantism. At the same time, Hanwell's accusers complained that she had slandered the entire church, as well as the consistory:

> Elizab. Hanwell rayled on the whole church as a generation of vipers saying she would set up a brief never to come in the church againe. [B]eing admonished that she had dwelt in gods houses & should not say so she sayd what evil she had learned it among us of this congregation. [B]eing sent for the consistory she sayd she would rather see them all hanged then come to them, and excepted againste the good men.

However, instead of accepting Ralph Matley's testimony against Hanwell, the consistory censored Rebecca Barlow "for bringing the testimony of R. Matley, who [as Hanwell complained] by [Barlow's] owne confession & report in many places, is a notorious knave."[148]

It also censured Barlow for her search for evidence against the defendant, concluding that "Mrs Barlowe hath done unwarrantably, being accessorie to the opening of Elizab. Hanwells chest in an other mans house, without the consent of the magistrates, and hath shewed weaknes by hard courses, in prosecuting this controversie, such as tended rather to harden her then to bring her to repentance."[149] This objection was grounded on the principle that presbyterians used to dismiss allegations of private offenses if there was insufficient evidence or witness. In addition presbyterians used it to deride congregational practice in the ordination controversy by claiming that it amounted to private usurpation of lawful authority. However, in the consistory's proceedings in this case, certain members made similar objections to presbyterian discipline. Adams not only insisted on the need for public satisfaction of offenses but more notably objected to the consistory's private hearing of witnesses individually according to canon law procedure where "the parties complayning & complayned of were not brought face to face in the consistory."[150] This low-status church member was ready to contest everything from the election of elders and the authority of the Dutch classis to the consistory's sentences and the procedure in hearing witnesses.

The consistory defended its procedure by claiming that "as for the confronting of persons before the consistory, though we did sometimes admit the same, yet we did sometimes also avoyd it as being in some cases a meanes of provocation unto further strife according to that of the whisemen, prov 27.17."[151] Its concern to bring reconciliation between parties cannot be overlooked. Not only did church officers provide mediation between members and between church officers, but members and nonmembers alike approached the consistory for more formal arbitration in settling their disputes.[152] More strikingly, even women and poorer members played a part as mediators. In

TABLE 8
Summary of Popular Participation (ERCA)

Status	Complaint	Disciplinary witness	Witness for new member	Nomination of officer	Total
High	12	9	136	6	163
Intermediary	22	18	168	12	220
Low	40	25	275	13	353
Unknown	21	13	117	6	157
TOTAL	95	65	696	36	893

NOTE: The gender of certain members who appeared before the consistory is unknown. Hence the total number of members listed in the tables exceeds the total of men and women in the same category.

the dispute between Rebecca Barlow and Elizabeth Hanwell, the consistory sent two mediators: John Paget's wife, Bridget, along with the upperman John Green, who was of the same occupation as Hanwell's husband.[153] Other members of the Church who held no official post acted as mediators. Just as the consistory became involved in the disputes that they mediated, so members became involved themselves. As in the case of Adam Dixon, the tailor Bartholomew Barrell and the stone-carver Robert Bulward claimed that they had mediated between Dixon and his wife. Within a month, the consistory's records reveal contention between Dixon and Barrell. The other mediator, Robert Bulward, had been involved in disputes with other members and been under the discipline of the Church for various offenses prior to his mediating activity. When the weaver Edward Hawkins privately admonished Bulward, he later came under the censure from the consistory himself for his "forward dealing" with Bulward.[154]

The mediating activity of women and the intervention of the poor in the personal affairs of other members reveals that they were not simply objects of censure or participants motivated by disaffection or by personal grievances. The active engagement of poorer men and women was integral to the effective functioning of ecclesiastical discipline.[155] Overall the participation of low-status members was 5 percent above their membership, constituting approximately 40 percent of all recorded activity in the Church. Women also demonstrated considerable participation with the exception of nominating or objecting to the nomination of church officers. They contributed to approximately 39 percent of the activity recorded in the consistory minutes, which was only 3 percent below their overall membership in the Church. This offers an alternative view to that which emphasizes the dominant role of the middling sort in the successful execution of church discipline. Not only did poorer members constitute a large proportion of church membership,

TABLE 9
Summary of Disciplinary Cases (ERCA)

		High status	Intermediary status	Low status	Unknown status	Total	Men	Women	Former Separatist	Officer
Religious Offences	Heresy	0	4	7	1	12	6	3	3	0
	Schism	0	1	4	2	7	3	3	1	0
	Absence from Service	5	10	17	9	41	24	16	3	1
	Absence from Communion	4	11	14	12	41	28	13	4	0
	Sabbath Observance	0	4	8	5	17	11	6	1	0
		9	30	50	29	118	72	41	12	1
Marital and Sexual	Concerning Marital Status	0	11	2	1	14	9	5	0	2
	Neglect of Family	0	6	9	1	16	10	6	0	1
	Adultery	3	2	5	4	14	11	3	0	0
	Fornication	1	2	6	4	13	7	6	0	0
	Other Sexual Misconduct	0	5	3	4	12	10	2	1	0
		4	26	25	14	69	47	22	1	3
Inter-personal Disputes	Violence	0	5	12	6	23	20	3	0	2
	Dispute	9	15	21	7	52	37	15	2	4
	Defamation	8	5	21	9	43	29	14	3	13
		17	25	54	22	118	86	32	5	19
Misbehavior	Disorderly Behavior	0	7	12	2	21	13	8	0	0
	Drinking and Drunkenness	1	7	12	6	26	22	3	1	0
	Other Misbehavior	1	2	2	2	7	6	1	0	1
		2	16	26	10	54	39	12	1	1
Pecuniary	Theft	0	1	2	0	3	2	1	0	0
	Economic Dispute	0	3	5	3	11	5	5	0	2
	Abuse of Alms	0	1	3	0	4	4	0	4	0
	Debt	1	7	11	6	25	15	8	2	1
		1	12	21	9	43	24	14	6	3
False Testimony	False Oath or Perjury	0	0	1	0	1	1	0	0	0
	Forgery	1	1	0	0	2	2	0	0	0
	Rash Testimony	0	1	1	0	2	1	1	0	1
		1	2	2	0	5	4	1	0	1
Totals		49	103	185	75	**407**	272	122	25	28

but they played a crucial role in the admission of new members; they shaped the priorities of church discipline by bringing matters to the attention of the consistory and accusing other members; they not only appeared before the consistory to contest ecclesiastical sentences and retaliate against others but also took the initiative to make confessions and to gain readmission to communion when suspended; they understood and engaged in theological controversies, shaping debates at a time when such issues have traditionally been regarded as moot even to many clerics. Poorer men and women objected to and worked within the ambiguities between private and public boundaries as defined by the consistory. Whereas, on the one hand Thomas Adams demanded public confessions from particular persons, on the other Florence Stevens expected the deacons to look after her children. In light of the energetic participation of members in this community, it is little wonder that it was here that the archetypical English presbyterian popularizer of the mid-seventeenth century, Thomas Edwards, ended his career.[156]

Conclusion

———◆◆◆———

Historians cannot always expect to find the missing pieces of a puzzle; when they do, it can cast further light on the parts that they already hold. English presbyterianism is one such piece. By the end of the sixteenth century Elizabeth and her bishops appeared to have effectively silenced presbyterians and driven them into obscurity. Presbyterians themselves contributed to this picture by carefully concealing themselves when in fact they remained active and their ideas continued to flourish. This has a range of implications for the broader interpretation of the period.

First, it modifies the trajectory of episcopal self-definition and action. It makes Richard Bancroft's aggression toward presbyterians before and after he became Archbishop of Canterbury seem much less effective, indeed counterproductive, making presbyterians more socially radical and keener to formulate legal objections to bishops. It shows that many of the anti-episcopal arguments often seen as the product of the civil-war years were fully developed in previous decades within a hidden presbyterian community. All this throws the emphasis away from the particular problems introduced by Laudianism and toward a more extended "war" over religion. Long before Laudian policies were articulated, George Downame had been engaged in an effective polemic aimed at disrupting the solidarity of the godly: the neglect of Downame is, indeed, a clear consequence of the failure of historians to identify the continued existence of presbyterianism. Reaction against Laudian obsessions with ceremonialism and sacerdotalism were to play their part in shaping the puritan program in the 1640s, but more important was the much longer lasting conflict over issues of ecclesiology rooted in both Scripture and in the English and continental protestant experience.

Equally, the rediscovery of the continuity and development of English presbyterianism has implications for understanding the dynamics of English nonconformity. Historians in search of the genesis of congregationalism have tended to explain its emergence through the specific influence of either separatism, the Elizabethan puritan tradition, or in reaction to episcopal juris-diction: some have pointed out that congregationalism could not have been inspired by separatism given the antiseparatist writings of congregational au-thors; others have turned to the Elizabethan puritan tradition.[1] However, it is quite as problematic to describe congregational development as an uncon-tested extension of Elizabethan puritanism. The continuation of presbyterian-ism is the missing link here. It is clear that by the early seventeenth century presbyterian and congregational exponents responded to each other as well as to others with different visions of the visible church. Their disagreements centered on the role of synods, but also involved differences over the nature and extent of common consent, the administration of the sacraments, the re-lationship between ecclesiology and soteriology, and elements of worship that were prescribed by the Second Commandment. Henry Jacob admitted that he consciously extended the continental reformation led by Calvin. According to his adversaries, he did more. His church in Southwark (and exposition of congregationalism) amounted to a silent ecclesiastical revolution: not only did it introduce novel claims to popular sovereignty and ecclesiastical inde-pendence into the puritan mainstream, but it also marked a turning point in history through the dissolution of the universal visible church. Rather than becoming a separatist by conviction, Jacob claimed to remain in fellowship with English parishes which enabled him to work out an ecclesiastical trans-formation within the Church of England. If English presbyterianism inspired congregational thinking in the early seventeenth century, it contributed to its development in a negative as well as positive sense by directly challenging it. Indeed, its challenges were as forceful as those of conformist critics.

The ecclesiology of the mid-seventeenth century was thus more than a result of circumstantial expediency.[2] However fluid ecclesiological disposi-tions may have been, these issues had already come under consideration and resulted in ideological divisions. At the same time, the opening decades of the seventeenth century were marked by a dynamism in which ecclesiological definition was in constant motion. Within the diverse spectrum of English protestant thought, varying ecclesiological formulations emerged, changed, and were reconfigured. Although some scholars (in line with Richard Bax-ter) would prefer to abandon the use of ecclesiological categories altogether for this period, contemporaries continued to employ them. It appears that the process by which ecclesiological views developed in relation to multiple parties gave increasingly precise definitions to various positions while it was modifying and realigning them. This took place as a multidimensional debate between conformists, congregationalists, and presbyterians, as well as separatists and those who represented elements from more than one category. There were also participants who were neither from the stock of erudite theologians nor necessarily from the early Stuart period.[3] If this points back to tensions within the godly community, it no less significantly demonstrates the constant stimulation and further articulation of ecclesiological positions by a range of participants.

This raises important questions for the mid-seventeenth century, particularly with regard to the influence of Scottish presbyterianism. A pan-British history could have been told, and there would have undoubtedly been value in pursuing this aspect of presbyterianism for the early seventeenth century. However, it has not been necessary to discuss the problems of multiple monarchy in order to explore conflict between multiple ecclesiologies.[4] Examination of English presbyterian developments during this period reveals several important distinctions between the English and Scottish versions. English presbyterians made concerted efforts to accommodate royal supremacy. They built an alliance with common lawyers and were particularly concerned to argue that their polity would not impinge on civil authority in response to conformist accusations of political sedition. English presbyterians also quarreled with congregationalists for an extended period before the Westminster Assembly. Yet in the course of these debates presbyterians came to stress congregational liberty, and they sustained continued debate even as their disagreements advanced in many directions. This practice was unique to English presbyterianism; Scottish presbyterians did not engage on this level before the mid-seventeenth century with such erastian and congregational arguments.[5] The continued existence of English presbyterianism should therefore provide an essential context for further investigations into the alliance with Scottish presbyterians instead of being replaced wholesale by Scottish explanations.

There is also value in pursuing an English history that is sensitive to continental and transatlantic experiences without being imperialistic. If English presbyterianism was not identical to Scottish presbyterianism, it too resembled international presbyterianism. It had a nature that was both international and national.[6] Hostility from religious authorities helped to stimulate the mobility of English presbyterians during this period, and under such circumstances the Netherlands provided a place of refuge for nonconformists across the spectrum. While the diaspora was significant in contributing to the international nature of English presbyterianism, it was not the only factor. At times English presbyterians left their native country in order to assist actively in church government overseas or migrated for economic, academic, and other reasons.[7] There were also international influences other than personal contact that reveal a closer relationship between English developments and those on the continent than is often recognized.[8] If this study has focused on the experience and continued correspondence of English presbyterians with the Netherlands and with New England, it has also recognized a wider reception of continental traditions. As in the example of Walter Travers and in the debates over common consent, English presbyterian thought drew on a range of continental examples. The view of the reformers and the example of the reformed churches played a crucial role in ecclesiological debate during the early seventeenth century. Yet English presbyterian internationalism must also be seen as more than the importation of foreign ideas. It developed within international and national contexts, actively engaging with those on the continent and across the Atlantic, and by the mid-seventeenth century those who had studied in England would carry their ideas across to Eastern Europe.[9]

The self-description of those who participated in activity outside of England suggests that international experiences did not necessarily conflict with English identification. The case study of the English Reformed Church in Amsterdam is one example which reveals that English history can extend beyond traditional boundaries and that distances overseas may not have been as far as they often seem.[10] The English church was incorporated into the Dutch Classis, but its members identified themselves as English.[11] Although not under the immediate authority of the Church of England, the English Reformed Church continued to identify itself in relation to the Church of England. Their criteria for admitting separatists into membership appears to have been their confession of the Church of England as a true church.

The continued movement of ecclesiological debate can be traced alongside the movement of people, goods, and books across the channel and the Atlantic. Ideas and debates extended across geographical boundaries as well as beyond the particular moments when they first took place. According to John Paget, members of the congregation broadcast their complaints against him in Amsterdam as well as in England.[12] Ecclesiological disputes that began in England also advanced to several theaters outside of England's own borders and outside of the British Isles. Issues initially raised by presbyterians in intrapuritan debates in England were central to later developments in the Netherlands and are essential for interpreting polemical exchanges with those in New England. Many of the disputants in these debates overlapped, and so did their arguments. Thomas Hooker referred directly back to Henry Jacob's definition of the visible church as a particular congregation. The establishment of English identity through history also became a distinct priority, even for those outside England. Both the early English protestant tradition and Elizabethan presbyterian writing were used as yardsticks for measuring the parameters of nonconformity in the early Stuart period. That English identity and history became inscribed in these debates suggests that this is an English history.

English presbyterianism therefore provides a crucial interpretive key to ecclesiological developments. What can be made of its impact? Perhaps it can be characterized as an agent of opposition that made a straightforward contribution to the outbreak of the English Civil War and to the development of an ideological faction in the Long Parliament. Presbyterians continued to set themselves up against the bishops and against godly clergy who tended toward ecclesiological variation. They stressed the conditional nature of ecclesiastical unity, which they based on "verity": as the "Reformed Church Government" noted, "[We] must not simply desire peace but such a peace as is acceptable unto god . . . that peace and unity then which is joined with truth. . . . If unity simply without any further regard, had been sufficient there was as much unity as might be in that that made the Golden Calfe."[13]

The controversial and conditional elements in presbyterianism seem to confirm a historiography that has depicted an innate tendency toward disagreement and division. Accounts of the movement during the 1570s and 1580s are marked by an absence of agreement among those who were themselves committed to advancing presbyterianism. Its failure, according to R. G. Usher, was as a result inevitable.[14] Historians have also argued that English presbyterians significantly contributed to social divisions within local communities by condemning the unregenerate mass of English society, believing in the elect as a narrow minority, and by maintaining a highly specified agenda for moral reform.

How can such impressions be reconciled with accounts that argue the opposite? Revisionist historians have drawn attention to the consensual nature of godly debate in the first two decades of the seventeenth century and of the political process at the beginning of the Long Parliament.[15] Anti-puritan writers endlessly complained of the popularity and organized underground of presbyterians.[16] To view presbyterian activity exclusively through a prism that fractures their activity obscures their broader objectives and ignores the degree to which they established alliances with those who did not conform to the highest standard of their rigorous discipline.[17] Whether dealing with theological controversies, intercongregational conflicts, or interpersonal disagreements, presbyterianism was as much a shared commitment to a means of coming to a resolution as it was an organized movement for further ecclesiastical and moral reformation. English presbyterianism was a process rather than a movement or series of moments. It should not be simplistically labeled as either a success or failure, nor should its impact be measured as either divisive or conciliatory.

During this period there was a commitment to unity embedded in English ecclesiology, yet many factors contributed to conflicting ecclesiological developments and divisions. In their definition of the visible church some of the godly (such as the presbyterians) presupposed that common consent in ecclesiological affairs was both national and ecumenical rather than merely congregational. The visible church as a general and universal body was a national cord that was not only politically defined but also ecclesiologically binding. It provided a theoretical and organizational basis for collective action that was not constructed simply on the basis of antithetical argument and opposition. It had implications including and beyond a potential usefulness for the mobilization of alliances. Belief in a universal ecclesiastical society bound the godly to a wider community outside the particular congregation, as well as to antiquity, and to a diverse spectrum of men and women that included those who claimed faith even if not a record of exemplary piety.

This was a presbyterianism before denominationalism and a Calvinism marked as much by collectivism as it was by individualism. These presbyterians neither saw themselves as being, nor behaved much like, a denomination. Rather than finding them to be a minority group whose actions were dictated by a concern for self-preservation and individualistic interest,[18] they worked within a wider set of circumstances that they had not welcomed. It is true that presbyterians played a central role in the formation of denomination: they gave some of the earliest definition to what would emerge as congregationalism as well as presbyterianism at the same time as they resisted a distinct denominational identity. What distinguishes ecclesiological debate during this period from that of later periods, however, is the continued refinement of ecclesiological views through disputation and argumentation. This took place because of the consensual nature of ecclesiology during this period and because ecclesiology had not yet evolved into fixed denominational parties and become enshrined in personal identity. That the godly could come closer to agreement on certain issues at the same time as becoming further divided on others suggests that discussion did not always straightforwardly and inevitably result in further division. Eventually ecclesiological debate would no longer need to be prohibited by the monarch, since uncompromising denominational loyalties would ultimately complete the enclosure of ecclesiology. But this was still not the case in the early seventeenth century.

The consensual nature of English ecclesiology becomes a fruitful base from which to observe the flexibility of presbyterianism, a flexibility that could range from attempts to reconcile a reformed polity with Elizabeth's supremacy to guarding the personal liberty of Elizabeth Hanwell, a humble member, whose children repeatedly came under discipline by the consistory. While presbyterians were attacking the hierarchy of the Church of England, they were making a conscientious attempt to reconcile their polity with the royal supremacy. While they developed an alliance with lawyers and members of the elites in town and countryside, their polity was adaptable to more humble lay participation and interest. This alternative view reveals that presbyterianism had a range of effects. In the case of ecclesiological controversy, they played a central role in deepening divisions and opening up new contentions, and contributed to the development of further ecclesiological ambiguities. Yet, in the course of their argument over the role of synods, puritans had come somewhat closer to an agreement as presbyterians conceded to congregational liberties while their opponents allowed for the authority of church councils under certain conditions.

Not only did presbyterian leaders speak in varied ways to different audiences, but they also played varying roles when dealing with them. They both arbitrated in and became involved in disputes. The story began with their role as defendants and their refusal to take the oath before the High Commission and the Court of Star Chamber. Following their trials in the late sixteenth century, presbyterians raised complaints against episcopacy and built a case against its church polity and exercise of civil authority as "plaintiffes."[19] Presbyterians drew attention to the multiple roles played by John Ball, who was "a plaintiffe for the Nonconformists against the corruptions in our Church" as well as a "defendant" of the Church of England against separatists.[20] In addition, presbyterians acted as leading prosecutors against congregational "defendants" in a series of what they considered to be trials for schism. Yet even here they could assume a dual role. Just as Martin Hanwell was both father and accuser of his children, so Henry Jacob's presbyterian "examiners" acted as his prosecutors as well as his spiritual kin whose duty it was to correct him. They believed that he ought to be grateful for their correction.[21]

Ecclesiological debate also closely intersected with politics and society.[22] Presbyterians used ecclesiastical, social, and constitutional arguments to attack episcopacy, to propose practical plans for the reordering of secular and ecclesiastical jurisdiction, and to direct all of this to judges and magistrates "specially of thes that be in Authoritye." Presbyterians' exhortations to a politicized audience came from their understanding that the role of ministers included advising magistrates. In their view, privy councillors were not the only ones who were supposed to counsel princes and parliaments. Increasingly, historians have found that a better understanding of the political actors during this period requires exploring their interactions with others.[23] Further investigation into the relationship between political and ecclesiastical figures will not restore a puritan choir to Elizabethan parliaments. Neither will it reconstruct a bipolar division between the crown and the parliament or between the court and the county. Puritan appeals to crown and parliament can be identified, as well as to common law and neo-Roman ideology. By extending analysis beyond episodic moments and motions passed in parliament, it has recovered a rich diversity in ecclesiological thought that intersected with a wider political culture.[24]

Further work on lay-clerical alliances would throw more light not only on political culture but also on religious culture and the role of the laity in the changes that ensued in both. Presbyterians shared more than a mutual hostility to episcopacy with sympathetic lay people. They exchanged notes and arguments. Presbyterians exhorted lay allies to take political action, and they also married into their families and depended upon them for financial and administrative support in their ministries. Even a cursory survey of these relationships demonstrates that there was no inevitable drift toward congregational autonomy when the laity took part in nonconformist activity. Puritan exercise of jurisdiction outside immediate localities in addition to wider concepts of the community counters the view that these relationships were based on individualistic impulses and necessarily led toward independency. Lay participation extended beyond patronage and material contributions.[25] Even relatively humble lay men and women could play an active role in theological developments. Moreover, lay men and women were not always wholly ignorant of ecclesiological issues; they also initiated and participated in deliberations over matters of church polity.

There is less of a tendency to overlook the active agency of the laity in general than of poorer men and women in particular. Humble folk have frequently entered into the narratives as at best passive recipients (or even victims) of reformation or as only half-understanding basic if not watered down protestant tenets.[26] In the English Reformed Church in Amsterdam, however, the meanest members appear among the most active agents in reformed discipline, and they understood it. Both poorer men *and* women witnessed for new members, reported the sins of their neighbors, testified in disciplinary cases, approached the consistory for arbitration, and redefined public and private boundaries. Their participation involved more than redressing personal grievances, as they expressed concern for the appointment of their church officers and could also play a role in mediating between members. Their interaction with the consistory was often born out of conviction, and they apparently felt competent in grasping theological concepts. Elizabeth Hanwell was in no doubt of her salvation. Although a poor women, Florence Stevens was not only sure of her salvation but also so sure of the soundness of her understanding of the doctrine of justification that she confidently assaulted the theological rationale of the consistory's demand for outward evidence of her repentance.

It has been possible to identify the convictions of Elizabeth Hanwell and Florence Stevens only because of their engagement with the consistory of the English Reformed Church in Amsterdam. If this book concludes with a case study of one particular community, it is also itself a microhistory. English presbyterianism operated within a broader social, political, ecclesiological, chronological, and geographical framework than many traditional accounts have allowed. It could appeal to diverse constituents with varying interests. It could also form alliances with many parties even if those parties did not always agree. To factor English presbyterianism back into the story, then, is to recover an extensive web of relationships and to weave an alternative narrative out of the diverse worlds that they inhabited.[27]

Appendix: Walter Travers's Papers

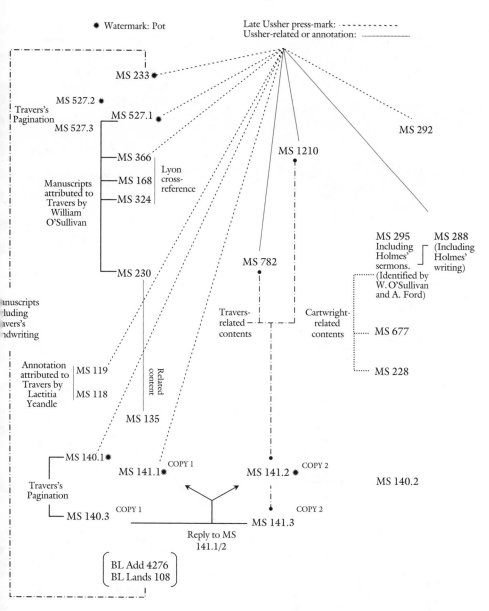

FIG. AI. Presbyterian-related Manuscripts, Trinity College Dublin Library.

192   Appendix

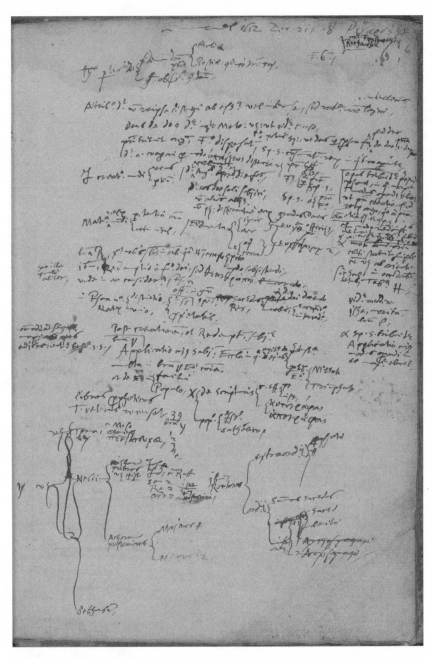

FIG. A2. Travers's Ramus Tree, TCD MS 366, fol. 6r. Courtesy of the Board of Trinity
College Dublin.

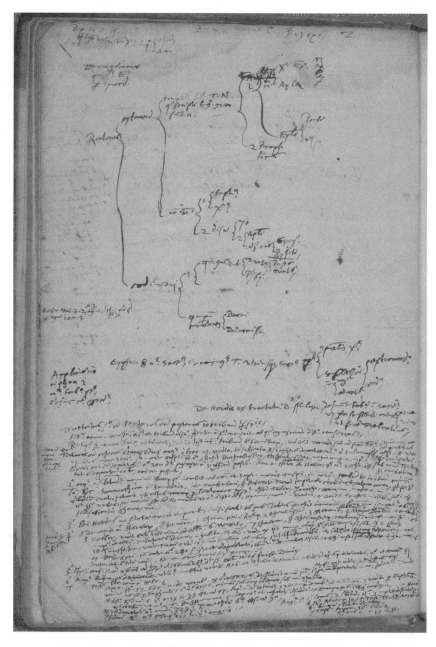

FIG. A3. Travers's Ramus Tree, TCD MS 366, fol. 6v. Courtesy of the Board of Trinity College Dublin.

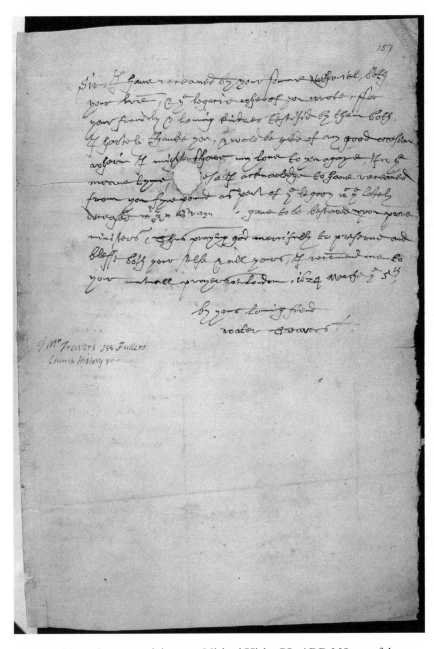

FIG. A4. Travers's autograph letter to Michael Hicks, BL, ADD MS 4276 fol. 157.
©The British Library Board.

Bibliographic Note: The Provenance
of Walter Travers's Papers

––––––––•◆•––––––––

Although the biographer S. J. Knox believed that Walter Travers's manuscripts could not be traced, Travers's student at Trinity College Dublin, James Ussher, later archbishop of Armagh, in fact procured them after his death, and they are now held in the library at Trinity College Dublin.[1] The late keeper of manuscripts there, William O'Sullivan, established that Travers's papers became part of Archbishop Ussher's collection, which was added to the library's manuscript holdings in 1661.[2] He identified several volumes as having belonged to Travers in his handwritten notes in the library's manuscript catalogue. These are listed under his predecessor T. K. Abbott's numbers 168 (*Analysis variorum locorum S.S.*), 324 (*Collectanea varia Theologica*), 366 (*Collectania varia de rebus Theologicis, Historicis*), and 527. Two of these volumes (366 and 527) still bear an old shelf-mark from Ussher's library, consisting of a triple letter, and another old shelf-mark that Samuel Foley assigned to the manuscripts in 1688. Travers's unbound papers were not included in the seventeenth-century catalogue of Ussher's collection, and it was only in the mid-eighteenth century that all of them were catalogued, when John Lyon bound the loose papers into volumes and rearranged all the Trinity manuscripts, mainly by provenance.[3] Lyon further indicated the distinct provenance of Travers's papers by cross-referencing manuscripts such as 186 with 324 and 366 in his catalogue.[4]

After O'Sullivan's retirement in 1980, Travers's manuscripts remained largely unrecognized, although in 1990 Laetitia Yeandle discussed them, and their provenance, in the Folger edition of Richard Hooker's *Works*:

> These four manuscripts (MSS 168, 324, 366, and 527) have only recently been identified as Travers's. None bears his name, and the attribution depends solely on a comparison of the handwriting, which is appalling, with the few known specimens of his hand. . . . These meager specimens were all that could be drawn on to determine the identity of the four manuscripts. The contents, however, help confirm the attributions. . . . Two of the other three manuscripts consisting of various notes and some daily entries (MSS 324, apparently dating from the last quarter of the sixteenth century, and 366, dating from about 1610 to about 1630) were written by a man with strong Puritan sympathies who was closely connected with a dissenting congregation.[5]

She also found that "in addition, two other manuscripts contain what seem to be notations in Travers's hand [on a copy of] Hooker's *Justification* (MS 118) and his

Answer (in MS 119) — the two of Hooker's works that most closely concerned Travers and that aroused widespread discussion at the time of their composition."[6] Despite this, neglect of these sources continued.[7] The most likely explanation is Travers's poor penmanship.

However, if Travers's handwriting is "appalling," it is also distinctive. My study of these manuscripts not only confirmed O'Sullivan's attributions to Travers through the contents of his papers but also led to the identification of several additional volumes of Travers's manuscripts in Trinity library through provenance, distinctive handwriting, and contents.[8] Travers's handwriting appears in his response to Richard Hooker as well as in response to a leading exponent of congregationalism in the early seventeenth century. These manuscripts, misidentified as antiseparatist polemic, were composed by a panel of English presbyterian "examiners" against a "defendant" of congregationalism, who can be identified almost certainly as Henry Jacob. Not only do the examiners accuse the defendant of establishing a congregational church, but the internal references correspond to the dates of Jacob's congregational experiment in Southwark and the points made by the defendant are the exact arguments made in Jacob's treatises, particularly his *Attestation*.[9]

These treatises were part of a prolonged exchange. Two copies are extant in Trinity College Library; throughout these Travers has marked corrections, annotations, and pagination. One copy also bears a residual late shelf-mark from Ussher's library.[10] The watermark that appears in both copies (a pot) matches that which appears in another collection of Travers's papers, manuscript 527. In addition to the presbyterian treatises are two copies of the defendants' response, one of which appears to have been in Travers's possession. Travers used numerals and capital letters to paginate the more complete text, which is in poorer condition than the second copy. Although there are no clues to the identity of the other presbyterian "examiners" in Jacob's writings, internal evidence from this reply confirms Travers's authorship of the examination. Not only does Travers's defense of his writing, "the declaracion," prove his involvement in the examination of Jacob, but his identity is also made clear by Jacob's mention of "Mr Traverse" as his opponent.[11]

Additional Travers-related papers can also be identified through their provenance and Travers's handwriting. These include translations of sermons ranging from those of the early church Father John Chrysostom, to the contemporary protestant Abraham Scultetus. Travers's handwriting further appears in his brother John's philosophical notebook in Trinity College Library, dating to the early seventeenth century. These specimens of Travers's handwriting share all the distinctive features of Travers's autograph letters in the British Library. Elisabeth Leedham-Green has confirmed that the handwriting samples included in these manuscripts match Travers's other writings and that the attribution is firm.[12]

Bound with one of Travers's copies of Henry Jacob's responses is another source, which provides insight into presbyterian activity following suppression in the early 1590s. A treatise entitled the "Reformed Church Government," which dates to the last days of Elizabeth's reign, sheds light on the presbyterians' campaign against episcopacy and their continued agitation for further ecclesiastical reform.[13] Although this manuscript was found with Travers-related papers and the arguments made in it closely correspond to earlier Elizabethan presbyterian works, the author remains unknown and there is no direct internal or external evidence of a relationship to other of Travers's papers held at Trinity.

There are several manuscript volumes relating to English presbyterianism at Trinity that bear no identifiable relationship to Travers through their provenance.[14] Thomas Cartwright's autograph letter to Arthur Hildersham is among other papers linked to Elizabethan presbyterianism. The contents of TCD MS 677 concern Thomas Cartwright, Matthew Holmes, Edmund Snape, and William Fludd. William O'Sullivan and Alan Ford identified Matthew Holmes's handwriting in TCD MS 295. Holmes's handwriting also appears in one of Ussher's manuscripts, TCD MS 288. In addition to manuscripts relating to Elizabethan presbyterianism, Trinity also holds other material concerning early Stuart ecclesiological deliberations. A prominent nonconformist text in the realm of ecclesiological debate in the early seventeenth century was *The Reply* to George Downame's defense of his sermon. Contemporaries identified Richard Sheerwood as its likely author, but aside from his participation in the petition at the accession of James I and VI to the English throne, little is known about him.[15] The third part of the *Reply* does not appear with existing copies of the first two parts and until now has remained unknown to historians. However, in Trinity Library, a manuscript copy of the last seven chapters of the third part is extant and bears Ussher's shelf-mark. Its contents confirm Thomas Paget's claim that the presbyterian writer John Paget had edited and then approved of the text as agreeing with the authority of synods and assemblies.[16]

Notes

———◆◆◆———

INTRODUCTION

1. Patrick Collinson, *The Elizabethan Puritan Movement* (London: Jonathan Cape, 1967), 101–8. Their proposed model of church government also included a hierarchy of ecclesiastical bodies ranging from the local consistory and the provincial classis to the national synod and ecumenical council.

2. Thomas Rogers, *Catholic Doctrine*, ed. J. J. S. Perowne, Parker Society (Cambridge: Cambridge University Press, 1854), 17. Considerable weight has also been given to Richard Baxter's claim that "the truth is *Presbytery* was not then known in *England*, except among a few studious Scholars, nor well by them": R. S. Paul, *Assembly of the Lord: Politics and Religion in the Westminster Assembly and the "Grand Debate"* (Edinburgh: T. and T. Clark, 1985), 112; Richard Baxter, *Reliquiae Baxterianae, or, Mr. Richard Baxters Narrative of the Most Memorable Passages of his Life and Times* (London: 1696), 3: 41.

3. *The Presbyterian Movement in the Reign of Queen Elizabeth as Illustrated by the Minute Book of the Dedham Classis, 1582–1589*, ed. R. G. Usher (London: Camden Society Publications, 3rd ser., 1905), 3: xxiv. W. A. Shaw claimed that "there are no traces of any inheritance of the ideas or influence of this Elizabethan Presbyterianism by the English Puritans of the days of James I and Charles I": *A History of the English Church during the Civil War and under the Commonwealth, 1640–1660* (London: Longmans, 1900), 1: 6.

4. According to Collinson, "[F]or most church puritans, the presbyterian polity, or any other scheme for the extensive reparation of the Church's structure, institutions and ministry, became a remote and irrelevant idea": *Elizabethan Puritan Movement*, 464–65.

5. S. R. Gardiner, *History of England: From the Accession of James I to the Outbreak of the Civil War* (London: Longmans, 1883–84).

6. Patrick Collinson, "Puritan Classical Movement" (Ph.D. diss., University of London, 1957), and *Elizabethan Puritan Movement*.

7. Patrick Collinson, *The Religion of Protestants: The Church in English Society, 1559–1625* (Oxford: Clarendon Press, 1982), and "Towards a Broader Understanding of the Early Dissenting Tradition," in *Godly People* (London: Hambledon Press, 1983), 527–50.

8. Nicholas Tyacke, *Anti-Calvinists: The Rise of English Arminianism c. 1590–1640* (Oxford: Clarendon, 1990). Tyacke's later stress on broader continuities across Eliza-

bethan and early Stuart puritanism is an important exception to the historiography that has argued for the redirection of puritanism in the early seventeenth century: "The Fortunes of English Puritanism, 1603–1640," in *Aspects of English Protestantism* (Manchester: Manchester University Press, 2001), 126. Jacqueline Eales also argued for an important line of continuity between Elizabethan and Jacobean puritan patronage and religious culture: "A Road to Revolution: The Continuity of Puritanism, 1559–1642," in *The Culture of English Puritanism, 1560–1700,* ed. Christopher Durston and Jacqueline Eales (Basingstoke: Macmillan, 1996), 184–209. My dissertation explored the relationship between Elizabethan and early Stuart presbyterianism and the overlap between theological and legal arguments against episcopacy in the early seventeenth century: "English Presbyterianism, c 1590–1640" (Ph.D. diss., University of Cambridge, 2006), ch. 1. Michael Winship's article, which addresses this issue to some extent, appeared while this book was in the press.

9. Tom Webster, *Godly Clergy in Early Stuart England: The Caroline Puritan Movement,* c. *1620–1643* (Cambridge: Cambridge University Press, 1997).

10. Heinz Schilling, "Confessionalization," in *Confessionalization in Europe,* ed. John M. Headley, Hans J. Hillderbrand, and Anthony J. Papalas (Aldershot: Ashgate, 2004), 21–37. See also "Post-Confessional Reformation History," *Archiv für Reformationsgeschichte* 97 (2006): 276–306.

11. "The religious dualistic cast of much recent scholarship on early Stuart religion, revolving around either an Anglican/puritan or Arminian/Calvinist paradigm, has served to obscure the extent to which a broad spectrum of different religious views did exist before the civil war": Anthony Milton, *Catholic and Reformed: The Roman and Protestant Churches in English Protestant Thought, 1600–1640* (Cambridge: Cambridge University Press, 1995), 7. For a study of ecclesiastical divisions between English protestants in the Jacobean church, see Charles Prior, *Defining the Jacobean Church: The Politics of Religious Controversy, 1603–1625* (Cambridge: Cambridge University Press, 2005).

12. Peter Lake, *Moderate Puritans and the Elizabethan Church* (Cambridge: Cambridge University Press, 1982). See also, for example, "Moving the Goal Posts? Modified Subscription and the Construction of Conformity in the Early Stuart Church," in *Conformity and Orthodoxy in the English Church, c. 1560–1660,* ed. Peter Lake and Michael Questier (Woodbridge: Boydell Press, 2000), 179–205.

13. David Como, *Blown by the Spirit: Puritanism and the Emergence of an Antinomian Underground in Pre-Civil-War England* (Stanford: Stanford University Press, 2004).

14. Peter Lake, "The Historiography of Puritanism," in *Cambridge Companion to Puritanism,* ed. John Coffey and Paul C. H. Lim (Cambridge: Cambridge University Press, 2008), 361.

15. S. J. Knox, *Walter Travers: Paragon of Elizabethan Puritanism* (London: Methuen, 1962), 141.

16. Thomas Fuller called Travers "The Neck" of the Presbyterian party and Cartwright "The Head," while Richard Bancroft, the puritans' chief antagonist, saw Travers as the "Paragon of Elizabethan Puritanism": *The Church History of Britain* (London: T. Tegg, 1837), 3: 26.

17. "[It] is very unlikely that much will ever be known of Travers' personal life during this period": Knox, *Walter Travers,* 146–47.

18. See Bibliographic Note.

19. Travers's distinctive handwriting has proved difficult for even the most skilled palaeographers, which is the most likely explanation for the neglect of these sources. In discussing MS 168 Laetitia Yeandle stated that "the hand and abbreviated form of these notes make them exceedingly difficult to read": *Works of Richard Hooker*, ed. W. Speed Hill (Cambridge: Harvard University Press: 1982), 5: xxi, note 21. Travers's poor penmanship may be partly explained by the fact that he never intended many of his papers to be read by others. I am grateful to Elisabeth Leedham-Green for her help in deciphering these passages.

20. According to Samuel Clarke, Herring "had many papers and letters (which he much prized) contained both the spirituall brethings of greacious hearts, and matters of great concernment: and those he durst not adventure to take with him [to the Netherlands] (fearing a search,) nor yet did he judge it safe to leave them [in England], because he knew not into what hands they might come; therefore upon advice he burnt many writings, though both then and afterwards he did with tears think of that Letter martyrdome, (for so he called it,)": *The Lives of Two and Twenty English Divines Eminent in Their Generations for Learning, Piety, and Painfulnesse in the Work of the Ministry, and for their Sufferings in the Cause of Christ* (London: 1660), 194. The self-censorship of sources for this period is discussed in the introduction to Richard Cust and Ann Hughes, *Conflict in Early Stuart England: Studies in Religion and Politics, 1603–1642,* (Harlow: Longman, 1989), 13.

21. This process did not necessarily apply to all presbyterian activity as seen in the polemical writing of the mid-seventeenth century. Ann Hughes noted that, in Thomas Edwards's *Gangraena,* "[t]here is no clear hierarchy of authorization—printed evidence is not necessarily preferred to oral or manuscript testimony": "Print, Persecution and Polemic: Thomas Edwards' *Gangraena* (1646) and Civil War Sectarianism," in *The Uses of Script and Print, 1300–1700,* ed. Julia Crick and Alexandra Walsham (Cambridge: Cambridge University Press, 2004), 263. However, the process of weighing historical evidence and personal testimony in theological deliberation and church discipline appears to be characteristic of presbyterians, especially in the manuscript sources surveyed in this study. J. G. A. Pocock commented that mental patterns of this sort were particularly acute in historical consciousness and that they were not limited to historical evidence: "British History: A Plea for a New Subject," *JMH* 47, no. 4 (1975): 611–12. For the role of history in theological debate, see Chapter 4, below; for the patterns used in theological debate reflected through the consistory records in the practice of presbyterian church government, see Chapter 7, below.

22. This passage instructed offended parties first to seek reconciliation with an obstinate brother individually, then to bring witnesses, failing which to "tell the church" and resolve the matter by ecclesiastical authority.

23. In addition to the revisionist historiographical trends noted above, Carol Schneider underscored "a point made by many scholars" that "it is more confusing than informative to attempt to delineate 'presbyterian' and 'congregational' clerical ideologies through most of the early Stuart period": "Roots and Branches: From Principled Nonconformity to the Emergence of Religious Parties," in *Puritanism: Transatlantic Perspectives on a Seventeenth-Century Anglo-American Faith,* ed. Francis Bremer (Boston: Massachusetts Historical Society, 1993), 171. While Schneider stressed fluidity in puritan thought to the exclusion of ecclesiological distinctions,

there has also been a tendency among historians to elide English nonconformist thought, taking congregational views to be its representative position. For example, see Stephen Brachlow, *The Communion of Saints: Radical Puritan and Separatist Ecclesiology, 1570–1625* (Oxford: Clarendon Press, 1988), Tom Webster, Godly Clergy, and Michael Watts, *Dissenters: From the Reformation to the English Revolution* (Oxford: Clarendon Press, 1978), 62

24. Judith Pollman, *Religious Choice in the Dutch Republic: The Reformation of Arnoldus Buchelius, 1565–1641* (Manchester: Manchester University Press, 1999), 7–9, 77–93. For another study of multiconfessionalism through the coexistence of and interaction between competing religious traditions on the continent, see Benjamin Kaplan, *Divided by Faith: Religious Conflict and the Practice of Toleration in Early Modern Europe* (Cambridge: Harvard University Press, 2007), esp. ch. 8. Rather than approaching England as a multiconfessional state, however, multiconfessionalism is used in this book as a viable position for individuals who maintained a series of allegiances to more than one confessional tradition.

25. See Chapter 4, below.

26. *Works of Hooker* (ed. Speed Hill), 4: 255–60.

27. Anthony Milton, *Laudian and Royalist Polemic in Seventeenth-Century England* (Manchester: Manchester University Press, 2007), 93–96.

28. Backlash against the presbyterian party of the 1570s and 1580s produced a host of anti-puritan treatises in the last decade of Elizabeth's reign, which Patrick Collinson has called "the nasty nineties": "Religious Satire and the Invention of Puritanism," in *The Reign of Elizabeth I: Court and Culture in the Last Decade*, ed. John Guy (Cambridge: Cambridge University Press, 1995), 153–54. If no puritan threat actually existed after the ministers were silenced, Bancroft and Sutcliffe created it. "In the 1590s it was flatly asserted that presbyterianism was a conspiracy to overthrow the state": John Guy, "The Elizabethan Establishment and the Ecclesiastical Polity," in *The Reign of Elizabeth*, 131.

29. Unlike his predecessors, George Downame, a defender of episcopacy, carefully outlined the difference between older and newer disciplinarians, before proceeding to argue separately against both in a sermon at St. Paul's Cross in 1608. His attempt to refute English presbyterians while also distinguishing them from congregationalists makes clear that at least some conformists knew the difference between the two: George Downame, *Two Sermons the One Commending the Ministerie in Generall: the Other Defending the Office of Bishops in Particular* (London: 1608), 5–7. See also his *A Defence of the Sermon Preached at the Consecration of the L. Bishop of Bath and Welles against a Confutation Thereof by a Namelesse Author* (London: 1611), 27.

30. Quentin Skinner, *The Foundations of Modern Political Thought* (Cambridge: Cambridge University Press, 1978), 2: 267–75; Martin van Gelderen, *The Political Thought of the Dutch Revolt* (Cambridge: Cambridge University Press, 1992), ch. 3.

31. Insofar as the presbyterians continued to direct their initiatives for further national ecclesiastical reform at lawyers and public authorities, they operated in the public domain, even if hidden from a wider audience. This does not assume a fixed dichotomy between public and private boundaries, but leaves room for the ambiguity, overlap, and constant construction of those boundaries. Jürgen Habermas's model of public and private spheres has come under attack and some have preferred to identify several or multiple spheres, but the terms are employed here because they were used

by contemporaries. Rather than proposing a direct parallel between Habermas and the early seventeenth century, his model is used to focus attention on these issues: *The Structural Transformation of the Public Sphere*, trans. Thomas Burger (Boston: Massachusetts Institute of Technology, 1992), 1–2.

32. All this was part of an intrapuritan debate, similar to that which Peter Lake and David Como discussed in another context as an underground in which the godly contested puritan orthodoxy, normally outside the purview of ecclesiastical authorities: "'Orthodoxy' and Its Discontents: Dispute Settlement and the Production of 'Consensus' in the London (Puritan) 'Underground,'" *JBS* 39, no. 1 (2000), 34–70.

33. See Chapter 3, below.

34. The introduction of "independency" into the presbyterians' vocabulary at this date bears witness to the novelty of Henry Jacob's ecclesiastical polity. As Quentin Skinner has remarked, "The surest sign that a group or society has entered into the self-conscious possession of a new concept is that a corresponding vocabulary will be developed, a vocabulary which can then be used to pick out and discuss the concept in question with consistency": "The Idea of a Cultural Lexicon," in *Visions of Politics* (Cambridge: Cambridge University Press, 2002), 1: 160.

35. Although the usefulness of the term "Second Reformation" has been debated by scholars seeking to explain the extension of Lutheran reform to Calvinism in central Europe, it is useful here for highlighting English presbyterian identification with the institutional development of reformed consistories on the continent and their concern for purifying worship by "completing" reformation of the Church of England. For the uses of the term "Second Reformation," see Harm Klueting, "Problems of the Term and Concept 'Second Reformation': Memories of a 1980s Debate," in *Confessionalization in Europe, 1555–1700*, ed. John M. Headley, Hans J. Hillerbrand, and Anthony J. Papalas (Aldershot: Ashgate, 2004), 37–50; and Bodo Nischan, *Prince, People, and Confession: The Second Reformation in Brandenburg* (Philadelphia: University of Pennsylvania Press, 1994).

36. This is one example of the connection between theory and practice. It marks a notable shift from the historiographical focus on disagreement over the role of synods, often virtually the single point of contrast between these competing forms of ecclesiastical government. See also Chapters 4, 7.

37. Regardless of the practical implications of congregationalism, Jacob distinguished his ecclesiology from separatism by refusing to "separate" from the Church of England and to condemn it as altogether corrupt. This ultimately posed more of a threat than separatism by redefining the very nature of the Church of England. This supports, contra Stephen Brachlow, Perry Miller's delineation between Jacob's ecclesiology and that of separatists: *Orthodoxy in Massachusetts, 1630–1650* (New York: Harper and Row, 1970), chs. 3–4. This has also been confirmed by Victoria Gregory's re-examination of congregational literature: "Congregational Puritanism and the Radical Puritan Community in England, *c.* 1585–1625" (Ph.D. diss., University of Cambridge, 2003), esp. ch. 6.

38. Philip Gorski, *The Disciplinary Revolution: Calvinism and the Rise of the State in Early Modern Europe* (Chicago: University of Chicago Press, 2003).

39. For a discussion of how covenanted membership did not necessarily lead to absolute congregational independence among the early exponents of separatism, see B. R. White, *The English Separatist Tradition: From the Marian Martyrs to the Pilgrim*

Fathers (Oxford: Oxford University Press, 1971), 29, 61, 81. For the currency of the neo-Roman concept of liberty among secular writers in early Stuart England and its potency in the mid-seventeenth century, see Quentin Skinner, "Classical Liberty, Renaissance Translation and the English Civil War," in *Visions of Politics*, 2: 309–12, and *Liberty before Liberalism* (Cambridge: Cambridge University Press, 1998).

40. D. A. Martin commented on the trend "dominated by the typology of church and sect proposed by Troeltsch." Whereas Richard Niebuhr's discussion of denomination, and subsequent scholarship, has tended "to regard the denomination as an advanced stage in the development of the sect," Martin distinguishes the denomination from both church and sect typologies, where "the denomination may even appear to retain some of the organizational forms and titles which belong to a church, but the content and understanding of these forms will be quite different": "The Denomination," *British Journal of Sociology* 13, no. 1 (1962): 1. For other examples of the tension between church and sect types, see Alastair Duke and Rosemary L. Jones, "Towards a Reformed Polity in Holland, 1572–1578," *Tijdschrift voor Geschiedenis* 3 (1976): 384.

41. Peter Lake and David Como have challenged the social limits of theological controversy by identifying the active role of relatively humble laity in early-seventeenth-century puritan debates: *The Boxmaker's Revenge: "Orthodoxy," "Heterodoxy" and the Politics of the Parish in Early Stuart London* (Stanford: Stanford University Press, 2001); David Como, *Blown by the Spirit*. Ann Hughes has argued that the popularization of presbyterianism through print and polemic during the mid-seventeenth century was not only directed to middling artisans but also extended to an audience of lower social order: "'Popular' Presbyterianism in the 1640s and 1650s: The Cases of Thomas Edwards and Thomas Hall," in *England's Long Reformation, 1500–1800*, ed. Nicholas Tyacke (London: University College London, 1998), and *Gangraena and the Struggle for the English Revolution* (Oxford: Clarendon Press, 2004). This book finds that men and women were actively involved in ecclesiastical discipline, not as might have been expected among left-wing godly, but among English presbyterians as they deliberated over church polity.

CHAPTER I

1. Patrick Collinson, "Episcopacy and Reform in England in the Later Sixteenth Century," in *Godly People*, 155. For the impact of presbyterianism on James's political thought, see Roger Mason, "James VI, George Buchanan, and 'The True Lawe of Free Monarchies,'" in *Kingship and the Commonweal: Political Thought in Renaissance and Reformation Scotland* (East Linton: Tuckwell, 1998), 215–41.

2. *The Letters of Queen Elizabeth and King James VI*, ed. J. Bruce (London: Camden Society, vol. xlvi, 1849), 63–64, cited in Clare Cross, *The Royal Supremacy in the Elizabethan Church* (London: George Allen and Unwin, 1969), 51. Although John Knox's *First Blast* against female rule was written against Mary, it coincided with Elizabeth's accession and its association with presbyterianism was no help for later Elizabethan presbyterian activists.

3. *Charles I in 1646*, ed. John Bruce (London: Camden Society, 1856), 26–27, cited in Conrad Russell, *The Causes of the English Civil War* (Oxford: Clarendon Press, 1990), 197. Anthony Milton has explained that "in rejecting presbyterian government as 'absolutely unlawful,' the king listed as one chief argument among many the fact

that it had never become established in any country save by rebellion, echoing the arguments of Heylyn": *Catholic and Reformed*, 522–23.

4. For the argument that the abolition of episcopacy would also allegedly overthrow the estates of the land in parliament and give rise to anarchy, see Michael Mendle, *Dangerous Positions: Mixed Government, the Estates of the Realm, and the Making of the Answer to the XIX Propositions* (Tuscaloosa: University of Alabama Press, 1985). For charges of potential resistance and conflict with royal supremacy, see Hooker in Lake's and Pearson's discussion on the relationship of this threat to Cartwright's doctrine of the two kingdoms: Peter Lake, *Anglicans and Puritans? Presbyterianism and English Conformist Thought from Whitgift to Hooker* (London: Unwin Hyman, 1988), ch. 4; and A. F. Scott Pearson, *Church and State: Political Aspects of Sixteenth Century Puritanism* (Cambridge: Cambridge University Press, 1928), ch. 2.

5. For conformists, the radical implications of presbyterianism were demonstrated by the political instability of Geneva: Richard Bancroft, *Daungerous Positions and Proceedings Published and Practised within the Iland of Brytaine* (London: [J. Windet for] Iohn Wolfe, 1593), 9. During the mid-seventeenth century the same argument was made against presbyterianism by Sir Thomas Aston in his *Remonstrance against Presbytery* (1641). For a discussion of this work, see John Morrill, *Cheshire, 1630–1660: County Government and Society during the English Revolution* (Oxford: Oxford University Press, 1974), 50.

6. Peter Lake, "Presbyterianism, the Idea of a National Church and the Argument from Divine Right," in *Protestantism and the National Church in Sixteenth Century England*, ed. Peter Lake and Maria Dowling (London: Croom Helm, 1987), 202.

7. "[J]ust as the Church in ancient Rome was spiritually independent of Nero's jurisdiction . . . so she ought always to be a free, spiritual society with her own spiritual head, namely, the pope, whether she lives amongst heathens or Christians": P. D. L. Avis, *The Church in the Theology of the Reformers* (London: Marshall Morgan and Scott, 1981), 156.

8. Pearson, *Church and State*, 20.

9. Ibid., 10.

10. Lake, "Presbyterianism," 197.

11. Collinson, "Puritan Classical Movement," 1122.

12. Alan Cromartie, *The Constitutionalist Revolution: An Essay on the History of England, 1450–1642* (Cambridge: Cambridge University Press, 2006), 137.

13. Regardless of its actual existence, the continued influence of presbyterianism in the late sixteenth and seventeenth centuries is undisputed. Some historians have drawn attention to the profound influence of presbyterianism in the refashioning of conformist identity. Peter Lake noted that the "major long term contribution [of presbyterianism] . . . lay in the reaction it provoked from other Elizabethan divines": "Presbyterianism," 206. Anthony Milton has described the subsequent development of conformist thought where "by the reign of James I, the doctrine that bishops were *iure divino* had become an established orthodoxy." He notes the considerable degree to which anti-presbyterians continued to feed upon the negative imagery of English presbyterianism in the first several decades of the seventeenth century and even after the 1640s through the work of Peter Heylyn: *Catholic and Reformed*, 456. William Abbott has also discussed the pressure exerted on the English by the reformed churches

on the continent: "The Issue of Episcopacy in the Long Parliament, 1640–1648: The Reasons for Abolition" (D.Phil. diss., University of Oxford, 1981).

14. For diverse readings of royal supremacy, see Cross, *Royal Supremacy*; Ethan Shagan, *Popular Politics and the English Reformation* (Cambridge: Cambridge University Press, 2003), ch. 1; and Jacqueline Rose, "Royal Ecclesiastical Supremacy and the Restoration Church," *Historical Research* 80, no. 209 (2007): 324–45. I am grateful to Ethan Shagan for his conversation on this subject.

15. Patrick Collinson, "The Monarchical Republic of Queen Elizabeth I," *Bulletin of the John Rylands University Library of Manchester* 69, no. 2 (1987): 394–424. See also *The Monarchical Republic of England: Essays in Response to Patrick Collinson*, ed. John F. McDiarmid (Aldershot: Ashgate, 2007).

16. Trinity College Dublin (TCD), MS 140, fols. 70v, 110v–111.

17. The perception that presbyterian radicals recklessly sought to set up an altogether different church has remained and is largely the result of the polemical legacies of their adversaries, despite discussion by Patrick Collinson, Peter Lake, and others of their intention to reform the existing church.

18. Walter Travers, *Fvll and Plaine Declaration of Ecclesiastical Discipline Ovt of the Word of God* (Geneva: 1580) (in all future references to this work the 1617 edition will be cited); Knox, *Walter Travers*, 33.

19. Although presbyterians were by no means the only ones to have used the language of mixed polity in England, they became associated with this form of government because they appropriated it into an ecclesiastical context with radical interests. Presbyterians such as Cartwright and Travers directly drew upon the model and secular language of mixed polity to describe presbyterian order. This is precisely why conformists could argue that the adoption of a mixed ecclesiastical polity equally threatened change in secular authority; Michael Mendle has discussed how the idea of a mixed polity as applied to the Church soon became equated with outright denial of the queen's supremacy: *Dangerous Positions*.

20. Avis, *Theology of the Reformers*, 102.

21. Lake, "Presbyterianism," 203.

22. TCD, MS 140, fols. 68r–v.

23. According the Peter Lake, "The iure divino claims of the presbyterians were no longer being matched with the cautious erastianism of Whitgift. . . . Rather the conformists had developed their own iure divino arguments which all but replicated the structure of the presbyterian case": *Anglicans and Puritans?*, 96.

24. David George Mullan, *Episcopacy in Scotland: The History of an Idea, 1560–1638* (Edinburgh: John Donald, 1986), 59.

25. Lake, *Anglicans and Puritans?*, 98.

26. TCD, MS 140, fol. 68v.

27. Ibid., fol. 104.

28. As David Mullan has said of the establishment of presbyterianism in Scotland, one "area of difficulty was that of appointments to vacant sees, a right which the crown had by no means relinquished": *Episcopacy in Scotland*, 53.

29. TCD, MS 140, fol. 104.

30. Whereas a national synod could be "summoned by Hir Majestyes Writ," a council within a province could be "summoned by the Bishop of the province," and a

bishop of a diocese likewise a council within a diocese: ibid., fol. 103v. For the use of the title bishop for all ministers, see 101 above and 234, n. 103 below.

31. According to A. S. Pearce there were two critical concessions by means of which James established moderate episcopacy in Scotland: the first compromised the "fundamental principle of ministerial equality" and the second acknowledged that "the episcopate had a priori justification for administrative pre-eminence in the church": "John Spottiswoode, Jacobean Archbishop and Statesman" (Ph.D. diss., University of Stirling, 1998), 86.

32. TCD, MS 140, fol. 68v. In determining matters of doctrine, the treatise insisted on the authority of synods, rejecting the singular rule of the bishop: "[T]he humane devise of erecting a Bishop or primate in a Nation to rule the rest (whereby all the rest were made subiect to one mans pleasure) was a very vayne devise & to intollerable in the Church, which ought to be governed (as St. Hierome hath before saide) by the *Pastors together in common* for the fource & sway of Many (in a Councell) must needes cary greater perswasion in the minds of all Christians then the pleasure of one preferred above the rest" (fol. 86).

33. Ibid., fol. 83.

34. Russell, *Causes of the English Civil War*, 48. Similarly, for the Channel Islands, James's "key aim was to secure a token acceptance of the episcopal principle. . . . Once again, argument centered on the question of a permanent or temporary moderator" (51).

35. "By most voyces one is to be chosen out from the rest to be the moderator, president or Ruler of the action, so long as that Synod lasteth, who is to propound the matter & cause of that their meetings, to gather their voices speaking in order, & at last to give sentence according to the most voices": TCD, MS 140, fol. 103v.

36. Downame, *Two Sermons*.

37. F. R. Boulton, "Archbishop Ussher's Scheme of Church Government," *Theology* 1, no. 310 (1947): 9–16. For Travers's and other presbyterian influences on Ussher's ecclesiology, see Alan Ford, *James Ussher: Theology, History, and Politics in Early Modern Ireland and England* (Oxford: Oxford University Press, 2007), 41–52.

38. Examples also included Acts 15 as well as Athanasius, Eusebius, and Jewel. Within this system the queen's authority was not forgotten, as she was said to hold the last appeal: "For as now there be appeales from the Archdeacon to the Bishop from the Bishop to the Archbishop and . . . to the Queene in hir High Court of chancerye . . . so then also (in steede of thes) there will be appeales from a particuler church to A Synod within a shire . . . from this to a synod within a Dioces . . . And from thence to a Synod within a province: and from thence to A Synod within the Nation. And from thence or from the provinciall synod (if it shalbe thought meter) to Hir Maiesty in the chancery. . . . This Reformed Church governement taketh not away Appeales (as the adversaryes suggest) but alloweth them": TCD, MS 140, fol. 104.

39. "[N]on auth*oritate* imp*er*ii sed potius ut Christianus imperator ex pot*est*ate eccl*esi*ae": ibid., MS 366, fol. 14v. See Figure 5, H*a*, "English Presbyterianism." This excerpt from Travers's theological commonplace book can be dated by internal evidence and cross-references to other texts to about the second decade of the seventeenth century. Travers appears to have been attracted to Bullinger's *De Origine Erroris* and *De Conciliis* for their focus on the Church as a visible institution in history.

40. Polly Ha, "Puritan Conciliarism: Why Walter Travers Read Heinrich Bullinger," *SCJ* 41, no. 4 (2010). For a summary of this article, see Franz Mauelshagen, "Heinrich Bullinger (1504–1575): Leben—Denken—Wirkung," *Zwingliana* 32 (2005): 95.

41. "[U]nde *tempore* factu*m* e*st*, ut tande*m* Imperat*ores* vendicare*nt* tenere*ntque* sibi ius co*n*vocandar*um* synodor*um*": TCD, MS 366, fol. 14v.

42. "*Quod* certe cessante et neglig*ente* eccl*esia* magistratus e*st*": ibid. I am grateful to David Money and Diarmaid MacCulloch for their help with the translation of this statement.

43. Instead of emphasizing the exceptional nature of civil authority in calling councils as Travers noted, Bullinger describes that when rulers "surrendered the power to call councils afterwards to the bishops, then this flowed out of indulgence, ignorance, negligence by seizure or similar cause": *De Conciliis* (Zurich: 1561), 24v–25.

44. See Ha, "Puritan Conciliarism."

45. Travers noted the strategy of Innocent III, who was responsible for "Phillip and Otto as equals committing their related battle lines and with brother against brother and son against parent, Germany almost died with mutual slaughter. . . . [T]he popes watched those arts of committing people and princes against each other . . . [and] with each side tired out the Roman seat triumphed"; "[N]am Phillipum et Otonem quosi paria committens et eorum cognatas acies atque fratrem cum fratre et filium cum parente ut Germania mutuis sedibus [caedibus] pene conciderit vidit eos spectabant hae artes committendi interse populos et principes ut de utraque parte fatigata Roma*na* sedis triumphet": TCD, MS 366, fol. 52. These notes also appear to have been dictated to a scribe, who mistook the word "caedibus" for "sedibus," which would have had the same pronunciation. I am grateful to David Money for identifying this error.

46. "Interea Alexander vocatus a romanis venit in urbem unde plereque Italiae urbes eo suadente contra fidem et iusiurandum ab imperatore deficiunt": ibid., fol. 52.

47. Heinrich Bullinger, *A Confutation of the Pope's Bull* (London, 1572).

48. For further discussion on this treatise, see David John Keep, "Henry Bullinger and the Elizabethan Church: A Study of the Publication of His 'Decades,' His Letter on the Use of Vestments and His Reply to the Bull Which Excommunicated Elizabeth" (Ph.D. diss., University of Sheffield, 1970), ch. 6.

49. Iames Peregrin, *The Letters Patents of the Presbyterie: With the Please and Frvits of the Prelacie* ([n.p.]: 1632), 4.

50. Ibid., 43.

51. Ibid., A2.

52. Ibid., 43.

53. Ibid., 53.

54. There is a notable contrast to Travers's former treatise, which stressed the prince's necessary subjection to the Scriptures in the *Declaration*.

55. As John Guy has commented, "In a very real sense, it was the threat of presbyterianism in the 1570s and 1580s which caused the regime belatedly to recognize the true implications of the undercurrents that swirled beneath the (superficially) calmer waters of Elizabethan political thought." In this respect, presbyterians such as Cartwright who posed a "threat of 'popularity' in religion . . . paved the way for the rehabilitation of the thesis of 'imperial' kingship": "Tudor Monarchy and Its Critiques," in *The Tudor Monarchy* (London: Edward Arnold, 1997), 101. See also Mason, "James VI," 215–41.

CHAPTER 2

1. Christopher Hill, *Society and Puritanism in Pre-Revolutionary England* (London: Panther Press, 1969), chs. 8, 10.

2. Collinson, *Religion of Protestants*, esp. ch. 2; Kenneth Fincham, *Prelate as Pastor: The Episcopate of James I* (Oxford: Oxford University Press, 1990).

3. Walter Travers, *Vindiciae Ecclesiae Anglicanae: or A Iustification of the Religion Now Professed in England* (London: 1630), 17. Despite its general argument that the Church of England remained a true church, the *Vindiciae* conspicuously remained silent on the institutional hierarchy of the Church of England. It was careful to endorse the Church of England insofar as it agreed with the apostolic church in essential Christian doctrines, rather than in its church government. For intrapuritan debate over the nature of the Church of England and the marks of a true church, see ch. 5 below.

4. This chapter seeks to build on previous studies by adding presbyterianism to the equation of puritan clerical-lay alliances in the early seventeenth century. There is no claim to originality here in exploring the relationship between puritan ministers and the laity more generally, which, for example, has been studied by Richard Cust: "Anti-Puritanism and Urban Politics: Charles I and Great Yarmouth," *HJ* 35, no. 1 (1992): 1–26.

5. Margaret Spufford, "Puritanism and Social Control?," in *Order and Disorder in Early Modern England*, ed. John Stevenson (Cambridge: Cambridge University Press, 1987), 41–57; Martin Ingram, "Reformation of Manners in Early Modern England," in *The Experience of Authority in Early Modern England*, ed. Steve Hindle (Basingstoke: Macmillan, 1996), 47–88; Marjorie McIntosh, *Controlling Misbehavior in England, 1370–1600* (Cambridge: Cambridge University Press, 1998), 3–6; Rosamund Oates, "Tobie Matthew and the Establishment of the Godly Commonwealth in England: 1560–1606" (Ph.D. diss., University of York, 2003). There is no question that there was a drive to correct moral behavior in the history of the English church prior to the emergence of presbyterianism, but the particularities that constituted moral reform became deeply contested by the late sixteenth century.

6. For a recent discussion of this view, and challenge to it, see William Abbot, "Anticlericalism and Episcopacy in Parliamentary Debates, 1640–1641: Secular Versus Spiritual Functions," in *Law and Authority in Early Modern England*, ed. Buchanan Sharp and Mark Charles Fissel (Newark: University of Delaware Press, 2007), 157–86.

7. For presbyterian reference to "bishop" as local minister, see Chapter 1, above. For the presbyterians' argument against episcopal hierarchy by the principle of common consent, see Chapter 4.

8. Gorski, *Disciplinary Revolution*. For a more nuanced discussion of reformed discipline, including variation among consistories, see Philip Benedict, *Christ's Churches Purely Reformed: A Social History of Calvinism* (New Haven: Yale University Press 2002), 455–59.

9. Quoted in R. G. Usher, *The Rise and Fall of the High Commission* (Oxford: Clarendon Press, 1913), 134.

10. TCD, MS 140, fol. 102.

11. Ruth Gilbert, *Early Modern Hermaphrodites: Sex and Other Stories* (Basingstoke: Palgrave, 2002), 20.

12. TCD, MS 140, fol. 99v.

13. "Wheras our savior himselffe off whose example we ought to learne refused to divide the herytage betwene the brethren as a thing not belonginge to his office and offten tymes refused to divide the herytage betwene the brethren as a thing not belonginge to his office and offten tymes reprouethe and repressethe the like desyer off the Apostles desyring and longyng after suche thinges he detested all this lordinge and exercisyng off domynion togither with the titles off princes and honorable personages and such like titles and names": Travers, *Fvll and Plaine Declaration*, 42.

14. Against the argument that not all but only supreme authority was forbidden to ministers, the writer insisted that the ministers desired not supreme or regal authority but "a delegate Authoritye . . . which sheweth that Christs answeare . . . was aswell against delegate Authority as supreme": TCD, MS 140, fols. 99r–v.

15. For the relationship between effeminacy and lack of self-control, see Alexandra Shepard, *Meanings of Manhood in Early Modern England* (Oxford: Oxford University Press, 2003), 28. For early modern readings of the hermaphrodite's gender, see Gilbert, *Early Modern Hermaphrodites*, 26–31.

16. Collinson, *Religion of Protestants*, 40–41.

17. Gordon Donaldson, "The Relations between the English and Scottish Presbyterian Movements to 1604" (Ph.D. diss., University of London, 1938), 114, 118.

18. Helen Pierce, "Anti-Episcopacy and Graphic Satire," *HJ* 47, no. 4 (2004): 835.

19. John King, "The Bishop's Stinking Foot: Milton and Antireplatical Satire," *Reformation* 7 (2002): 188.

20. For the association between infatuation and effeminacy, see Elizabeth Foyster, *Manhood in Early Modern England: Honour, Sex and Marriage* (London: Longman, 1999), 56.

21. As R. G. Usher noted in regard to Bancroft, "It is significant that his ecclesiastical functions were to be secondary in importance to his political, that he was to display not administrative ability in ecclesiastical affairs, but discretion and tact in the performance of certain onerous and delicate duties of a quasi-political character which the Privy Council had been in the habit of entrusting to the Bishop of London": *The Reconstruction of the English Church* (Farnborough: Gregg International Publishers, 1910), 114.

22. TCD, MS 140, fol. 100r–v. Bishop John Hooper's concern for the preaching ministry served as a supporting example: "Mr Hooper therefore is bould even to reprooue Princes herein for their* bestowinge of civill offices upon ministers of the worde" (fol. 100v). There were also examples in the ancient church where ministers were rebuked for taking on civil responsibility: Jerome and Bernard evidently disliked it. Jerome was cited as writing that "Being the soldiers of Christ they binde themselues to worldly affayres & offer up one Image to Goed and Caesar." And, according to St. Bernard, "[It] is plaine that unto the Apostles Lordship or temporall Magistracy is forbidden." There were also specific instances where this practice was condemned: "As appeareth in the person of Samosatenus . . . condemned as one that was *like to men in worldly dignitye*, whereby he brought a slander to the gospel. . . . A like example and likewise reprooved is in Ruffinus of one Gregory a Bishop" (fols. 100–101v).

23. William Stoughton, *An Abstract, of Certain Acts of Parliament: Of Certaine Her*

Maiesties Iniunctions: [Etc.] for the Peaceable Gouernment of the Church (London: 1583), 15.

24. Donaldson, "The Relations between the English and Scottish Presbyterian Movements," 102.

25. Abbott, "Issue of Episcopacy," 69–70. Among Travers's personal papers dating from the first two decades of the seventeenth century is a passage that reveals that he continued to reject the pluralities of bishops and their civil responsibilities. He first writes that the apostolic definition of a bishop was of "a pastor of either one church or parish." After criticizing the office of a bishop over more than one particular church, what follows in Travers's fragmented notes is a statement that in the Church the primary responsibility of the pastor is preaching the gospel: TCD, MS 366, fol. 36.

26. "While the desire of some MPs and lords to participate in ecclesiastical governance had received a decisive impetus from the imposition of Laudian policies, it had been growing well before the 1630's": Abbott, "Issue of Episcopacy," 69–70, 91.

27. Members of the Long Parliament did not simply object to abuse of the temporal authority but also argued that civil office conflicted with the nature of spiritual responsibilities, viewing civil office "not simply as a distraction from the clerical function but as morally incompatible with it": ibid., 70–71.

28. Travers, *Fvll and Plaine Declaration*, 40–41.

29. TCD, MS 140, fol. 111.

30. Dudley Fenner (*A Counter-Poyson, Modestly Written For the Time, To Make Aunswere to the Obiections and Reproches, Wherewith the Aunswerer to the Abstract, Would Disgrace the Holy Discipline of Christ* [London: 1584]) defended the presbyterian position against Richard Cosin's objections to Stoughton's *Abstract* in *An Answer to the Two First and Principall Treatises of a Certeine Factious Libell, Put Foorth Latelie, Without Name of Author or Printer, and Without Approbation by Authoritie, vnder the Title of An Abstract of Certeine Acts of Parliament* (London: 1584).

31. Stoughton, *An Abstract*, 222–23.

32. Peregrin, *Letters Patents*, D2.

33. Travers, *Fvll and Plaine Declaration*, 42.

34. TCD, MS 140, fol. 98. Another exception was "the Examples of Eli . . . being both priest & Iudge, is extraordinary . . . as also contrary to comen use & practise of the comen Weale of Israell." There were other exceptional periods such as "the examples of Esaras the priest who had civill magistracy and of the priests in the maccabees. They are all examples of ruinous tymes & decayed comon weales & therefore neither rules nor yet meete examples to be followed of peaceable & well setled kingdomes" (fol. 98v).

35. It is noteworthy that the understanding of two distinct offices did not suggest that the two officers act entirely independently and without consultation. The active relationship that presbyterians envisioned between minister and magistrate is explored further below. At this point it is more helpful to discuss the distinction between the two offices.

36. TCD, MS 140, fol. 98.

37. Usher, *Reconstruction*, 106–7.

38. Gilbert, *Early Modern Hermaphrodites*, 20.

39. TCD, MS 140, fol. 109v.

40. This is not to say that secular punishment was to be withheld altogether, since

presbyterians such as Travers affirmed the civil magistrates' use of force to back church censure in certain circumstance.

41. 1. Cor. 6.4, Travers, *Fvll and Plaine Declaration*, 88.

42. Ibid.

43. For example, Christopher St. German, *A Treatise Concernynge the Diuision Betwene the Spiritualtie and Temporaltie* (London: 1532), 6, 9, 13v.

44. Ibid., 103.

45. J. S. Morrill, "The Attack on the Church of England in the Long Parliament, 1640–1642," in *History, Society and the Churches*, ed. Geoffrey Best (Cambridge: Cambridge University Press, 1985), 113.

46. Pierce, "Anti-Episcopacy," 841, 847.

47. This compares with continental reformed protestants who defended their practices on constitutional grounds according to local custom.

48. Stoughton, *An Abstract*, 15.

49. Ibid., 211–12.

50. Ibid., fol. 107v.

51. See Mendle, *Dangerous Positions*, ch. 4.

52. Ibid.

53. David Smith has described the confusion created by England's bicameral parliamentary structure. In contrast with "the conventional definition of the three estates (spirituality, nobility, commonalty)" in most European models, the English bicameral structure consisted of lords spiritual and temporal in one House and the Commons in the other. Competing interpretations of parliament emerged most visibly during the mid-seventeenth century. While those defending the prerogative of the king tended to interpret the three estates of parliament according to the conventional model, their opponents argued that the three estates consisted of the king, the lords, and the commons. As "the unresolved confusion [over England's bicameral structure] remained benign and was not of great political moment" before the mid-seventeenth century, it is of particular significance that the writer of the "Reformed Church Government" gave an extended defense of the latter position at the very end of the sixteenth century: *The Stuart Parliaments, 1603–1689* (London: Edward Arnold, 1998), 81–84.

54. TCD, MS 140, fol. 111v.

55. The writer continued to argue thus: "Secondly . . . by the manner of the Endorsing of the Bills the parliament . . . doth show that Acts of parliament by consent of the Queene the lords the commons may very well passe, notwithstanding thes Lords spirituall be Extinct. Thirdly, many & divers statuts themselves are found to be made in this forme, by the Kinge the Lords, and the Commons (without mentioning of any lords spirituall) & so may they be still made & have their due force. Fourthly Some statuts are founde to be made, by the assent of the Lords Temporall expressely & only . . . Fiftly, when Any is to be attainted by Act of parliament, The lorde spirituall may not consent by the law of the lande, and yet it is a perfect act notwithstandinge Sixtly Mr Foxe citeth divers parliament Rolls & out of them sheweth Divers Acts & statuts made in the tyme of kinge Edward the Third, And yet the consent of Bishops neither required nor expressed (which he wisheth his Reader to note & observe) Seventy Mr Juwell . . . against Harding the papist [doth] Justify & affirme that the parliament holde the first yeare of the Queenes Maiestyes raigne that now is (when the religion was restored) and the Acts thereof were good & of full strength, though the

Bishops refused to agree thereun[ ] Eight[hly] Amongst the ould & Antient Statuts of England This terme of Lords spirituall, is not founde, being (as it should seeme) as yet unhatched . . . I conclude therefore that Acts of Parliament both have beene, and may be made without Lords spirituall, most undoubtedly, And that the three estates of the . . . Lande do still remayne visible and in their splendent and absolute perfection (though Lords spirituall be utterly extinct)": ibid., fols. 111–12.

56. Ibid., fol. 101v.

57. Ibid.

58. Ibid., fol. 105v.

59. According to Patrick Collinson, between 1588 and 1593 "the alliance of the puritans and the common lawyers, of which the full implications were to be seen in the succeeding two reigns was knit . . . when the legal and constitutional aspects of the struggle between the puritans and the established church were first explored": "Puritan Classical Movement," 831. By contrast, he has observed the absence of legal arguments in earlier Elizabethan vestiarian controversy where there was "no concerted effort to challenge the dubious legality of the proceedings taken against them. At this stage we are not witnessing the alliance with the lawyers which was to be so marked a feature of the puritan movement in the eighties and in the early seventeenth century": *Elizabethan Puritan Movement,* 82.

60. Cited in Hill, *Society and Puritanism,* 330.

61. Allen D. Boyer, "Coke, Sir Edward (1552–1634), *Oxford Dictionary of National Biography*. Coke's opposition to church courts was not argued along the lines of divine right, but on the antiquity and supremacy of the English common law, which inclined markedly toward erastianism rather than toward presbyterian government: J. G. A. Pocock, *The Ancient Constitution and the Feudal Law: English Historical Thought in the Seventeenth Century* (New York: : W. W. Norton and Company, 1967), ch. 2. See also Allen Boyer, *Sir Edward Coke and the Elizabethan Age* (Stanford: Stanford University Press, 2003), ch. 7. However, as Boyer has pointed out (176), "On matters of religion, Coke's record reflects a peculiar tension." He is seen to have "linked himself to the Puritan cause" shortly following Travers's lectureship in the Temple Church. Boyer noted (182–84) that "[f]amily connections probably drew Coke in," for Anne Stubbe (*née* Coke), the separatist and sister-in-law of Thomas Cartwright was Coke's own sister.

62. These alliances did not always and necessarily work together against bishops, since they could also have conflicting interests. As Ann Hughes has pointed out for the mid-seventeenth century, "[T]he central issue is not how political actors should be classified, but how minorities are able to impose their vision or programme on those whose views are less developed or less committed": *Gangraena,* 331. Paul Seaver, who found that lay magistracy in Elizabethan Suffolk fits no traditional ecclesiological category, has noted that "we still know all too little about the impact of the Reformation on the godly magistracy and on those laity who experienced Biblical Protestantism as a species of liberation": "Community Control and Puritan Politics in Elizabethan Suffolk," *Albion* 9, no. 4 (1977): 315. For caution about aligning patronage with particular religious beliefs, see also Pauline Croft, "The Religion of Robert Cecil," *HJ* 34 (1991): 773–96; and David L. Smith, "Catholic, Anglican or Puritan? Edward Sackville, Fourth Earl of Dorset and the Ambiguities of Religion in Early Stuart England," *Transactions of the Royal Historical Society* 6th ser., 2 (1992): 105–24.

63. W. D. J. Cargill Thompson, "Sir Francis Knollys' Campaign against the *Jure Divino* Theory of Episcopacy," in *The Dissenting Tradition: Essays for Leland H. Carlson*, ed. Michael E. Moody (Athens: Ohio University Press, 1975), 43–44. Although the term "disciplinarian" did not necessarily refer to presbyterianism, Knollys used it in the context of discussing Whitgift's and Bancroft's controversy with the presbyterians. His attack on *jure divino* episcopacy was made at the height of Bancroft's obsessive drive against presbyterianism, in which he tended to refer to virtually all forms of dissent that stopped short of separatism as presbyterian.

64. Beale claimed "that the 'principal cause' for his disfavour was that he was suspected of being 'a plotter of a new Ecclesiastical government'": Guy, "Elizabethan Establishment," 137.

65. Mark Taviner, "Robert Beale and the Elizabethan Polity" (Ph.D. diss., St. Andrews University, 2000), 245.

66. Morice's example of vindictive action taken by an ecclesiastical judge toward the presbyterian John Knewstubs indicated not only that he defended the presbyterians as attorney but also that he listened to Knewstubs's preaching. After Knewstubs's sermon, "Morice was going out of the church along with the suffragan and heard him give 'some fewe wordes of commendacion both of the sermon and of the preacher himself'": James E. Hampson, "Richard Cosin and the Rehabilitation of the Clerical Estate in Late Elizabethan England" (Ph.D. diss., University of St. Andrews, 1997), 173. There is also evidence that, like Coke, Morice attended and took notes at Travers's lectures in the Temple Church: "Mr James Morrice, Mr Ameredith, Benchers of that house, and Sr James Altham of Grays Inn Constituted a Baron of the Excheqr in 1606. and others of the Other Societyes tooke notes from his [Travers's] mouth": DWL, Morrice MS I, fol. 431.

67. Travers's interpretation of Cartwright's later years is telling. He used Cartwright's example to argue that he lawfully abided within the Church of England and that congregationalists wrongly interpreted his teaching on the Church of England: TCD, MS 141, 189.

68. Cartwright's continued presbyterian activity in the later years of Elizabeth's reign is most clearly demonstrated by his role in reconciling the Guernsey and Jersey presbyteries in the Channel Islands: A. F. Scott Pearson, *Thomas Cartwright and Elizabethan Puritanism* (Cambridge: Cambridge University Press, 1925), 373–86. See also conclusion below.

69. BL, Sloane MS 271, fol. 22.

70. Boyer, *Sir Edward Coke*, 176. Christopher Hill stated that the puritan critique of episcopacy could have "appealed to an erastian anti-clerical public which was not in the usual sense of the word 'Puritan,' but which shared Puritanism's enemies": *Intellectual Origins of the English Revolution* (Oxford: Clarendon Press, 1965), 271.

71. "Cartwright in Ecclesiasten. STC. 4710. On t-p Edw: Coke Ex dono Authoris": W. O. Hassall, *A Catalogue of the Library of Sir Edward Coke* (New Haven: Yale University Press, 1950), 7.

72. Richard Rogers, *A Commentary Vpon the VVhole Booke of Iudges* (London, 1615).

73. *Two Elizabethan Puritan Diaries: By Richard Rogers and Samuel Ward*, ed. M. M. Knappen (Gloucester: Peter Smith, 1966), 28.

74. Rogers, *Commentary*, 2. Knappen comments on Rogers's participation in

presbytery meetings for the purpose of edification, where in his diary "he very rarely alludes to the business that was transacted at these gatherings, but rather concentrates on the spiritual exercises that were another feature of them": *Two Elizabethan Puritan Diaries*, 28. For Rogers and practical divinity, see Jason Yiannikkou, "Protestantism, Puritanism, and Practical Divinity in England, 1570–1620" (Ph.D. diss., University of Cambridge, 1999), ch. 3. Travers's reading and use of Heinrich Bullinger's writings in the early seventeenth century similarly reveals a concern to prompt parliamentarians to take political action on behalf of presbyterian ministers: Ha, "Puritan Conciliarism."

75. TCD, MS 140, fol. 66.

76. On impulse the writer reduces the entire controversy to this one issue, only to later refine the argument and cross out the initial blanket statement: "[T]his controversy is about church censures (namely reprehension of a synner, suspention of him from the communion, and Excommunication) who ought to be the minister of them, or who ought to be the church governors for the exercise & ministery thereof": ibid., fol. 68v. As can be seen in the manuscript, the writer places the institution of church courts, along with the bishops, at the center of opposition. Accusation is originally placed against "our Bishops." On second thought the writer inserts with a caret "& their courts," followed by two charges against their practice: first that they have taken the execution of church censures away "from the Pastor & other Elders of every Congregation." Secondly, "they also exercise civill magistracy and Jurisdiction": ibid., fol. 67v.

77. Ibid., fol. 74v.

78. Richard Cosin, *An Apologie: of, and for Sundrie Proceedings by Iurisdiction Ecclesiasticall of Late Times by Some Challenged, and also Diuersly by Them Impugned* (London: 1591); James Morice, *A Briefe Treatise of Oathes Exacted by Ordinaries and Ecclesiastical Iudges, to Answere Generallie to All Such Articles or Interrogatories, as Pleaseth Them to Propound* (Middelburg: 1590?); C. W. Brooks, *Law, Politics and Society in Early Modern England* (Cambridge: Cambridge University Press, 2009), 103–5. On Cosin's *Apologie*, see Ethan Shagan, "The English Inquisition: Constitutional Conflict and Ecclesiastical Law in the 1590s", *HJ* 47, no. 3 (2004): 541–65.

79. R. H. Helmholz, *The Roman Canon Law in Reformation England* (Cambridge: Cambridge University Press, 1990), 50–51.

80. The transfer of cases from church courts to common law would reduce occupational rivalry and increase the commission earned in cases tried by common lawyers: Hill, *Society and Puritanism*, 292.

81. R. B. Outhwaite, *Rise and Fall of the English Ecclesiastical Courts, 1500–1860* (Cambridge: Cambridge University Press, 2006), 23–27.

82. TCD, MS 140, fol. 105v. For one discussion of the variation within puritan complaints over tithes, see Laura Brace, *The Idea of Property in Seventeenth-Century England: Tithes and the Individual* (Manchester: Manchester University Press, 1998).

83. Ibid., 108.

84. Another case to be transferred to temporal courts was "administrations of goods granted by ordinaryes." By Richard Cosin's own confession this came under the Church's jurisdiction in the time of Edward III and therefore was "but a late upstart . . . of no great Antiquity." The writer argued (ibid., fol. 107) that at the time of Edward III the common law resisted the encroachment of the Church on secular

cases, "and consequently [ecclesiastical officers] were not appointed to entermeddle in civil causes or affayes of this world, as afterward they encroached, who encroachments princes tolerated so long, till prelates brought it to a custome: and custome bred a law."

85. Ibid., fols. 108v–109.

86. That Stoughton was the author of both *The Abstract* and the *Assertion* is noted in the *epistle dedicatory* of his *Assertion* (1642 edition), which refers to the "abstract written in the time of famous Queene *Elizabeth* (a Book well knowne to learned King *Iames*) by the same Author," which was "seemingly answered by the rayling stile of a then Doctor *Cozens*": *An Assertion for True and Christian Church-Policie. Wherein Certaine Politike Obiections Made against the Planting of Pastors and Elders in Every Congregation, Are Sufficientlie Aunswered* (London: 1642), epistle dedicatory.

87. Ibid., 35.

88. Stoughton's list specified, as being triable in both courts: "[B]ee punishable partly by temporall and partly by Ecclesiasticall authoritie, so drunkennesse, absence from divine service and prayer, fighting, quarrelling, and brawling in Church and Churchyard; defamatorie words and libels; violent laying on of hands upon a Clarke, &c. may not onely bee handled and punished in a court ecclesiasticall, but they may also be handled and punished by the King, in his temporall courts": ibid., 49. By contrast, cases that were strictly to be tried in ecclesiastical courts were defined as "1. things properly Triable by the law of the conisance of sinner & offences against the law of god, 2. the conisance of synnes & offences against the law of god, so farre forth only as the censures of reprehension suspention, & excommunication are . . . awardable and publick confession . . . & the only execution thes things belong . . . to the ecclesiastical jurisdiction": TCD, MS 140. fol. 109v.

89. Peter Milward, *Religious Controversies of the Jacobean Age: A Survey of Printed Sources* (London: Scolar Press, 1978), 2.

90. "Bills hostile to the jurisdiction of the church courts were put forward in the House of Commons throughout James's first English parliament, which sat in several sessions between 1603 and 1610": Brooks, *Law, Politics and Society*, 110, 113.

91. Quoted in Hill, *Society and Puritanism*, 292.

92. Peregrin, *Letters Patents*, 27.

93. I am grateful to Christopher Brooks for his comment on this.

94. Stoughton, *An Abstract*, 227.

95. In his speech at the end of the sixteenth century against the bishops' claims to exercise their jurisdiction by divine right, Sir Francis Knollys argued that "it is true, that the Bishops may prescribe that K: Henry 8. gaue them authority, by the Statute of the 25 of his reigne, to have authority & rule over their inferiour brethren . . . But this was no special warrant for them to keep their courts by & that in their owne names. And yet they haue no other warrant to keep their courts." Knollys's speech was reprinted by Stoughton in 1604 and again in response to Downame's *jure divino* claims for episcopacy in 1608: *Informations, or a Protestation, and a Treatise from Scotland with D. Reignoldes His Letter to Sir Francis Knollis* (1608), 90. Christopher Hill describes Stoughton's steadfast efforts to continue this argument: *Society and Puritanism*, 326. For *jure divino* episcopacy, see Chapter 1, above.

96. TCD, MS 140, fol. 105.

97. John Whitgift, *The Works of John Whitgift*, ed. John Ayre (Cambridge: Cambridge University Press, 1851), 2: 408–9.

98. Whitgift, *An Ansvvere to a Certen Libel Intituled, An Admonition to the Parliament* (London 1572), 224, quoted in Stoughton, *Assertion*, 15.

99. TCD, MS 140, fols. 107r–v.

100. Stoughton, *An Abstract*, 26. The Newcastle merchant John Fenwick was another layman who referred back to the Admonition controversy in denouncing episcopacy and its roots in roman canon law: John Fenwicke, *The Downfall of the Pretended Divine Authoritie of the Hierarchy into the Sea of Rome. From Some Arguments, and Motives, to the Finall Extirpation of That Unlawfull Government of the Prelacy: as Having No Foundation in the Scriptures, but Onely in That Filthy Dung-Hill of the Canon Law of the Popes Authorities, and Therefore Antichristian* (London: 1641), 2–5. Although Fenwick's treatise was published in 1641, he expressed presbyterian and anti-episcopal affinities prior to this date by his subscription to the Scottish national covenant in 1638: Andrew J. Hopper, "Fenwick, John (1593–d. c. 1670)," *ODNB*. I am indebted to David Como for this reference.

101. Stoughton, *Assertion*, 15.

102. Cosin, *Apologie*, 4.

103. Stoughton, *Assertion*, 19.

104. Ibid., epistle dedicatory.

105. Shagan, "English Inquisition," 552.

106. According to Patrick Collinson, Stoughton's *Assertion* was written "to prove that a presbyterian Church polity was not inconsistent with English law or custom": "The Authorship of *A Brieff Discours off the Troubles Begonne at Franckford*," in *Godly People*, 206, n. 4. Although Cosin's *Apologie* was not directed exclusively toward presbyterians, "many of the puritan derogators of ecclesiastical proceedings were Presbyterians who routinely filled out their arguments against ecclesiastical jurisdiction with calls for the new discipline. . . . Cosin often referred to his opponents as the 'innovators,' or, on occasion, 'innovating Disciplinarians' when addressing a particularly Presbyterian argument": Hampson, "Richard Cosin," 76–78.

107. Milward, *Religious Controversies*, 2.

108. Stoughton, *An Abstract*. Furthermore, Victoria Gregory has pointed out that "it could not have been written before 1589, as the tract answers Cooper's Admonition, published in that year": "Congregational Puritanism," 67.

109. 1604 edition 23318 [Huntington Library Call number: 438876], 50–51, 63.

110. John G. Rechtein, "Antithetical Literary Structures in the Reformation Theology of Walter Travers," *SCJ* 8, no. 1 (1977): 53. Gordon Donaldson has similarly recognized in Scotland that "'discipline,' of the 'lives of the clergy,' of their 'manners' and their 'morals' . . . meant primarily the reform of ecclesiastical polity": *The Scottish Reformation* (Cambridge: Cambridge University Press 1960), 1.

111. Gorski, *Disciplinary Revolution*. Although Philip Benedict discusses the drift from lay leadership to clericalism in some reformed consistories, as well as disciplinary variance and contingency, he nonetheless observes the distinctive impact on local communities by reformed church government compared with other confessional traditions: *Christ's Churches Purely Reformed*, 451–59. For another overview that addresses variance in consistorial discipline, see Graeme Murdock, *Beyond Calvin: The Intellectual, Political and Cultural World of Europe's Reformed Churches, c. 1540–1620* (Basingstoke: Palgrave, 2004), 82.

112. TCD, MS 140, fol. 75v.

113. Ibid., fol. 76.

114. The deaths of Elizabeth's privy councilors indicate that the treatise was written in the late 1590s. I am grateful to Keith Wrightson for bringing to my attention that mention of the recent dearth indicates that this treatise must be dated after 1598, as the dearth of the 1590s reached its height in 1596–98.

115. *The First and Large Petition of the City of London and of Other Inhabitants Thereabouts: For a Reformation in Church-Government, as Also for the Abolishment of Episcopacy* (London: 1641), 11.

116. *Puritan Manifestos: A Study of the Origin of the Puritan Revolt: With a Reprint of the Admonition to the Parliament and Kindred Documents, 1572,* ed. W. H. Fere and C. E. Douglas (London: Society for Promoting Christian Knowledge, 1907), 17–18.

117. TCD, MS 140, fol. 86.

118. Travers, *Fvll and Plaine Declaration,* 99.

119. Shaw, *History of the English Church,* 216ff.

120. Ronald A. Marchant, *The Church under the Law: Justice, Administration, and Discipline in the Diocese of York, 1560–1640* (Cambridge: Cambridge University Press, 1969), 242.

121. Travers, *Fvll and Plaine Declaration,* 49.

122. *Puritan Manifestos,* 15.

123. TCD, MS 140, fol. 102.

124. Travers, *Fvll and Plaine Declaration,* 85.

125. Act. 20.28, 1 Thes. 5.12, Heb. 13.17, 1 Pet. 5.1, 1. Tim. 5.17. Ibid.

126. For reported deaths immediately following Cartwright's rebuke (in private and in public sermons), see Pearson, *Thomas Cartwright,* 295–96.

127. Lake, *Anglicans and Puritans?,* 31.

128. TCD, MS 140, fol. 88.

129. The impression of a negative agenda in abolishing church courts without the activism of implementing a new system has resulted in the caricature put forward by adversaries. As Whitgift stated, "[T]hey proceed . . . not of minds desirous to reform, but of stomachs seeking to deform and confound that which is in due form and order by lawful authority established": *Works,* 1: 141.

130. Stoughton, *An Abstract,* 199.

131. Pearson, *Church and State,* 22.

132. F. Douglas Price has argued that the failure to incorporate the laity in ecclesiastical discipline led to its decline in England in the sixteenth century, "since only by an effective use of the assistance of the temporal power could its authority have been maintained": "The Abuses of Excommunication and the Decline of Ecclesiastical Discipline under Queen Elizabeth," *EHR* 47, no. 225 (1942): 114.

133. Stoughton, *An Abstract,* 93. "In case they of the ministerie shalbe herein remisse & negligent, then to punish them with such paines, as either by hir lawes is prouided, or by hir wisdom shalbe thought expedient in that behalf, for the contempt of hir gratious commandement, & neglect of the Lords seruice. In which diuersitie of punishments, the diuersitie of the offices, of magistracie and ministery, doth manifestly appeare. Magistracie hauing euermore regarde to the bodye and outwarde man: but ministery always to the soule, and inner man. the magistrate punisheth with bodily chastisement, the minister with spiritual discipline, neither doth thone hereby derogate from the other, or any whit weaken the other, but rather ech one strengthneth & fortifieth the other" (199).

134. Rogers, *Commentary,* 9.

135. Marchant, *Church under the Law*, 242.

136. "It had no public competence to deal with the problem of tramps, 'the multitude of roges wherewith the cuntrey was charged at their dores', this being a matter for the magistrate (13M)": *Conferences and Combination Lectures in the Elizabethan Church: Dedham and Bury St. Edmunds, 1582–1590*, ed. Patrick Collinson, John Craig, and Brett Usher (Woodbridge, Church of England Record Society: Boydell Press, 2003), lxxxix.

137. P. D. L. Avis, "Moses and the Magistrate: A Study in the Rise of Protestant Legalism," *JEH* 26 (1975): 168–69.

138. Pearson, *Thomas Cartwright*, 90–91.

139. J. H. Primus, *Holy Time: Moderate Puritanism and the Sabbath* (Macon, GA: Mercer University Press, 1989), 33.

140. Harro Höpfl, *The Christian Polity of John Calvin* (Cambridge: Cambridge University Press, 1982), 154. Bullinger also shared this understanding. As Pamala Biel noted, he "envisioned the clergy as preachers, priests, teachers, pastors as well as advisers to kings and councils": *Doorkeepers at the House of Righteousness: Heinrich Bullinger and the Zurich Clergy, 1535–1575* (Bern: Peter Lang, 1991), 5.

141. TCD, MS 141, 404.

142. John Fielding, "Conformists, Puritans and the Church Courts: The Diocese of Peterborough, 1603–1642" (Ph.D. diss., University of Birmingham, 1989), 240–41.

143. The puritan reformation of manners "involve[d] the enthusiastic participation of magistrate, minister and people in bringing about a new order of reformation and national regeneration": Wrightson, "Puritan Reformation of Manners," 13, 16.

144. Ibid., 15.

145. Robert Brenner, *Merchants and Revolution: Commercial Change, Political Conflict, and London's Overseas Traders, 1550–1653* (Princeton: Princeton University Press, 1993), 462.

146. "Presbytery of the year 1647 took cognisance of the morals of the congregation, held investigations in regular form, and decreed punishment by suspension, being further empowered to call in the civil arm for the enforcement of this sentence": Shaw, *History of the English Church*, 1: 4.

147. Wrightson, "Puritan Reformation of Manners," 14.

148. For one case study, see Mark Valeri, "Religious Discipline and the Market: Puritans and the Issue of Usury," *William and Mary Quarterly*, 3rd ser. 54, no. 4 (1997): 747–68.

149. "Civil magistrates were needed to censure spiritual assemblies civilly for the sake of order and decency": Gregory, "Congregational Puritanism," 154, 176–77. The role of the civil magistrate in congregational thought is important given the similarities between presbyterian and congregational views of him. Margaret Sommerville has argued that presbyterian and congregational views of the civil magistrate "did not lead to differing assessments of the scope of the civil magistrate's authority": "Independent Thought, 1603–1649" (Ph.D. diss., University of Cambridge, 1981), 194. However, presbyterians such as John Paget objected to the congregationalists' appeal to the civil magistrate as an alternative to synods and councils, arguing that the civil magistrate could be heathen and was therefore no good substitute for a system of spiritual appeals through synods: *A Defence of Chvrch-Government, Exercised in Presbyteriall, Classicall, & Synodall Assemblies* (London 1641), 31–32.

CHAPTER 3

1. Downame, *Two Sermons*. For Downame's distinction between elder and newer disciplinarians, see 5–7. He argued that primitive churches were "not parishes properly but Dioceses" and that "the word *Ecclesia* . . . [signified] generally, any assembly, company or congregation of men whatsoeuer." From this argument, he went on to claim that elder disciplinarians in the tradition of Cartwright, Calvin, and Beza "doe herein join with vs against our new sect of Disciplinarians." For English and continental responses to Downame, see Milton, *Catholic and Reformed*, and Willem Nijenhuis, "The Controversy between Presbyterianism and Episcopalianism surrounding and during the Synod of Dordrecht, 1618–1619," in *Ecclesia Reformata: Studies on the Reformation* (Leiden: E. J. Brill, 1972), 207–20.

2. Although debate over the nature of the Church included discussion of the invisible church, the debate between presbyterian and congregational writers during this period centered chiefly on the nature of the visible church. Sommerville is one exception who has drawn attention to the importance of this concept in distinguishing between presbyterian and congregational thought: "The controversy over the Catholic visible church is significant because it highlights the depth of the difference between Independent and Presbyterian theory": "Independent Thought," 59.

3. For example, Carol Schneider, "Godly Order in a Church Half-Reformed: The Disciplinarian Legacy, 1570–1641" (Ph.D. diss., Harvard University, 1986); and Brachlow, *Communion of Saints*.

4. "In the first definitive treatment of presbyterian government . . . Walter Travers was neither full nor plain in his treatment of this problem, and virtually left it on one side, either because his own tendencies were Congregationalist, or because it was still too much in dispute": Collinson, *Elizabethan Puritan Movement*, 107–8; Travers, *A Full and Plaine Declaration* (1580), 98. The most extreme version of this elision of presbyterian and congregational ecclesiologies has been maintained by Stephen Brachlow, who argues for an "ecclesiological continuum running between the disciplinarian puritanism of Cartwright and strict separatism in early Stuart England," where "the ecclesial ideals of left-wing Puritanism [including Cartwright and Travers] were entirely compatible with those of the separatists." Although Brachlow acknowledged the potential "dangers in this method of viewing the Elizabethan material too narrowly through the interpretative glasses of two Jacobean radicals [Henry Jacob and John Robinson]," his study is an example of how a concern to maintain fluidity within puritan ecclesiology by withdrawing from distinctions in puritan thought has often failed to resolve the problem of ecclesiology and even led to greater distortion by representing all puritan ecclesiology through a single ecclesiological category that is by default congregational: *Communion of Saints*, 5, 16ff.

5. See Figures 2 and 3, above.

6. Although modern notions of individualism have almost automatically become attached to discussions of the doctrine of predestination, the predestinarianism mapped out in this tree refers to the whole redeemed community. Particular definitions of the Church as an institution and as a community could result in multiple views of which the individualism associated with Calvinism is only one reading.

7. Miller, *Orthodoxy*; Gregory, "Congregational Puritanism." This is not to suggest that such circumstances and polemical arguments were the only factors that contributed to Jacob's ecclesiology.

8. "Congregationes dicuntur Ecclesia per synecdochicus": TCD, MS 366, fol. 6v. See Figure 3, above.

9. Henry Jacob, *Reasons Taken out of Gods Word and the Best Humane Testimonies Prouing a Necessitie of Reforming Our Churches in England Framed and Applied to 4: Assertions Wherein the Foresaid Purpose Is Contained* (Middelburg: 1604), 6. "This sense of the word (Ecclesia) in Math 18.17" could not be understood through synecdoche according to Jacob, for "this word Ecclesia was taken but only for the whole Assembly of the Church" (B3v).

10. Lake, "Presbyterianism," 195.

11. See Chapter 4.

12. John Von Rohr, "The Congregationalism of Henry Jacob," *Transactions of the Congregational Historical Society* 19, no. 3 (1962): 107.

13. Stephen Brachlow, "The Elizabethan Roots of Henry Jacob's Churchmanship: Refocusing the Historiographical Lens," *JEH* 36 (1985): 237; Champlain Burrage, *Early English Dissenters in the Light of Recent Research, 1550–1641* (Cambridge: Cambridge University Press, 1912), I: 313; Murray Tolmie, *The Triumph of the Saints: The Separate Churches of London, 1616–1649* (Cambridge: Cambridge University Press, 1977), 12–13; Schneider, "Godly Order," 153.

14. TCD, MS 141, 62–63.

15. Ibid., 2.

16. Ibid.

17. Henry Jacob, *A Confession and Protestation of the Faith of Certaine Christians in England Holding it Necessary to Observe, & Keepe All Christes True Substantiall Ordinances for His Church Visible and Politicall (That Is, Indued with Power of Outward Spirituall Government) under the Gospel* (Amsterdam: 1616), B2v.

18. Jacob, *Reasons Taken Out of Gods Word*, B3.

19. Jacob, *The Divine Beginning and Institution of Christs Church* (Leiden: 1610).

20. Jacob, *A Confession and Protestation*, Bv.

21. TCD, MS 141, 3.

22. Ibid., 69.

23. Sommerville, "Independent Thought," 1, n. 1.

24. TCD, MS 141, 413.

25. Ibid., 67.

26. Ibid., 414.

27. Ibid., 413.

28. Ibid., 15.

29. Ibid., 16–18.

30. They further argued (ibid., 68–69) that "the towne clarke or secretary of Ephesus a greeke orator as it seemeth by his speech reported in the Acts by this word[e] doth signify the courts of Justice . . . which agreeth well with our sense taking it for ecclesiasticall courts of iustice."

31. Ibid., 30.

32. "Hee speaketh of those who were chosen by the consent of the church to heare causes which in all reason could not bee the whole congregation": ibid., 69–70. Thomas Cartwright offered the same interpretation of this passage in his *Confutation*: "To *tell the Church* is to *tell the gouernours* euery seueral assembly in the time of the Law. . . . I conclude therefore that to tell the Church, is not to tell the Bishop or Minister of the word onely: but a company which hath ouersight of the Church; by

whom, or by whose mouth, which is the minister of the word, the rest of the body of the Church is to be advertised": *A Confutation of the Rhemists Translation, Glosses and Annotations on the Nevv Testament* (Leiden: 1618), 92.

33. TCD, MS 141, 30.

34. Ibid., 23–24.

35. "Sometymes it is taken for the whole Catholique church in heaven and earth as when christ is sayde to bee the heade of the church. Some tymes for the whole church militant as when it is sayde bee with out offence to the church of Christ and sometimes otherwise": ibid., 69. Richard Hooker had similarly described his controversy with Travers: "But what if in the end it be found that he judgeth my words, as they do colours, which look upon them with green spectacles, and think that which they see is green, when indeed that is green whereby they see": *The Works of That Learned and Judicious Divine Mr. Richard Hooker,* ed. John Keble (Oxford: Clarendon Press, 1841), 3: 576.

36. Examples included "spirit for the third person in god and for the guifts of the same spirit election for predestination to salvation, redemption for deliverance from spiritual enemies, faith for a perswation of the truth of god promises hope for an expectation of the performance of the promises believed, baptisme for a sacrament of the new testament signing": *Works of Hooker* (ed. Keble), 3: 67. For Calvin's use of pagan and Christian authors, see Irena Backus, *Historical Method and Confessional Identity in the Era of the Reformation, 1378–1615* (Leiden: E. J. Brill, 2003), ch. 2.

37. TCD, MS 141, 68.

38. They argued that "whereas you infer upon it that it is taken in the new testament . . . for a parochiall assembly independent this wee utterly deny neither doth it any where in the new testament signify any matter of independancy": ibid., 69.

39. Ibid. The presbyterians declared (18–19) that "the question then betweene us is not whether any synods bee the ordinances of god for it is graunted that Synods for councill are devine, but the question is altogether about the* authoritie of Synods."

40. "I grant Synods may discusse and determine of errors, and may pronounce them wicked and accursed errors. But actually excommunicat mens persons, the Apostles never did without the concurrence and consent of that Congregation where they were members": Henry Jacob, *An Attestation of Many Learned, Godly, and Famous Divines, Lightes of Religion, and Pillars of the Gospell Iustifying This Doctrine, Viz. That the Church-Governement Ought to Bee Alwayes with the Peoples Free Consent. Also This; That a True Church Vnder the Gospell Contayneth No More Ordinary Congregations but One* (Middelburg: 1613), 117.

41. Ibid., 86.

42. Ibid., 153.

43. TCD, MS 141, 410.

44. "For both every perticuler congregation may bee ordered by an outward spirituall government in the affayres that odenarily doe conscerne that congregation, and also perticuler congregations of a sheire, diocesse, province or nation yea and of all nations subiect to one & the same civill government may by their owne common & free consent agree of assemblyes to bee held at convenient tymes & places for yealding their mutuall help and adise in matters that may conscerne the churches of each combination both to debate them and to determine according to gods word of them by iust authoritie": ibid., 14–15.

45. They further argued that "this power wee doe also acknowledge to belong to such perticuler churches as are compleate and are able to order the administration of their owne perticuler congregation according to gods word": ibid., 96.

46. "But this argument is of no force at all for to prove that such congregations are not also subiect to the authority of synods": ibid.

47. Ibid.

48. Ibid., 97.

49. Ibid., 429. For the importance of independence to Jacob's ecclesiology in contrast to earlier separatist literature, see 7 and 203n39 above. A fuller discussion of Jacob's independent ecclesiology and the separatist tradition will appear in my forthcoming essay "Ecclesiastical Independence and the Freedom of Consent."

50. Skinner, "Classical Liberty", 309–12.

51. TCD, MS 141, 130.

52. Ibid., 423. See also ibid., MS 140, fol. 152.

53. While Hugh Peter's candidacy in 1629 was quickly overturned, Paget drafted a formal set of questions to test Thomas Hooker's views, which succeeded in disqualifying him by November 1631. Paget then used the same interrogatories against John Davenport, whom he finally managed to exclude by May 1634.

54. According to Alice Carter, "[It] appears more than likely, that Paget deliberately framed the questions [to Hooker] to show up the differences between the Independents and the Reformed Churches": *The English Reformed Church in Amsterdam in the Seventeenth Century* (Amsterdam: Scheltema and Holkema, 1964), 78. Keith Sprunger stated that Paget intended to "minutely examine Davenport in the same manner used so successfully on Hooker. . . . All of these maneuvers of Paget 'shuffled the cards' against Davenport, and by the summer of 1634 Boswell could report to England that Davenport was wholly excluded at Amsterdam": *Dutch Puritanism: A History of English and Scottish Churches of the Netherlands in the Sixteenth and Seventeenth Centuries* (Leiden: E. J. Brill, 1982), 115.

55. For example, see John Davenport's responses to Paget: *A Just Complaint Against an Uniust Doer: Wherein is Declared the Miserable Slaverie & Bondage That the English Church of Amsterdam is Now In, By Reason of The Tirannicall Government and Corrupt Doctrine, of Mr. Iohn Pagett Their Present Minister* (Amsterdam: 1634).

56. Paget, *A Defence of Chvrch-Government*, 186–87.

57. Ibid., 37.

58. Ibid.

59. Ibid., 41.

60. Ibid., 37. For further discussion on this subject, see Chapter 7, below.

61. Ibid., 38.

62. Rembert Carter, "The Presbyterian-Independent Controversy with Special Reference to Dr. Thomas Goodwin and the Years 1640–1660" (Ph.D. diss., University of Edinburgh, 1961), 92; Thomas Cartwright, *Helpes for Discovery of the Truth in Point of Toleration: Being the Judgment of That Eminent Scholler Tho. Cartwright, Sometimes Divinity-Professor in the University of Cambridge in the Reigne of Queen Elizabeth of Happy Memory, and Then A Famous Non-Conformist, For Which Through the Tyranny of the Bishops He Suffered Exile* (London: 1648), 12.

63. In his critique of Henry Ainsworth's use of rabbinical sources, Paget also admitted that "there is some use of the Rabbines for understanding and learning of

the holy tongue." He did, however, qualify this statement and recommend a critical use of such sources: "And a principall vse of them is, thereby to refute the Jewes themselves from their owne writings": *An Arrow Against the Separation of the Brownists: Also an Admonition Touching Talmudique & Rabbinical Allegations* (Amsterdam: 1618), 339. There are also hints at the presbyterians' argument for the continuity between the Old and New Testaments in their insistence on the perpetuity, unalterable nature, and continuity of ecclesiastical discipline. Travers asserted that "touching the originall of discipline, that it commeth from God, and therefore is vnchangeable and perpetual & common to all churches with that earnest charge which S. Paul giueth Timothie touching the keeping and maintaining thereof, who hauing taught his scholar all the order of ruling the house of God which is the Church I charge thee saith he in the sight of thee God which quickneth all things ": *Fvll and Plaine Declaration,* 7. "I note furdr also that this order of discipline is constant and unchangeable which may neither bee broken for any mans power or authority, nor altered for any mans fauour: seeing that it is not onely called a commandement, but is giuen also with such a charge. . . . Last of all, that it is no commandement belonging to any certain time, but perpetuall, and pertaining to all times and states of the Church. Seeing it is so expresly commanded, that it should be kept unto the coming of our Lord Iesus Christ": ibid.

64. Paget, *A Defence of Chvrch-Government,* 214.

65. "I will begin with the ordinary offices of the Church, whereof seing some bee simple, and others some compounded, I will in the first place more fully and at large as the matter it selfe requireth speake of the first and more simple part whence also the latter doth wholy spring": Travers, *Fvll and Plaine Declaration,* 38.

66. Paget, *A Defence of Chvrch-Government,* 85.

67. Ibid., 147.

68. TCD, MS 141, 19.

69. See 52, 57–58, 64 above and following.

70. TCD, MS 141, 83.

71. Ibid.

72. Ibid., 13–14.

73. Carter, *English Reformed Church,* 53.

74. Schneider, "Roots and Branches," 178.

75. Webster, *Godly Clergy,* 311. Tom Webster uses the term "Amesian" to refer to puritans in a tradition marked by the ambiguities in the ecclesiology of William Ames during the early seventeenth century.

76. Ibid., 303.

77. Simeon Ashe and William Rathband signed this letter and were involved in printing Ball's treatises during the mid-seventeenth century. For these publications, see 66, below.

78. Schneider, "Roots and Branches," 193.

79. Webster, *Godly Clergy,* 296–97.

80. Ibid., 297.

81. Ibid., 298.

82. Schneider, "Roots and Branches," 193.

83. John Ball, *A Friendly Triall of the Grounds Tending to Separation in a Plain and Modest Dispute Touching the Lawfulnesse of a Stinted Liturgie and Set Form of Prayer,*

Communion in Mixed Assemblies, and the Primitive Subject and First Receptacle of the Power of the Keyes (London: 1640), 299.

84. Ibid., 297–98, and Ball, *A Letter of Many Ministers in Old England, Requesting the Judgement of Their Reverend Brethren in New England Concerning Nine Positions* (London: 1643), 35.

85. Ball, *A Letter of Many Ministers*, 35.

86. Schneider, "Roots and Branches," 193.

87. Robert Parker's sister, Sara Parker, also remained a member of the English Reformed Church in Amsterdam long after her brother had departed: GAA, ERCA, no. 84. I am grateful to William Boylan for his conversation on the early religious life of Newbury, Massachusetts.

88. James Noyes, *The Temple Measured: Or, a Brief Survey of the Temple Mystical* (London: 1646), 5.

89. "Independency in point of Iurisdiction upon earth is but Temporal, and it hindreth Humility and Love (in particular Churches) which are perfections eternal. It is no perfection to be so independent as to become insolent and impotent": ibid., 56.

90. "If we look upon the type or patern of the Christian Church in the State of *Israel*, we shall finde that the lesser cities in *Israel* had their particular Presbyters, though consisting but of three Elders [the Triumvirale Synedrium], such was their frame of Policie": ibid., 5.

91. Ibid., B.

92. Ibid., 2.

93. Ibid., 41. Thomas Cartwright offered this interpretation in his *Confutation* (92): see 221, n. 32 above.

94. Noyes, *Temple Measured*, 41.

95. Ibid., 3.

96. "It is most probably that the synedrion of Elders was called the Congregation, because there was wont to be an assembly of people present in the place and at the time of Judicature; we call the Presbyterie the representative church, upon another consideration": ibid., 42. All those who viewed the visible church as both a particular congregation and a general body applied this principle to the collective jurisdiction of congregations through synods. The relationship between the universal nature of the visible church and collective ecclesiastical government can be seen in Noyes's examples. He affirmed (4) that "all Churches have power to act together, and to exert power of Jurisdiction in a General Councel. Calvin is expresse, Instit. l 4. c 8": *Institutes of Christian Religion*, ed. John T. McNeill (Philadelphia: Westminster Press, 1960), book 4, ch. 8. Noyes explicitly established (54) the relationship between the general nature of the visible church and the authority of synods, asserting, "All the Arguments which prove an universal visible Church, do prove the power of Councels and Synods."

97. Joseph Felt, *The Ecclesiastical History of New England* (Boston: Congregational Library Association, 1855), 1: 431.

98. Thomas Parker, *The True Copy of a Letter: Written by Mr. Thomas Parker, a Learned and Godly Minister, in New-England, unto a Member of the Assembly of Divines now at Westminster. Imprimatur. Ja. Cranford* (London: 1644), 3.

99. "And upon conference had with them about the particulars controverted betwixt them, finding himself still unsatisfied both in their Arguments against him,

and Answers to him (in neither of which he could perceive so much truth, as might convince him of Error, or move him from his own principles) but perceiving rather that jealousies and misunderstandings of him did arise in the hearts of his Reverend fellow-Presbyters": Noyes, *Temple Measured,* epistle.

100. Felt, *Ecclesiastical History,* 490.

101. Parker stated on this occasion that "there wee have proposed our arguments, and answered theirs; and they proposed theirs, and answered ours: and so the point is left to consideration": *True Copy of a Letter,* 4. Peter Hobart, the minister in Hingham, Massachusetts, was also renowned for his presbyterianism by the late 1630s: John J. Waters, "Hingham, Massachusetts, 1631–1661: An East Anglian Oligarchy in the New World," *Journal of Social History* 1, no. 4 (1968): 362.

102. Paul, *Assembly of the Lord,* 111–13.

103. The convention decided against "'some parts of the Presbyterian way,' and the Newbury elders took their arguments into consideration": Felt, *Ecclesiastical History,* 1: 490.

104. Ibid., 1: 493.

105. William Rathband, *A Briefe Narration of Some Church Courses* (London: 1644), A2v–A3.

106. Ibid., 4.

107. Ibid.

108. Sargent Bush, Jr., *The Writings of Thomas Hooker: Spiritual Adventure in Two Worlds* (Madison: University of Wisconsin Press, 1980), 108.

109. Ibid.

110. Andrew Thomas Denholm, "Thomas Hooker: Puritan Preacher, 1586–1647" (Ph.D. diss., Hartford Seminary Foundation, 1961), 409. My thanks to Deborah Hart Stock for this reference.

111. I am grateful to Ann Hughes for drawing my attention to those involved in the publication of Ball's treatises.

112. Richard Heyricke, *Three Sermons preached at the Collegiate Church in Manchester by Richard Heyricke* (London: 1641), 2–6. I thank Chad van Dixhoorn for directing me to the earlier writings of the Westminster divines as a source for their definition of the visible church.

113. Ibid., 105.

114. Vernon also comments that "Stephen Marshall and Richard Vines could rebut the Independents by arguing that as the church was *a priori* a united and catholic body, the presbytery represented the aggregate of the members of that body": ibid.

115. Carter, "Presbyterian-Independent Controversy," 105, n. 11; Thomas Edwards, *Gangraena: or A Catalogue and Discovery of Many of the Errours, Heresies, Blasphemies and Pernicious Practices of the Sectaries of This Time, Vented and Acted in England in These Four Last Years: As Also, A Particular Narration of Divers Stories, Remarkable Passages, Letters; An Extract of Many Letters, All Concerning the Present Sects* (London: 1646), 19.

116. Carter, "Presbyterian-Independent Controversy," 100.

117. Ibid., 106.

118. Ibid., 90, 94.

119. Criticism of varying beliefs among avant-garde congregationalists was made by both John Paget and William Rathband: John Paget, *An Answer to the Unjust Com-*

plaints of William Best, and of Such Others as Have Subscribed Thereunto (Amsterdam: 1635), 23–24; Rathband, *Briefe Narration*, sig. A3.

120. Susan Hardman Moore, "Arguing for Peace: Giles Firmin on New England and Godly Unity," in *Unity and Diversity in the Church*, ed. R. N. Swanson (Oxford: Blackwell, 1996), 258.

121. Massachusetts Historical Society, MS SBd-76, fol. 22.

122. Hardman Moore, "Arguing for Peace," 251.

123. Gregory, "Congregational Puritanism," 66. Thomas Parker referred to a *"Mr. Sh."* as "The Author of the Reply to D. Down": "An Humble Advertisment to the High Court of Parliament," in *A Defence of Chvrch-Government*, ****2. For Sheerwood's authorship, see Sommerville, "Independent Thought," 12.

124. Richard Sheerwood, *A Replye Answering a Defence of the Sermon, Preached at the Consecration of the Bishop of Bathe and Welles, by George Downame, Doctor of Divinitye In Defence of an Answere to the Foresayd Sermon Imprinted Anno 1609* (Amsterdam: 1614), book 1, part 2, 90–91; book 2, part 2, 104.

125. Paget quoted Sheerwood "as writing of himself in the third person . . . for better security in those dangerous times: *I am sure his meaning is not to comfirme H.Ia. against whom he disputed by writing, about the subject you speake of*": "An Humble Advertisement," ****2v.

126. According to Thomas Paget, the author sent "the Copie [of the Reply] to Mr P. for the amending or altering of what they conceived to be amisse. Mr P. returned the Copie, with these words, *I have corrected (as I might) the maine point of your scruple*": ibid.

127. Sheerwood, *A Replye*, part 2, book 2, 113.

128. "[T]hat it was in the power and libertie of all Bishops to rule alone, as Moses did and that Hieromes owne words doe importe so much although he would have them to use the help of their Presbiters and therein to imitate Moses "believing that "they might by Apostolicall ordinance as lawfully have ruled as Moses by Divine calling did wherein how absurd he is I have before shewed cap 2": TCD, MS 292, fols. 40–41v.

129. Ibid., fol. 30v.

130. Paget, *A Defence of Chvrch-Government*, 105.

131. Sprunger, *Dutch Puritanism*, 344; Miller, *Orthodoxy*.

132. Bodleian Library, Oxford, Parker MS English Th.e.158, fol. 137v.

133. Ibid.

134. Ibid., fol. 131v.

135. Travers, *Fvll and Plaine Declaration*, 38.

136. Bodl. Lib., Parker MS English Th.e.158, fol. 113.

137. Ibid., fol. 115.

138. Ibid.

139. Ibid., fol. 155v; Richard Field, *Of the Church Fiue Bookes* (London: 1606).

140. Bodl. Lib., Parker MS English Th.e.158., fol. 115.

141. Ibid.

142. Ibid., fol. 116v.

143. Ibid., fol. 107. See also Frank Benjamin Carr, "The Thought of Robert Parker (1564?–1614) and his Influence on Puritanism before 1650" (Ph.D. diss., University of London, 1964), 170.

144. Bodl. Lib., Parker MS English Th.e.158., fol. 105v.

145. Ibid.

146. Ibid., fol. 110.

147. Ibid., fol. 99v. Parker further denied the conformists' "distinction between power of jurisdiction & exercise of it: in which dotage fell that noble witted Field who learned of Stapleton that Bishop & Presbyters are of one order & power & may ordained, but that the Apostles by decree restrained them from exercise of that power fearing schisme." He argued (fol. 101) against "downam who maketh [presbyters] a simple presbyter by ordination without all Pastorall power till the Bishop by institution assigne him into part of his owne cure." For the conformist career and anti-presbyterian arguments of Thomas Bilson, see Lake, *Anglicans and Puritans?*

148. Bodl. Lib., Parker MS English Th.e.158, fol. 168.

149. Ibid., fol. 117. For the moderate puritanism of William Whitaker, see Lake, *Moderate Puritans*.

CHAPTER 4

1. TCD, MS 141, 105.

2. See, for example, Downame, *Two Sermons*.

3. Ibid., dedicatory epistle, A1; book four, ch. four, 75. Downame himself claimed to have studied the Elizabethan ecclesiastical controversies and proved to be well versed in these writings when responding to objections to his sermon.

4. Ibid., book four, ch. four, 89. "Although vpon speciall and extraordinary occasions they were by the Apostle called to other places," Downame argued that "yet these were the places of their ordinary residence, And that I proue, because they both liued and died ther." Furthermore, he reasoned that "Paul required them both, to continue there," "supplying substitutes in their absence," 1. Tim. 1.3; Tit. 1.5: Davenport, *A Defence of the Answer and Arguments of the Synod Met at Boston in the Year 1662* (Cambridge: 1664); Sheerwood, *A Replye*, part 2, book 2: 116–17.

5. Travers, *Fvll and Plaine Declaration*, 25, 27.

6. "Timothy was not fixed & bounde to any one particular church & sea in certayne (as bishops be) but employed sometyme here sometyme there in the Church & in that church" (2 Cor. 8.23, Act 19.22, 1 Cor. 4.17, 1 Thes. 3.2): TCD, MS 140, fol. 79.

7. Ibid., 292, fol. 28.

8. Ibid., fol. 27v.

9. David Mullan noted in Theodore Beza's counsel to the Scots that "superiority of bishops was directly proportional to ecclesiastical decay": *Episcopacy in Scotland*, 48. English presbyterians had long maintained that the slightest introduction of ranking among ministers gave way to nothing less than popery: "[F]or as at the first one Presbiter was prefered before the rest, and made a Bishop, soe afterwards one Bishop was sett aboue the rest, and soe this Custome bred the Pope and his monarchie": TCD, MS 292, fol. 30. Travers interpreted the papal monarchy as having resulted from the introduction of superiority among ministers in small increments: "Neither durst the Bishops arrogate thus much to themselues in the beginning but by little and little, as ambition, and desire of bearing rule did increase in them, and the care of the Church did decrease in their fellows, at the last they came to this unspeakable pride": *Fvll and Plaine Declaration*, 99. It is evident that even a moderate episcopal model could not be reconciled with arguments that forbade the slightest degree of superiority among

ministers. And, of course, presbyterians were not simply concerned to guard equality among ministers when attacking the superiority of bishops, but also to include lay elders in ecclesiological deliberations. The "Reformed Church Government" argued that a superior ecclesiastical officer such as the bishop could not be found in the New Testament and that it was necessary to establish equality among ministers and to elect lay elders. George Downame centered his attack against presbyterianism on the inclusion of lay elders in synods: *Two Sermons*. For further discussion of lay elders, see Chapter 2, above.

10. "This is the true history of the confusion of Ecclesiastical offices: This was the cradle and the beginning of the ambition of Church-men. . . . [If] they think this shamefull in the Pope to do to Generall Councels, they would not play the petty-Popes in Convocations, or Provinciall Synodes, and taking away the liberty of the Ecclesiasticll Synodes and Assemblies, rule, governe and appoint all alone by tyrannie": Travers, *Fvll and Plaine Declaration*, 101.

11. Peregrin, *Letters Patents*, 24.

12. The writer continued: "and that such was the practize of the primitive & Ancient Church in such cases I conclude it is the best & only good course that can betake in this behalfe": TCD, MS 140, fol. 86.

13. Ibid.

14. Ibid.

15. Peregrin, *Letters Patents*, F3.

16. TCD, MS 141, 7.

17. "This was also ordinary, that the church of Anteoche, and the other that were likewise so troubled adviseth of this remedy against this mischeife, that is to send from their churches chosen men to Jerusalem, to advise with that church about this businesse, and to procure a resolution therein": ibid., 6.

18. Ibid.

19. Ibid., 27.

20. Ibid., 7.

21. Ibid.

22. Ibid., 33. They further reasoned (25) that "taken out of the 1 Cor 14.32. to wit in these words The Spirits of the prophets are subiect to the prophets hereby wee argued only this much that the pastors of such separate congregations ought to bee subiect to the iudgement of the prophets of other churches assembleed in . . . [a] synode."

23. Jacob, *An Attestation*, 10.

24. Ibid., 10. See Chapter 3, above.

25. Jacob, *An Attestation*, 85.

26. Jacob, *Divine Beginning*, B3v.

27. Ibid., A3–A3v.

28. Jacob, *A Confession and Protestation*, B4v.

29. Jacob, *An Attestation*, 25.

30. Jacob, *Divine Beginning*, D8v. Francis Oakley, "Legitimation by Consent: The Question of the Medieval Roots," in *Politics and Eternity* (Leiden: E. J. Brill, 1999), 132.

31. TCD, MS 141, 49.

32. Jacob, *A Confession and Protestation*, B4v.

33. Even if they denied that power or authority rested in congregational consent, the presbyterians had long argued that churches were at liberty to consent and "to order the administration of their owne perticuler congregation": TCD, MS 141, 96.

34. TCD, MS 141, 76.

35. Travers, *Fvll and Plaine Declaration*, 28.

36. Ibid., 105.

37. See 145–46, above; and Ha, "Puritan Conciliarism."

38. Irena Backus, "These Holy Men: Calvin's Patristic Models for Establishing the Company of Pastors," in *John Calvin and the Company of Pastors: Papers presented at the 14th Colloquium of the Calvin Studies Society, May 22–24 2002: University of Notre Dame, Indiana*, Grand Rapids, MI: Calvin Studies Society, 2004.

39. As a puritan spokesman in the Lambeth Palace Conference of 1584, Travers warned that in divine service the Church of England might "soe much more to proferre the Apocrypha before the canonicall." This, he argued, was "not be farre from blasphemie, the difference of honor being as grate betweene theme & the other as between divine & humane writings, and in respect of the Authors of them betweene god & man": BL, MS Add 48064, fol. 52.

40. "It was a common tactic of Cartwright's, when confronted with a patristic source cited against him by Whitgift, simply to write the author off, if not as a papist, then as a member of the church much beset by popish error and therefore not to be trusted": Lake, *Anglicans and Puritans?*, 18.

41. In response to Bancroft's sermon of 1588–89, "Cartwright and Reynolds wrote to [him] to confute his ideas of the Church Fathers, and when Cartwright was later imprisoned, he kept up the dispute in private conversation as well as by letters." "Thus you say," wrote Bancroft, "if you . . . had ever read ye ecclesiasticall historye, ye might have found easily the eldership most flourishing in Constantyne's tyme[.]" "[In] my poore iudgment, you [Cartwright] mistook the meaning of Eusebius and that marvelously": Usher, *Reconstruction*, 2: 54.

42. TCD, MS 140, fol. 77.

43. In light of Calvin's misgivings about Origen, Travers's citations of him are noteworthy, as are references to him in the "Reformed Church Government": ibid., MS 366, fol. 14v; MS 140, fol. 67. Whereas the same quotation from Augustine writing against the Donatists appears in both Travers's notes and the "Reformed Church Government," there was also variation. Instead of quoting, like Travers, from Athanasius to affirm the sole authority of Scripture and the secondary use of the testimony of the fathers, the "Reformed Church Government" cited Ambrose: ibid., MS 140, fol. 67.

44. TCD, MS 140, fol. 67.

45. Ibid.

46. Ibid.

47. Eugene Rice, *Saint Jerome in the Renaissance* (Baltimore: Johns Hopkins University Press, 1985), 138, 139–43ff.

48. TCD, MS 140, fol. 81v.

49. Travers also referred to Greek fathers, including Athanasius for the doctrine of *sola scriptura*, in addition to translating Chrysostom's sermons (see Chapter 7, below): ibid., 233.

50. Ibid., fol. 81v.

51. Early English protestant debate with papists was also introduced to discount conformist examples from early church history: "They proclayme it an other while to be the heresy of Aerius to deny the superiority of a Bishop above a pastor . . . out of the testimony of Epiphanius who so reckoneth it. . . . [T]his is the very allegation of Pigglimus that notorious papist even in the very selfe same cause which we have now in hande ffor against the Waldenses first, and after against Wicliffe who held that a Bishop was not superior to a pastor": ibid., fol. 80.

52. TCD, MS 141, 7.

53. "Ita prima ecclesia episcopi et ministri, vicini admoniti, necessitate postulante convenerunt sponte, et synodos habuerunt, minores et Particulares. Oecumenicae et universales": ibid., MS 366, fol. 14v. Heinrich Bullinger, *De Conciliis* (Zurich: 1561), book 1, ch. 21, provided Travers with further detail concerning provincial synods, as he headed fol. 47 of his notes with the title "synodi particulares et provinciales." He proceeded to catalogue examples of provincial synods on this page: "Romani a Victore episcopi de paschale, Cesareae in Palestina a Traphilo, Ponto a Palmate, Gallia a Ireneo, Achaia a Bacchylo."

54. "[De] eo an filius dei fuerit Christus ante incarnationem. . . . Quod cum Beryllus Arabum Bestroensium episcopus negaret in ea synodo ab Adamantio Origene convictus et conversus est ad rectam fidem": TCD, MS 366, fol. 47.

55. "[A]lia in qua idem Origenes convicit qui dicit animas ad resurrectionem cum corporibus interire": ibid. Given the controversy over his ministry as a laymen and his contested ordination, Origen's example was useful, especially for Travers, whose presbyterian ordination in Antwerp had also been challenged: Knox, *Walter Travers*, 82–85.

56. TCD, MS 141, 113–14.

57. "In the Councill of Nice there are reported to have been above 300 Bishops beside a great number of the worthy persons. Amongst these were Athanasius of imortall memory for his invincible constancie in the truth and Paphnasius that noble confessor whose blind ieyes that religious and most renowned Emperor Constantine the great kissed in reverence and honor that hee had lost them for Christ and his gospell sake. Likewise there were many other of excellent pietie and lerning": ibid.

58. "These and the like circumstances being duely considered would easyly yeld another manner of weight for that authorytye of the synods and councills where at they were and generally for all the lawfull synods then . . . would be counter poysed with any testimony agaynst them saue only of the holy scriptures": ibid., 104.

59. S. J. Knox has recounted Beza's high regard for Cartwright: "The sun, I think, does not see a more learned man." Beza's friendship with Travers is also documented by Knox through a letter dated in the 1580s referring to "our ancient friendship," where "there does not pass a day in which I do not think caringly of you and your affairs . . . my very dear brother": *Walter Travers*, 27–28. Travers also developed a close friendship with Beza while he was in Geneva, and maintained contact with him after he returned to England. A letter from Beza to Travers appears in *The Seconde Parte of a Register*, ed. Albert Peel (Cambridge: Cambridge University Press, 1915).

60. Travers's booklist also included Nicolaus Hemmingius, *De Pastore, siue Pastoris Optimus Viuendi Agendique Modus* (Leipzig: 1574), AD H 210; and Wilhelm Zepper, *De Politia Ecclesiastica* (Herborn: 1595), AD Z 135.

61. Ha, "Puritan Conciliarism." There is also evidence of Travers's personal con-

cern for continental churches in his translation of Abraham Scultetus's sermons on the Psalms. "[T]wo sermons upon Psalme 74.l One upon Psal 79. One upon the 80 & also One upon the 83 three upon the 89 & one which is the last upon the 102 Psalme. He expressed his concern for the trials faced by the reformed churches during the early seventeenth century in explaining that these sermons he translated into Englishe for the good uses they may yeelde of instruction and comfort in respect of the reformed churches in many parts beyond the seas, most grievously afflicted. All which were first made by the worthy & reverend preacher Mr \/ Bartilmeu Pitiscus & \/ Mr Abraham Scultetus": TCD, MS 135, fols. 40–41v.

62. The writer continued by adding, "Yea not only thes before named (with whom not any of them no nor all our Bishops together, are to be compared) but also Bullinger, Musculus, & even Guwalter himselfe do testifye with us (as they know) that the order of Church government in the primitive church, both in respect of Elders as also in other respects was as we teach and flat contrary to them and their government doctrine, and assertions in this behalf": TCD, MS 140, fol. 70v.

63. Ibid., MS 292, fols. 120r–v.

64. Ibid., fols. 144r–v.

65. Milton, *Catholic and Reformed*, chs. 8, 9.

66. Hooker, *Works* (ed. Keble), 3: 558.

67. Ibid., 559. For the Spanish protestant Anthony de Corro, see ibid., n. 16.

68. Paul Christianson, "Reformers and the Church of England under Elizabeth I and the Early Stuarts," *JEH* 31 (1980), 471.

69. Bodl. Lib., Parker MS English Th.e.158, fol. 51v.

70. Ibid., fol. 54.

71. Ibid., fol. 54v.

72. TCD, MS 141, 105.

73. "They are (as hath beene shewne) without all warant from gods word and without all consent not only of any nation or perticular country state or province but of many godly and learned writer that wee know; did not Bucer and peter Martyr two very worthy servants of god live and preach in our church and thereby discerne of the state thereof; yet if all the writings where is there one word that may teach men this doctrine that they ought to ceperate them selues from it and ioyne together in perticuler congregations that rule themselues and bee ruled by no other. Calvin and Beza as it appeareth by their Epistles were well acquainted also with the state of our church but have they let fall from them in all their writings any thing that may give incongruent to this disorder": ibid., 119.

74. Ibid.

75. Paget, *A Defence of Chvrch-Government*, 30.

76. Rathband, *Briefe Narration*.

77. Chad van Dixhoorn, "Reforming the Reformation" (Ph.D. diss., University of Cambridge, 2004), 4: 393.

78. TCD, MS 141, 107.

79. Ibid.

80. Ibid., 107–8.

81. Ibid., 62.

82. Ibid., 70. The *Replye* similarly responded to the example of "Melancthon . . . singled out from all the rest by the D. and his Surveyour," by asking, "[C]an the sin-

gular opinion and practise of such a one make good the D. his indefinite and general assertion viz. that the godly and learned Protestants wch reformed religion in this last age, did both allow the Episcopall function": TCD, MS 292, fol. 122.

83. For Cartwright, it was an "injury . . . to leave the public works of Bucer, and to fly unto the apocryphas; wherein also they might drive us to use the like, and to set down likewise his words which we find in his private letters": Whitgift, *Works*, 3: 124.

84. As Irena Backus has pointed out from the example of Abraham Scultetus, conciliar judgments were regarded as "of greater authority than all writings of a private nature": "The Fathers and Calvinist Orthodoxy: Patristic Scholarship," in *The Reception of the Church Fathers in the West: From the Carolingians to the Maurists* (Leiden: E. J. Brill, 1997), 845. Laurence Chadderton's regard for familiarity with ancient councils is reflected in his list of six gifts that would equip students of divinity for the ministry, where the fifth was the "reading of the learned commentaries of the old and new writers and of the ancient Councils with due examination of their interpretations and judgments; not differing from them but upon just occasion, whereof good reason may be rendered by the means aforesaid": Lake, *Moderate Puritans*, 37.

85. TCD, MS 295, fol. 37v. This letter is also printed in Thomas Cartwright, *Cartwrightiana*, ed. Albert Peel and Leland H. Carlson (London: George Allen and Unwin, 1951).

86. TCD, MS 141, III.

87. Ibid., MS 292, fol. 128v. Other sources included "the Schinalkaldicke Articles subscribed by the Divines of the augustane confession, [which] doe plainely shew, that they taught the power of ordination and Jurisdiction to pertaine in common to all Ministers, and that it was tyranny in Bps to draw unto themselues any superioritie therein" (fol. 119).

88. Ibid., 141, 114.

89. Ibid., 112. "Thus in this age have . . . Churches in ffrance held many nationall councils and other provinciall and smaller synods. This also have done the churches in other parts to their infinite commoditi in the low cuntryes at dort and assisted by many worthy personages, of excellent pietie and learning send unto it from sundry parts of Europe which increased the countenance of it as if it had bene a council of many nations" (8).

90. "Notwithstanding any power given to particular congregations ordinarily to governe themselves yet are they subiect to give account of such their government to higher ecclesiasticall authority that is to the synods of the churches wherein they are combined even to the nationall Synode of the kingdome or country where they are. And here of as all the tymes have examples so of late wee had a notable example in Holland wherein the nationall synode tooke godly orders for suppressing the errors that had so sprunge up amongst them": ibid., 77.

91. Jacob, *An Attestation*, 117.

92. Ibid., 116.

93. For discussion of the English delegation at the Synod of Dort, see the introduction to *The British Delegation and the Synod of Dort* (1618–1619), ed. Anthony Milton (Woodbridge: Boydell, 2005).

94. See Chapter 2, above.

95. Lake, *Anglicans and Puritans?*, 26.

96. TCD, MS 140, fol. 74. For competing claims to the Edwardian Reformation in the late sixteenth century, see Diarmaid MacCulloch, *The Boy King: Edward VI and the Protestant Reformation* (Berkeley: University of California Press, 2002), 195–96.

97. TCD, MS 140, fol. 74.

98. Ibid., fol. 71.

99. Ibid., fol. 71v.

100. Ibid., fol. 80.

101. D. Barnes, "a famous Man & most constant martyr saith thus . . . I cannot believe, neither will I ever believe that any man may by the law of god be a Bishop of a provance much lesse of a Whole cuntrey: for that it is contrary to the doctrine of St. Paul commanding Titus to ordeyne a Bishop in every Towne": ibid., fol. 81; MS 292, fol. 213v.

102. While the appeal to English writers was prompted by conformist polemicists, it nevertheless serves as a powerful reminder and example of English presbyterian independence from Scottish tradition, which is often ascribed more influence over the English than is warranted: ibid., MS 292, fol. 212v.

103. The writer continued by calculating that "this was almost an Eleven hundreth yeares after Christ, namely about Anno adnni 1076. Whereby apeareth how new & howe farre degenerated one sort of Bishops be from the ancient Bishops of Englande . . . every pastor hath as much authoritye both to binde & lo[ose] as an other. (Mr. Foxe in the story of Wickliffe)": ibid., 140, fol. 82v.

104. Stoughton, *Assertion,* A3v. The *Reply* to Downame made the same argument in part 1, book 1, 34–35. Carr points out this argument in Robert Parker's *De Politeia Ecclesiastica: The Thought of Robert Parker*, 146.

105. Paget, *A Defence of Chvrch-Government,* 173.

106. On the authority of synods, Paget cited Cartwright in arguing for the possibility of excommunicating an entire community: "To excommunicate a whole Church together, is indeed a hard thing, and such a thing as I never heard of in the practise of the Reformed Churches: yet this intimates that he [Cartwright] thought they had a power of excommunicating at least some, if not all, upon a just occasion": ibid., 82–83.

107. TC [Thomas Cartwright] Repl 2 pag 575: Thomas Cartwright, *The Second Replie of Thomas Cartwright: Agaynst Maister Doctor Whitgiftes Second Answer, Touching the Church Discipline* (Heidelburg: 1575); TCD, MS 141, 516.

108. They argued that he "meaneth that the whole congregation is not to be tould first nor first to heere the complaint nor to iudg, neither any ought to examine the busines by the people by the elders apart first, to say that hee heere meaneth to exclude finally & absolutely the whole congregacon, and the peoples full consent, to excommunicacon in the laste act [Thomas Cartwright Repl, 176; Repl pag 183]": Thomas Cartwright, *A Replye to An Ansvvere Made of M. Doctor Whitegifte: Againste The Admonition to the Parliament* (Hemel Hempstead?: 1573); TCD, MS 141, 417.

109. TCD, MS 141, 44.

110. Ibid.

111. Ibid., 184.

112. Neither can recourse to history be understood as inconsistent with protestant belief in the doctrine of *sola scriptura*. As Irena Backus has demonstrated for the reformers, "[H]istory became a means of constructing and expressing their confessional identity": *Historical Method,* 61.

113. As Arnaldo Momigliano wrote: "[In] the Church conformity with the origins is evidence of truth. This doctrine may be interpreted differently in the various denominations; but it is never absent in any of them": *The Classical Foundations of Modern Historiography* (Berkeley: University of California Press, 1990), 136.

114. Momigliano argued that "in no other history does precedent mean so much as in ecclesiastical history" and that "the very importance of precedent and tradition in ecclesiastical history compelled the ecclesiastical historians to quote documentary evidence to an extent which is seldom to be found in political historians": ibid., 136–37.

115. Ibid., 93.

116. Ibid., 96.

117. Jacob cited passages including 1 Corinthians 5: 4, 1 Corinthians 11: 18, 20, and 14: 23 to describe the physical meeting of the congregation in one place: *A Confession and Protestation*, Biv.

118. Paget, *A Defence of Chvrch-Government*, 99. In countering Henry Jacob's citation of modern writers, the presbyterians similarly argued that "the cheife of these blessed instruments by whose ministery it pleased god to discover unto us the manyfold errors and the floud of inormytyes that had beene brought into the service of god and doctrine of the church by the sea of Roome. Heere are named Luther, and Zuingulus, Melancton, and Chemnitius, Calvin and Beza, Viret and Martyr and chiefely the churches agreeing and Dveus, Martyr and Bucer, Cartwright and whittacor, beside divers others and chiefely the churches agreeing to both the Helvetian confesions": TCD, MS 141, 105.

119. Paget, *A Defence of Chvrch-Government*, 96.

120. According to Paget, "[In] none of his latter writings he doth use that peremptory phrase, in limiting Synods, or Churches combined in Classes or Synods, *onely to counsell or advise*, in such manner as was done in that first writing. . . . Now as in particular Congregations the greatest acts of power and jurisdiction which are exercised therein, receive their strength from *common consent*, and doe consist therein: so if in matters of greater weight the *common consent* of Synods is to be used, then is a power and authority asscribed unto them; then ought not particular Churches to proceed without and against the authority of common consent in Synods." Paget proceeded to claim that Ames conceded to the right of suffrage, that "he confesseth that to have a definitive voyce is a matter of greater authority, then to counsell and advise; and seeing withall that this power of suffrages and definitive voyces belongs unto the deputies of Churches in Synods, and that by his confession; it is evident that herein he asscribes more power unto Synods then he did in that book of English Puritanisme": ibid., 106–7.

121. "D. Ames according to the receyved opinion of the Protestants, allowes unto them also the right and authority of suffrages, when they are deputed and sent as the Delegates of their Churches unto Synods": ibid., 107.

122. Ibid.

123. Ibid., 111.

124. Hall's observation of an increased sacerdotalism among the New England clergy has not gone unchallenged. James Cooper has instead argued that the character of New England congregationalism had always been marked by its nature as a mixed polity and that the distribution of power between governing elders and the congregation continued following the Antinomian controversy: "'A Mixed Form': The Es-

tablishment of Church Government in Massachusetts Bay, 1629–1645," *Essex Institute Historical Collections* 123, no. 3 (1987): 233–59. Perry Miller and other historians have on the other hand traced oligarchic tendencies among the colonists in Massachusetts prior to the Antinomian controversy.

125. David D. Hall, *The Faithfull Shepherd: A History of the New England Ministry in the Seventeenth Century* (Chapel Hill: University of North Carolina Press, 1972), 20.

126. H. M. Dexter, *The Congregationalism of the Last Three Hundred Years, as Seen in Its Literature: With Special Reference to Certain Recondite, Neglected or Disputed Passages* (New York/Boston: Harper and Bros., 1880), 433–34. The process of discipline outlined in this treatise identified a parallel between the admonition among individuals ultimately deferred to the Church and the unresolved disputes among particular congregations that were brought to neighboring churches: "If the Church offending doe heare the Church admonishing they have gained their Brethren and their desire." However, John Cotton described, "[If] the Church heare them not, then that other Church may take one or two 1 Churches moe 2 to assist them in the conviction of that sinne. If yet the Church heare them not, then upon due notice therof given, all the Churches thereabout may so meet together; and after judicious 3 inquirie into the cause, may by the Word of God confute and condemne such errours in doctrine or practise, as are found offensive, to prevent the spreading either of the 4 gangren of Heresie or of the leprosie of 5 sin": *The Doctrine of the Church, to Which is Committed the Keyes of the Kingdome of Heaven* (London: 1643), 12.

127. Cotton, *Doctrine of the Church*, 12.

128. Noyes, *Temple Measured*, 56.

129. Ibid., 43–44.

130. One of the notes in his treatise also described withdrawal from a heretical congregation (that is, "non-communication") as "a defensive Excommunication with such as formerly enjoyed communion": ibid., 57, 79.

131. "*To withdraw from a Church, or peccant party therein, after due means, with patience used, obstinately persisting in Errours or Scandals*; this must be taken with a grain of Salt": John Davenport, *Another Essay for Investigation of the Truth, in Answer to Two Questions* (Cambridge: 1663), 52.

132. Like others, Davenport argued, "but Neighbour-Churches may not withdraw from a true Church for every Errour and Scandal, though persisted in, and, in their opinion, obstinately": ibid., 53–54.

133. Ibid., 54.

134. He continued that they "are obstinately persisted in, against due means regularly used with patience for their conviction . . . from whence they may be justly denominated *Heretical*, Tit. 3.10.11. 2 Joh. ver 10,11. Or to the *communion of Saints*; from whence they may be justly styled *Schismatical*, Rom 16.17.18": ibid., 55.

135. Ibid., 63. "It is not the bare Consent, or mutual Agreement of Churches, but *the nature of the thing consented to*, as, *viz. The Power they agree to be stated under*, that makes it a Classical Combination, or puts those Churches *under a Classical Jurisdiction*. What though the *voluntary Combination*, mentioned by Mr. *Rutherfurd*, in his sense doth inferre *a Classical Membership and Jurisdiction?*": John Davenport, *A Defence of the Answer and Arguments of the Synod Met at Boston in the Year 1662* (Cambridge, 1664), 101.

136. Arnaldo Momigliano drew attention to the connection between history and contemporary events, where "the very continuity of the institution of the Church through the centuries makes it inevitable that anything which happened in the church's past should be relevant to its present": *Classical Foundations*, 136.

137. For the relative weight placed on various historical sources by theologians, see Backus, *Historical Method*.

138. See 161–63, 166–68, 172–74, above.

139. Pocock, *Ancient Constitution*; D. R. Woolf, *The Idea of History in Early Stuart England: Erudition, Ideology, and 'The Light of Truth' from the Accession of James I to the Civil War* (Toronto: University of Toronto Press, 1990), ch. 2.

140. J. G. A. Pocock, "The History of British Political Thought: The Creation of a Center," *JBS* 24, no. 3 (1985): 290. Glenn Burgess has argued that the impetus of ecclesiastical antiquarianism not only contributed to the development of history among humanists but also helped set a context from which the "classic phase" of ancient constitutionalism in the first half of the seventeenth century emerged: "[T]he Elizabethan defences of the *ecclesia Anglicana* explored themes that were essential features of ancient constitutionalism. . . . Perhaps they provide the 'missing link' between St German and Selden or Coke. . . . It is possible, then, to see the central conceptual nexus of ancient constitutionalism given its first full examination in Elizabethan ecclesiology": *The Politics of the Ancient Constitution: An Introduction to English Political Thought, 1603–1642* (Basingstoke: Macmillan, 1992), 102–5. Anthony Grafton has also discussed the legacy of ecclesiastical history on historical scholarship through the prioritization of documentation and primary sources: *The Footnote: A Curious History* (London: Faber and Faber, 1997), 168–70.

141. See 31–32, above.

142. Ole Grell has drawn attention to the historical interest that helped to establish links between merchants and Calvinist clerics: "Merchants and Ministers: The Foundations of International Calvinism," in *Calvinism in Europe*, ed. Andrew Pettegree, Alastair Duke, and Gillian Lewis (Cambridge: Cambridge University Press, 1994), 266–70. See also his *Calvinist Exiles in Tudor and Stuart England* (Aldershot: Scolar Press, 1996).

CHAPTER 5

1. Oakley, "Legitimation by Consent," 132.

2. Henry Jacob, *A Christian and Modest Offer of a Most Indifferent Conference, or Disputation, about the Maine and Principall Controversies Betwixt the Prelats, and the Late Silenced and Deprived Ministers in England* (London: 1606), A2v. This reading of Jacob's ecclesiology draws from Philip Pettit's discussion of freedom as nondomination and interference with choice as a form of domination in *Republicanism: A Theory of Freedom and Government* (Oxford: Clarendon Press, 1997), 52–53.

3. TCD, MS 141, 439.

4. Jacob, *A Confession and Protestation*, B10.

5. TCD, MS 141, 439.

6. Ibid.

7. Ibid., 440.

8. Jacob, *An Attestation*, 86.

9. For a discussion of the development of individual natural rights in the early

seventeenth century, see Richard Tuck, *Natural Rights Theories: Their Origins and Development* (Cambridge: Cambridge University Press, 1979), chs. 3–4.

10. "King Vzziah was striken with the leaprosie, for that being not content with his kingly office, hee would haue taken vpon him the Priests office also." He added further examples, which he argued "ought to be a lesson to vs for euer, not onely as *Moses* writeth, that no man burne incense before the Lord, but onely they which are of the stock of *Aaron*, and are thereby called thereunto, but also that no man bee so bold as to pervert or alter that order which God hath established in his Church, and to arrogate vnto him that honour which he hath by no right and lawfull calling obtained": Travers, *Fvll and Plaine Declaration*, 10.

11. "For that sentence of the Apostle is generall, that no man ought to take this honour vnto him but he that is called thereto as was *Aaron*": ibid., 9.

12. Ibid., 37.

13. TCD, MS 141, 46. This corresponds to their ranking of formal ecclesiastical acts above the private writings of ecclesiastical scholars.

14. Richard L. Greaves, "The Ordination Controversy and the Spirit of Reform in Puritan England," *JEH* 21, no. 3 (1970): 238.

15. Ibid., 236.

16. TCD, MS 141, 135. For "as the Apostle declareth saying to the Corinthians though you have ten thousand teachers in Christ yet you have not many fathers. For in christ Jesus I have begotten you by the gospell." The presbyterians continued (136): "To plant churches then is a matter above the ordinary dignity of a common minister much more of a common professer." The presbyterians argued against private church planting in direct response to Henry Jacob's justification for his erection of a congregational church in Southwark. See 98, 100, above

17. Paget, *An Answer to Unjust Complaints*, 58.

18. TCD, MS 141, 136.

19. Travers, *Fvll and Plaine Declaration*, 9.

20. "And as for Election that it is necessary to the giving of any of these offices, it may appeare even of that, that S. Paul ioyneth it with examination and triall, and diligently warneth *Timothy*, that he lay not on his hands upon them that be unworthy, but onely upon those that after a iust triall being had, are found meet and chosen," 1. Tim. 3.10.15: ibid., 23.

21. Ibid., 34.

22. He also explained that through ordination "the party chosen was warned by this ceremony, that he was separated and set, apart to the worke of God, as appeareth in the 13 of Acts, and that hee was taken out of the rest of the people to the doing of that office, as it were by the hand of God himselfe." Yet, for Travers, this action was not to impart "the Holy Ghost, which no man gaue them, no nor could giue them, vnlesse it were extraordinarily, this being proper to those times and to the Apostles onely": ibid., 35–36.

23. "[T]he Consistorie or Councell of the Church . . . heere is no one man hath any office or authority to doe any thing as in the former: But there is one office of all, which they all doe execute in common together: For the Consistory or Councell of the Church is the company and assembly of the Elders of the Church, who by common councell and authority doe rule and governe the same": ibid., 23, 86.

24. Nevertheless, argument from common consent could be used as a presbyte-

rian argument against episcopacy and in favor of church councils. For instance, in *Letters Patents* (24), Peregrin had argued for common consent and condemned the singular rule of prelates on the grounds that it replaced the role of synods.

25. Travers, *Fvll and Plaine Declaration*, 24–25.

26. TCD, MS 140, fol. 96v.

27. Whitgift, *Works*, 1: 296.

28. Ball, *A Friendly Triall*, 86.

29. Milton, *Catholic and Reformed*, 475.

30. Prior to writing the *Supplication*, Travers had refused to be reordained as a condition for appointment as Master of the Temple Church as Archbishop Whitgift required. He explained that "the calling to the ministry is such an action, as he, that in a Church orthodox, and not heretical or schismatical, hath once received sufficiently, for the substantial points to be observed in it, by the ordinance of God, in any part of the holy Catholic Church, wheresoever he may after be required to any place, wherein he may exercise that calling, is not to be urged to any new imposition of hands, and vocation to the ministry": Hooker, *Works* (ed. Keble), 3: 115–16.

31. Ibid., 3: 552–53.

32. Ibid., 3: 553.

33. Ibid. Travers also pointed out that "a doctor created in any university of Christendom, is acknowledged sufficiently qualified to teach in any country."

34. Congregational consent had been a central principle for rejecting diocesan authority: "For where the peoples free consent is orderly and conveniently practised alwayes in the Church government, there the Body of the Church can not be so large as a Diocese, much less as a Province or Nation, and least of all so large as a Universall Church": Jacob, *An Attestation*, 85. Jacob further argued (86) that "where each ordinarie Congregation hath their free consent in their ordinarie governement, there certainly each Congregation is an intire and independent Body politike Spirituall, and is indued with power in it selfe immediately vnder Christ."

35. Sommerville "Independent Thought," 74, 76; Gregory, "Congregational Puritanism," 158.

36. Jacob, *A Confession and Protestation*, B4v.

37. Thus, church officers gathered in synods held only a consultative and not coercive power over particular congregations.

38. van Dixhoorn, "Reforming the Reformation", 32.

39. Ibid., 252.

40. Slayden A. Yarbrough, "Henry Jacob, a Moderate Separatist, and His Influence on Early English Congregationalism" (Ph.D. diss., Baylor University, 1972), 61, 75.

41. Henry Jacob, A *Defence of the Churches and Ministery of Englande Written in Two treatises, Against the Reasons and Obiections of Maister Francis Iohnson, and Others of the Separation Commonly Called Brownists* (Middelburgh: 1599), 85.

42. Yarbrough, "Henry Jacob," 77.

43. TCD, MS 141, 53.

44. Ibid., 53–54.

45. Ibid., 98.

46. Ibid., 97. They continued to argue that this was "as if one should say. This town by their charter doth chose their owne officers and bringeth in many witnesses

to prove that point and having so done would there upon conclude and infere that therefore it dependeth not on any higher authority neither is bound to recive & obey any acts of Parlament."

47. Paget, *Answer to Unjust Complaints*, 19. He argued that "election of Ministers is an action belonging to severall Congregations, and not to Classes and Synods."

48. Ibid.

49. Ibid.

50. This applied in all ecclesiastical appointments: "But the Elders in elections, as also in all the rest of the government of the Church, are as eies unto the rest: and leade and direct them that either through ignorance, or being blinded with their owne desires they slide not in the way": Travers, *Fvll and Plaine Declaration*, 29.

51. Paget, *Defence of Chvrch-Government*, 68.

52. John Davenport, *An Apologeticall Reply to a Booke Called an Answer to the Unjust Complaint of W.B.* (Rotterdam: 1636), 244. Davenport asked (249), "[W]ho ever heard that it is an act of Schysme for a man to preach at the desire of any Church, onely as an assistant, without the consent of the Classis?"

53. "When neither Elders can satisfy me, nor I perswade them in that which I beleeve to be just and necessary, then in such case the judgement of others is nedfull for determination of the question": Paget, *Answer to Unjust Complaints*, 66. He observed (65) that "if I should not protest against the concordant judgment of Elders, and bring the matter to further tryall, when I conceave their resolutions to be unlawfull & hurtfull to the Church, I should sinne against God and mine owne conscience, in following a multitude to doe evill."

54. Given the tendency for scholars to overlook the distinctions between late medieval and early modern conciliar theory, it is highly significant that Paget emphasized the distinction between Roman and Protestant councils to underpin the need for them. "Seeing we maintaine against the Romish Church, that Synods and Councells are subject unto errour sometimes . . . seeing in such cases there is liberty for the servants of Christ, to protest against those resolutions and decrees, which they are in conscience perswaded to be erroneous: how much more may we thinke that a Consistory, where 3 or 4 Elders make an agreement and decree, without consent of their Minister, are subject to errour, and therefore in such case may lawfully be protested against by the same Ministers": ibid., 66.

55. Travers, *Fvll and Plaine Declaration*, 12–13. John Paget had argued that his dispute with Davenport involved "such weighty points of government, as doe concerne the good estate not of our Church onely, but of other reformed Churches in these countries": *Answer to Unjust Complaints*, 12.

56. By.

57. TCD, MS 141, 46–47.

58. Paget, *An Arrow*, 100.

59. "The Ministers of the Gospell is not made absolutely a Minister by the choice or election of this or that people, but onely their Minister for the time of his abode and continuance with them": John Ball, *An Ansvver to Two Treatises of Mr. Iohn Can, the Leader of the English Brownists in Amsterdam* (London: 1642.), 87.

60. van Dixhoorn, "Reforming the Reformation," 4: 685.

61. Ibid., 4: 687. "The words [fixed or unfixed] may stand as in the proposition; we have noted them already as to the poynt of ordination. A congregation having a

perfect eldership yet may be under a presbyteriall government, for ther may be complaints, matters of maladministration" (4: 696–97).

62. Ibid., 4: 689. On the same page William Rathband raised the question "whether a third [distinction] may be added to those 2 fixed or unfixed, namely mixt. Not alwayes fixed, yet more ordinarily fixed. All pastors, elders, & deacons of that one, yet the severall care distributed."

63. Ibid., 4: 697.

64. Ibid., 4: 661.

65. Noyes, *Temple Measured*, 49.

66. Schneider, "Roots and Branches," 180.

67. Ball further argued that "it seemeth somewhat strange, that you should cite those texts of Scripture, as if the Apostle had said, feed one flock, or feed that flock of God onely." In reference to Acts 20: 28, he wrote that "Ordinary Pastors and Teachers it is true . . . are tied ordinarily to one flock, as the Text proveth. . . . But that a Pastor is so tied to his flock, that he can perform no ministeriall act to any other upon any occasion that it proveth not, nor can we find that it was ever so understood by Divines ancient or modern." He also asserted that "the function or power of exercising that Function in the abstract, must be distinguished from the power of exercising it, concretely, according to the divers circumstances of places. The first belongeth to a Minister every where in the Church, the latter is proper to the place and people where he doth minister. The lawfull use of his power is limited to that congregation ordinarily. The power it self is not so limited and bounded": *A Friendly Triall*, 76, 32–33.

68. Ball, *An Ansvver to Two Treatises*, 71.

69. Ibid.

70. Ball, *A Friendly Triall*, 35.

71. Ibid., 32–33.

72. Ibid., 80.

73. van Dixhoorn, "Reforming the Reformation," 4: 639.

74. Ibid.

75. Ibid., 4: 661.

76. Ibid., 4: 639–40.

77. Ibid., 4: 664.

78. Ibid., 4: 657.

79. Whitgift, *Works*, 1: 208.

80. Ibid., 2: 508–9.

81. Ibid., 1: 207.

82. Ibid., 2: 530.

83. Ibid., 2: 529.

84. Ibid., 2: 525.

85. Lake, *Anglicans and Puritans?*, 28–34. For puritanism and the principle of edification, see John Coolidge, *The Pauline Renaissance in England: Puritanism and the Bible* (Oxford: Clarendon Press, 1970).

86. Whitgift, *Works*, 2: 529–30.

87. As Robert Browne wrote, "Master Cartwright commeth to that point, concerning the dumbe minister. . . . [H]ere he prooueth the Sacraments, ministred by such, to be Gods Sacraments, and that men may receiue them lawfully": *An Ansvvere*

to Master Cartvvright His Letter for Ioyning with the English Churches: Whereunto the True Copie of His Sayde Letter is Annexed (London: 1585), 45.

88. TCD, MS 141, 89.

89. Hooker, *Works* (ed. Keble), 3: 119.

90. TCD, MS 141, 58.

91. Ibid.

92. For "hee acknowledgeth the peoples consent in the calling of their preists . . . [and] holdeth the calling of popish priests in that respect for the essence of it good; where as the very forme and end of it is most corupt which is . . . that they are ordayned not to minister the gospell but to offer sacrifice for the quicke and the dead": ibid., 89–90.

93. Whitgift, *Works*, 3: 102.

94. Ibid., 3: 139.

95. Ibid., 3: 140.

96. Ibid.

97. Here there is a crucial qualification in the traditional binary distinction between the godly and ungodly. Between the exemplary "sheep" and the openly profane "swine" were the conforming yet ultimately unregenerate "goats" as well as the less than exemplary yet ultimately regenerate sheep who submitted to the discipline of the Church: Lake, *Anglicans and Puritans?*, 31. A significant subsection of the Church could fall into this category, between the supergodly and scandalous.

98. Sprunger, *Dutch Puritanism*, 104, 107.

99. Ibid., 115.

100. Paget, *Answer to Unjust Complaints*, 139. Complaining of Davenport's opposition to infant baptism, Paget wrote: "Hereby in the administration of Baptisme, in stead of an Assistant, I should have had a Resistant: his dayly example in refusing to baptise such as I should, serving to strengthen others in their opposition and contention against me": ibid., 69.

101. See Chapter 7, below.

102. Sprunger, *Dutch Puritanism*, 25–27.

103. Ibid., 101, 104, 107. Sprunger noted (101) that "because the Ancient Church of Johnson and Ainsworth had a congregational covenant, Paget was under some compulsion to prove that his own church had a similar deep commitment to righteousness. His vision, however, as explicated in debate with Ainsworth, was an implied covenant by which members in the course of joining were assumed to be promising 'to separate from knowen evils, and to serue the Lord in the Gospel of his Son, so far as it is revealed vnto you.' To Ainsworth such covenant talk was only 'generals'—where were the 'particulars'?"

104. Robert Lord Goodman, "Newbury, Massachusetts, 1635–1685: The Social Foundations of Harmony and Conflict" (Ph.D. diss., Michigan State University, 1974), 120.

105. Ibid., 121. The presbyterians in Hingham also used less stringent criteria for membership admission. For more on Hingham, see Edward Franklin Ripley, *Shepherd in the Wilderness: Peter Hobart, 1604–1679: A Founder of Hingham Plantation in Massachusetts* (Lanham: University Press of America, 2001), 110.

106. Webster, *Godly Clergy*, 302–3.

107. Paget, *Answer to Unjust Complaints*, 135.

108. Ibid., 134. "Hereby he doth plainely refute himself, and that divers wayes; for, 1. If the communion of particular Churches amongst themselves doe warrant him to baptise their infants, who are no members of his Church, then is it an errour to thinke that a Pastour may not exercise his ministery in some act of it, toward those who are no members of his Church; and all his allegations to that end are vaine and idle" (135–36); "Mr Davenport hath resigned his Pastorall or Ministeriall charge in London, and is now no established Minister of any particular Congregation, having no calling elsewhere, and doth yet upon occasion preach sometimes for others, as for Mr. Balms. and Mr. Pet. &c., it were worthy to be knowne, upon what ground he doth administer the word unto them" (136).

109. Ball, *A Letter of Many Ministers*, 16–17.

110. Ibid., 18–19.

111. Ibid., 19.

112. Patrick Collinson, "The English Conventicle," in *Voluntary Religion*, ed. W. J. Sheils and Diana Wood (Oxford: Basil Blackwell, 1986), 244.

113. Richard Bancroft, *A Survay of the Pretended Holy Discipline* (London: 1593), 127.

114. Brachlow, *Communion of Saints*, 43; R. T. Kendall, *Calvin and the Calvinists* (Oxford: Oxford University Press, 1980), chs. 2–3.

115. Webster, *Godly Clergy*, 312.

116. Browne, *An Answvere to Master Cartvvright*, 25.

117. Ibid., 33.

118. Jacob, *A Defence*, 11.

119. Travers, *Fvll and Plaine Declaration*, 7–8.

120. "They know not, who being content with the doctrine of the Gospell, neglect discipline, that the disposition and nature of these two, is like the disposition of two sisters who are twins: or of those brethren of whom Hypocrates speaketh, who beganne to bee sicke together, and to amend together. . . . [T]hey were affected one with the others health and infirmity": ibid.

121. Lake, *Anglicans and Puritans?*, 77.

122. Brachlow, *Communion of Saints*, 35.

123. Henry Jacob, *A Plaine and Cleere Exposition of the Second Commandement* (Leiden: 1610), 'Third Part of Discourse.'

124. Ibid., n.p.

125. TCD, MS 141, 185–86.

126. Ibid., 189.

127. Ibid. They further insisted (186) that they "confesse in deede if this ordr bee wanting any church that it is the most unperfect, and marked with a naughty blot, but yet nevethelesse we hold it for a church and continew in the communion of it and affirme that it is not for singuler persons to separate themselves from it."

128. Ibid., 119.

129. Ibid., 121.

130. Ibid., 120–21.

131. They continued that Jacob taught men "ought to ceperate them selues from it and ioyne together in perticuler congregations that rule themselves and bee ruled by no other": ibid., 119.

132. Ibid., 120.

133. Ball, *A Letter of Many Ministers*, epistle.
134. Ibid., 5.
135. Ibid., 4.
136. Ibid., 6.
137. Ball, *A Friendly Triall*, 24.
138. Ibid., 306.
139. TCD, MS 141, 437.
140. Ibid., 123.
141. Ibid.
142. Ibid., 401.
143. As John Paget had argued in his writing against the separatists in Amsterdam, "[It] is one thing to neglect the counsel of some godly men, another to renounce communion of all true Churches": *An Arrow*, 43.
144. TCD, MS 141, 119.

CHAPTER 6

1. Patrick Collinson's analysis of voluntary religious exercises has identified varying tendencies in these practices: "Godly Preachers and Zealous Magistrates in Elizabethan East Anglia: The Roots of Dissent", in *Religious Dissent in East Anglia*, ed. E. S. Leedham-Green (Cambridge: Cambridge Antiquarian Society, 1991), *The Religion of Protestants*, and "English Conventicle." However, the view that nonconformity in England overwhelmingly gravitated toward congregationalism in practice has subsequently become an assumption in many works. For example, Tai Liu has argued that classical and synodical government "was but an artificial superstructure without sociohistorical roots in the City's parishes," and so the entire presbyterian government was reliant on individual congregations making "the transition from theory to practice": *Puritan London: A Study of Religion and Society in the City Parishes* (Newark: University of Delaware Press, 1986), ch. 2.
2. Collinson, "Puritan Classical Movement," 386.
3. Travers's presbyterian ordination drew public attention following his famous dispute with Richard Hooker in the Temple Church during the mid-1580s: Sprunger, *Dutch Puritanism*, 21–22; BL, Landsdowne MS 50, fol. 171.
4. Sprunger, *Dutch Puritanism*, 234.
5. Knox, *Walter Travers*, 46.
6. "De precibus initio et fine." "De caena prox[imo] Dominico denuncianda, ubi seniores adm[oniti]o de off[icin]o gratia suos cons[istorum]": TCD, MS 324, fol. 86.
7. "Electibus seniorum et diacorum": ibid., fol. 86.
8. Ibid., fol. 42v.
9. One disciplinary case during Travers's ministry is mentioned in the few reports remaining of the Antwerp Church in the Boswell papers. "Leonard Walker was dealt with all at sundry times about his mariadge with the widow of William Horne deceased for marrying her in a popish church & by ministry of a popish priest not attending the time nor order prescribed by the Reformed Churches though he had warning thereof given before by the [blank space] of this church. And after many admonitions to consider & repent him of the fault (which he of long time would not confesse to be a fault) in the end he confessing it & desiring to be prayed for that he might be pardoned of God, & the Church": BL, Add. MS 6394, fol. 106v.

10. Knox, *Walter Travers*, 46; TCD, MS 324, fols. 4r–v.

11. Knox, *Walter Travers*, 48.

12. Ibid., 49.

13. Ibid.

14. TCD, MS 324, fol. 2v.

15. Collinson, *Elizabethan Puritan Movement*, 227.

16. Knox, *Walter Travers*, 47–49; BL, Cotton Galba C, VI (Walsingham letter in defense of Travers's ministry at Antwerp).

17. TCD, MS 324, fol. 4.

18. Earlier in his career, Grindal had written urging a preacher of the Merchant Adventurers in Antwerp, William Cole, to conform to the Book of Common Prayer: Patrick Collinson, *Archbishop Grindal, 1519–1583: The Struggle for a Reformed Church* (London: Jonathan Cape, 1979), 171.

19. He recorded "limina venimus": TCD, MS 324, fol. 31.

20. This is probably a Latinized spelling of Margate, on the east coast of England.

21. TCD, MS 324, fol. 31.

22. Sprunger, *Dutch Puritanism*, 25–28.

23. Since the Merchants' congregation had "closed during the dispute . . . Hence we request you to ask the Governor and Deputy of the Company of merchants adventurers to send a Minister who would agree with us in Church-government, and to send him as soon as possible": *Ecclesiae Londino-Batavae Archivum*, ed. Joannes Henricus Hessels (Cambridge: Cambridge University Press, 1887), 937.

24. Theodore Rabb, *Enterprise and Empire: Merchant and Gentry Investment in the Expansion of England, 1575–1630* (Cambridge: Harvard University Press, 1967).

25. TCD, MS 324, fol. 32.

26. Ibid., fol. 31v.

27. "Se[niores] et dia[coni] ordinandi": ibid., fol. 32.

28. Ibid., MS 295, fol. 50v.

29. Ibid., fol. 65.

30. Edward Gellibrand of Kent matriculated at Magdalen College, Oxford, 1571, minister of English Church Middelburg, Holland d. 1601: NA Kew, PROB 11/98.

31. *Calendar of State Papers Domestic, Great Britain*. Series 2. 1625–1702. London: Longman, 1858–1897., 234: fol. 10.

32. G. W. Sprott and Alan R. MacDonald, "Forbes, John (*c.* 1565–1634)", *ODNB*.

33. "(Though they have not had one together 16 monthes, as I am informed) with the Deputy, who offereth to joyne charitably with them for amendment of all, if all will meet to mend, which I cannot hope to worke by my mediacion. The minister and Company abandoning him for scandalizing and (as they object) affronting theyr Church, and the Deputy challenging them for want of Lyturgye Catechisme, Confiscian set formes of prayers for marriage or for celebracion of the Sacrament, exercise of the Lord Prayer solemne Thanksgiving and Anniversaryes for the Birth and Death of our Saviour &c": *Calendar of State Papers Domestic, Series 2 1625–1702*, 234: fols. 10v–11.

34. Sprunger, *Dutch Puritanism*, 237.

35. Ibid.

36. Hugh Goodyear of Manchester became minister to the English reformed

church at Leiden in 1617/18 and stayed there until 1661. Sprunger related that while in the Low Countries, "Goodyear hesitated to take a stand between the old Puritanism of John Paget and the new Puritanism of [Thomas] Hooker and [John] Davenport": ibid., 131. Goodyear is commonly perceived to have tended more toward semisepa-ratism than toward presbyterianism: "During the early 1630s, however, Goodyear, in spite of his traditional Presbyterian stance, showed sympathy for the Hooker-Dav-enport program" (ibid.). He is also known to have maintained strong ties with the pastor to the American Pilgrims, John Robinson. Yet, at the same time, Goodyear continued to maintain good relations with presbyterians personally as well as institu-tionally: "Goodyear and Paget got along tolerably well," and "Goodyear had no deep opposition to classis government and was one of the first English preachers to apply for Dutch classis membership" (ibid.).

37. Ibid., 342.

38. Ibid., 185–86.

39. GAD, MS 110/5, consistory records, fol. 12.

40. Sprunger, *Dutch Puritanism*, 164.

41. Ibid., 201.

42. Ibid., 202.

43. Ibid., 222.

44. Ibid., 195.

45. Carter, *English Reformed Church*, 19–21; Sprunger, *Dutch Puritanism*, 91.

46. Webster, *Godly Clergy*, 311. See also Watts, *Dissenters*, 89.

47. Hughes, *Gangraena*, 35.

48. Webster, *Godly Clergy*, 311.

49. "When I was yet a childe, before I was 12 yeares old, I felt this impression & this ardent affection to that calling; and that for this cause to instruct the people of God": Paget, *An Answer to Unjust Complaints*, 16.

50. Lake and Como, *The Boxmaker's Revenge*, 4.

51. Sprunger, *Dutch Puritanism*, 93. See also Paget, *An Arrow*, 34.

52. R. C. Richardson, *Puritanism in North-West England: A Regional Study of the Diocese of Chester to 1642* (Manchester: Manchester University Press, 1972). Although I was not able to incorporate her notes into the present chapter, I am grateful to Barbara Coulton for sharing her work and extensive knowledge on puritanism in Cheshire with me.

53. Morrill, *Cheshire*, 4.

54. Ibid., 18.

55. Ibid., 19.

56. Ibid.

57. Ruthin, Denbighshire Record Office, Plas Power MS DD/PP/839, 154–56. I am indebted to Jane Dawson for her recovery of Goodman's correspondence and for sharing her transcription of these citations. For a discussion of these papers, see Jane Dawson and Lionel K. J. Glassey, "Some Unpublished Letters from John Knox to Christopher Goodman." *Scottish Historical Review* 84, no. 218 (2005): 166–201.

58. The Queen's College, Oxford, MS 280, fols. 179v–180.

59. Clarke, *Two and Twenty English Divines*, 161.

60. Ibid., 163.

61. Ibid., 161.

62. Carter, *English Reformed Church*, 85.

63. A letter to the consistory by an unknown author complained of his preaching on this subject from Acts during the late 1630s. The writer's objection that members of the Church should be allowed greater involvement in the process of election reveals the continued controversy over this subject that extended beyond Paget's ministry: GAA, ERCA 318, no. 27.

64. Clarke, *Two and Twenty English Divines*, 161.

65. Ibid., 166.

66. Ibid., 95.

67. NA Kew, PROB 11/98. Of Herring's thirteen children, one daughter married Edward Richardson, who was an ejected minister from Ripon, Yorkshire, and was minister to the English Church in Leiden from 1670 to 1674: J. A. Venn, *Alumni Cantabrigienses: A Biographical List of All Known Students, Graduates and Holders of Office at the University of Cambridge, From the Earliest Times to 1900* (Cambridge: Cambridge University Press, 1922–54).

68. Clarke, *Two and Twenty English Divines*, 167.

69. J. P. Earwaker has noted that "he is stated to have been descended from the Pagets of Rothley, co. Leicester, but no proof of this is offered": *East Cheshire: Past and Present; or a History of the Hundred of Macclesfield, in the County Palatine of Chester* (London: 1877), 1: 390.

70. Robert Halley, *Lancashire: Its Puritanism and Nonconformity* (Manchester: Tubbs and Brook, 1872), 244.

71. GAA, ERCA 318, no. 3, 99.

72. Vernon, "Sion College Conclave," 51; Edmund Calamy, *The Righteous Man's Death Lamented: A Sermon Preached at St. Austins, London, Aug. 23. 1662, at the Funeral of That Eminent Servant of Jesus Christ, Mr. Simeon Ash Late Minister of the Gospel There.* London: 1662.

73. Clarke, *Two and Twenty English Divines*, 166.

74. Richardson, *Puritanism in North-West England*, 56.

75. William Urwick, *Nonconformity in Herts: Being Lectures upon the Nonconforming Worthies of St. Albans and Memorials of Puritanism and Nonconformity in ALL the Parishes of the County of Hertford* (London: Hazel, Watson, and Vinery, Ltd., 1884), 399–400.

76. Michael Mullett, "Herrick, Richard (1600–1667)," *ODNB*.

77. Leicester Public Record Office, BR II/18/1, fol. 157.

78. Michael Mullett, "Thomas Case (bap. 1598, d. 1682)," *ODNB*.

79. Richardson, *Puritanism in North-West England*, 54.

80. Ann Hughes, *Politics, Society and Civil War in Warwickshire, 1620–1660* (Cambridge: Cambridge University Press, 1987), 79.

81. William Sheils, *The Puritans in the Diocese of Peterborough, 1558–1610* (Northampton: Northamptonshire Record Society, 1979). The handwriting in Robert Smart's commonplace book in the British Library appears to match that found in another commonplace book in the British Library that may have belonged to Smart. Contents in the latter are explicitly presbyterian, including notes on Cartwright's lectures on Acts dating to the 1580s. These notes provide the closest account of Cartwright's exposition on these passages to his lectures delivered on Acts at Cambridge during the early 1570s.

82. See Robert Paget to Hugh Goodyear, 3 February 1661: GAL, LB(66751)Zie BE.

83. See Clarke, "Julines Herring," in *Two and Twenty English Divines*, 188–98.

84. J. F. Merritt, "Tuke, Thomas (1580/81–1657)," *ODNB*.
85. Collinson, *Elizabethan Puritan Movement,* 320, 412.
86. Vernon, "Sion College Conclave," 48.
87. Ibid., 62.
88. Hughes, *Gangraena,* 48.
89. Ibid., 33.
90. Lake and Como, "Orthodoxy."
91. Ibid., 46.
92. Ibid., 45.
93. Ibid., 63.
94. Samuel Clarke, *The Lives of Thirty-Two English Divines Famous in Their Generations for Learning and Piety, and Most of Them Sufferers in the Cause of Christ* (London: 1677), 117. See also Ian Atherton and David Como, "The Burning of Edward Wightman: Puritanism, Prelacy and the Politics of Heresy in Early Modern England," *EHR* 120 (2005): 1215–50. I am grateful to the authors for allowing me to read a version of this article before publication, and to Peter Lake and Lesley Rowe for directing me to this reference.

95. Michael Winship, *Making Heretics: Militant Protestantism and Free Grace in Massachusetts, 1636–1641* (Princeton: Princeton University Press, 2002), 133.

96. Roger Howell, *Puritans and Radicals in North England: Essays on the English Revolution* (Lanham: University Press of America, 1984), 114.

97. Paget, *An Arrow,* epistle. This was also a tactic of Thomas Edwards, if not of a long tradition of heresiographers.

98. Robert Jenison, *The Height of Israels Heathenish Idolatrie, in Sacrificing their Children to the Deuill Diuided into Three Sections* (London 1621), prefatory epistle.

99. Howell, *Puritans and Radicals,* 114.

100. "He responded by publishing a sermon denouncing 'that spreading gangrene of Anabaptism which unless timely prevented may prove fatall to the whole body of this church' (*The Doctrine and Practice of Paedobaptisme,* 1645, preface). This was followed by a stream of further publications between the mid-1640s and mid-1650s in which he sought to provide an "antidote" against the "dangerous and damnable errours . . . broken in upon us"—for example, *A Looking Glass for Good Women* (1645), *Standstill, or, A Bridle for the Times* (1647), and *An Antidote Against the Poisonous Weeds of Heretical Blasphemies* (1650). Brinsley found the threat posed by heretics to be both theological and physical: "In a letter which was later published in Thomas Edwards's *Gangraena,* Brinsley described how in mid-1645 he was assailed in his own house by Anabaptists and antinomians who refused to accept the authority of the Christian magistrate (Edwards, 2.161)": Richard Cust, "Brinsley, John (1600–1665)," *ODNB*.

101. Patrick Collinson, "Puritanism and the Poor," in *Pragmatic Utopias: Ideals and Communities, 1200–1630,* ed. Rosemary Horrox and Sarah Rees Jones (Cambridge: Cambridge University Press, 2001), 246.

102. Paul Seaver, *The Puritan Lectureships: The Politics of Religious Dissent* (Stanford: Stanford University Press, 1970), 72. Heylyn's concern that lay involvement would easily translate into a presbyterian system should obviously be read with caution. His comment is nonetheless relevant by drawing attention to the threat that such involvement posed by its potential conversion to presbyterian government. As Anthony Milton commented, Heylyn's "claims that parish officials were behaving as

the equivalents of lay elders and deacons had a grain of truth in them, however paranoid his assumptions of crypto-presbyterianism. When the Westminster Assembly debated the creation of the presbyterian system, it was suggested that 'in the church of England ther is some vestige of ruling elders in church wardens'": *Laudian and Royalist Polemic*, 96. The potential for converting existing offices to alternate ecclesiastical establishments can be compared to Tadhg Ó hAnnrachin's discussion of how bishops later served as the spine of a Catholic shadow church in Ireland: "Lost in Rinuccini's Shadow: The Irish Clergy, 1645–9," in *Kingdoms in Crisis: Ireland in the 1640s*, ed. Micheál Ó Siochrú (Dublin: Four Courts Press, 2001), 178.

103. In the late sixteenth century the presbyterian movement in London "appears to have attracted the wives of the merchants more than their husbands," while Stephen Egerton's ministry at St. Anne's Blackfriars in the early seventeenth century was notorious for its number of godly merchant wives: Seaver, *Puritan Lectureships*, 103.

104. Collinson, *Puritan Classical Movement*, 773, quoting DWL, MS Morrice B II, fol. 17v.

105. Hill, *Economic Problems*, 267.

106. Collinson, *Puritan Classical Movement*, 802. According to W. H. Mildon, "On the whole it appears that the strength of Puritanism in Hampshire was not in its clergy, though there were several who were making a courageous witness for the Puritan faith, its strength lay in the laity": "Puritanism in Hampshire and the Isle of Wight from the Reign of Elizabeth to the Restoration" (Ph.D. diss., University of London, 1934), 88.

107. Howell, *Puritans and Radicals*, 113.

108. Cited in Seaver, *Puritan Lectureships*, 108.

109. Hopper, "Fenwick, John (1593–d. c. 1670)." For the overlap between Fenwick's anti-episcopacy and other presbyterian arguments, see Chapter 2, above.

110. Barbara Coulton, "Rivalry and Religion: The Borough of Shrewsbury in the Early Stuart Period," *Midland History* 28 (2003): 31.

111. In 1618 one of the bailiffs, Richard Hunt, asked the advice of Laurence Chaderton on behalf of the corporation when they were seeking to fill the vacancy at St. Chad's. Hunt and another bailiff, John Nicholls, were brothers-in-law to Rowland Heylyn.

112. Wilfred Prest, *The Inns of Court under Elizabeth I and the Early Stuarts, 1590–1640* (London: Longman, 1972), 36.

113. Cust, "John Brinsley."

114. Mullett, "Thomas Case," *ODNB*.

115. Mary Wolffe, "George Hughes (1603/4–1667)," *ODNB*. Nicholas Tyacke has explored the distribution of lay bequests through ministers like Arthur Hildersham and the patronage of other laity, including the godly London merchant Rowland Heylyn, who supported Herring, and was Peter Heylyn's uncle: "Fortunes of English Puritanism," 121–23.

116. The laity as well as clerics acted as local agents in placing lecturers. As Jacqueline Eales has noted, Thomas Pierson (Harley's chaplain) "acted as a local agent for the London based feoffees for impropriations and in 1631 and 1632 asked Harley to deal with two of their members, Alderman Rowland Heylin and John Geering on his behalf": "Thomas Pierson and the Transmission of the Moderate Puritan Tradition," *Midland History* 20 (1995): 90.

117. Hill, *Economic Problems*, 261.

118. Ibid.

119. Richardson, *Puritanism in North-West England*, 13.

120. "Blakiston's correspondence . . . suggests fairly long stays in London": Roger Howell, *Newcastle upon Tyne and the Puritan Revolution: A Study of the Civil War in North England* (Oxford: Clarendon Press, 1967), 71.

121. "John Cosins and John Fenwick were both resident on the Continent for a period": ibid., 71–72.

122. Quoted in Kenneth Wayne Shipps, "Lay Patronage of East Anglian Puritan Clerics in Pre-Revolutionary England" (Ph.D. diss., Yale University, 1971). 224.

123. When the servant Pierce Powell decided to transfer his membership from Blackfriars church in London to the English Reformed Church in Amsterdam in 1627, William Gouge supplied him with a testimonial: "[F]or many years [having] beene a member of the church . . . and ever caried himself for ought that ever [heard] to the contrary, as a good Christian." In addition to producing a testimonial from "the Parish of Stratford Bow neere London" the joyner William Norrice was received into the Church by the witness of the poor widow Joyce Bird, a member of the English Reformed Church: GAA, ERCA 318, no. 3, 1; no. 104. n.p.

124. See 152, below, and GAA, ERCA 318, no. 3, 38.

125. Ethyn W. Kirby, "The Lay Feoffees: A Study in Militant Puritanism." *JMH* 14 (1942): 16.

126. Isabel M. Calder, "A Seventeenth Century Attempt to Purify the Anglican Church," *AHR* 53, no. 4 (1948): 765.

127. NA Kew, SP 16/259/78, State Papers Domestic, Charles I.

128. Dorothy Whitney attaches Aldersey's Bunbury trust given at the end of the sixteenth century to the Elizabethan Classical movement, which became a success "between 1610 and 1640" and under the security of the Company, remained "an outstanding center of nonconformity." Here are two examples then, where the managers of lay impropriations were carrying out activity that was similar to the interest that Elizabethan presbyterians [clerics] had taken in placing ministers at the end of the sixteenth century: "London Puritanism: The Haberdashers' Company," *CH* 32 (1963): 304.

129. Seaver, *Puritan Lectureships*, 95.

130. Whitney, "London Puritanism," 306–9.

131. Sprunger, *Dutch Puritanism*, 95.

132. "Vicar Alvey . . . alleged that Stephenson had left his post because of 'some of our fiery zealots' harsh carriage towards him.' The mayor had then summoned a special Common Council and elected a new lecturer without consulting Alvey. This was John Bewick, a relative of the mayor and of Dr. Jenison": Howell, *Newcastle upon Tyne*, 111.

133. Cust, "John Brinsley."

134. Seaver, *Puritan Lectureships*, 98.

135. Ibid., 108.

136. Ibid., 94.

137. Ibid., 94–95.

138. Ian Archer, *The History of the Haberdashers' Company* (Chichester: Phillimore, 1991), 32.

139. For the increase in litigation and centralization of legal life in the late sixteenth century, see C. W. Brooks, *Pettyfoggers and Vipers of the Commonwealth: the "Lower Branch" of the Legal Profession in Early Modern England* (Cambridge: Cambridge University Press, 1986), ch. 5 at 93, 96.

140. Craig Muldrew, *The Economy of Obligation: The Culture of Credit and Social Relations in Early Modern England* (London: Macmillan Press, 1998), 40.

141. For the linguistic overlap between presbyterian clerics and the laity, see ch. 7, note 129 (p. 259).

142. Huntington Library, San Marino, EL 35 b 34. n.p.

143. Ibid.

144. Cynthia Herrup, *The Common Peace: Participation and the Criminal Law in Seventeenth-Century England* (Cambridge: Cambridge University Press, 1987), 59.

145. Addressing civil magistrates, Jenison urged that "it belongs to your care, Right Worshipfull, who must still take your selues bound to the vse your sword and authority against two sorts of men especially: Enemies 1) of Truth 2) of Holinesse": *Israels Heathenish Idolatrie*, C3.

146. "[So] surely, you must also awake and not suffer the house of God to be broken and digged through by theeues and robbers": ibid., C3v.

147. Ibid., epistle. For, as Jenison argued (B2v): "Each Kingdome, Commonwealth, Citie, Towne, Corporation, is onely and so farre safe and settled, as it rests it selfe by weldoing vpon God by a continuall reliance and dependence on him." According to W. H. Mildon this vision of ministry and magistracy had also developed in Hampshire by the 1620s: "The Reformation idea that the Magistrate must come to the aid of the minister in securing morality was fairly gaining ground": "Puritanism in Hampshire," 139.

148. Richardson, *Puritanism in North-West England*, 116.

CHAPTER 7

1. Benedict, *Christ's Churches*, 467.

2. Rather than testing the level of disciplinary activity in the English Reformed Church over time, this case study tests the level and nature of participation by the lowest standing members. For comparative levels of consistorial activity in early modern Europe, see ibid., ch. 14.

3. See Chapter 2, above.

4. Keith Lindley, *Popular Politics and Religion in Civil War London* (Aldershot: Scolar Press, 1997), 15–16.

5. Hughes, "'Popular' Presbyterianism," 249–50.

6. Anne Hughes has argued that "we have not sufficiently grasped the degree to which Presbyterians themselves had a very radical programme. . . . Presbyterians sought a drastically purified social order, yet in order to achieve this ideal they were prepared to risk the disorder of disruptive, socially inclusive campaigns": *Gangraena*, 21–22.

7. Hughes, "'Popular' Presbyterianism," 248.

8. Paget, *Defence of Chvrch-Government*, 37.

9. Paget, *An Answer to Unjust Complaints*, 90. Paget's nephew, Robert, also noted "the extraordinary diligence & paines he tooke there, both in publick & private, with persons of all sorts, and the blessed successe, hath bene already witnessed by the

lively Epistles of Christ ministred by him": *Meditations of Death Wherein a Christian is Taught How to Remember and Prepare for His Latter End: by the Late Able & Faithfull Minister of the Gospel, Iohn Paget* (Dort: 1639), *3.

10. Paget, *An Answer to Unjust Complaints*, 95.

11. TCD, MS 233, fol. 23; cf. John Chrysostom, *On Wealth and Poverty*, trans. and intro. Catharine Roth (New York: St. Vladimir's Seminary Press, 1984).

12. Paul Slack, *Poverty and Policy in Tudor and Stuart England* (London: Longman, 1988), 9; Steve Hindle, *On the Parish? The Micro-Politics of Poor Relief in Rural England c. 1550–1750* (Oxford: Clarendon, 2004), 100.

13. Hindle, *On the Parish?*, 102.

14. Travers's example can be added to a few other documentations of puritan concerns for indiscriminate relief and defense of the poor by Richard Baxter and Thomas Carew. As Paul Slack noted, "Richard Baxter was ready to disobey the laws against indiscriminate charity if overseers failed to relieve all the poor: 'I will take myself as guilty of their death, if I relieve them not when I am able'": *Poverty and Policy*, 21. For Thomas Carew, see Patrick Collinson, "Christian Socialism in Elizabethan Suffolk: Thomas Carew and His Caveat for Clothiers," in *Counties and Communities: Essays on East Anglian History*, ed. Carole Rawcliffe, Roger Virgoe, and Richard Wilson (Norwich: Centre of East Anglian Studies, University of East Anglia, 1996), 161–78, and "Puritanism and the Poor," 242–58.

15. TCD, MS 233, fol. 3. See Figure 8, above.

16. The sermon went on to say that "therefore, thou also seeing a man, that upon the land is fallen, & cast away, by the wracke of poverty, doe not sit like a iudge upon him, nor call him not to accounts: but releive his calamity why dost thou make thy selfe business, more then thou needest, God hath freed thee, from all curiosity & busy dealing & questioning. How many things would many men speake & aske & dislike, if god had commanded them, first to examine dilligently their life & their conversation, & curiosly to inquire into the things that havve bene down by every one: & then to shew them mercy. But now, we are freed from all such difficulties, Why then doe wee draw upon our selves superfluous cares/A iudge is one thing, & a man that sheweth mercy, & giveth almes, is another. For this cause, wee sy, a man doth give almes & sheweth mercy, because he giveth even unto the unworthy": ibid., fols. 34v–35.

17. Andy Wood, *Riot, Rebellion and Popular Politics in Early Modern England* (Basingstoke: Palgrave, 2002), 171.

18. "In trying to reconstruct the social interaction of the godly and faithful with their allegedly ungodly and unfaithful neighbours, we have not yet progressed much beyond the primitive stage of reporting the contents of what might be called religious courtesy books, consisting of exhortation and casuistry on what ought to have been the case (according to their authors) rather than descriptive accounts of what was actually the case": Patrick Collinson, "The Cohabitation of the Faithful with the Unfaithful," in *From Persecution to Toleration: The Glorious Revolution and Religion in England*, ed. Ole Peter Grell, Jonathan I. Israel, and Nicholas Tyacke (Oxford: Clarendon Press, 1991), 52.

19. Keith Wrightson and David Levine, *Poverty and Piety in an English Village: Terling, 1525–1700* (Oxford: Oxford University Press, 1995).

20. Ian Archer, *The Pursuit of Stability: Social Relations in Elizabethan London* (Cambridge: Cambridge University Press, 1991), 74–82, 154–63.

21. On October 14, 1615, Paget initially noted the acceptance of English liturgy to test conversion from separatism to the Church of England where "The three above-mentioned, Jacob Johnson, Edward Clyfton and Mary Clyfton have testified that they are resolved to hear the faithful preachers in the Church of England and not to forsake the worship of God where read prayer is used": Carter, *English Reformed Church*, 57. However, Carter points out that "in the margin is a further note, 'Not binding themselves hereby to approve of any errors or abuses in the Book of Common Prayer', which obviously relates to what is written at the beginning about the use of read prayer, and which shews the compromise nature of this settlement."

22. From Cartwright's letter to his sister-in-law who turned separatist, Ann Stubbes, to Thomas Parker's letter to his sister who turned Quaker, presbyterian ministers can be seen attempting in vain to reclaim family members and close friends from separatism. Antiseparatist efforts can be written off as either a lost cause or simply as a defensive denial of radical tendencies within nonconformity. However, it is crucial to recognize that the stigmatization of separatism in early modern England could have a powerful effect. Paget's antiseparatist propaganda that generated support for presbyterianism in Amsterdam is one example, while the writings of Thomas Edwards against schism and heterodoxy during the mid-seventeenth century is another: Hughes, *Gangraena*.

23. As Sprunger explained, "The move to establish the English church was largely an anti-Brownist strategy supported by the Dutch Reformed Church and the leading English citizens of the city." Furthermore, "The chief promoter of the new English church was rector Mathew Slade of the Latin School, excommunicated ex-Separatist of the Ancient Church, now an esteemed scholar and citizen": *Dutch Puritanism*, 91.

24. According to Alice Carter, "The major schism among the Brownists, after which Johnson retreated to Emden, took place while Paget's effective attack on the Separatists . . . was in preparation." Moreover, "the spectacular ostensible Act of God which destroyed the Brownists' Church building, was not without its effect": *English Reformed Church*, 55.

25. Ibid., 56.

26. Sprunger, *Dutch Puritanism*, 100.

27. "As the younger members of the Separatist assembly grew older, and especially as the responsibilities of parenthood came upon some of them, they began to want traditional baptism for their children": Carter, *English Reformed Church*, 56. There was an irony in how this particular question of baptism became caught up in the controversy between presbyterian and congregationalist sympathizers. Whereas Paget was concerned to defend the promiscuous baptism of infants that the Church had performed in the case of separatist members, it was primarily those former separatists who supported the candidates who objected to the practice of baptizing the infants of nonmembers. Among the fifteen members who joined from the Ancient church in August 1621, "Four signatories, Thomas Adams, Romein, Symons and Attley, later developed views directly contrary to those of Paget on the question of the power of the Classis, and the first three, with another man of the name of Pinnock, were among those who favoured the appointment of one or other of the left-wing, independent-minded preachers proposed for ministers after 1631." See also Michael Moody, "Trials and Travels of a Nonconformist Layman: The Spiritual Odyssey of Stephen Offwood, 1564–ca. 1635," *CH* 51, no. 2 (1992): 157–71.

28. Carter, *English Reformed Church*, 57. The information that follows was drawn from the Book of Baptism and membership lists: GAA, ERCA 318, nos. 82–88.

29. Carter, *English Reformed Church*, 57.

30. These members included "William Pinnock & Helina his wife, John Whithead, Thomas Adams & Elizabeth his wife, William Masier, Richard plater and joane his wife, Gregorie Atlee, edward Romie and Mary his wife, Henry Gasken & Elizabeth his wife, Comfort simons & Persiste his wife": ibid., no. 2, p. 5.

31. Of these former separatists, roughly 33 percent can be identified as relatively well off and at least 30 percent as poorer members.

32. Sprunger, *Dutch Puritanism*, 91.

33. Carter, *English Reformed Church*, 20.

34. Ibid., 20, 22. In 1607 Jonas Thomson served as elder and Richard Owen and Jonas Harwood as deacons.

35. See Table 1.

36. For example, some of the children who became members of the Church are not recorded upon their entrance into the membership rosters beginning in 1623.

37. I am grateful to Alice Wolfram, Craig Muldrew, Ken Sneath, John Walter, and Keith Wrightson for discussing occupations with me and for advising on these categories.

38. This was particularly the case for the low-status category.

39. According to Mary Sprunger, during this period contemporaries in Amsterdam classed together "the well-to-do, which included non-ruling notables and rich merchants in the highest category, as well as city officials such as town clerks and army captains, businessmen, shopowners and intellectuals": "Rich Mennonites, Poor Mennonites: Economics and Theology in the Amsterdam Waterlander Congregation during the Golden Age" (Ph.D. diss., University of Illinois at Urbana-Champaign, 1993), 40. I am grateful to Keith and Mary Sprunger for answering questions concerning status in Amsterdam during the seventeenth century.

40. Ibid., 38.

41. J. G. Frederiks and P. J. Frederiks, *Kohier van den tweenhonderdsten penning voor Amsterdam en onderhoorige plaatsen over 1631* (Amsterdam: Ten Brink and De Vries, 1890).

42. Vivien Brodsky Elliot, "Mobility and Marriage in Pre-Industrial England: A Demographic and Social Structural Analysis of Geographic and Social Mobility and Aspects of Marriage, 1570–1690, with Particular Reference to London and General Reference to Middlesex, Kent, Essex and Hertfordshire" (Ph.D. diss., University of Cambridge, 1979), chs. 3, 4.

43. There is no indication that the two millers included in this number either owned or leased a mill.

44. Slack, *Poverty and Policy*, 7.

45. This leaves a total of twenty-five members who received alms in the years 1640 and 1641 prior to becoming members in 1630. Sixteen of these were either widows or of unknown occupation, while the occupation of others ranged from tailor, hatmaker, stoolmaker, and silk-thrower to chain-maker.

46. Paul Seaver, *Wallington's World: A Puritan Artisan in Seventeenth-Century London* (Stanford: Stanford University Press, 1985); Lake and Como, *The Boxmaker's Revenge*.

47. GAA, ERCA 318, no. 3, 38.

48. Ibid.

49. Several came from London, and one merchant brought a testimonial from Norwich.

50. Eight of these testimonials came from the Dutch Reformed Church in Amsterdam and six from London.

51. Of the twenty testimonials that came from England, at least fourteen were from London parishes. Although the status of each Londoner who presented a testimonial letter is unknown, it is possible to identify a range of occupations from merchant to servant in addition to the many in between, such as the printer Randall Evans, the embroiderer Hugh Cave, the painter Pierce Powell, and the tobacco-pipe maker Thomas Townsend.

52. The most likely reason for migration among the poorer members of the congregation is the high level of poverty in England during this period. In discussing British overseas migration for the period 1600 to 1800, Alison Games has described the high proportion of Englishmen: "[It] was a surplus *English* population that traveled disproportionately overseas in this period. It was not merely fortuitous that English enterprises overseas (in Mediterranean, in India, in the Americas) coincided with population growth": "Migration," in *The British Atlantic World*, ed. David Armitage and Michael J. Braddick (Basingstoke: Palgrave, 2002), 36.

53. GAA, ERCA 318, no. 2, 27.

54. Ibid., 30.

55. Ibid., 31. In another instance "Mary Oldham was not admitted because William Bon & N. Sherock had complayned that John Sherock upon his death bed had confessed whoredome with her. [Witnesses Adam Oldham her husband & Mary Tod.]" Her husband and witnesses were again rebuked for testifying on behalf of Oldham: ibid., no. 3, 85; no. 2, 30–31.

56. Shaw, *History of the English Church*, 216ff.

57. "That for this present the minister that dwelleth on the new side viz Mr Jo. Pagett shall with the elder that dwelleth on that side viz. Jonas Thomas visitt all the members of that side: And mr jo. dowglas who dwelleth on the olde side shall with one of the Elders which dwelleth on the sam side & for this tymThomas Armitage visitt the members on the olde side": GAA, ERCA 318, no. 1, 10–11.

58. "1. Ministers & Elders shall have theire severall Quarters for visitations, both before the sacrament & uppon other occasions, 2. One minister is to visit the old syde; with 2 Elders; each in theire severall Quarters, & the other minister is to visit the New syde with the other twoe Elders, at the same tyme": ibid., no. 45 ("The Standing orders off the Consistory," 5).

59. Ibid., no. 2, 28.

60. Ibid., 79.

61. Ibid., 94.

62. Ibid., no. 1. 18.

63. See Table 8.

64. Peter Holmes, *Resistance and Compromise: The Political Thought of the Elizabethan Catholics* (Cambridge: Cambridge University Press, 1982), ch. 6.

65. GAA, ERCA 318, no. 2, 28.

66. For the conflict over Sabbatarianism between the English and Dutch, see Keith

Sprunger, "English and Dutch Sabbatarianism and the Development of Puritan Social Theology (1600–1660)," *CH* 51, no. 1 (1982): 24–38.

    67. Carter, *English Reformed Church*, 122.

    68. Paget, *An Answer to Unjust Complaints*, 5.

    69. Ibid., 5–6.

    70. Ibid., 9.

    71. Ibid.

    72. Ibid., 18.

    73. Ibid., 29.

    74. Sprunger, *Dutch Puritanism*, 101. GAA, ERCA 318, no. 2, 86.

    75. GAA, ERCA 318, no. 2, 7.

    76. Ibid., no. 3, 92.

    77. Ibid., no 1, 48.

    78. This contrasts with the Scottish Kirk's high volume of cases relating to sexual offences. See Michael F. Graham, *The Uses of Reform: 'Godly Discipline' and Popular Behavior in Scotland and Beyond, 1560–1610* (Leiden: E. J. Brill, 1996), ch. 5.

    79. For a summary of disciplinary cases, see Table 9, 176, above. The high proportion of interpersonal disputes in relation to cases involving immoral behavior compares to William Naphy's study of the Geneva Consistory Minutes from 1542 to 1550: *Calvin and the Consolidation of the Genevan Reformation* (London: Westminster John Knox Press, 1994), table 14, 109. It also corresponds to Raymond Mentzer's analysis of disciplinary patterns in the consistory at Nimes: "Disciplina Nervus Ecclesiae: The Calvinist Reform of Morals at Nimes," *SCJ* 18, no. 1 (1987): 108–9. For comparative studies on consistorial activity and moral reform, see: Raymond Mentzer, ed., *Sin and the Calvinists: Morals Control and the Consistory in the Reformed Tradition* (Kirksville, MO: Truman State University Press, 1994); and Benedict, *Christ's Churches*, 467–82.

    80. Members of the Church could also report against nonmembers. In December 1637, Elizabeth Lucas complained against her husband who was not a member, for his "violence towards her, in beatinge her & threateninge to kill her, & desiring assistance & advise." The consistory decided to "acquaynt the ministers & Elders of the Lutheran Church with his misdemenors (hee being a member ther,) & in case helpe ther fails then to seke to the Magistrats for help from them": GAA, ERCA 318, no 3, 79.

    81. Ibid., no. 2, 65.

    82. Ibid., 61.

    83. Ibid., no. 3, 93.

    84. Ibid., 62.

    85. On October 31, 1629, "Martin Hanwell & Alice Trowte coming to the consistory complayned that Edward Hanwell (son of Martin Hanwell) had profaned the Sabath & kept evill company in time of Gods worship, & had also bene overcome with drink, & being admonished by them did not answer them nor give such satisfaction as they desired Edward Hanwell being by the eldership admonished hereof did acknolwedge his fault & his greefe for it, promising by the grace & help of God that he would avoyd the like offence": ibid., 6.

    86. When John Davenport drew on Samuel Balmford's testimony to prove John Paget's unlawful proceeding against his candidacy, Paget objected that at least two witnesses were required: "[If] Mr. Balmford should affirm his answer to have bene

the very same: yet ought not his affirmation to be taken against my denyall in such case as this. The reason is evident from the expresse ordinance of God, who hath appointed, that for determining the truth in controversies, touching matter of fact, two witnesses at the least should be had. Deut. 19.15, Mat. 18.16, Joh. 8.17": ibid., 75. For the quality and quantity of evidence and testimony, see 166–69, 173–74 below.

87. GAA, ERCA 318, no 1, 105.

88. Several months later, in August 1613, Hawkins had again come into conflict after admonishing another member, where "Alexander browne being acused by edward hawkins of usual sleping in the church & of dispysing his admonysion with oathes & threats of revenge . . . promy[sed] ammendement & to reconcyle hymself to his admonysh*ion*ur": ibid., 77, 79.

89. Ibid., 86. Dixon appeared before the consistory again in April 1621, "having bene admonished of his contention with his wife & confessed his fault therein, [Dixon] was formerly required to abstaine from the communion . . . but in the meane time he absented himself from the church & went unto the Anabaptists": ibid., no. 2, 1.

90. Ibid., no. 2, 2.

91. Ibid., 6.

92. Ibid., 28.

93. Ibid., no. 3, 27.

94. Ibid., no. 2, 45–46.

95. On September 6, 1623, "Jacob Smith being reproved for keeping his doore open to 12 a clocke commonly & letting men drinke in his house, acknowledgeth that he hath done evill therein, and that he is sorie for it, and promiseth for the time to come to follow the order of the magistrates in sutting his door at 9 a clocke in the night": ibid., 35. James Cameron has pointed out that in Scotland, "the Kirk Session was determined 'to put sin' down, particularly sin that was a cause of public scandal.'" He also commented more generally that in "ecclesiastical discipline in the reformed tradition" there was a distinct concern for "the public face of the Church, for the well-being of society, for public morals": "Godly Nurture and Admonition in the Lord," in *The Danish Reformation against Its International Background*, ed. Leif Grane and Kai Hørby (Gottingen: Vandenhoeck and Ruprecht, 1990), 273.

96. GAA, ERCA 318, no 1, 65.

97. Ibid., no. 3, 11b. In 1631 "Susanna bullard coming unto the consistory demaunded an ackt of her suspention. . . . [S]he was admonished to forsacke her sin, she acknowliged itt to bee a sin yet would nott promise to leave her standing in the markett publikly upon the lords daye selling of her wares, to ye greatt offence of our members who complayned thereof, she answered if ye Lords did forbid itt shee would refrayne & wished itt weare so itt was sheewed her yt shee esteemed more ye commandements of men then gods which was her great sin & was even agaynst her owne contcence her sin & the greevosnes thereof was shewed here in disobayeng gods comandement & yeat shee remayned obstinate & without remorse departed": ibid., 12.

98. Ibid., 99.

99. On September 2, 1607, "after calling on the name of god: Francis blackwell & his wife being sent for before us, about a great & long Iar which had continued between them they were both reproved for their faults & did promise hereafter to live better together which god of his mercy graunt them to doe": ibid., 23.

100. Ibid., 95.

101. Ibid.

102. In response, Francis James "confesseth that he hath smitten her but is sory for it. . . . [He] denyeth that ever he cast any meat on the flour" and explained that "he saith he would not work yf she should give her goods so to her children as she hath done": ibid., no. 2, 34.

103. Ibid., no. 3, 74.

104. "It was sayd unto him that he must shew his repentance by his good conversation & amendment of life, that we must have yet some further time to take triall thereof & that we would then signify unto him what we required for the maner of confessing his fault": ibid., no. 2, 68.

105. Ibid., 29. On August 23 "Jone Phillips & margaret Ted being sent for unto the Eldership & enquired of touching the behaviour of Ambrose Kettring did testify that they had seene him overcome with drink, & rayling, & Jone Phillips did also signify that he had acknolwedged his being overcome with drink & that he was very sory for it. The Eldership apoynted him to absteyne from the communion untill he had shewed better fruits of his rpentance" (35). Two months later, on October 25, "Ambrose Kettring desiring to be admitted to the Lords table it was signifyed unto him that he must first confesse his fault openly againe, & give us better proofe of his amendment for some time, seing he fell so quickly into the scandall of drunkenes after his first confession whereupon he desired us to put his name out of the church booke that he might be no more troubled with us nor we with him. And being reproved for that speech, he sayd he was content to tary away" (37).

106. Ibid., no. 1, 104.

107. Ibid., no. 2, 6.

108. Thomas Ward also testified "that he was brailling with his wife almost continually": ibid., 63. Whereas "John Stephens being spoken unto by Mr Pot & Mr Allen at his house, according to his promise unto them came unto the consistory & confessed his fault of drunkenness & disquietnes in his house, saying that through extreme provocation of his wife he was drawne thereunto & that he would endevour to amend the same": ibid.

109. "And for so much as she then accused him of drunkennes, & cutting her clothes with his knife, & of further violence done unto her. He denying the same she was appoyunted to bring her witnesses, & he to be at the consistory upon the Wednesday following": ibid., 63–64. On October 22, 1625, "Mr Pot & Mr Allen were deputed by the consistory to go unto John Stephens to admonish him of his scandall, to require him to come unto the consistory, & to signify unto him withall that if he persisted in his course, he must be further proceeded with all; seing he had bene divers times sent for & had refused to come unto the consistory" (63).

110. "She was required to bring witnesses of his drunkennes that we might deale further with him": ibid., consistory minutes, 1621–27, 64.

111. Ibid., 68.

112. This was in order that "she might go unto the Dutch": ibid.

113. "She notwithstanding persisting in her evill without any shew of repentance, wished us to excommunicate her with speede, that she might have a seale thereof & to go to the rasp house for maintenance": ibid., no. 3, 5.

114. Ibid., 6.

115. Ibid., 69.

116. The consistory decided as early as 1607, on November 28, that Francis Blowfield "shalbe sent for against the next wensday to be delt with about his continuall absence from the church": ibid., no. 1, 25. In April 1609 "Francis blowfield being also sent for & demanded them Reasn of his absence from the church could make no answer: being admonished to amendment was dismissed" (45). Meanwhile, in June 1608, the consistory took note that Blowfield's "master had a complynt about him that he would not worke & it was said he was gone to harlem to the Reims" (33). In the following month he had fallen out with another member (35).

117. Ibid., 35. Francis Blowfield's wife, Elizabeth, was also brought under discipline for her absence in October 1622, being "admonished for negligence in coming to the church and admonished to fit her selfe to come to the table againe": ibid., no. 2, 24.

118. Ibid., no. 3, 52, 71.

119. Ibid., 92.

120. "[It] was thought meet by the Eldership that he should at the next communion confesse his fault for wounding the man, & for his drunkenes & disorder; & that the communion after he should be admitted to the Lords supper, if no exception came against him": ibid., no. 2, 30.

121. Ibid., 31.

122. The following year, in 1623, Humfrey Bromly, "having also brought a certificate touching the death of Mary Augstine, as being executed by the report of her mother, & desired therfore to be admitted to the Lords table: it was answered unto him that this testimony was insufficient both because it came but from the mouth of one witnesse; & because there was nothing in it touching his agreement with the foresayd Mary Augstines friends as had bene required of him . . . besides these things there were other matters & offences for which also he was withheld from the communion": ibid., 20, 36.

123. Ibid., no. 1, 29.

124. Ibid.

125. Ibid., 31.

126. Ibid., no. 2, 19.

127. Ibid., no. 3, 52.

128. Ibid.

129. The significant point here is the illocutionary dimension of Stevens's speech, as Quentin Skinner has distinguished it from the motivation of the speaker. Not only did Stevens draw on the language commonly used by puritans as a resource that held currency among her contemporaries, but her language also functioned as a "speech act" as she exploited this language to her advantage: "Interpretation and the Understanding of Speech Acts," in *Visions of Politics*, 1: 103–27.

130. Scholars have explored the ways in which the puritan community empowered women through their models of exemplary piety and ability to act as patronesses of godly clergy. In addition, Amanda Porterfield has argued that women could potentially hold an exalted role in society through the domestic sphere, which was central in the puritans' worldview. She has also discussed the variation in relationships between godly men and women and argued for the effectiveness of those women who appropriated "puritan rhetoric" instead of directly subverting the authority exercised

by men in puritan communities: "Women's Attraction to Puritanism," *CH* 60, no. 2 (1991): 205–6, 209. See also Diane Willen, "Godly Women in Early Modern England: Puritanism and Gender," *JEH* 43 (1992): 561–80; Patrick Collinson, "The Role of Women in the English Reformation Illustrated by the Life and Friendships of Anne Locke," in *Godly People*, 273–87; and Peter Lake, "Feminine Piety and Personal Potency: The 'Emancipation' of Mrs Jane Ratcliffe," *Seventeenth Century* 2, no. 2 (1987): 143–65.

131. Studies of women within nonconformity have largely focused upon those of higher social status, otherwise known as "ladies elect," and their pietistic and material contributions over their directly theological or ecclesiological interactions. However, as Jacqueline Eales has found in her examination of the women in Clarke's *Lives*, godly women were also active readers: "Samuel Clarke and the 'Lives' of Godly Women," in *Women in the Church*, ed. W. J. Sheils and Diana Wood (Oxford: Basil Blackwell, 1990), 365–76.

132. GAA, ERCA 318, no. 3, 8–9.

133. Ibid., no. 1, 64.

134. Ibid., 107. On February 10, 1621, "gilbet Much having made confession of his heresie desyreth to be receaved againe into the bosome of thr church, which is agreed upon [when] no lawful exception come against him ere the next lords day" (110).

135. Ibid., 94.

136. Ibid., no. 3, 6.

137. Ibid., no. 1, 61.

138. Ibid., no. 2, 23.

139. Ibid.

140. Ibid., no. 1, 3.

141. Ibid., no. 2, 86.

142. Adams also objected to Samuel Meridith's readmission to communion "without satisfaction given to the party offended" and argued that in addition other "members of the church were suspended without the knowledge of the congregation & so receyved againe without knowledge of the church": ibid.

143. In the next month, the surgeon John Nicholas also "charged the [consistory] with sin for admission of Elizabeth Hanwell to the Lo. table & yet being demanded for his ground to show the particular sins for which she should be excluded, his answer was that he knew them not . . . but sayd the matters were well knowne & publique though he knew them not": ibid., 87. If all the particulars surrounding Elizabeth Hanwell's case were unknown to the general membership of the Church, the level of discontent with the consistory's verdict was clear. As the consistory noted, "[We] think that it had bene more christianly & godlines in them not to have published so much in their disordered courses as some of them have done already both in the church & out of the church to the scandall of many. We exhort them therefore in the name of Ch. that they desist from such courses whereunto the spirit of God will never constraine them. And as for this their writing & gathering of hands which subscription of names, we think it tends to make a faction in a church & to the rending of the same & is therfore to be avoyded as a contentious practise not beseeming those that are godly persons & seek the edificaiton & peace of gods church" (91).

144. Ibid., 88.

145. Ibid., 86.

146. Ibid., 72.

147. Ibid., 76.

148. John Green and John Whitehead confirmed that "diverse persons of the separation say that Raph Matley hath dealt dishonestly in sundry things, but they will not come to particulers, because they know him to be a politick man and dangerous to be dealt with all": ibid., 81.

149. Ibid., 84.

150. Ibid., 85.

151. Ibid. What is particularly notable in the case of Elizabeth Hanwell is the reverse flexibility exhibited in the presbyterians' disciplinary sentences. Presbyterians relied on ecclesiastical reinforcement from outside of their particular congregation in prosecuting heresy or excluding undesirable ministers when other attempts had failed. Here the presbyterian discipline is protecting the reputation of officers or penitents by guarding private confessions where members demanded public confession before the entire church community. English presbyterians had apparently mastered the art of concealing everything, from their own identity and attack against episcopacy in alliance with jurists to their consistorial proceedings and the personal affairs of paupers such as Elizabeth Hanwell.

152. On July 17, 1624, "John Jordan & Eleazar Clifton his servant coming to the consistory did ech of them desire that for ending of the controversy betwixt them the consistory would choose some good men to heare the matter." It was understood that parties seeking arbitration would submit to the judgment of the elders, "whereupon the consistory nominated these three, John Webster, Richard Beauchamp, & William Watson, with which good men the sayd John Jordan & Eleazar Clifton professed that they were content & promised to stand unto their sentence & arbitrement & to rest therein": GAA, ERCA 318, no. 2, 43–44. Those outside the membership of the Church were also aware of the consistory's role in resolving disputes. When secular arbitration failed to bring a resolution, "a duch woman comminge to the consistory, complayned of Persist Simons, yt notwithstandinge the sentence giuen by the Magistrates, yet she giues her no contentment in paying her housrent which ammounts to 40 s. & therfore desired the advise & councel of the consistory that in a frendly maner the difference may bee ended betwixt them": ibid., no. 3, 76. In March 1633, the consistory recorded that "Margret Allen having made a complaynt of Henry Poulter each haueing reproached on another it was ordered that Mr Whitaker and Richard Beauchamp should see if they could mack reconsiliation between them without brining the buysenese further in questyon" (38). If they failed to bring reconciliation through their mediation, the work of the consistory also provided more formal arbitration. Craig Muldrew has described how arbitration was a step up from mediation in economic disputes: "The Culture of Reconciliation: Community and the Settlement of Economic Disputes in Early Modern England," *HJ* 39, no. 4 (1996): 931. Margo Todd has described the popular service of arbitration provided by the Scottish Kirk and "the frequency with which people resorted to the session. . . . So popular was resort to sessions for arbitration that in many parishes they replaced some of the more traditional mediators, like crafts guilds or fraternities": *The Culture of Protestantism in Early Modern Scotland* (New Haven: Yale University Press, 2002), 258. I am grateful to John Craig for his discussions of the role of reconciliation in puritan studies.

153. John Green was nominated to act as mediator by Barlow: GAA, ERCA 318, no. 2, 72.

154. Ibid., no. 1, 77.

155. As Bruce Lenman has argued, "[It] was above all in relatively simple and homogenous societies where local communities internalized the spiritual and moral values of a national church that Godly Discipline was most effective. Such were Scotland and Sweden, and it is no accident that both laid heavy emphasis on education as a means of access to God's Word": "The Limits of Godly Discipline in the Early Modern Period with Particular Reference to England and Scotland," in *Religion and Society in Early Modern Europe, 1500–1800,* ed. Kaspar von Greyerz (London: George Allen and Unwin, 1984), 142.

156. Edwards must have felt vindicated by the elder Henry Whitaker, who hosted him before his death, since Whitaker appears to have been the former separatist who became a member of the English Reformed Church in 1625: Carter, *English Reformed Church*, 59.

CONCLUSION

1. Brachlow, *Communion of Saints.* See also 202, n. 23, above.

2. See 199, n. 2, above. For the preoccupations that shaped Richard Baxter's ecclesiology during this period, see Paul Lim, *In Pursuit of Purity, Unity, and Liberty: Richard Baxter's Puritan Ecclesiology in Its Seventeenth-Century Context,* (Leiden: Brill, 2004), chs. 5–7.

3. These debates extended to the continent and to New England, and they were also shaped in reference to Roman Catholic and foreign reformed churches: Milton, *Catholic and Reformed.*

4. The competing ecclesiological views within England can be compared with what John Morrill has described in writing a history of religion in the three kingdoms as "a curdled mix in which the elements will not gel however stiffly beaten the historical whisk": "The War(s) of the Three Kingdoms," in *The New British History*, ed. Glenn Burgess (London: Tauris Academic Studies, 1999), 85.

5. As Brian Levack has observed, "English presbyterians were too Erastian for their Scottish co-religionists," and "the rise of the English Independents, who were feared and abhorred in Scotland, sealed the fate of presbyterianism in England, driving the Scottish presbyterians into a temporary alliance with the royalists and ending, for all practical purposes, the last real hope of religious union in the history of the two nations": *The Formation of the British State: England, Scotland and the Union, 1603–1707* (Oxford: Clarendon Press, 1987), 129.

6. This can be compared to Patrick Collinson's comment that "Protestant nationalism and internationalism were two sides of the same coin": "Europe in Britain: Protestant Strangers and the English Reformation," in *From Strangers to Citizens,* ed. Randolph Vigne and Charles Littleton (Brighton: Sussex Academic Press, 2001), 64.

7. It is important to note that foreigners resident in England (with backgrounds in reformed polity) made contact with international presbyterianism possible for those who never left England. For the crucial role that stranger churches in London played in the development of English Protestantism, see Andrew Pettegree, *Foreign Protestant Communities in Sixteenth-Century London* (Oxford: Clarendon Press,1986), 272–76; and Patrick Collinson, "The Elizabethan Puritans and the Foreign Reformed Churches in London," in *Godly People,* 245–72. As Pettegree points out, there were diverse reasons for migration to England. John Paget claimed that this was the case for Amsterdam

in the early seventeenth century: puritans did not come "out of England for the same cause. Each might have their peculiar reason": Paget, *An Answer to Unjust Complaints,* 23; Carter, *English Reformed Church,* 117; Sprunger, *Dutch Puritanism,* 7–8.

8. Owen Chadwick, "The Sixteenth Century," in *The English Church and the Continent,* ed. C. R. Dodwell (London: Faith Press, 1959), 62, 64. English presbyterian involvement in church government outside of England is seen in the Channel Islands. Disputes within the presbytery of the Channel Islands kept the churches there from holding a synod for more than a decade between the years 1585 and 1597, and it was ultimately English intercession that helped to resolve the dispute. After procuring release from prison in May 1592 and recovering from ill health, Cartwright was summoned to serve as chaplain at Castle Cornet in Guernsey. Edmund Snape, another outspoken presbyterian who was imprisoned along with Cartwright, was stationed at Jersey as the governor's chaplain in 1595. The two English ministers worked alongside the local congregations, acting as mediators to resolve the ongoing conflict between the two churches. Once reconciliation was achieved, a revised form of Presbyterian Discipline was agreed in 1597 by the churches of Sark, Guernsey, and Jersey: Helen Mary Elizabeth Evans, "The Religious History of Jersey 1558–1640" (Ph.D. diss., University of Cambridge, 2002), 97–98; D. M. Ogier, *Reformation and Society in Guernsey* (Woodbridge: Boydell, 1996), 89–90.

9. Graeme Murdock, *Calvinism on the Frontier, 1600–1660: International Calvinism and the Reformed Church in Hungary and Transylvania* (Oxford: Clarendon Press, 2000); Diarmaid MacCulloch, *Reformation: Europe's House Divided, 1490–1700* (London: Allen Lane, 2003), 461–63. I am grateful to Diarmaid MacCulloch for bringing this aspect of English presbyterianism to my attention.

10. As Francis Bremer has written, "[T]he puritan experience in one place—whether it be London, New Haven, or Arnhem in the Netherlands—illumines Puritanism wherever we find it": "Introduction," in *Puritanism: Transatlantic Perspectives,* xii. See also Bremer, *Congregational Communion: Clerical Friendship in the Anglo-American Puritan Community, 1610–1692* (Boston: Northeastern University Press, 1994). See also Sprunger, *Dutch Puritanism,* ch. 17; and Susan Hardman Moore, *Pilgrims: New World Settlers and the Call of Home* (New Haven: Yale University Press, 2007), esp. chs. 4, 6.

11. The self-identification of the "English Reformed Church" that appears in its title was documented in its records and procedure. The consistory minutes recorded that on June 24, 1607, "in the forenoon being the Lords daye was celebrated the holy supper of the Lord being the first tyme that it ever was celebrated by the english nation in this place": GAA, ERCA 318, no. 1. 16. That the English separatist community had celebrated the Lord's Supper long before this date reveals that the English association in this statement meant more than English people celebrating the Lord's Supper together.

12. "To proove that formerly they have not bene silent men, I have many witnesses; and first I alledge these two witnesses against them, the Damme, & the Burse, the Market-place and the Exchange. . . . I alledge two other witnesses England, and Netherlands, through both which the clamours that are here raysed by them are scattered abroad": Paget, *An Answer to Unjust Complaints,* 14.

13. TCD, MS 140, fol. 67.

14. Usher, *Elizabethan Presbyterian Movement,* xxvi–xxvii.

15. Tyacke, *Anti-Calvinists*; Mark Kishlansky, "The Emergence of Adversary Politics in the Long Parliament," *JMH* 49 (1977): 617–40.

16. Complaints of presbyterian popularity did not come only from conformists but also from religious radicals during the Interregnum: Ann Hughes, "The Meanings of Religious Polemic," in *Puritanism: Transatlantic Perspectives*, 221.

17. Historians have increasingly cautioned against overlooking the rhetorical function and polemical context of puritan complaint literature. As Alexandra Walsham has argued, such reading of religious writings, which sought to construct a single confessional identity, can misrepresent diversity within the early modern English community: *Church Papists: Catholicism, Conformity and Confessional Polemic in Early Modern England* (Woodbridge: Boydell and Brewer, 1999), ch. 2.

18. According to Richard Neibuhr, "[T]he evil of denominationalism lies in the conditions which makes the rise of sects desirable and necessary: in the failure of the churches to transcend the social conditions which fashion them into caste-organizations, to sublimate their loyalties to standards and institutions only remotely relevant if not contrary to the Christian ideal, to resist the temptation of making their own self-preservation and extension the primary object of their endeavor": *The Social Sources of Denominationalism* (Cleveland: Meridian Books, 1968).

19. Downame complained, "[In] affection wholly alienated from our Church-governours [the presbyterians] have studied these things as opponents and plaintiffes": *Two Sermons* (Second sermon, epistle.)

20. Ball, *An Ansvver to Two Treatises,* A2.

21. "[A] due reproofe, wherby one that is out of the good way wherein hee ought to walke is called upon to returne into the path of the lords obedience, ought to esteeme him selfe beholden to him that reprehended him": TCD, MS 141, 1.

22. Presbyterian ministers used an interesting array of metaphors to attack episcopacy, including a comparison of their civil and religious responsibilities to "Hermaphroditas." They also introduced political language to attack congregational polity, describing it as "anarchy," "democracy," and, in its worst possible sense, a "monarchy." They compared synods and assemblies in presbyterian government to a "parliament of saints." In response Henry Jacob employed a neo-Roman argument for ecclesiastical liberty to underpin congregational polity. The novelty in Jacob's use of neo-Roman ideology is his theoretical and practical application of it to ecclesiology, not his employment of a political analogue to a nonpolitical description per se. "The importance of analogical thinking," as J. P. Sommerville has explained, "should not be overrated," since most early Stuart writers used analogy to illustrate rather than to prove an argument or to identify the origin of authority: *Politics and Ideology in England, 1603–1640* (London: Longman, 1986), 48.

23. For example, see Guy, "Tudor Monarchy and Its Critiques," 78–109; and Stephen Alford, *The Early Elizabethan Polity: William Cecil and the British Succession Crisis, 1558–1569* (Cambridge: Cambridge University Press, 1998).

24. McDiarmid, *Monarchical Republic*, esp. chs. 1, 6, 10.

25. For the active agency of the laity in the religious development of the period, see Todd, *Culture of Protestantism*; Lake and Como, *The Boxmaker's Revenge*; Como, *Blown by the Spirit*; and Andrew Pettegree, *Reformation and the Culture of Persuasion* (Cambridge: Cambridge University Press, 2005).

26. Commenting on poorer men and women in England during the mid-seven-

teenth century, Richard Niebuhr stated that "the abstract theological terminologies of Presbyterian confessions and sermons were not only unintelligible to them, they were irrelevant": *Social Sources,* 43. See also Christopher Haigh, *English Reformations: Religion, Politics, and Society under the Tudors* (Oxford: Clarendon Press, 1993); and Wrightson and Levine, *Poverty and Piety.*

27. This can be compared to the multifaceted nature of the English parish during this period in general, which Keith Wrightson has described as "a political forum—not simply as a unit of secular or ecclesiastical administration, nor even as a complex of institutions focusing social interaction intensely within a specific geographical area, but as a tangled, messy, skein of overlapping and intersecting social networks, most of which extended beyond its boundaries outwards and upwards into the larger society, and many of which were networks of power: "The Politics of the Parish in Early Modern England," in *The Experience of Authority in Early Modern England,* ed. Paul Griffiths, Adam Fox, and Steve Hindle (Basingstoke: Macmillan, 1996), 11.

BIBLIOGRAPHIC NOTE

1. Knox, *Walter Travers,* 146–47.

2. William O'Sullivan, "Introduction," in *Trinity College Dublin: Descriptive Catalogue of Mediaeval and Renaissance Latin Manuscripts at Trinity College Library Dublin,* ed. Marvin L. Colker (Aldershot: Scolar Press for Trinity College Library, Dublin, 1991), 24, 29.

3. Vincent Kinane and Anne Walsh, eds., *Essays on the History of Trinity College Library Dublin* (Dublin: Four Courts Press, 2000), 108.

4. TCD, MUN/Lib/1/53, fols. 17, 47.

5. Laetitia Yeandle, *Works of Richard Hooker,* ed. W. Speed Hill (Cambridge: Harvard University Press, 1982), 5: xxi, note 21.

6. Ibid., xxi.

7. I was unaware of William O'Sullivan's attributions when I began my own research on Walter Travers at Trinity College Dublin in August 2001 with the intention of examining Ussher's notes on Travers's sermons and searching for further sources. At this point, Alan Ford drew my attention to O'Sullivan notes in the Abbott catalogue, which in fact proved to be his "untraceable papers." I am indebted to him for this help.

8. These are written in his distinctive handwriting, which can be compared to autograph letters in the British Library. The contents also confirm his authorship. For example, in addition to the extensive notes on presbyterian government dating in the late sixteenth century, the papers unmistakably include notes on the controversies in the Merchant Adventurer Church during Travers's ministry in the early 1580s. See Chapter 6, above.

9. See Chapter 3, above.

10. TCD, MS 140.

11. Ibid., 141, 423.

12. Another Travers-related manuscript that shares the provenance of his other papers and includes Travers's pagination is a theological discourse on the invocation of saints. There is also a possibility that Travers owned and paginated a petition to Parliament in behalf of the godly deprived of their ministry by the 1604 canons. Examples of the affinity between Travers's autograph letter (BL, Add MS 4276, fol. 157)

and his translation of Chrysostom's sermons (TCD, MS 233, fol. 3) can be found in his minuscule italic letters. The "w" begins at a sharp angle and is followed by a curved loop. Other features shared with Travers's autograph letter include the "t," which is usually not completely crossed and is marked by a horizontal serif and a slightly hooked ascender. The second stroke of the "h" is broken and followed by a leftward curving descender that finishes on an upward stroke. Further examples include the stem of the "b," which is completely looped, and the descender in the "y," which is also consistently finished with a backward hook. Handwriting samples can be found in Ha, "English Presbyterianism, c 1590–1640," 282–84.

13. TCD, MS 140.

14. O'Sullivan pointed out that certain manuscripts from Ussher's library were borrowed and later returned, with other collections, to Trinity Library: "Ussher's Manuscripts: The Cataloguing of Ussher Manuscripts," (Unpublished typescript, Reading Room, Trinity College Library, Dublin), 1–11. See also his "Ussher as a Collector of Manuscripts," *Hermathena* 88 (1956): 34–58.

15. Gregory, "Congregational Puritanism," 66. Thomas Parker referred to a *"Mr. Sh."* as "The Author of the Reply to D. Down." ****2. For further discussion of Sheerwood's authorship, see Sommerville, "Independent Thought," 12.

16. It is noteworthy that these manuscripts reveal more than the continued argumentation of English presbyterianism: they also bear witness to the continuance of presbyterian practice. It appears from the contents of the "Reformed Church Government" that it was an extension of presbyterian agitation for further reformation. The continued disputation of ecclesiastical questions can be understood as a part of the presbyterians' deliberative process and "artifacts" of presbyterianism itself. As Margo Todd recently discussed, the usefulness of Scottish Kirk session minutes: "[T]he abundance of kirk session minutes, their remarkable detail, the earthiness of much of the language and the availability of corroborating evidence in depositions, journals, correspondence and other records, makes them a source enviable to historians of the English protestant parish whose records are so sparse and narrow": *Culture of Protestantism,* 20. The consistory minutes of the English Reformed Church in Amsterdam can be compared to the kirk session minutes in the nature and extent of their detail. These records were not simply a historic archive for the consistory's own reference, but an object of the presbyterians' disciplinary system. John Paget, for example, appealed to the minutes in defense of the consistory's ecclesiastical sentences: *An Answere to Unjust Complaints,* 67.

Bibliography

———•◆•———

UNPUBLISHED PRIMARY SOURCES

Amsterdam, Gemeentearchief (GAA)
  English Reformed Church Archive 318 (ERCA 318)
  1   Consistory Minutes, 1607–21
  2   Consistory Minutes, 1621–27
  3   Consistory Minutes, 1628–1700
  45   "The Standing orders off the Consistory"
  81   Book of Matrimony
  82   Book of Baptism
  84   Membership Lists, 1623–33
  85   Membership Lists, 1629–42
  86   Membership Lists, 1634
  87   Membership Lists, 1636–42
  88   Membership Lists, 1641
  104   Testimonials, 1618–29
Boston, Massachusetts Historical Society
  MS SBd- 76 Notes on sermons (Ipswich)
Dordrecht, Gemeentearchief (GAD)
  MS 110/5 Consistory Records
Dublin, Trinity College Library (TCD)
  MS 118   Richard Hooker's Sermon on Justification
  MS 119   Richard Hooker's Answer to Travers
  MS 121   Richard Hooker's Sixth Book of Ecclesiastical Polity
  MS 135   Theological Treatises (including Travers's translation of Abraham Scult-etus's sermons)
  MS 140   A Treatise of Conformitie, The Reformed Church Government Desired, on Church Government, against "The Examiner"
  MS 141   "A Defence of Certain Christians"
  MS 168   Analysis of Various Scriptures by Walter Travers
  MS 230   Expositions (including poems by Walter Haddon and notes by Walter Travers)
  MS 233   Theological Treatises
  MS 292   A Discourse of Church Government (Third Part of the Replye to George Downame)

MS 295 Articles of Religion and Discipline Observed in Guernsey, Jersey, etc.

MS 324 A Theological Note-book (Walter Travers)

MS 366 Collectanea de rebus theologicis (commonplace book of Walter Travers)

MS 391 John Travers, Collectanea Philosophica.

MS 527 Papers on Ecclesiastical Matters (containing *Justification for the Religion Now Professed in England* by Walter Travers.)

MS 677 Questions in Divinity Discussed (notes of sermons by puritan ministers, including Snape and Fludd)

MS 782 Tractatus Anonymi de Disciplina Ecclesiae

MS 1210 Micellanea Theologica (including notes on Travers's sermons by Archbishop Ussher)

MS 1708 Henry Joseph Monck Mason Catalogue of Manuscripts Trinity College Library, Dublin.

MUN/LIB/1/53 John Lyon catalogue of manuscripts Trinity College Library, Dublin, *c.* 1743. (Abbreviated notes from, or based on, T. K. Abbott's *Catalogue* (1900) are cited above)

Leicester, Public Record Office

MS BR II/18 Letter Attempting to Secure Travers as Minister

Leiden, Gemeentearchief (GAL)

LB(66751)Zie BE Goodyear Papers (letter to Goodyear by Robert Paget dated 1661)

London, British Library (BL)

Add. MS 4276 Letter by Travers Thanking Arthur Hildersham for Received Benevolences

Add. MS 6394 Extracts from the Register Book of the English Congregation at Antwerp

Add. MS 48064 Records of the Lambeth Palace Conference with Travers, Sparke, and Whitgift

Add. MS 4930 West Riding Sermons

Cotton Galba,

C, VI Walsingham Letter in Defense of Travers's Ministry at Antwerp

Harleian MS 4888 Petition from Walter Travers to Queen and Council about Conformity

Harleian MS 6849 Court Record of Cartwright and Seven Others' Subscription to the Book of Discipline

Landsdowne MS 50 Petition from Walter Travers to the Council for the Continuance of his Ministry and Notes on the Hooker-Travers Controversy with Annotations by Hooker

Landsdowne MS 64 Letter Regarding Marprelate Tracts, Thomas Cartwright and Articles against Presbyterian Ministers of Northampton and Warwickshire

Landsdowne MS 108 Travers Letter Asking for Support of Trinity College

Landsdowne MS 120 Proceedings against Presbyterian Ministers

Landsdowne MS 847 Speech by Adam Loftus on the Appointment of Travers as Provost of Trinity College, Dublin

Sloane MS 271 Letters, Petitions &c. Collected by Robert Smart

Yelverton MS LXX   Records of the Lambeth Palace Conference with Travers, Sparke, and Whitgift
London, Dr Williams's Library (DWL)
Morrice MS I   An Account of the Careers of Travers and Wilcocks
Morrice MS A   A Petition on Conformity from Travers to the Queen and Council
London, Lambeth Palace Library (LPL)
Carte Misc. IV   Charges Drawn against Walter Travers
Carte Misc. IV, 191 Summary of Answers by the Charged Presbyterian Ministers, Thomas Cartwright and Six Others
MS 2006   Notes on Hooker-Travers Controversy
Sion Arc L40.2/E58(1)   Books Removed, 1666
Sion Arc L40.2/E60   Book of Benefactors, a List of Books Bequeathed to Sion College by Travers
London, The National Archives, Kew (NA Kew)
PROB 11/103   Prerogative Court of Canterbury Wills (Thomas Cartwright)
PROB 11/112   Prerogative Court of Canterbury Wills (Edmund Snape)
PROB 11/129   Prerogative Court of Canterbury Wills (Thomas Wilcox; Thomas Sparke)
PROB 11/167   Prerogative Court of Canterbury Wills (Walter Travers)
SP 16/259/78   State Papers Domestic, Charles I.
Oxford, Bodleian Library
Parker MS English Th.e.158 English Translation of Robert Parker's *De Politeia Ecclesiastica*.
Oxford, Corpus Christi College Library
MS 294   Codex chartaceus (including letters from Thomas Cartwright to Mrs. D.B. and on doubts concerning a man's entry into the ministry.)
Oxford, The Queen's College
MS 280   On Church Government
San Marino, California, Huntington Library
EL 35 b 34   Reasons Shewing that the Companye of Marchaunts Aduenturers of England are Necessarye members for the Prince and State.
438876   William Stoughton, *An Assertion for True and Christian* 1604 edition. 23318
Ruthin, Denbighshire Record Office
Plas Power MS DD/PP/839   Correspondence and notes of Christopher Goodman

PRINTED PRIMARY SOURCES

Calendar of State Papers Domestic, Great Britain. Series 2. 1625–1702. London: Longman, 1858–97.
Calvin, John. *Institutes of Christian Religion*. Edited by John T. McNeill. Philadelphia: Westminster Press, 1960.
Cartwright, Thomas. *Cartwrightiana*. Edited by Albert Peel and Leland H. Carlson. London: George Allen and Unwin, 1951.
Charles I in 1646: letter of Charles the first to Queen Henrietta Maria. Edited by John Bruce. London: Camden Society, 1856.

Conferences and Combination Lectures in the Elizabethan Church: Dedham and Bury St. Edmunds, 1582–1590. Edited by Patrick Collinson, John Craig, and Brett Usher. Woodbridge, Church of England Record Society: Boydell Press, 2003.

Ecclesiae Londino-Batavae Archivum. Edited by John Henry Hessels. Cambridge: Cambridge University Press, 1887.

Hooker, Richard, *The Works of Richard Hooker.* Edited by W. Speed Hill. Cambridge: Harvard University Press: 1982.

———. *The Works of That Learned and Judicious Divine Mr. Richard Hooker.* Edited by John Keble. Oxford: Clarendon Press, 1841.

John Chrysostom, *On Wealth and Poverty.* Translated and Introduced by Catharine Roth. New York: St. Vladimir's Seminary Press, 1984.

The Letters of Queen Elizabeth and King James VI. Edited by John Bruce. London: Camden Society, 1849.

Milton, Anthony, ed. *The British Delegation and the Synod of Dort (1618–1619).* Woodbridge: Boydell, 2005.

The Presbyterian Movement in the reign of Queen Elizabeth as Illustrated by the Minute Book of the Dedham Classis, 1582–1589. Edited by R. G. Usher. London: Camden Society, 1905.

Puritan Manifestos. A Study of the Origin of the Puritan Revolt: With a Reprint of the Admonition to the Parliament and Kindred Documents, 1572. Edited by W. H. Fere and C. E. Douglas. London: Society for Promoting Christian Knowledge, 1907.

Rogers, Thomas. *Catholic Doctrine.* Edited for the Parker Society by J. J. S. Perowne. Cambridge: Cambridge University Press, 1854.

The Seconde Parte of a Register. Edited by Albert Peel. Cambridge: Cambridge University Press, 1915.

Strype, John. *The Life and Acts of John Whitgift, D.D.* Oxford: Clarendon Press, 1822.

Two Elizabethan Puritan Diaries: By Richard Rogers and Samuel Ward. Edited by M. M. Knappen. Gloucester: Peter Smith, 1966.

Whitgift, John. *The Works of John Whitgift.* Edited by John Ayre. Cambridge: Cambridge University Press, 1851.

Winthrop, John. *The History of New England from 1630 to 1649.* Edited by James Savage. Boston: Little, Brown and Company, 1853.

CONTEMPORARY BOOKS

Ball, John. *An Answer to Two Treatises of Mr. Iohn Can, the Leader of the English Brownists in Amsterdam.* London: 1642.

———. *A Friendly Triall of the Grounds Tending to Separation in a Plain and Modest Dispute Touching the Lawfulnesse of a Stinted Liturgie and Set Form of Prayer, Communion in Mixed Assemblies, and the Primitive Subject and First Receptacle of the Power of the Keyes.* London: 1640.

———. *A Letter of Many Ministers in Old England, Requesting the Judgement of Their Reverend Brethren in New England Concerning Nine Positions.* London: 1643.

———. *A Tryall of the Nevv-Church VVay in New-England and in Old.* London: 1644.

Bancroft, Richard. *Daungerous Positions and Proceedings Published and Practised within the Iland of Brytaine.* London: [J. Windet for] Iohn Wolfe, 1593.

————. *A Suruay of the Pretended Holy Discipline.* London: 1593.

Baxter, Richard. *Reliquiae Baxterianae, or, Mr. Richard Baxters Narrative of The Most Memorable Passages of His Life and Times.* London: 1696.

Brinsley, John. *An Antidote Against the Poysonous VVeeds of Heretical Blasphemies, which During the Deplorable Interval of Church-Government Have Grown up in the Reforming Church of England.* London: 1650.

Browne, Robert. *An Ansvvere to Master Cartvvright His Letter for Ioyning with the English Churches: Whereunto the True Copie of His Sayde Letter is Annexed.* London: 1585.

Bullinger, Heinrich. *De Conciliis.* Zurich: 1561.

————. *A Confutation of the Pope's Bull.* London: 1572.

————. *De Origine Erroris.* Zurich: 1539.

Calamy, Edmund, *The Righteous Man's Death Lamented: A Sermon Preached at St. Austins, London, Aug. 23. 1662, at the Funeral of That Eminent Servant of Jesus Christ, Mr. Simeon Ash Late Minister of the Gospel There.* London: 1662.

Cartwright, Thomas. *Christian Religion: Substantially, Methodicalli[e,] [Pla]inlie, and Profitablie Treatised.* London: 1611.

————. *A Commentary vpon the Epistle of Saint Paule Written to the Colossians. Preached by Thomas Cartwright, and Now Published for the Further Vse of the Church of God,* London: 1612.

————. *A Confutation of the Rhemists Translation, Glosses and Annotations on the Nevv Testament.* Leiden: 1618.

————. *Helpes for Discovery of the Truth in Point of Toleration: Being the Judgment of That Eminent Scholler Tho. Cartwright, Sometimes Divinity-Professor in the University of Cambridge in the Reigne of Queen Elizabeth of Happy Memory, and Then A Famous Non-Conformist, For Which Through the Tyranny of the Bishops He Suffered Exile.* London: 1648.

————. *A Replye to An Ansvvere Made of M. Doctor Whitegifte: Againste The Admonition to The Parliament.* Hemel Hempstead?: 1573.

————. *The Second Replie of Thomas Cartwright: Agaynst Maister Doctor Whitgiftes Second Answer, Touching the Church Discipline.* Heidelburg: 1575.

Clarke, Samuel. *The Lives of Thirty-Two English Divines Famous in Their Generations for Learning and Piety, and Most of Them Sufferers in the Cause of Christ.* London: 1677.

————. *The Lives of Two and Twenty English Divines Eminent in Their Generations for Learning, Piety, and Painfulnesse in the Work of the Ministry, and for their Sufferings in the Cause of Christ.* London: 1660.

Cosin, Richard. *An Answer to the Two First and Principall Treatises of a Certeine Factious Libell, Put Foorth Latelie, Without Name of Author or Printer, and Without Approbation by Authoritie, vnder the Title of An Abstract of Certeine Acts of Parliament.* London: 1584.

————. *An Apologie: of, and for Sundrie Proceedings by Iurisdiction Ecclesiasticall of Late Times by Some Challenged, and also Diuersly by Them Impugned.* London: 1591.

————. *Conspiracie, for Pretended Reformation viz. Presbyteriall Discipline.* London: 1592.

Cotton, John. *The Doctrine of the Church, to Which is Committed the Keyes of the Kingdome of Heaven.* London: 1643.

Davenport, John. *Another Essay for Investigation of the Truth, in Answer to Two Questions.* Cambridge: 1663.

———. *An Apologeticall Reply to a Booke Called an Answer to the Unjust Complaint of W.B.* Rotterdam: 1636.

———. *A Defence of the Answer and Arguments of the Synod Met at Boston in the Year 1662.* Cambridge: 1664.

———. *A Just Complaint Against an Uniust Doer: Wherein is Declared the Miserable Slaverie & Bondage That the English Church of Amsterdam is Now In, By Reason of The Tirannicall Government and Corrupt Doctrine, of Mr. Iohn Pagett Their Present Minister.* Amsterdam: 1634.

Downame, George. *A Defence of the Answer and Arguments of the Synod Met at Boston in the Year 1662.* Cambridge: 1664.

———. *A Defence of the Sermon Preached at the Consecration of the L. Bishop of Bath and VVelles against a Confutation Thereof by a Namelesse Author.* London: 1611.

———. *Tvvo Sermons the One Commending the Ministerie in Generall: the Other Defending the Office of Bishops in Particular.* London: 1608.

Edwards, Thomas. *Gangraena: or A Catalogue and Discovery of Many of the Errours, Heresies, Blasphemies and Pernicious Practices of the Sectaries of This Time, Vented and Acted in England in These Four Last Years: As Also, A Particular Narration of Divers Stories, Remarkable Passages, Letters; An Extract of Many Letters, All Concerning the Present Sects.* London: 1646.

Fenner, Dudley. *A Counter-Poyson, Modestly Written For the Time, To Make Aunswere to the Obiections and Reproches, Wherewith the Aunswerer to the Abstract, Would Disgrace the Holy Discipline of Christ.* London: 1584.

Fenwicke, John. *The Downfall of the Pretended Divine Authoritie of the Hierarchy into the Sea of Rome. From Some Arguments, and Motives, to the Finall Extirpation of That Unlawfull Government of the Prelacy: as Having No Foundation in the Scriptures, but Onely in That Filthy Dung-Hill of the Canon Law of the Popes Authorities, and Therefore Antichristian.* London: 1641.

Field, Richard. *Of the Church Fiue Bookes.* London: 1606.

The First and Large Petition of the City of London and of Other Inhabitants Thereabouts: For a Reformation in Church-Government, as Also for the Abolishment of Episcopacy. London: 1641.

Informations, or a Protestation, and a Treatise from Scotland. [n.p.] 1608.

Hemmingius, Nicolaus. *De Pastore, siue Pastoris Optimus Viuendi Agendique Modus.* Leipzig: 1574 [Travers's edition: 1562].

Heylyn, Peter. *Aerius Redivivus, or, The History of the Presbyterians Containing the Beginnings, Progress and Successes of that Active Sect.* Oxford: 1670.

Heyricke, Richard. *Three Sermons Preached at the Collegiate Church in Manchester by Richard Heyricke.* London: 1641.

Jacob, Henry. *An Attestation of Many Learned, Godly, and Famous Divines, Lightes of Religion, and Pillars of the Gospell Iustifying This Doctrine, Viz. That the Church-Governement Ought to Bee Alwayes with the Peoples Free Consent: Also This; That a True Church Vnder the Gospell Contayneth No More Ordinary Congregations but One.* Middelburg: 1613.

———. *A Christian and Modest Offer of a Most Indifferent Conference, or Disputation, about the Maine and Principall Controversies Betwixt the Prelats, and the Late Silenced and Deprived Ministers in England.* London: 1606.

————. *A Confession and Protestation of the Faith of Certaine Christians in England Holding it Necessary to Observe, & Keepe All Christes True Substantiall Ordinances for His Church Visible and Politicall (That Is, Indued with Power of Outward Spirituall Government) under the Gospel.* Amsterdam: 1616.

————. *A Defence of the Churches and Ministery of Englande Written in Two treatises, Against the Reasons and Obiections of Maister Francis Iohnson, and Others of the Separation Commonly Called Brownists.* Middelburgh: 1599.

————. *The Divine Beginning and Institution of Christs Church.* Leiden: 1610.

————. *A Plaine and Cleere Exposition of the Second Commandement.* Leiden: 1610.

————. *Reasons Taken Out of Gods Word and the Best Humane Testimonies Prouing a Necessitie of Reforming Our Churches in England Framed and Applied to 4. Assertions Wherein the Foresaid Purpose is Contained.* Middelburg: 1604.

Jenison, Robert. *The Height of Israels Heathenish Idolatrie, in Sacrificing their Children to the Deuill Diuided into Three Sections.* London: 1621.

Knollys, Francis. *Informations, or a Protestation, and a Treatise from Scotland with D. Reignoldes His Letter to Sir Francis Knollis.* 1608.

A Letter of Many Ministers in Old England, Requesting the Judgement of their Reverend Brethren in New England Concerning Nine Positions: Written Anno Dom. 1637: Together with Their Answer Thereunto Returned, anno 1639: And the Reply Made unto the Said Answer, and Sent Over Unto Them, anno 1640. London: 1643.

Mather, Cotton. *Magnalia Christi Americana: or The Ecclesiastical History of New England.* London: 1702.

Morice, James, *A Briefe Treatise of Oathes Exacted by Ordinaries and Ecclesiastical Iudges, to Answere Generallie to All Such Articles or Interrogatories, as Pleaseth Them to Propound.* Middelburg: 1590?

Noyes, James. *The Temple Measured: Or, a Brief Survey of the Temple Mystical.* London: 1646.

Paget, John. *An Answer to the Unjust Complaints of William Best, and of Such Others as Have Subscribed Thereunto.* Amsterdam: 1635.

————. *An Arrow Against the Separation of the Brownists: Also an Admonition Touching Talmudique & Rabbinical Allegations.* Amsterdam: 1618.

————. *A Defence of Chvrch-Government, Exercised in Presbyteriall, Classicall, & Synodall Assemblies.* London: 1641.

————. *Meditations of Death Wherein a Christian is Taught How to Remember and Prepare for His Latter End: by the Late Able & Faithfull Minister of the Gospel, Iohn Paget.* Dort: 1639.

Paget, Thomas. "An Humble Advertisment to the High Court of Parliament." In *A Defence of Chvrch-Government.*

Parker, Robert. *De Politeia Ecclesiastica: Libri Tres.* Frankfurt: 1616.

Parker, Thomas. *The Copy of a Letter Written by Mr. Thomas Parker, Pastor of the Church of Newbury in New-England, to His Sister, Mrs Elizabeth Avery: Imprimatur John Downame.* London: 1649.

————. *The True Copy of a Letter: Written by Mr. Thomas Parker, a Learned and Godly Minister, in New-England, unto a Member of the Assembly of Divines now at Westminster: Imprimatur. Ja. Cranford.* London: 1644.

Peregrin, Iames. *The Letters Patents of the Presbyterie: With the Please and Frvits of the Prelacie.* [n.p.]: 1632.

Rathband, William. *A Briefe Narration of Some Church Courses.* London: 1644.

Rogers, Richard. *A Commentary Vpon the VVhole Booke of Iudges.* London: 1615.

St German, Christopher. *A Treatise Concernynge the Diuision Betwene the Spiritualtie and Temporaltie.* London: 1532.

Sheerwood, Richard. *A Replye Answering a Defence of the Sermon, Preached at the Consecration of the Bishop of Bathe and Welles, by George Downame, Doctor of Diuinitye In Defence of an Answere to the Foresayd Sermon Imprinted Anno 1609.* Amsterdam: 1614.

Stoughton, William. *An Abstract, of Certain Acts of Parliament: Of Certaine Her Maiesties Iniunctions: [Etc.] for the Peaceable Gouernment of the Church.* London: 1583.

———. *An Assertion for True and Christian Church-Policie: Wherein Certaine Politike Obiections Made against the Planting of Pastors and Elders in Every Congregation, Are Sufficientlie Aunswered.* Middelburg: 1641.

Travers, Walter. *Fvll and Plaine Declaration of Ecclesiastical Discipline Ovt of the Word of God.* Geneva: 1580; Leiden: 1617.

———. *A Supplication Made to the Priuy Counsel.* Oxford: 1612.

———. *Vindiciae Ecclesiae Anglicanae: or A Iustification of the Religion Now Professed in England.* London: 1630.

Whitgift, John. *An Ansvvere to a Certen Libel Intituled, An Admonition to the Parliament.* London: 1572.

Zepper, Wilhelm. *De Politia Ecclesiastica.* Herborn: 1595.

SECONDARY SOURCES

Abbot, William. "Anticlericalism and Episcopacy in Parliamentary Debates, 1640–1641: Secular Versus Spiritual Functions." In *Law and Authority in Early Modern England,* ed. Buchanan Sharp and Mark Charles Fissel, 157–86. Newark: University of Delaware Press, 2007.

Alford, Stephen. *The Early Elizabethan Polity: William Cecil and the British Succession Crisis, 1558–1569.* Cambridge: Cambridge University Press, 1998.

Archer, Ian. *The History of the Haberdashers' Company.* Chichester: Phillimore, 1991.

———. *The Pursuit of Stability: Social Relations in Elizabethan London.* Cambridge: Cambridge University Press, 1991.

Atherton, Ian, and David Como. "The Burning of Edward Wightman: Puritanism, Prelacy and the Politics of Heresy in Early Modern England." *EHR* 120, no. 489 (2005): 1215–50.

Avis, P. D. L. *The Church in the Theology of the Reformers.* London: Marshall Morgan and Scott, 1981.

———. "Moses and the Magistrate: A Study in the Rise of Protestant Legalism." *JEH* 26 (1975): 149–72.

Backus, Irena. "The Fathers and Calvinist Orthodoxy: Patristic Scholarship." In *The Reception of the Church Fathers in the West: From the Carolingians to the Maurists,* ed. Irena Backus, 2: 839–62. Leiden: E. J. Brill, 1997.

———. *Historical Method and Confessional Identity in the Era of the Reformation, 1378–1615.* Leiden: E. J. Brill, 2003.

———. "These Holy Men: Calvin's Patristic Models for Establishing the Company of Pastors." In *John Calvin and the Company of Pastors. Papers presented at the 14th Colloquium of the Calvin Studies Society, May 22–24, 2003. University of Notre Dame, Indiana,* ed. David Foxgrover, 25–51. Grand Rapids, MI: Calvin Studies Society, 2004.

Bangs, J. D. *The Auction Catalogue of the Library of Hugh Goodyear English Reformed Minister at Leiden*. Utrecht: Hes Publishers, 1985.

Benedict, Philip. *Christ's Churches Purely Reformed: A Social History of Calvinism*. New Haven: Yale University Press, 2002.

Biel, Pamela. *Doorkeepers at the House of Righteousness: Heinrich Bullinger and the Zurich Clergy, 1535–1575*. Bern: Peter Lang, 1991.

Boulton, F. R. "Archbishop Ussher's Scheme of Church Government." *Theology* 1, no. 310 (1947): 9–16.

Boyer, Allen D. "Coke, Sir Edward (1552–1634)." In *ODNB*.

———. *Sir Edward Coke and the Elizabethan Age*. Stanford: Stanford University Press, 2003.

Brace, Laura. *The Idea of Property in Seventeenth-Century England: Tithes and the Individual*. Manchester: Manchester University Press, 1998.

Brachlow, Stephen. *The Communion of Saints: Radical Puritan and Separatist Ecclesiology, 1570–1625*. Oxford: Clarendon Press, 1988.

———. "The Elizabethan Roots of Henry Jacob's Churchmanship: Refocusing the Historiographical Lens." *JEH* 36 (1985): 228–54.

Bremer, Francis. *Congregational Communion: Clerical Friendship in the Anglo-American Puritan Community, 1610–1692*. Boston: Northeastern University Press, 1994.

———. "Introduction." In *Puritanism: Transatlantic Perspectives on a Seventeenth-Century Anglo-American Faith*, ed. Francis Bremer, xi–xvii. Boston: Massachusetts Historical Society, 1993.

———. *Shaping New Englands: Puritan Clergymen in Seventeenth Century England and New England*. London: Prentice Hall International, 1995.

Brenner, Robert. *Merchants and Revolution: Commercial Change, Political Conflict, and London's Overseas Traders, 1550–1653*. Princeton: Princeton University Press, 1993.

Brooks, C. W. *Law, Politics and Society in Early Modern England*. Cambridge: Cambridge University Press, 2009.

———. *Pettyfoggers and Vipers of the Commonwealth: The 'Lower Branch' of the Legal Profession in Early Modern England*. Cambridge: Cambridge University Press, 1986.

Burgess, Glenn. *The Politics of the Ancient Constitution: An Introduction to English Political Thought, 1603–1642*. Basingstoke: Macmillan, 1992.

Burrage, Champlin. *Early English Dissenters in the Light of Recent Research, 1550–1641*. Cambridge: Cambridge University Press, 1912.

Bush, Sargent, Jr. *The Writings of Thomas Hooker: Spiritual Adventure in Two Worlds*. Madison: University of Wisconsin Press, 1980.

Calder, Isabel M. "A Seventeenth Century Attempt to Purify the Anglican Church." *AHR* 53, no. 4 (1948): 760–75.

Cameron, James. "Godly Nurture and Admonition in the Lord." In *The Danish Reformation against Its International Background*, ed. Leif Grane and Kai Hørby, 264–76. Gottingen: Vandenhoeck and Ruprecht, 1990.

Cargill Thompson, W. D. J. "Sir Francis Knollys' Campaign against the *Jure Divino* Theory of Episcopacy." In *The Dissenting Tradition: Essays for Leland H. Carlson*, ed. Michael E. Moody, 39–77. Athens: Ohio University Press, 1975.

Carter, Alice. *The English Reformed Church in Amsterdam in the Seventeenth Century*. Amsterdam: Scheltema and Holkema, 1964.

———. "John Paget and the English Reformed Church in Amsterdam." *Tidschrift voor Geschiedenis* 70 (1957): 349–58.

Chadwick, Owen. "The Sixteenth Century." In *The English Church and the Continent*, ed. C. R. Dodwell, 60–72. London: Faith Press, 1959.

Christianson, Paul. "Reformers and the Church of England under Elizabeth I and the Early Stuarts." *JEH* 31 (1980): 463–82.

Cliffe, J. T. *The Puritan Gentry: The Great Puritan Families of Early Stuart England*. London: Routledge and Kegan Paul, 1984.

Coffey, John. *Politics, Religion and the British Revolution: The Mind of Samuel Rutherford*. Cambridge: Cambridge University Press, 1997.

Coffin, Joshua. *A Sketch of the History of Newbury, Newburyport, and West Newbury: From 1635 to 1845*. Boston: Samuel G. Drake, 1845.

Collinson, Patrick. *Archbishop Grindal, 1519–1583: The Struggle for a Reformed Church*. London: Jonathan Cape, 1979.

———. "The Authorship of *A Brieff Discours off the Troubles Begonne at Franckford*." In *Godly People*.

———. "Christian Socialism in Elizabethan Suffolk: Thomas Carew and His Caveat for Clothiers." In *Counties and Communities: Essays on East Anglian History*, ed. Carole Rawcliffe, Roger Virgoe, and Richard Wilson, 161–78. Norwich: Centre of East Anglian Studies, University of East Anglia, 1996.

———. "The Cohabitation of the Faithful with the Unfaithful." In *From Persecution to Toleration: The Glorious Revolution and Religion in England*, ed. Ole Peter Grell, Jonathan I. Israel, and Nicholas Tyacke, 51–76. Oxford: Clarendon Press, 1991.

———. "Ecclesiastical Vitriol: Religious Satire in the 1590s and the Invention of Puritanism." In *The Reign of Elizabeth I*, ed. John Guy, 150–70.

———. *The Elizabethan Puritan Movement*. London: Jonathan Cape, 1967.

———. "The Elizabethan Puritans and the Foreign Reformed Churches in London." In *Godly People*.

———. "The English Conventicle." In *Voluntary Religion*, ed. W. J. Sheils and Diana Wood, 223–59. Oxford: Basil Blackwell, 1986.

———. "Episcopacy and Reform in England in the Later Sixteenth Century." In *Godly People*.

———. "Europe in Britain: Protestant strangers and the English Reformation." In *From Strangers to Citizens*, ed. Randolph Vigne and Charles Littleton, 57–67. Brighton: Sussex Academic Press, 2001.

———. *Godly People: Essays on English Protestantism and Puritanism*. London: Hambledon Press, 1983.

———. "Godly Preachers and Zealous Magistrates in Elizabethan East Anglia: The Roots of Dissent." In *Religious Dissent in East Anglia*, ed. E. S. Leedham-Green, 5–27. Cambridge: Cambridge Antiquarian Society, 1991.

———. "The Jacobean Religious Settlement: The Hampton Court Conference." In *Before the English Civil War*, ed. Howard Tomlinson, 27–52. London: Macmillan Press, 1983.

———. "The Monarchical Republic of Queen Elizabeth I." *Bulletin of the John Rylands University Library of Manchester* 69, no. 2 (1987): 394–424.

———. "Puritanism and the Poor." In *Pragmatic Utopias: Ideals and Communities, 1200–1630*, ed. Rosemary Horrox and Sarah Rees Jones, 242–58. Cambridge: Cambridge University Press, 2001.

———. *The Religion of Protestants: The Church in English Society, 1559–1625*. Oxford: Clarendon Press, 1982.

———. "The Role of Women in the English Reformation Illustrated by the Life and Friendships of Anne Locke." In *Godly People.*

———. "Towards a Broader Understanding of the Early Dissenting Tradition." In *Godly People.*

Como, David. *Blown by the Spirit: Puritanism and the Emergence of an Antinomian Underground in Pre-Civil-War England.* Stanford: Stanford University Press, 2004.

Coolidge, John. *The Pauline Renaissance in England: Puritanism and the Bible.* Oxford: Clarendon Press, 1970.

Cooper, J. F., Jr. "'A Mixed Form': The Establishment of Church Government in Massachusetts Bay, 1629–1645." *Essex Institute Historical Collections* 123, no. 3 (1987): 233–59.

Coulton, Barbara. "Rivalry and Religion: The Borough of Shrewsbury in the Early Stuart Period." *Midland History* 28 (2003): 28–50.

Croft, Pauline. "The Religion of Robert Cecil." *HJ* 34 (1991): 773–96.

Cromartie, Alan. *The Constitutionalist Revolution: An Essay on the History of England, 1450–1642.* Cambridge: Cambridge University Press, 2006.

———. "The Constitutionalist Revolution: The Transformation of Political Culture in Early Stuart England." *P&P* 163 (1999): 76–120.

Cross, Claire. *The Royal Supremacy in the Elizabethan Church.* London: George Allen and Unwin, 1969.

Cust, Richard. "Anti-Puritanism and Urban Politics: Charles I and Great Yarmouth." *HJ* 35, no. 1 (1992): 1–26.

———. "Brinsley, John (1600–1665)." In *ODNB.*

——— and Ann Hughes. "Introduction: After Revisionism." In *Conflict in Early Stuart England: Studies in Religion and Politics 1603–1642*, ed. Richard Cust and Ann Hughes, 1–46. Harlow: Longman, 1989.

Dawson, Jane, and Lionel K. J. Glassey. "Some Unpublished Letters from John Knox to Christopher Goodman." *Scottish Historical Review* 84, no. 218 (2005): 166–201.

Dexter, H. M. *The Congregationalism of the Last Three Hundred Years, as Seen in Its Literature: With Special Reference to Certain Recondite, Neglected or Disputed Passages.* New York/Boston: Harper and Bros., 1880.

Donaldson, Gordon. *The Scottish Reformation.* Cambridge: Cambridge University Press, 1960.

Drysdale, A. H. *History of the Presbyterians in England: Their Rise, Decline, and Revival.* London: Presbyterian Church of England, 1889.

Duke, Alastair, and Rosemary L. Jones. "Towards a Reformed Polity in Holland, 1572–1578." *Tijdschrift voor Geschiedenis* 89, no. 3 (1976): 373–93.

Eales, Jacqueline. *Puritans and Roundheads: The Harleys of Brampton Bryan and the Outbreak of the English Civil War.* Cambridge: Cambridge University Press, 1990.

———. "A Road to Revolution: The Continuity of Puritanism, 1559–1642." In *The Culture of English Puritanism, 1560–1700*, ed. Christopher Durston and Jacqueline Eales, 184–209. Basingstoke: Macmillan, 1996.

———. "Samuel Clarke and the 'Lives' of Godly Women." In *Women in the Church*, ed. W. J. Sheils and Diana Wood, 365–76. Oxford: Basil Blackwell, 1990.

———. "Thomas Pierson and the Transmission of the Moderate Puritan Tradition." *Midland History* 20 (1995): 75–102.

Earwaker, J. P. *East Cheshire: Past and Present; or a History of the Hundred of Macclesfield, in the County Palatine of Chester.* London: 1877.

Felt, Joseph. *The Ecclesiastical History of New England*. Boston: Congregational Library Association, 1855.

Fincham, Kenneth. *Prelate as Pastor: The Episcopate of James I*. Oxford: Oxford University Press, 1990.

Ford, Alan. *James Ussher: Theology, History, and Politics in Early Modern Ireland and England*. Oxford: Oxford University Press, 2007.

Foster, Stephen. *Notes from the Caroline Underground: Alexander Leighton, the Puritan Triumvirate, and the Laudian Reaction to Nonconformity*. Hamden, CT: Archon Books, 1978.

Foyster, Elizabeth. *Manhood in Early Modern England: Honour, Sex and Marriage*. London: Longman, 1999.

Frederiks, J. G., and P. J. Frederiks. *Kohier van den tweenhonderdsten penning voor Amsterdam en onderhoorige plaatsen over 1631*. Amsterdam: Ten Brink and De Vries, 1890.

Fuller, Thomas. *The Church History of Britain*. London: London: T. Tegg, 1837.

Games, Alison. "Migration." In *The British Atlantic World*, ed. David Armitage and Michael J. Braddick, 31–50. Basingstoke: Palgrave, 2002.

Gardiner, S. R. *History of England: From the Accession of James I to the Outbreak of the Civil War, 1883–1884*. London: Longmans, 1883–84.

Gilbert, Ruth. *Early Modern Hermaphrodites: Sex and Other Stories*. Basingstoke: Palgrave, 2002.

Gorski, Philip. *The Disciplinary Revolution: Calvinism and the Rise of the State in Early Modern Europe*. Chicago: University of Chicago Press, 2003.

Grafton, Anthony. *The Footnote: A Curious History*. London: Faber and Faber, 1997.

Graham, Michael F. *The Uses of Reform: "Godly Discipline" and Popular Behavior in Scotland and Beyond, 1560–1610*. Leiden: E. J. Brill, 1996.

Greaves, Richard L. "The Ordination Controversy and the Spirit of Reform in Puritan England." *JEH* 21, no. 3 (1970): 225–41.

Grell, Ole Peter. *Calvinist Exiles in Tudor and Stuart England*. Aldershot: Scolar Press, 1996.

———. "Merchants and Ministers: The Foundations of International Calvinism." In *Calvinism in Europe*, ed. Andrew Pettegree, Alastair Duke, and Gillian Lewis, 254–73. Cambridge: Cambridge University Press, 1994.

Guy, John. "The Elizabethan Establishment and the Ecclesiastical Polity." In *The Reign of Elizabeth*, 126–49.

———. ed. *The Reign of Elizabeth I: Court and Culture in the Last Decade*. Cambridge: Cambridge University Press, 1995.

———. "Tudor Monarchy and Its Critiques." In *The Tudor Monarchy*, ed. John Guy, 78–109. London: Edward Arnold, 1997.

Ha, Polly, "Puritan Conciliarism: Why Walter Travers Read Heinrich Bullinger." *SCJ* 41, no. 4 (2010).

Habermas, Jürgen. *The Structural Transformation of the Public Sphere*. Translated by Thomas Burger. Boston: Massachusetts Institute of Technology, 1992.

Haigh, Christopher. *English Reformations: Religion, Politics, and Society under the Tudors*. Oxford: Clarendon Press, 1993.

Hall, David D. *The Faithful Shepherd: A History of New England Ministry in the Seventeenth Century*. Chapel Hill: University of North Carolina Press, 1972.

Halley, Robert. *Lancashire: Its Puritanism and Nonconformity*. Manchester: Tubbs and Brook, 1872.

Hassall, W. O. *A Catalogue of the Library of Sir Edward Coke*. New Haven: Yale University Press, 1950.

Helmholz, R. H. *The Roman Canon Law in Reformation England*. Cambridge: Cambridge University Press, 1990.

Herrup, Cynthia. *The Common Peace: Participation and the Criminal Law in Seventeenth-Century England*. Cambridge: Cambridge University Press, 1987.

Hill, Christopher. *Economic Problems of the Church from Archbishop Whitgift to the Long Parliament*. Oxford: Clarendon Press, 1956.

———. *Intellectual Origins of the English Revolution*. Oxford: Clarendon Press, 1965.

———. *Society and Puritanism in Pre-Revolutionary England*. London: Panther Press, 1964.

Hindle, Steve. *On the Parish? The Micro-Politics of Poor Relief in Rural England, c. 1550–1750*. Oxford: Clarendon Press, 2004.

Holmes, Peter. *Resistance and Compromise: The Political Thought of the Elizabethan Catholics*. Cambridge: Cambridge University Press, 1982.

Höpfl, Harro. *The Christian Polity of John Calvin*. Cambridge: Cambridge University Press, 1982.

Hopper, Andrew J. "Fenwick, John (1593–d. c. 1670)." *ODNB*.

Houlbrooke, Ralph. *Church Courts and the People during the English Reformation*. Oxford: Clarendon Press, 1979.

Howell, Roger. *Newcastle upon Tyne and the Puritan Revolution: A Study of the Civil War in North England*. Oxford: Clarendon Press, 1967.

———. *Puritans and Radicals in North England: Essays on the English Revolution*. Lanham: University Press of America, 1984.

Hughes, Ann. *Gangraena and the Struggle for the English Revolution*. Oxford: Clarendon Press, 2004.

———. "The Meanings of Religious Polemic." In *Puritanism: Transatlantic Perspectives on a Seventeenth-Century Anglo-American Faith*, ed. Francis Bremer, 201–29. Boston: Massachusetts Historical Society, 1993.

———. *Politics, Society and Civil War in Warwickshire, 1620–1660*. Cambridge: Cambridge University Press, 1987.

———. "'Popular' Presbyterianism in the 1640s and 1650s: The Cases of Thomas Edwards and Thomas Hall." In *England's Long Reformation, 1500–1800*, ed. Nicholas Tyacke, 235–260. London: University College London, 1998.

———. "Print, Persecution and Polemic: Thomas Edwards' Gangraena (1646) and Civil War Sectarianism." In *The Uses of Script and Print, 1300–1700*, ed. Julia Crick and Alexandra Walsham, 255–73. Cambridge: Cambridge University Press, 2004.

Ingram, Martin. *Church Courts, Sex and Marriage in England, 1570–1640*. Cambridge: Cambridge University Press, 1987.

———. "Reformation of Manners in Early Modern England." In *The Experience of Authority in Early Modern England*, ed. Steve Hindle, 47–88. Basingstoke: Macmillan, 1996.

Kaplan, Benjamin. *Divided by Faith: Religious Conflict and the Practice of Toleration in Early Modern Europe*. Cambridge: Harvard University Press, 2007.

Kaufman, Peter. "How Socially Conservative Were the Elizabethan Religious Radicals?" *Albion* 30, no. 1 (1998): 29–48.

———. *Thinking of the Laity in Late Tudor England.* Notre Dame: University of Notre Dame Press, 2004.

Kendall, R. T. *Calvin and the Calvinists.* Oxford: Oxford University Press, 1980.

Kinane, Vincent, and Anne Walsh, eds. *Essays on the History of Trinity College Library Dublin.* Dublin: Four Courts Press, 2000.

King, John N. "The Bishop's Stinking Foot: Milton and Antireplatical Satire." *Reformation* 7 (2002): 187–96.

Kingdon, Robert M. "Social Welfare in Calvin's Geneva." *AHR* 76, no. 1 (1971): 50–69.

Kirby, Ethyn W. "The Lay Feoffees: A Study in Militant Puritanism." *JMH* 14, no. 1 (1942): 1–25.

Kishlansky, Mark. "The Emergence of Adversary Politics in the Long Parliament." *JMH* 49 (1977): 617–40.

Klueting, Harm. "Problems of the Term and Concept 'Second Reformation': Memories of a 1980s Debate." In *Confessionalization in Europe, 1555–1700,* ed. John M. Headley, Hans J. Hillerbrand, and Anthony J. Papalas, 37–50. Aldershot: Ashgate, 2004.

Knox, S. J. *Walter Travers: Paragon of Elizabethan Puritanism.* London: Methuen, 1962.

Lake, Peter. *Anglicans and Puritans? Presbyterianism and English Conformist Thought from Whitgift to Hooker.* London: Unwin Hyman, 1988.

———. *The Boxmaker's Revenge: "Orthodoxy", "Heterodoxy" and the Politics of the Parish in Early Stuart London.* Stanford: Stanford University Press, 2001.

———. "Conformist Clericalism? Richard Bancroft's Analysis of the Socio-Economic Roots of Presbyterianism." In *The Church and Wealth,* ed. W. J. Sheils and Diana Wood, 219–29. Oxford: Basil Blackwell, 1987.

———. "Defining Puritanism—Again?" In *Puritanism: Transatlantic Perspectives on a Seventeenth-Century Anglo-American Faith,* ed. Francis Bremer, 3–29. Boston: Massachusetts Historical Society, 1993.

———. "Feminine Piety and Personal Potency: The 'Emancipation' of Mrs Jane Ratcliffe." *Seventeenth Century* 2, no. 2. (1987): 143–65.

———. "The Historiography of Puritanism." In *The Cambridge Companion to Puritanism,* ed. John Coffey and Paul C. H. Lim, 346–71. Cambridge: Cambridge University Press, 2008.

———. *Moderate Puritans and the Elizabethan Church.* Cambridge: Cambridge University Press, 1982.

———. "Moving the Goal Posts? Modified Subscription and the Construction of Conformity in the Early Stuart Church." In *Conformity and Orthodoxy in the English Church, c. 1560–1660,* ed. Peter Lake and Michael Questier, 179–205. Woodbridge: Bydell Press, 2000.

———. "Presbyterianism, the Idea of a National Church and the Argument from Divine Right." In *Protestantism and the National Church in Sixteenth Century England,* ed. Peter Lake and Maria Dowling, 193–224. London: Croom Helm, 1987.

Lake, Peter, and David Como. "'Orthodoxy' and Its Discontents: Dispute Settlement and the Production of 'Consensus' in the London (Puritan) 'Underground.'" *JBS* 39, no. 1 (2000): 34–70.

Laurence, Anne. "A Priesthood of She-Believers: Women and Congregations in Mid-Seventeenth-Century England." In *Women in the Church,* ed. W. J. Sheils and Diana Wood, 345–63. Oxford: Basil Blackwell, 1990.

Lenman, Bruce. "The Limits of Godly Discipline in the Early Modern Period with Particular Reference to England and Scotland." In *Religion and Society in Early Modern Europe, 1500–1800,* ed. Kaspar von Greyerz, 124–42. London: George Allen and Unwin, 1984.

Levack, B. P. *The Formation of the British State: England, Scotland and the Union, 1603–1707.* Oxford: Clarendon Press, 1987.

Lim, Paul. *In Pursuit of Purity, Unity, and Liberty: Richard Baxter's Puritan Ecclesiology in Its Seventeenth-Century Context.* Leiden: E. J. Brill, 2004.

Lindley, Keith. *Popular Politics and Religion in Civil War London.* Aldershot: Scolar Press, 1997.

Liu, Tai. *Puritan London: A Study of Religion and Society in the City Parishes.* Newark: University of Delaware Press, 1986.

Luoma, John K. "Who Owns the Fathers? Hooker and Cartwright on the Authority of the Primitive Church." *SCJ* 8, no. 3 (1977): 45–59.

MacCulloch, Diarmaid. *The Boy King: Edward VI and the Protestant Reformation.* Berkeley: University of California Press, 2002.

———. *Reformation: Europe's House Divided, 1490–1700.* London: Allen Lane, 2003.

McDiarmid, John F., ed. *The Monarchical Republic of England: Essays in Response to Patrick Collinson.* Aldershot: Ashgate, 2007.

McIntosh, Marjorie. *Controlling Misbehavior in England, 1370–1600.* Cambridge: Cambridge University Press, 1998.

Marchant, Ronald A. *The Church under the Law: Justice, Administration, and Discipline in the Diocese of York, 1560–1640.* Cambridge: Cambridge University Press, 1969.

Martin, D. A. "The Denomination." *British Journal of Sociology* 13, no. 1 (1962): 1–14.

Mason, Roger. "James VI, George Buchanan, and 'The True Lawe of Free Monarchies.'" In *Kingship and the Commonweal: Political Thought in Renaissance and Reformation Scotland,* ed. Roger Mason, 215–41. East Linton: Tuckwell, 1998.

Mauelshagen, Franz. "Heinrich Bullinger (1504–1575): Leben—Denken—Wirkung." *Zwingliana* 32 (2005): 89–106.

Mendle, Michael. *Dangerous Positions: Mixed Government, the Estates of the Realm, and the Making of the Answer to the XIX Propositions.* Tuscaloosa: University of Alabama Press, 1985.

Mentzer, Raymond. "Disciplina Nervus Ecclesiae: The Calvinist Reform of Morals at Nimes." *SCJ* 18, no. 1 (1987): 89–116.

———, ed. *Sin and the Calvinists: Morals Control and the Consistory in the Reformed Tradition.* Kirksville, MO: Truman State University Press, 1994.

Merritt, J. F. "Tuke, Thomas (1580/81–1657)." In *ODNB.*

Miller, Perry. *Orthodoxy in Massachusetts, 1630–1650.* New York: Harper and Row, 1970.

Milton, Anthony. *Catholic and Reformed: Roman and Protestant Churches in English Protestant Thought, 1600–40.* Cambridge: Cambridge University Press, 1995.

———. "The Creation of Laudianism: A New Approach." In *Politics, Religion and Popularity in Early Stuart Britain,* ed. Tom Cogswell, Richard Cust, and Peter Lake, 162–84. Cambridge: Cambridge University Press, 2002.

————. *Laudian and Royalist Polemic in Seventeenth-Century England*. Manchester: Manchester University Press, 2007.

Milward, Peter. *Religious Controversies of the Jacobean Age: A Survey of Printed Sources*. London: Scolar Press, 1978.

Momigliano, Arnaldo. *The Classical Foundations of Modern Historiography*. Berkeley: University of California Press, 1990.

Moody, Michael. "Trials and Travels of a Nonconformist Layman: The Spiritual Odyssey of Stephen Offwood, 1564–ca. 1635." *CH* 51, no. 2 (1992): 157–71.

Moore, Susan Hardman. "Arguing for Peace: Giles Firmin on New England and Godly Unity." In *Unity and Diversity in the Church*, ed. R. N. Swanson, 251–61. Oxford: Blackwell, 1996.

————. *Pilgrims: New World Settlers and the Call of Home*. New Haven: Yale University Press, 2007.

Morrill, J. S. "The Attack on the Church of England in the Long Parliament, 1640–1642." In *History, Society and the Churches*, ed. Geoffrey Best, 105–24. Cambridge: Cambridge University Press, 1985.

————. *Cheshire 1630–1660: County Government and Society during the English Revolution*. Oxford: Oxford University Press, 1974.

————. "The Religious Context of the English Civil War." In *The English Civil War*, ed. Richard Cust and Ann Hughes, 155–78. London: Edward Arnold, 1997.

————. "The War(s) of the Three Kingdoms." In *The New British History*, ed. Glenn Burgess, 65–91. London: Tauris Academic Studies, 1999.

Muldrew, Craig. "The Culture of Reconciliation: Community and the Settlement of Economic Disputes in Early Modern England." *HJ* 39, no. 4 (1996): 915–42.

————. *The Economy of Obligation: The Culture of Credit and Social Relations in Early Modern England*. London: Macmillan Press, 1998.

Mullan, David George. *Episcopacy in Scotland: The History of an Idea, 1560–1638*. Edinburgh: John Donald, 1986.

Mullett, Michael. "Case, Thomas, (bap. 1598, d. 1682)." In *ODNB*.

————. "Herrick, Richard (1600–1667)." In *ODNB*.

Murdock, Graeme. *Beyond Calvin: The Intellectual, Political and Cultural World of Europe's Reformed Churches, c. 1540–1620*. Basingstoke: Palgrave, 2004.

————. *Calvinism on the Frontier, 1600–1660: International Calvinism and the Reformed Church in Hungary and Transylvania*. Oxford: Clarendon Press, 2000.

Naphy, William. *Calvin and the Consolidation of the Genevan Reformation*. London: Westminster John Knox Press, 1994.

Neale, J. E. *Elizabeth I and Her Parliaments, 1584–1601*. London: Jonathan Cape, 1957.

Niebuhr, H. Richard. *The Social Sources of Denominationalism*. Cleveland: Meridian Books, 1968.

Nijenhuis, Willem. "The Controversy between Presbyterianism and Episcopalianism surrounding and during the Synod of Dordrecht, 1618–1619." In *Ecclesia Reformata: Studies on the Reformation*, Leiden: E. J. Brill, 1972.

Nischan, Bodo. *Prince, People, and Confession: The Second Reformation in Brandenburg*. Philadelphia: University of Pennsylvania Press, 1994.

Oakley, Francis. "Legitimation by Consent: The Question of the Medieval Roots." In *Politics and Eternity: Studies in the History of Medieval and Early Modern Political Thought*, ed. Francis Oakley, 96–137. Leiden: E. J. Brill, 1999.

Ó hAnnracháin, Tadhg. "Lost in Rinuccini's Shadow: The Irish Clergy, 1645–9." In *Kingdoms in Crisis: Ireland in the 1640s*, ed. Micheál Ó Siochrú, 176–91. Dublin: Four Courts Press, 2001.

O'Sullivan, William. "Introduction." In *Trinity College Dublin: Descriptive Catalogue of Mediaeval and Renaissance Latin Manuscripts at Trinity College Library Dublin*, ed. Marvin L. Colker, 21–33. Aldershot: Scolar Press for Trinity College Library, Dublin, 1991.

———. "Ussher as a Collector of Manuscripts." *Hermathena* 88 (1956): 34–58.

Ogier, D. M. *Reformation and Society in Guernsey*. Woodbridge: Boydell, 1996.

Outhwaite, R. B. *Rise and Fall of the English Ecclesiastical Courts, 1500–1860*. Cambridge: Cambridge University Press, 2006.

Parker, K. L. *The English Sabbath: A Study of Doctrine and Discipline from the Reformation to the Civil War*. Cambridge: Cambridge University Press, 1988.

——— and Eric Carlson. *"Practical Divinity": The Works and Life of Revd Richard Greenham*. Aldershot: Ashgate, 1998.

Paul, R. S. *Assembly of the Lord: Politics and Religion in the Westminster Assembly and the "Grand Debate."* Edinburgh: T. and T. Clark: 1985.

Pearson, A. F. Scott. *Church and State: Political Aspects of Sixteenth Century Puritanism*. Cambridge: Cambridge University Press, 1928.

———. *Thomas Cartwright and Elizabethan Puritanism*. Cambridge: Cambridge University Press, 1925.

Pettegree, Andrew. *Foreign Protestant Communities in Sixteenth-Century London*. Oxford: Clarendon Press, 1986.

———. *Reformation and the Culture of Persuasion*. Cambridge: Cambridge University Press, 2005.

Pettit, Philip. *Republicanism: A Theory of Freedom and Government*. Oxford: Clarendon Press, 1997.

Pierce, Helen. "Anti-Episcopacy and Graphic Satire." *HJ* 47, no. 4 (2004): 809–48.

Pocock, J. G. A. *The Ancient Constitution and the Feudal Law: English Historical Thought in the Seventeenth Century*. New York: W. W. Norton and Company, 1967.

———. "British History: A Plea for a New Subject." *JMH* 47, no. 4 (1975): 601–28.

———. "The History of British Political Thought: The Creation of a Center." *JBS* 24, no. 3 (1985): 283–310.

Pollmann, Judith. *Religious Choice in the Dutch Republic: The Reformation of Arnoldus Buchelius, 1565–1641*. Manchester: Manchester University Press, 1999.

Porterfield, Amanda. "Women's Attraction to Puritanism." *CH* 60, no. 2 (1991): 196–209.

"Post-Confessional Reformation History." *Archiv fur Reformationsgeschichte* 97 (2006): 276–306.

Prest, Wilfrid. *The Inns of Court under Elizabeth I and the Early Stuarts, 1590–1640*. London: Longman, 1972.

Price, F. Douglas. "The Abuses of Excommunication and the Decline of Ecclesiastical Discipline under Queen Elizabeth." *EHR* 57, no. 225 (1942): 106–15.

Primus, J. H. *Holy Time: Moderate Puritanism and the Sabbath*. Macon, GA: Mercer University Press, 1989.

Prior, Charles. *Defining the Jacobean Church: The Politics of Religious Controversy, 1603–1625*. Cambridge: Cambridge University Press, 2005.

Rabb, Theodore. *Enterprise and Empire: Merchant and Gentry Investment in the Expansion of England, 1575–1630.* Cambridge: Harvard University Press, 1967.

Rechtein, John G. "Antithetical Literary Structures in the Reformation Theology of Walter Travers." *SCJ* 8, no. 1 (1977): 51–60.

Rice, Eugene. *Saint Jerome in the Renaissance.* Baltimore: Johns Hopkins University Press, 1985.

Richardson, R. C. *Puritanism in North-West England: A Regional Study of the Diocese of Chester to 1642.* Manchester: Manchester University Press, 1972.

Ripley, Edward Franklin. *Shepherd in the Wilderness: Peter Hobart, 1604–1679: A Founder of Hingham Plantation in Massachusetts.* Lanham: University Press of America, 2001.

Rose, Jacqueline. "Royal Ecclesiastical Supremacy and the Restoration Church." *Historical Research* 80, no. 209 (2007): 324–45.

Russell, Conrad. *The Causes of the English Civil War.* Oxford: Clarendon Press, 1990.

———. *Unrevolutionary England, 1603–1642.* London: Hambledon Press, 1990.

Schilling, Heinz. "Confessionalization." In *Confessionalization in Europe, 1555–1700*, ed. John M. Headley, Hans J. Hillderbrand, and Anthony J. Papalas, 21–36. Aldershot: Ashgate, 2004.

Schneider, Carol G. "Roots and Branches: From Principled Nonconformity to the Emergence of Religious Parties." In *Puritanism: Transatlantic Perspectives on a Seventeenth-Century Anglo-American Faith*, ed. Francis Bremer, 167–200. Boston: Massachusetts Historical Society, 1993.

Seaver, Paul. "Community Control and Puritan Politics in Elizabethan Suffolk." *Albion* 9, no. 4 (1977): 297–315.

———. *The Puritan Lectureships: The Politics of Religious Dissent.* Stanford: Stanford University Press, 1970.

———. *Wallington's World: A Puritan Artisan in Seventeenth-Century London.* Stanford: Stanford University Press, 1985.

Shagan, Ethan. "The English Inquisition: Constitutional Conflict and Ecclesiastical Law in the 1590s." *HJ* 47, no. 3 (2004): 541–65.

———. *Popular Politics and the English Reformation.* Cambridge: Cambridge University Press, 2003.

Shaw, W. A. *A History of the English Church during the Civil War and under the Commonwealth, 1640–1660.* London: Longmans, 1900.

Sheils, William. *The Puritans in the Diocese of Peterborough, 1558–1610.* Northampton: Northamptonshire Record Society, 1979.

Shepard, Alexandra. *Meanings of Manhood in Early Modern England.* Oxford: Oxford University Press, 2003.

Skinner, Quentin. "Classical Liberty, Renaissance Translation and the English Civil War." In *Visions of Politics*: II.

———. *The Foundations of Modern Political Thought.* Vol. II. Cambridge: Cambridge University Press, 1978.

———. "The Idea of a Cultural Lexicon." In *Visions of Politics*: I.

———. "Interpretation and the Understanding of Speech Acts." In *Visions of Politics*: I.

———. *Liberty before Liberalism.* Cambridge: Cambridge University Press, 1998.

———. *Visions of Politics*. Cambridge: Cambridge University Press, 2002. Vols. I and II.

Slack, Paul. *Poverty and Policy in Tudor and Stuart England*. London: Longman, 1988.

Smith, David L. "Catholic, Anglican or Puritan? Edward Sackville, Fourth Earl of Dorset and the Ambiguities of Religion in Early Stuart England." *Transactions of the Royal Historical Society* sixth ser., 2 (1992): 105–24.

———. *The Stuart Parliaments, 1603–1689*. London: Edward Arnold, 1998.

Sommerville, J. P. *Politics and Ideology in England, 1603–1640*. London: Longman, 1986.

Sprott, G. W., and Alan R. MacDonald. "Forbes, John (c. 1565–1634)." In *ODNB*.

Sprunger, Keith. *Dutch Puritanism: A History of English and Scottish Churches of the Netherlands in the Sixteenth and Seventeenth Centuries*. Leiden: E. J. Brill, 1982.

———. "English and Dutch Sabbatarianism and the Development of Puritan Social Theology (1600–1660)." *CH* 51, no. 1 (1982): 24–38.

Spufford, Margaret. "Puritanism and Social Control?" In *Order and Disorder in Early Modern England*, ed. John Stevenson, 41–57. Cambridge: Cambridge University Press, 1987.

Stock, Deborah Hart. "Thomas Hooker's Journey through English Congregationalism to the New England Way." *International Congregational Journal* 3, no. 1 (2003): 55–75.

Todd, Margo. *The Culture of Protestantism in Early Modern Scotland*. New Haven: Yale University Press, 2002.

Tolmie, Murray. *The Triumph of the Saints: The Separate Churches of London, 1616–1649*. Cambridge: Cambridge University Press, 1977.

Tuck, Richard. *Natural Rights Theories: Their Origin and Development*. Cambridge: Cambridge University Press, 1979.

Tyacke, Nicholas. *Anti-Calvinists: The Rise of English Arminianism, c. 1590–1640*. Oxford: Clarendon, 1990.

———. "The Fortunes of English Puritanism, 1603–1640." In *Aspects of English Protestantism*. Manchester: Manchester University Press, 2001.

———. "The 'Rise of Puritanism' and the Legalizing of Dissent." In *From Persecution to Toleration: The Glorious Revolution and Religion in England*, ed. Ole Peter Grell, Jonathan I. Israel, and Nicholas Tyacke, 17–49. Oxford: Clarendon Press, 1991.

Urwick, William. *Nonconformity in Herts: Being Lectures upon the Nonconforming Worthies of St. Albans and Memorials of Puritanism and Nonconformity in All the Parishes of the County of Hertford*. London: Hazell, Watson, and Vinery, 1884.

Usher, R. G. *The Reconstruction of the English Church*. Farnborough: Gregg International Publishers, 1910.

———. *The Rise and Fall of the High Commission*. Oxford: Clarendon Press, 1913.

Valeri, Mark. "Religious Discipline and the Market: Puritans and the Issue of Usury." *William and Mary Quarterly* 3rd ser. 54, no. 4 (1997): 747–68.

van Gelderen, Martin. *The Political Thought of the Dutch Revolt*. Cambridge: Cambridge University Press, 1992.

Venn, J. A. *Alumni Cantabrigienses: A Biographical List of All Known Students, Graduates and Holders of Office at the University of Cambridge, from the Earliest Times to 1900*. Cambridge: Cambridge University Press, 1922–54.

Von Rohr, John. "The Congregationalism of Henry Jacob." *Transactions of the Congregational Historical Society* 19, no. 3 (1962): 107–17.

Walsham, Alexandra. *Church Papists: Catholicism, Conformity and Confessional Polemic in Early Modern England.* Woodbridge: Boydell and Brewer, 1999.

Waters, John J. "Hingham, Massachusetts, 1631–1661: An East Anglian Oligarchy in the New World." *Journal of Social History* 1, no. 4 (1968): 351–70.

Watts, Michael. *Dissenters: From the Reformation to the English Revolution.* Oxford: Clarendon Press, 1978.

Webster, Tom. *Godly Clergy in Early Stuart England: The Caroline Puritan Movement, c. 1620–1643.* Cambridge: Cambridge University Press, 1997.

White, B. R. *The English Separatist Tradition: From the Marian Martyrs to the Pilgrim Fathers.* Oxford: Oxford University Press, 1971.

Whitney, Dorothy Williams. "London Puritanism: The Haberdashers' Company." *CH* 32, no. 3 (1963): 298–321.

Willen, Diane. "Godly Women in Early Modern England: Puritanism and Gender." *JEH* 43 (1992): 561–80.

Winship, Michael. *Making Heretics: Militant Protestantism and Free Grace in Massachusetts, 1636–1641.* Princeton: Princeton University Press, 2002.

Wolffe, Mary. "Hughes, George (1603/4–1667)." In *ODNB.*

Wood, Andy. *Riot, Rebellion and Popular Politics in Early Modern England.* Basingstoke: Palgrave, 2002.

Woolf, D. R. *The Idea of History in Early Stuart England: Erudition, Ideology, and 'The Light of Truth' from the Accession of James I to the Civil War.* Toronto: University of Toronto Press, 1990.

———. *The Social Circulation of the Past: English Historical Culture, 1500–1730.* Oxford: Clarendon Press, 2003.

Wrightson, Keith. "The Politics of the Parish in Early Modern England." In *The Experience of Authority in Early Modern England,* ed. Paul Griffiths, Adam Fox, and Steve Hindle, 10–46. Basingstoke: Macmillan, 1996.

——— and David Levine. *Poverty and Piety in an English Village: Terling, 1525–1700.* Oxford: University Press, 1995.

UNPUBLISHED DISSERTATIONS AND OTHER WORKS

Abbott, W. M. "The Issue of Episcopacy in the Long Parliament, 1640–1648: The Reasons for Abolition." D.Phil. diss., University of Oxford, 1981.

Brodsky Elliot, Vivien. "Mobility and Marriage in Pre-Industrial England: A Demographic and Social Structural Analysis of Geographic and Social Mobility and Aspects of Marriage, 1570–1690, with Particular Reference to London and General Reference to Middlesex, Kent, Essex and Hertfordshire." Ph.D. diss., University of Cambridge, 1979.

Carr, Frank Benjamin. "The Thought of Robert Parker (1564?–1614) and His Influence on Puritanism before 1650." Ph.D. diss., University of London, 1964.

Carter, Rembert. "The Presbyterian-Independent Controversy with Special Reference to Dr. Thomas Goodwin and the Years, 1640–1660." Ph.D. diss., University of Edinburgh, 1961.

Collinson, Patrick. "The Puritan Classical Movement in the Reign of Elizabeth I." Ph.D. diss., University of London, 1957.

Denholm, Andrew Thomas. "Thomas Hooker: Puritan Preacher, 1586–1647." Ph.D. diss., Hartford Seminary Foundation, 1961.

Donaldson, Gordon. "The Relations between the English and Scottish Presbyterian Movements to 1604." Ph.D. diss., University of London, 1938.

Evans, Helen Mary Elizabeth. "The Religious History of Jersey, 1558–1640." Ph.D. diss., University of Cambridge, 2002.

Fielding, John. "Conformists, Puritans and the Church Courts: The Diocese of Peterborough, 1603–1642." Ph.D. diss., University of Birmingham, 1989.

Goodman, Robert Lord. "Newbury, Massachusetts, 1635–1685: The Social Foundations of Harmony and Conflict." Ph.D. diss., Michigan State University, 1974.

Gregory, Victoria. "Congregational Puritanism and the Radical Puritan Community in England *c*. 1585–1625." Ph.D. diss., University of Cambridge, 2003.

Ha, Polly. "English Presbyterianism." Ph.D. diss., University of Cambridge, 2006.

Hampson, James E. "Richard Cosin and the Rehabilitation of the Clerical Estate in Late Elizabethan England." Ph.D. diss., University of St. Andrews, 1997.

Keep, David John. "Henry Bullinger and the Elizabethan Church: A Study of the Publication of His 'Decades,' His Letter on the Use of Vestments and His Reply to the Bull Which Excommunicated Elizabeth." Ph.D. diss., University of Sheffield, 1970.

Mildon, W. H. "Puritanism in Hampshire and the Isle of Wight from the Reign of Elizabeth to the Restoration." Ph.D. diss., University of London, 1934.

O'Sullivan, William. "Ussher's Manuscripts: The Cataloguing of Ussher Manuscripts." Unpublished typescript, Reading Room, Trinity College Library, Dublin.

Oates, Rosamund. "Tobie Matthew and the Establishment of the Godly Commonwealth in England: 1560–1606." Ph.D. diss., University of York, 2003.

Pearce, A. S. Wayne. "John Spottiswoode, Jacobean Archbishop and Statesman." Ph.D. diss., University of Stirling 1998.

Richardson, Roger C. "Puritanism in the Diocese of Chester to 1642." Ph.D. diss., University of Manchester, 1968.

Schneider, Carol. "Godly Order in a Church Half-Reformed: The Disciplinarian Legacy, 1570–1641." Ph.D. diss., Harvard University, 1986.

Shipps, Kenneth Wayne. "Lay Patronage of East Anglian Puritan Clerics in Pre-Revolutionary England." Ph.D. diss., Yale University, 1971.

Sommerville, Margaret. "Independent Thought, 1603–1649." Ph.D. diss., University of Cambridge, 1981.

Sprunger, Mary. "Rich Mennonites, Poor Mennonites: Economics and Theology in the Amsterdam Waterlander Congregation during the Golden Age." Ph.D. diss., University of Illinois at Urbana-Champaign, 1993.

Taviner, Mark. "Robert Beale and the Elizabethan Polity." Ph.D. diss., St. Andrews University, 2000.

Vage, Jonathan. "The Diocese of Exeter, 1519–1641: A Study of Church Government in the Age of the Reformation." Ph.D. diss., University of Cambridge, 1991.

van Dixhoorn, Chad. "Reforming the Reformation." Ph.D. diss., University of Cambridge, 2004.

Vernon, Elliot. "The Sion College Conclave and London Presbyterianism during the English Revolution." Ph.D. diss., University of Cambridge, 1999.

Wrightson, Keith. "The Puritan Reformation of Manners with Special Reference to the Counties of Lancashire and Essex, 1640–1660." Ph.D. diss., University of Cambridge, 1973.

Yarbrough, Slayden A. "Henry Jacob, a Moderate Separatist, and His Influence on Early English Congregationalism." Ph.D. diss., Baylor University, 1972.

Yiannikou, Jason. "Protestantism, Puritanism, and Practical Divinity in England, 1570–1620." Ph.D. diss., University of Cambridge, 1999.

General Index

Biblical References